COMPUTERS AND WRITTEN TEXTS

𝕁𝔹

Applied Language Studies
Edited by David Crystal and Keith Johnson

This new series aims to deal with key topics within the main branches of applied language studies – initially in the fields of foreign language teaching and learning, child language acquisition and clinical or remedial language studies. The series will provide students with a research perspective in a particular topic, at the same time containing an original slant which will make each volume a genuine contribution to the development of ideas in the subject.

Series List

COMPUTERS AND WRITTEN TEXTS

Edited by
Christopher S. Butler

BLACKWELL
Oxford UK & Cambridge USA

Copyright © Basil Blackwell Ltd 1992
Copyright © Introduction and editorial matter, C. S. Butler 1992

First published 1992

Basil Blackwell Ltd
108 Cowley Road
Oxford OX4 1JF
UK

Basil Blackwell, Inc.
Three Cambridge Center
Cambridge, Massachusetts 02142
USA

P
3 02.3
.C66
1992

A CIP catalogue record for this book is available from the British Library.

Library of Congress Cataloging in Publication Data

Computers and written texts / edited by Christopher S. Butler.
     p. cm. — (Applied language studies)
   Includes bibliographical references and index.
   ISBN 0–631–16381–6 (hardback) – ISBN 0–631–16382–4 (pbk.)
   1. Discourse analysis—Data processing.   2. Philology—Data
processing.   I. Butler, Christopher, 1945–   .   II. Series.
P 302.3.C66   1992
402′.85—dc20
                                                           91–23292
                                                              CIP

Typeset in 10 on 12pt Ehrhardt
by TecSet Ltd, Wallington, Surrey

Printed in Great Britain by Biddles Ltd, Guildford, Surrey

This book is printed on acid-free paper.

Contents

Contributors

JOHN A. BATEMAN, Project Leader at Gesellschaft für Mathematik- und Datenverarbeitung, and member of the Penman project at the Information Sciences Institute, University of Southern California.

LOU BURNARD, Consultant with Oxford University Computing Service.

JOHN F. BURROWS, Director, Centre for Literary and Linguistic Computing. University of Newcastle, New South Wales. Also Emeritus Professor of English at that University.

STEVEN FLIGELSTONE, Research Associate, Department of Linguistics and Modern English Language, Lancaster University.

EDUARD H. HOVY, Project Leader at Information Sciences Institute, University of Southern California, and Research Professor of Computer Science at University of Southern California.

REX LAST, Professor and Head of Department of Modern Languages, University of Dundee. Also freelance writer and software programmer, and editor of the *Amstrad PCW Magazine*.

GEOFFREY LEECH, Professor of Linguistics, Department of Linguistics and Modern English Language, Lancaster University.

DEREK LEWIS, Lecturer, Department of German, University of Exeter.

WILLEM MEIJS, Lecturer in English and Computational Linguistics. Department of English, University of Amsterdam.

WILHELM OTT, Leiter, Zentrum für Datenverarbeitung, Abteilung Literarische und Dokumentarische Datenverarbeitung, University of Tübingen.

TERRY PATTEN, Assistant Professor, Department of Computer and Information Science, The Ohio State University.

NOEL WILLIAMS, Senior Lecturer in Communication Studies, Sheffield City Polytechnic. Also Director of the Communication and Information Research Group at that Polytechnic.

Editorial Introduction

Computer: the very word misleads. The first computers were, it is true, used extensively for numerical purposes, as instruments for the complex calculations required, for example, to control missile projection in the Second World War. In the intervening half-century, the pattern has undergone a fundamental and immensely important change. Of course, computers are still heavily used in applications, largely within the mathematical, physical and natural sciences, which require the performance of vast numbers of mathematical operations, often dubbed 'number-crunching'. Today, however, a very sizeable proportion of our global computing activity is concerned with the manipulation of non-numerical data. Naturally, such activities can lead to the counting of items, and subsequent numerical analysis.

Foremost among the symbols which are at the heart of 'non-numerical computing' are, of course, alphabetic characters. Even among those academics in humanities faculties who would consider themselves essentially non-numerate (sadly, still a rather large proportion of our number), most now regard the word-processor as an indispensable tool of their trade. And yet there is still widespread ignorance, even in the ranks of those whose business is words, of the contribution which has so far been made by computers to the study of natural language texts, and the exciting possibilities for the future of such endeavours. This book is an attempt to remedy this situation, by providing an up-to-date survey which will, it is hoped, be accessible to those who already know something of applied language studies, but little about the computer and its uses. The book should therefore be of use, not only to lecturers and researchers within the applied fields represented here, but also to undergraduates and postgraduates on the increasing number of courses concerned with information technology in relation to language. Each chapter ends with a list of suggestions for further reading; and a very extensive integrated bibliography is provided at the end of the volume.

The field is a dauntingly large one, and restrictions thus have to be imposed if a worthwhile survey is to be achieved within the confines of a single volume. Although 'the study of natural language texts' will be interpreted fairly widely here, to include, for example, both text generation and computer-assisted language learning, the focus of all the chapters is the study of *written* texts. The areas of speech recognition and synthesis merit separate consideration, and have indeed been the topic of a number of volumes (e.g. Witten, 1982; Cater, 1983; Sclater, 1983; Allen, Hunnicutt and Klatt, 1987; Holmes, 1988).

The book deliberately brings together methods of inquiry which have traditionally been regarded as separate. The earliest techniques of computational analysis depended solely on the sequence of graphological symbols in a text (alphanumeric characters, punctuation marks), and produced word-lists, indexes (giving locational information about occurrences of words in the text) and concordances (giving a certain amount of context for each occurrence, as well as locational information). However, as the power and sophistication of computers (and their programmers!) increased, so a new breed of 'computational linguists' emerged, whose concern was the simulation of human linguistic activities by computers. In this sense of the term, computational linguistics is one part of the discipline of artificial intelligence, which also includes the computational modelling of vision, robotics, etc. Some practitioners of this newer and trendier art (or is it a science? Perhaps certain of the chapters in this book may begin to provide an answer) have been somewhat scathing about the contribution of the humbler indexing and concordancing work. The following quotation illustrates a by no means uncommon position:

> As those who count sheep know well, counting is a very boring task. Even the very earliest computers counted fast and accurately, and they did not get bored. They could, for example, count how many times *the* occurs in *Hamlet*. Some of the earliest work that came to be known as CL [computational linguistics – CSB] did exactly this kind of counting. A typical application was the attempted attribution of authorship to texts whose authorship was in doubt.
>
> Other work then considered to be CL involved the use of computers to derive indexes and concordances from computer-readable texts. Nowadays such work no longer counts as computational linguistics, or even as an academic activity, since humble word-processing programs often come equipped with sophisticated indexing utilities. (Gazdar and Mellish, 1987: 225–6)

In my view, such contempt for the less sophisticated techniques is not only arrogant, but also ill-founded, for a number of reasons.

As this book will clearly demonstrate, indexing and concordancing techniques are not simply relics of an earlier Stone Age of linguistic computing, but are still extremely versatile tools which form the basis of many imaginative studies in areas as diverse as stylistics, lexicography and textual editing. Of course, it is true that the main intellectual challenge of such studies is not concerned with the computational stage itself, but with the interpretation of data obtained by computational means. But this does not lessen the contribution which these 'humble' techniques have made, and continue to make, to our knowledge of texts.

A further important point often overlooked by the artificial intelligence-oriented computational linguists is the increasing convergence of the older and newer techniques in several areas of application. As will be apparent from chapter 6 of this book, the work of computational lexicographers is now making an extremely valuable contribution to the 'natural language processing' activities of the artificial intelligence community; nevertheless, concordancing techniques have been of great value in recent computer-based work in lexicography. An article by Cercone and Murchison (1985) envisages the development of the 'intelligent' programs known in the AI world as 'expert systems', in the area of literary stylistics, in which the main contribution of the computer has so far been to provide qualitative and quantitative information by means of fairly simple sorting and counting routines. And although Last, in chapter 9, is somewhat sceptical of the feasibility of applying artificial intelligence techniques to computer-assisted language learning, attempts to integrate the older and newer methodologies in this area will no doubt continue. It is, then, one of the aims of this book to show the value, and the compatibility, of the various types of technique, from simple to highly sophisticated, which are used in computer-based studies of written texts.

This wide range of techniques forms the subject-matter explored by Lou Burnard in chapter 1. After mapping out the area to be covered in the chapter, he describes the methods available for preparing textual material for analysis by the computer. There follows a discussion of the need for widely accepted standards in the encoding of texts. Pre-written 'package programs' for the quantitative analysis of texts are then described. Detailed consideration is given to the use of relational databases and text retrieval systems, as well as to hypertext systems, which provide a mechanism for making and exploiting links between parts of a single text, and between texts. Basic information is then provided on computer programming and programming languages, for those whose needs are not served by pre-written materials. The chapter ends with a useful review of sources of information, including those relevant to humanities computing in general.

In chapter 2, Terry Patten selects from the overall range of computational text analysis techniques those that are used for grammatical analysis, or 'parsing'. He begins with a review of key concepts, including top-down vs. bottom-up processing (that is, whether the system starts with the top node in a constituent structure tree and attempts to construct the branches by expansion, or rather starts with the terminal lexical items and attempts to move up the tree; or, indeed, combines both techniques), the use of concepts derived from work in transformational generative grammar, the ATN (augmented transition network) formalism, and grammars based on logic and on the idea of 'unification'. Attention is then given to the role of semantic and pragmatic analysis in guiding the parser.

With chapter 3, we move from the analytical to the generative perspective. The question addressed here by John Bateman and Eduard Hovy is how the computer can be used to produce naturalistic written text. As the authors observe, answers to this question have been rather slower to emerge than those to the problems of parsing. The generation problem is seen in terms of three basic dimensions: the tasks to be performed by the system, the ways in which these tasks might be achieved, and the role of information derived from the context of text production. The generator task involves three aspects: what is to be said, how it should be said, and why it needs saying. Under the heading of the 'how?' of generation, the authors review techniques of increasing sophistication: the use of templates, 'cascaded' generation using patterns of increasing generality, and construction based on a set of features for each unit in the text. The content of the text to be generated is discussed in similar terms: the use of 'canned' text, template-based paragraph construction and cascaded techniques. The authors then describe recent work which attempts to answer the 'why?' question by importing the concept of 'register'.

Chapter 4 follows naturally from the previous two chapters in that its topic, machine translation (MT), requires both parsing and text generation. After a brief introduction to the history of the subject, Derek Lewis outlines the role of machine-readable dictionaries and parsers in MT. He then discusses the three main approaches to the translation of source language into target language: the direct restructuring of information derived from analysis of the source text; the interlingual approach, which uses a highly abstract, ideally universal, inter-mediate representation between source and target; and the later transfer model, in which the initial source language analysis does not aim to capture all the information which would be needed for translation into all other languages. Lewis then considers some of the linguistic models which have been used in representing lexical, morphological and syntactic information for MT, and some of the software tools available for the implementation of these representations. The role of semantics and knowledge-based systems in MT is discussed. A number of current MT systems are then described, and the concept of machine-aided translation is introduced. Criteria for the evaluation of MT systems are outlined, and the chapter ends with an account of the availability and use of online termbanks.

Chapter 5, by Geoffrey Leech and Steven Fligelstone, examines the role of machine-readable corpora in present-day linguistic research, and the techniques for their exploitation. The authors present a useful account of the scope and availability of corpora in English and other languages, and then go on to consider some of the areas in which corpora have been used. There is a discussion of the kinds of information which can be incorporated into corpora (word-tags, syntactic analyses, labels for phonological and discoursal units), and the kinds of analysis which can be performed on them (concordancing; annotation; the induction of data structures such as a grammatically tagged frequency lexicon and frequency list of tag sequences; training the computer to learn how to analyse corpora more successfully).

In chapter 6, Willem Meijs discusses the important role now played by computers in the compilation and exploitation of dictionaries. This work has clear links with the topics of chapters 2–5, in that machine-readable dictionaries are an essential aspect of language understanding, text generation and machine translation systems, while the computer-aided analysis of corpora has played a key role in the compilation of recent printed dictionaries. After summarizing the types of information normally contained in a dictionary, Meijs illustrates the development of computer involvement in dictionary making, culminating with the COBUILD dictionary, in which computerized techniques were involved at all stages. The roles of computerized corpora, concordancing techniques and databases are then discussed, and practical applications such as word-processor spelling-checkers, on-line word-lists and CD-ROM ('read-only-memory compact disk') dictionaries are outlined. There then follows a detailed discussion of the ways in which the information available in machine-readable dictionaries can be used in work on 'natural language processing' (that is, text understanding, text generation and related activities).

Beginning with chapter 7, we move more clearly into the area of applied linguistics, as broadly conceived. John Burrows, in his chapter on 'Computers and the study of literature', first presents a careful analysis of the advantages and the pitfalls of computational approaches to literary stylistics. He then illustrates his claims from a wide range of studies, including not only computer-aided literary criticism, but also studies of disputed authorship. A particularly attractive feature is the account of Burrows' own fascinating work on the stylistic traits of writers in English from Defoe to the present day.

Chapter 8, by Wilhelm Ott, discusses the revolution made possible by computers in the area of textual editing. Having distinguished the various stages in the production of a critical edition of a text, Ott details the role of the computer in publishing (including typesetting, page make-up, and the use of special characters and fonts), manuscript preparation (involving the use of indexing and concordancing facilities, statistical work, automatic text collation), and the integration of the individual stages into a streamlined process. The discussion is informed by detailed reference to the TUSTEP suite of programs developed by Ott and his colleagues at the University of Tübingen.

In chapter 9, Rex Last reviews the use of computers in computer-assisted language learning and instruction (CALL/CALI). He first describes some of the early attempts to harness the power of the computer to teach languages, and outlines the reasons for the rather slow progress made. He then gives an account of some of the more successful work in CALL, covering topics such as tutorial programs, cloze testing, word-processing in relation to CALL, the 'electronic book' concept, and the teaching of languages to the business community. He ends with a review of new approaches in both hardware and software, and an assessment of the likely developments in CALL during the next decade.

Finally, in chapter 10, Noel Williams gives an overview of the rapidly growing application of computers to the area of writing. Having distinguished the three stages in the writing process which have been traditionally recognized (pre-writing, composing and post-writing), and noted that the division may be to some extent an artificial one, Williams discusses the tools which have been developed to help writers at each stage. At the pre-writing stage, dialogue and prompting programs help the writer to generate ideas, outliners ease the job of planning and organizing the text, while note-taking tools allow the writer to jot down ideas even while engaged in other aspects of the writing process. Williams discusses the advantages offered by modern word-processors at the composing and post-writing stages. He also describes recent work on grammar and style checkers. Other tools, including hypertext and desk-top publishing software, are also discussed.

1 Tools and Techniques for Computer-assisted Text Processing

Lou Burnard

1.1 Introduction

This chapter surveys software tools and analytic techniques which have been widely used in the domain of computer-aided language research. As other chapters in this volume demonstrate, computing and computational methods are now so pervasive, both in linguistics and in other traditionally 'soft' academic disciplines, that a complete overview would require a small volume in itself, and would moreover be out of date as soon as published. This chapter will address in detail only a few topics, while adumbrating several more, and will thus, it is hoped, be representative and suggestive rather than exhaustive. Where specific software packages or tools are mentioned, they should be taken as illustrative of a generic family, rather than as the only exemplars.

1.2 Areas Addressed

Researchers in every subject area have clearly benefited from the increased availability of effective data processing facilities over the last decade. The availability of computer networks, of easy-to-use word processing facilities, of improved access to library catalogue systems and of better software for the management of personal notes and bibliographies have all made the day-to-day business of language research easier and more productive, much as it has for every other academic discipline form archaeology to zoology. These topics are not therefore discussed here, except tangentially; instead, I focus on computing methods and applications which have been found particularly important by those working with language, though they may have ramifications for other disciplines.

Lexicographers and lexicologists alike have found the computer an indispensable tool for managing the enormous amounts of information they now need to manipulate. The use of a large corpus of running text in dictionary building, rather than the traditional collection of slips, and the consequent possibilities for quantitatively-based generalization about usage have radically altered the art of lexicography. At the same time, the availability of existing dictionaries in machine-readable form has provided theoretical and computational linguists with new and far richer sources of information about the structure of language. For more detailed discussion, see the chapter by Meijs in the present volume.

Many of those concerned with textual criticism (that is, the establishment of an authoritative version of a text) have come to appreciate the infinite plasticity of computer-held texts and the facilities it offers for the tabulation and analysis of variation. For discussion, see the chapter by Ott in this volume. Many of those concerned with quantitative stylistics or more broad-based literary analysis have attempted to reformulate their goals and their analyses in terms susceptible of computational analysis. See, for example, Potter (1989a) and chapter 7 by Burrows in the present volume.

The largest group, however, includes all those concerned with descriptive or historical linguistics, socio-linguistics and others attempting to describe language as a phenomenon. The emergence of such phrases as 'natural language processing' or 'the language industries' to describe such work is perhaps indicative in itself of the view of language as something akin to an industrial process or system, which must be analysed statistically before it can be understood. See, for examples, Oostdijk (1988) and chapter 5 by Leech and Fligelstone in this volume.

These areas have benefited most because they are characterized by the following three modes of operation, all of which are readily susceptible to computer processing:

- The quantitative description of linguistic features for comparative or analytic purposes;
- The search for evidence in a large reference corpus, used in support of linguistic intuitions;
- The development of new, pragmatically derived, linguistic models.

Different kinds of software may be used for each of these modes of operation. In each case, purpose-built programs may be developed or available software packages customized to particular requirements. For quantitative description, there are now several easy-to-use packages aimed specifically at the novice computer user, the capabilities of which are discussed in section 1.5. For text retrieval, there are many more, as discussed in section 1.6. The development of linguistic models, however, is not itself such an easily packaged process, generally requiring programming skill and the use of specialized programming languages. In section 1.7 I therefore give some examples of the kinds of programming languages available for developing special purpose software of this kind. Of course, the same tools can also be used for other purposes as well.

Such information must generally be extracted from a known corpus of text. The preliminary requirement for each mode of operation is thus the availability of some body of text in a form that can be processed by computer. Before discussing software tools appropriate to these three goals, therefore, a general discussion of the basic problems involved in preparing electronic texts is given in section 1.3, followed by some consideration of what is needed to make such texts truly useful in section 1.4.

1.3   Preparing Texts for Computer Analysis

Before any text can be processed by computer, it must first be converted to a computer-readable form. There are three methods by which this may be done: keying (that is, effectively, typing the material directly into a suitable word-processor or text editor); scanning (that is, using a special device capable of recognizing characters from a scanned image of the text); re-use of existing machine-readable resources prepared for other purposes.

1.3.1   Scanning

The availability of effective optical character recognition (OCR) systems has reduced some, but not all, of the problems involved in the task of preparing electronic texts. There are two components to such systems: an optical scanner, which produces a digitized image of a document placed on it,[1] and a recognition system, which analyses that image using sophisticated pattern-recognition algorithms to identify alphabetic characters and punctuation marks within it, which are then output as ordinary computer-encoded characters. Optical scanning technology is now remarkably accurate and sophisticated, as users of desk-top publishing systems know; character recognition systems, although equally sophisticated, have a technically much more difficult task to perform, and are correspondingly less successful at it.

One of the first and most successful OCR systems was the Kurzweil 4000 (Hockey, 1986), which has been installed at many research centres in the United Kingdom and North America. By comparison with more recent systems, this machine now seems slow and expensive; its slowness was to some extent caused by its need to learn each new character to be recognized, rather than rely on hardware-held dictionaries of character shapes. Similar, less flexible, but much faster and cheaper systems are now available. Scanners vary considerably in the speed with which they can recognize characters, and also in the range of different characters that can be recognized. The more expensive systems can generally distinguish several different fonts, though few systems are capable of learning new fonts. Recent experimental work has shown that even microform images can be scanned, though with limited accuracy.

It is important also to remember that an OCR device can only recognize (and hence can only store) what is visibly present on the page: it cannot edit out unwanted elements of a text such as running headings or end-of-line hyphenation; neither can it distinguish structurally different components of the printed page (such as footnotes or marginalia) even if these are visually distinct. The accuracy of such devices is also crucially dependent on the regularity and clarity of the typeface used: for older printed material, manuscripts or material using many mixed fonts, the error rate of even the most sophisticated multi-font recognizing systems may be unacceptably low. Nevertheless, for data entry where the material to be captured is extensive and its format comparatively simple or regular, there is no doubt that such devices have much to recommend them.

1.3.2 Keying

In cases where the texts to be processed by computer cannot be prepared using OCR, the only alternative is to key them in directly, using a word-processor or text editor of some kind. This is not such a disaster as it may appear: when the full costs of preparing a really useful computer-held text are calculated, it is often the case that the editorial costs (of checking that the text is correctly transcribed, that the editorial conventions or tagging system employed have been correctly observed, and so forth) far outweigh the cost of retyping the material. Where the texts concerned are spoken material, manuscripts or rare printed books, it is probable that some kind of diplomatic transcript would in any case be necessary, whether or not computer analysis were anticipated. It makes sense, therefore, to share the cost of preparing such a transcript across as many potential uses as possible.

1.3.3 Text Archives

Just as software can be obtained at very low cost from 'shareware' archives, so electronic tetxts and other data sets may be made available on a non-commercial basis. There are now several institutions around the world which distribute electronic texts, of individual well-studied literary works, of uniform samples or collections of language use and even of modern dictionaries. For linguists, the International Computer Archive of Modern English (ICAME) at the University of Bergen is probably the best known: this distributes well-established English language corpora such as the Brown Corpus, the Lancaster-Oslo-Bergen (LOB) corpus and the London-Lund corpus at low cost for scholarly use. The Oxford Text Archive (Burnard, 1988; Proud, 1989) maintains a very large number of texts of all kinds, many of them prepared by individuals rather than large projects, and distributes them at cost; it is one of the longest lived of a number of attempts to set up a general-purpose international distribution centre and deposit archive for electronic texts, and currently holds about 1,000 different texts in some forty different languages. A survey carried out at Georgetown University (Washington, DC) recently reported over 300 different major research projects whose main purpose is the creation of large textual databases (Neuman, forthcoming). Among languages for which substantial research projects, aiming to collect together full text corpora in excess of a million words, have been in existence for at least five years are Old English, Mediaeval and Classical Latin, Armenian, Classical Greek, Dutch, French, German, Italian, Swedish and Hebrew (Lancashire and McCarty, 1988). Recognizing the growing importance of lexical resources of this kind, the European Commission is currently funding a project to set up a formal network of European corpora and has already funded a survey of the texts and other lexicographical resources available. Many of these large research projects have experimented with the notion of distributing their corpora, either directly or by employing a publisher as agent, and some of them will already make individual texts available for a small fee. There is a growing awareness among commercial publishers of the potential market for electronic texts. Small, specialized publishers are beginning to emerge, whose stock in trade are cheap electronic editions of standard literary and other works, often bundled with a simple text retrieval package. At the other end of the scale are the large CD-ROM publishers, some of whom started as vendors of on-line services, whose market-place is the specialist library or information service. Both the *Guardian* and the *Independent* newspapers have recently announced publication of the full texts of their newspapers on CD-ROM: a development of immense potential for students of contemporary English. More conventional publishers, notably Oxford University Press with the electronic version of the OED, have also ventured into this area. The economics of the situation are not clear, some arguing that the current high retail cost of CD-ROM media limits the expansion of the market, others that the technology is not yet ripe enough for anything other than a small dedicated audience.

1.4   Re-using Texts and Encoding Standards

This re-use of resources is, however, likely to be effective only if the text has been captured in a way that is independent of any one particular usage. The pressure to produce published results can sometimes lead to a focus on one particular way of processing an electronic text (usually the production of a printed edition) at the expense of other, perhaps more scholarly, ways of using it. Coombs, De Rose and Renear (1987) argue, for example, that the net effect of recent enormous advances in the sophistication of the software at the disposal of most academics has been to distort traditional scholarly values, by focusing on matters of presentation at the expense of content. There are several signs that this trend may be reversible, as electronic publication and communication become increasingly the norm within the research community (Feeney and Merry, 1990). Certainly, electronic texts can be prepared in such a way as to facilitate a far richer range of types of analysis and application than the simple production of nicely printed conventional editions.

For such analytic purposes, even if a text has already been stored in computer-readable form (perhaps for typesetting purposes), it may still need reformatting. Equally, where a text has been prepared for one specific analytic purpose, its representation or encoding may be too impoverished to support any other. There is a clear need for generally accepted minimal standards, both as to what features of a text should be encoded, and as to how these features should be represented, before the full potential of electronic texts in research is likely to be achieved. Attempts to establish such standards are currently being undertaken by the Text Encoding Initiative, which is a major international research project, jointly sponsored by the ACH, ALLC and ACL (Ide and Sperberg-McQueen, 1990; Burnard, forthcoming). Some of the issues addressed by this initiative are discussed in this section.

1.4.1 Describing the Features of a Text

Language may be described at many different levels, not all of which are equally easily rendered into computer tractable form. A computer is essentially a machine for identifying, classifying and counting symbols: it accepts a string of symbols of some kind (words, numbers, arbitrary codes or a mixture) as input, performs a pre-defined set of operations upon them, and produces some further set of symbols as its output. Though having some similarity with the process by which language is heard, understood and realized, this is clearly a long way removed from the full complexity of human symbol processing. For human beings, the alphabetic strings of which a text is composed are invisibly enhanced by information not explicitly present in it: at a simple linguistic level, by an understanding of the language in which the text is written; at a higher semantic level, by an understanding of the context in which the text is intended to be read. An analysis which wishes to take heed of such levels of description must therefore make them explicit within the text in some way.

When spoken language is converted to written language, features of spoken language for which there is no clear written analogue, such as timing, emphasis, articulation, intonation, etc., must be either suppressed or encoded in some way. Punctuation and use of different typefaces or styles provide some obvious ways of doing this; non-standard spellings (*varmint, dahlin*), enrichment of the framing narrative information (such as *he shouted, he murmured through clenched teeth*, etc.) some others. In an analogous way, when written language is converted to computer tractable symbols, some set of conventions must be defined to represent the information not explicit in the written text, but brought to it by the reader. This set of conventions is known as the *markup* or *encoding system* of the text.

1.4.2 Markup

We are all so familiar with one particular style of markup that it has become almost transparent to us, though it might look fairly strange to someone unacquainted with the technology that depends on it. The introduction of fixed width spaces between lexical units, the organization of text into a series of line units which are syntactically meaningless, though not necessarily metrically so, the use of a special form of letter to mark the beginning of some (but not all) syntactic units and also to distinguish proper nouns from common – these are all ways of 'marking up' text used by typewriters and similar writing machines. Such conventions also change over time, in the same way as language itself: for example, the kinds of textual features marked by a shift to italic typeface are no longer the same as those which would have been thus signalled in the seventeenth century, and variant orthographic forms of the letter s, or of letter pairs such as 'ct', are rarely used except for antiquarian effect.

The function of typographic markup (like that of punctuation) is to guide the reader, by providing clues as to how the text should be interpreted. In an exactly analogous way, the function of markup in an electronic text is to simplify its processing, by making explicit a particular set of (human) interpretations of the text. Quite what that set of interpretations will include will to some extent be determined by the intended uses for the marked-up text. If all that is required is the preparation of a list of discrete tokens in the text, or a concordance (that is, a specialized form of index in which each reference for each term indexed is replaced by the actual context within which it appears), then some set of conventions must be adopted for the representation of the following:

- Characters or symbols not present in the computer's character set;
- Lexical tokens;
- Reference points within the text;
- Possibly some further categorization of lexical tokens.

If, additionally, the text itself is to be output or displayed in some more sophisticated format than its input form or the output from the concordance program itself, then some set of conventions must be determined for such things as:

- Ways of laying out the text on a page or screen;
- Ways of rendering groups of tokens in the text in ways appropriate to their functions:
- Ways of identifying subdivisions within the text for retrieval or display purposes.

1.4.3   Standardized Markup

A standardized markup scheme must try to achieve two goals: it must first specify *what* textual features should be distinguished, and then propose *how* those features should be encoded. The list in the previous section gives some indication of the range of textual features customarily distinguished in simple text analysis applications, but has not addressed the question of how they may be marked up. De Rose, Durand and Mylonas (1990) give a good introduction to the basic notions underlying modern theories of text markup, arguing that markup should describe what a text actually is – an ordered hierarchy of textual objects, each of which has a distinct type. The Text Encoding Initiative referred to above has chosen a particularly powerful markup language, the ISO Standard Generalized Markup Language (ISO, 1986; Goldfarb, 1990), as the vehicle for its recommendations, largely because of its expressive power, its flexibility and its independence of any particular software system or application. A readable introduction to SGML is provided by van Herwijnen (1990), and an interesting example of its use in a literary context is given by Barnard (1988). The TEI's final report is not due until 1992, but an initial draft (Sperberg-McQueen and Burnard, 1990) already indicates the immense range of textual structures which can be supported by it.

1.5   Packages for Quantitative Description of Text

Many easy-to-use packages (general-purpose programs) are now available to aid in the processing of texts which have been prepared to the requirements listed above, if not in their preparation. The Oxford Concordance Program (OCP) is one of the most popular such packages, available for mainframe and microcomputers; other examples include WordCruncher and TACT. Such packages typically operate in three steps: in the first, the input text is divided up into individual tokens, and each token is associated with a reference point in the text. In the second phase, these tokens are sorted alphabetically. Finally, the resulting list is processed to produce a simple frequency count for each distinct type found, an index showing the location of every occurrence, or a concordance, as defined above. In more modern systems, the computer-held index is used as an aid in browsing the text interactively; in others the index or concordance is the finished product.

1.5.1   Token Definition and Identification

Tokens are usually defined by user-supplied rules about how input characters may be combined. As a trivial example, the user must decide whether to count *user-supplied* as two tokens or as one, by stating whether or not the hyphen is to count as a token separator. Flexibility in the significance of individual characters is of particular importance when languages using more than the subset of characters generally available on the keyboard are to be processed. The treatment of characters other than the 'usual' alphabetic, numeric and punctuation symbols is unlikely to be consistent across different computer programs, let alone different computer systems; the tradition of using a transliteration scheme is likely therefore to continue. If a transliteration system has been used, as is most likely the case for Greek or for alphabets using accented letters, the concordance program must be made aware of which characters in the scheme are letters, which mark accents, which may be discarded or regarded as insignificant, and so on.

In most systems, the user can also specify selectional restraints such as 'only strings beginning with A or ending with G are to be considered as tokens' or 'only strings of length between 4 and 12' or 'discounting any token enclosed in brackets' or 'looking only at positions 12 to 48 on every input record', and so forth. As well as their obvious usefulness, these facilities allow for the processing of texts containing information of different kinds, for example, a running text to which a parallel translation has been added, or within which sets of grammatical or part of speech codes have been embedded.

At the same time as defining the substrings of the input to be regarded as tokens, it is necessary to specify a reference point in the original source text. For printed concordances, where only a limited amount of the original context can be reproduced, and still more for indexes, such reference points provide crucial ways of restoring the instance to its full context. This does not, of course, apply when the text itself is held electronically, distinct from the ordered list of tokens, as in a free text retrieval system. Even in this case, it may still be necessary to maintain complex referencing information with each token – to give corresponding page numbers in different versions of the same text for example.

In most cases, each token is associated with a fixed set of numerical or string values which together identify its position in the text: for example, 'chapter 2 line 312' or 'Book ABC Part Four Section 123'. In some schemes, markers are inserted in the text to show where the value of one or other of these values is to change; in others, each input record is tagged explicitly with all the values required in fixed positions. It should be noted that such packages regard text as simply a sequence of records, divided up into lines for referencing convenience only. They do not, for the most part, support more complex kinds of structural markup.

Sorting the tokens can be a time-consuming process if the text is large and the computer small. Options are usually available to sort by a user-specified collating sequence (necessary for non-standard transliteration schemes), to sort tokens either left-to-right or right-to-left (which has the effect of bringing together words with similar endings), to treat specific variant forms (upper and lower case or spelling variations) as identical, and so on. For concordances, it should also be possible to specify an independent sorting sequence for the contexts given under each headword: sorting the contexts by alphabetic order of the words following the headword occurrence that they contain is particularly useful as a means of identifying common collocations, for example.

1.5.2   Automatic Categorization of Tokens

In some cases, the categorization or analysis of input tokens can be specified by an algorithm. Some crude kinds of phonemic analysis for some languages can be performed on the basis of spelling alone, perhaps with the addition of a small set of rules about exceptions or ways of deducing particular phonemic phenomena from the orthographic evidence. For other languages, particularly highly agglutinative ones, automatic morphological analysis may be also be carried out simply by applying sets of rules, for example about affix stripping, to determine how individual morphs may be identified and combined.

More sophisticated and effective ways of automatically adding lexical classifications to the words in a text have also been developed, often as an aid in 'lemmatization', that is, the process of grouping together all the related forms or morphological variants of a word under a single head, and the very similar task of separating out homonyms. Other applications of the same principle have been as an aid in stylistic analysis: packages such as ARRAS or Lexico allow the user to specify groups of semantically- or stylistically-related tokens and thus produce counts, indexes, etc. in terms of these.

From the strictly linguistic perspective, an effective approach to this problem is that described in Biber (1988). This uses a kind of on-line dictionary in which the surface tokens of the input stream can be looked up, and from which a categorization can be derived. Sometimes this will be unambiguous (the string *the* is unlikely to be assigned to more than one class in any analysis of Modern English); more often, there will be several possibilities for any given input string (the string *lead* could represent a noun, a verb or even an adjective); this is particularly true if the classification scheme used makes more than trivial distinctions or attempts to categorize words by their syntactic function, distinguishing for example -*ing* forms of verbs which are participles from those which are gerunds.

To resolve such ambiguities, the usual practice is to inspect the context in which the ambiguous token has been found, and apply rules derived from collocational data (for example, that determiners such as *the* cannot be immediately followed by verbs, or that neither nouns nor verbs can follow immediately after any form of such verbs as *be*, *seem*, etc.). These collocational rules may be derived from formal grammars of the language concerned, or from that old stand-by 'linguistic intuition', and can rapidly become very complex. They could also be derived empirically from statistical observation of a pre-existing tagged corpus, which is one of the more interesting future possibilities as work in corpus linguistics develops.

So far, no general-purpose software package for analysis of this kind has been made widely available, though a number of such systems are widely used in research, for example, CLAWS (Garside, Leech and Sampson, 1987), which is described in Chapter 5 by Leech and Fligelstone in the present volume. Once texts have been enriched in this way, of course, a number of further analytic possibilities open up: observations derived from such corpora can be used as raw input for general purpose statistical packages, such as SAS or SPSS to quantify the linguistic evidence; syntactic analysis can proceed on the basis of observed feature clusters within the text; language understanding and language-generating systems can be made more accurate; better statistical models of the way language is used can be built. Such operations are, however, still the subject of specialized research and thus not discussed further here.

1.6 The Search for Evidence

When very large text corpora are used, either as objects of study in their own right or to provide comparative evidence, the capabilities of simple text processing packages of the type discussed so far can be severely stretched. Fortunately, the information handling needs of the linguist are not fundamentally different from those of many other computer users: general-purpose software systems designed to handle massive amounts of text and data can therefore be used by linguists with advantage. Conventional wisdom draws a distinction between systems designed primarily to handle text and those designed to handle more abstract or more tightly structured types of data. Though to some extent adventitious, deriving more from historical accident than any deep-seated difference between text and any other kind of recorded information, this distinction is observed in the following discussion.

1.6.1 Databases

After word-processors and spreadsheets, database management systems (DBMS) are probably the most widely sold, analysed, discussed, enthused over and hyped of software packages. Originally designed to streamline information handled within large industrial or government organizations, they are now available in a hundred different varieties on machines of all sizes. Whether used to manage an individual shopping list, to keep track of the brass widgets at the disposal of a multinational corporation or monitor air traffic over Heathrow Airport, all database management sytems share a common approach to the basic problems of managing large amounts of information. That approach may be summarized as follows:

- Data abstraction – a formal conceptual model of the information to be processed exists independently of the data itself.
- Data independence – the data to be processed are stored independently of any particular program or application.

- Application independence – applications can access data only via a predefined interface managed by the DBMS.

These characteristics originally arose out of the need to integrate disparate collections of data files and programs within a single organization so that a single shared resource could be made available to many different people simultaneously. They also make very good sense when any complex set of information is to be managed, particularly if more than one computing system is likely to be involved – which will inevitably be the case when a project lasts more than a few years.

The theory of database design has provided several formal techniques by which the complexities of real-life information may be abstracted and simplified to the point that they can be directly represented by the basic constructs of a database management system. The most commonly used such technique is known as 'entity-relationship modelling', after its primitives which are 'enti-ties' – objects about which information is to be held and 'relation-ship' – information about how entities of different types may be meaningfully related. In Burnard (1987) I have given a simplifed account of this process of abstraction, which is sometimes dignified with the name of 'conceptual analysis' and which, to quote Sowa (1984), is 'the work of philosophers, lawyers, lexicographers, systems analysts and database administrators'. It may also be thought of as a conveniently neutral meeting-place for the user of a database system and its designer to articulate their common concerns. Most 'user-unfriendly' systems are the way they are as a result of a very human tendency to think of information-modelling problems in terms of some notion of the way a computer might represent them. Even for the simplest of systems, the construction of a conceptual model enforces the discipline of considering a problem on its own terms.

Once a clear model of the information which a database is to represent has been determined, it is possible to re-express that model in terms appropriate to the particular database management system used. Every DBMS uses a structural model, or in perhaps more familiar terminology, a metaphor, to specify the ways in which the data it manages can be stored and manipulated. DBMS can thus be categorized by the particular metaphor on which they are based. The simplest systems store data as a series of records, each of which can be subdivided into the same pre-defined set of fields. They may be thought of as electronic analogues to conventional filecards, each one pre-printed with a set of boxes to be filled in. There are probably hundreds of such systems now available for microcomputers. Although adequate to many simple tasks, such a system cannot effectively cope with data that require more than one such set of filecards. Attempts to extend this metaphor include the notion of 'hierarchical' databases, in which records of one type are said to 'own' (or be 'owned by') records of another type, and an extension of it, the 'network' or CODASYL[2] model in which records of different types can be linked together in arbitrary networks by chains of pointers. Almost all commercial database systems now in use are, however, characterized by the 'relational' metaphor, a good introduction to which is provided by Date (1987).

In a relational database, data are organized as a number of differently sized tables, each consisting of an indeterminate number of rows. Each row of a particular table contains the same, pre-defined, set of columns. Each column contains a single, atomic, data item. The relational data model also requires that there should be some column (or group of columns) for every table, the values in which uniquely identify the row in which they appear; this is known as the primary key of the table.

Unlike earlier types of database system, relational systems do not process anything other than data held as tables. There are no pointer chains or hierarchies to maintain. Relationships, therefore, must also be represented explicitly by data, as we shall see. All operations in a relational system are carried out on, and result in, tables. As well as the ability to add or remove table definitions and contents, and alter the structure or contents of existing tables, relational database languages support three primitive relational operations: *select*, which extracts a subset of the rows in a table using some procedure that can be evaluated against each row in isolation; *project*, which extracts a subset of the columns in a table eliminating any duplicate rows; and *join*, which combines two tables to form a third by means of some shared column.

As a simple example of the use of relational database systems, consider how we might manage information about a corpus of interviews carried out over a number of years with several hundred people. We will assume that transcripts of the interviews have been made by different people and that descriptive keywords have been allocated to each one; quite a lot of information has also been gathered about the respondents. As a first step in the database design, we have identified four entities: Respondent, Interview, Transcript and Topic. For each of these, we will define a separate table. Within each such table we will define a column for each distinct category of the information held about a particular entity (for example, the age, sex or socio-economic status of a Respondent; the date, location or length of an Interview, the transcriber, encoding or location of a Transcript). In such a database, the select operation might be used to select only interviews given by female respondents while the project operation could be used to list all the different locations at which interviews were given. The join operation might be used to link interviews given by respondents of a specific socio-economic class with topics discussed. It is important to note that column values are the most elementary items in this taxonomy and cannot contain multiple occurrences of the same sort of information. If, for example, the topics discussed in an interview are to be recorded as a series of keywords, it is highly probable that more than one such keyword will need to be recorded for a given interview. Rather than a multi-valued column 'topic-keywords', it would normally be preferable to define 'topic-used' as a table in its own right. Each row of this table will contain two columns: one for a single keyword, and one to identify the interview to which that keyword applies. There will be one row in this table for each keyword used in a particular interview: only the combination of keyword and interview number will be unique.

To understand this way of structuring data, it is helpful to distinguish identifying columns and descriptive columns. The former can be used to stand for individual rows in a table, whereas the latter simply contain additional descriptive information about the entity defined by a particular row. For example, an interview might be allocated a number to distinguish it uniquely from all others, whereas its date or length might be the same as those of many others. The interview number can then be used in any other table as a shorthand for all the information contained in the row of the Interview table which it identifies. This is very useful when we wish to combine information from different tables, for example, to correlate information about respondents with information about the topics discussed in interviews with them.

Database management systems implementing the relational metaphor to a greater or lesser extent are available on almost every kind of computer. A correspondingly large variety of books exists, covering the full range from introductory overviews to full length instructional manuals and theoretical textbooks. Both non-specialist and specialist computer magazines (such as *DataBase Advisor*) include regular reviews and updates. Among the facilities which a modern database management system should provide are the following: user-definition of record structure in one or more files; interactive queries of records from one or more related files; sorting, summarizing and single or multiple updating of records from one or more files; user-defined and default data entry or query screens; user-defined and default reporting programs, preferably based on the internationally defined standard language SQL (Structured Query Language: Date, 1988).

SQL offers facilities for querying such databases and for transferring data between different DBMS in a way independent of particular software or hardware, and is thus at the core of all serious database systems. Unlike some other programming languages, SQL is not difficult to learn, because it is a very high-level, non-procedural language, in which the user simply specifies what is to be done rather than how the system is to implement it. The semantics of SQL extend, however, only to manipulating tabular data: it contains no way of formatting or doing more than elementary arithmetic calculations for example. For these, SQL must be embedded within some other programming language.

A major perceived weakness of most current database systems based on SQL is their lack of direct support for textual data. This is being addressed by some vendors (for example, Oracle (Ashford, 1987)), but is to a large extent an inherent characteristic of the relational model. This is not to say that textual data cannot be handled by relational systems: only that it provides no particular facilities for doing so. Textual objects, as discussed above, have several properties that make them difficult to fit into regular tables without consider-able fragmentation and consequent complexity of programming. For that reason, if textual data alone are to be processed, a system designed specifically for handling text may be preferable. The next section considers such systems.

1.6.2 Mainframe Text Retrieval Systems

Most mainframe text searching software was originally designed to cope with enormous numbers of individually distinct documents in such applications as bibliographic databases, library cataloguing or office automation. The object of such applications is to retrieve individual documents, or parts of documents, by specifying combinations of words or substrings contained within them. An accessible overview of such systems is provided by Ashford and Willett (1988). A typical enquiry in such a system might be: 'Recover all documents in which the word *nuclear* and the word *energy* both appear with no more than two other words intervening.' A typical response to such a query might indicate that 1,003 documents in the database being searched contain the word *nuclear* somewhere, that 2,034 contain the word *energy*, but only 68 contain both words in the required proximity. The user is then usually able to operate further on the set of documents thus identified, either to reduce its size further, for example, by selecting from it only those documents with a date later than January 1980, or to expand it by adding also any documents which contain the word *plutonium*. When a suitably defined set of documents has been identified, the user can browse through them, displaying all or part of each document, or passing them to some other processor for further analysis.

Typical examples of software designed to achieve these ends are packages such as BASIS, BRS-Search and Status, which were also the subject of a recent very detailed evaluation by an inter-university software committee (Bain et al., 1989). All such systems work in a very similar way, by maintaining in parallel two (or more) files: one containing the texts of the documents themselves, and the other an index file. In the index file, lexical items are associated with sets of pointers indicating where in the document file an occurrence of each item is to be found. In principle, every distinct word or phrase in every document in the database might be regarded as a distinct lexical item for this purpose; in most systems, however, very high frequency tokens such as *the* or *to* are disregarded, presentational variations are ignored and numbers and dates treated in a special way, for reasons of economy.

When a new document is added to the database, new entries are added to the index for any terms not already in it, and new pointers added for terms already present. Because such systems tend to be very large, handling perhaps millions of words of text, they generally use technically complex indexing schemes, which may be very expensive to update. Again for reasons of economy, the resolution of the index may be quite coarse; that is, it may simply record the fact that a term occurs at least once somewhere within a document, or part of a document, but not record its exact location, nor distinguish different occurrences within the same document. With such systems, retrievals requiring (for example) that two retrieval terms must be adjacent can only be done in two stages: first to recover all the possibly relevant documents by using the index, and then to scan the relevant text files sequentially, which can be very slow.

To cope with the obvious limitations of an index derived from a very simple tokenization algorithm, most such systems allow for pattern-matching searches of the index (find every document containing a word beginning with *comput*) or simple display of the terms in the index itself. In theory, by inspecting the index directly, the user can determine which search terms actually appear in the database and thus improve both the precision and recall of the query he or she poses. In practice, of course, it is very difficult to know in advance all the terms which are likely to be relevant for a particular enquiry, and much research has gone into ways of improving the performance of such retrieval systems: for a detailed description, see Salton (1989).

For the most part, such systems support a comparatively simple view of the structure of text. A document may be subdivided into fields or named subdivisions (for example, the abstract or title of a report may be distinguished from the body of the report itself), so that terms appearing in one part of a document may be indexed (or not indexed) differently from the same term appearing elsewhere. This is essential if (for example), a search for *London* as the author of a bibliographic citation is not to recover also every citation with the word *London* noted as its place of publication; this facility also allows the user to display (say) only the abstract for each recovered document, rather than the whole of it.

However, because every part of a document may be assigned to only one such subdivision, it can be quite difficult to deal with more complex structures such as those of a narrative or dramatic text. Changing the structure of an existing database is not easy, and may be impossible.

The greatest attraction of such systems is probably their sheer power as ways of providing more or less instantaneous access to millions of words of running text. They are well suited to the serendipitous browser, who wishes to engage with the language of a corpus in a spontaneous way, in which the results of one query determine the content of the next. Another major attraction lies in the facilities such systems generally include for the control and analysis of the index terms used. As already mentioned, the user can browse the index file as a retrieval aid. A separate thesaurus or word-list can also be used simply as a means of controlling terminology in a given field, allowing only certain pre-specified terms to be entered in a document. For subject indexing, where a specialized vocabulary must be used, this is a particularly useful facility.

In many systems, a more ambitious thesaurus can be used as a retrieval aid, in which terms are organized into semantically-related groups. Different semantic relations may be supported, including not just synonymy (so that requests for *human* will also recover *man*, *woman* or *person*), but also broadening or narrowing of concept (so that requests for *bird* can be automatically expanded to include documents which use the terms *robin*, *thrush*, *albatross*, etc.). A thesaurus of this kind could also usefully be employed as a means of disambiguating homographs, indexing inflected versions of terms under their stem, and so forth.

Historically, such systems have been developed and sold largely to the large-scale commercial or academic information science community. Consequently, they tend to be expensive and monolithic software packages, which attempt to do as much as possible within a single and often idiosyncratic software environment. This will usually include a simple query language interface, designed largely for use by librarians or other professionals, with some pre-defined screens for data entry or report formatting. For uses not anticipated by the software designers, or customizing of existing interfaces to a particular application area, specialist programming interfaces will usually be provided, but these will not always be very easy to learn for the novice, and may be designed very much on the assumption that a professional data processing service will be on hand to implement them.

1.6.3   Object-oriented DBMS and Hypertext

The data models (or metaphors) so far discussed all share a common view of information as a static network of entities and relationships amongst them. A third model is emerging in which the processes carried out on data objects are regarded as a part of their definition. This so-called *object-oriented* model has yet to be applied in any major commercial database system, but even limited applications of its principles provide striking examples of its potential. The object-oriented approach allows information to be held as a network, in which text, graphics, sound or more traditional types of data are stored at particular nodes. The properties of individual nodes (which, as noted above, include the processing that may be carried out on them as well as their appearance to the user) may be inherited from those of other nodes of different types. This capability is of particular importance where complex data objects, such as graphical images, are to be manipulated: rather than define both square and rectangle independently in terms of primitives such as points and lines, in an object-oriented design database, a square can be defined as a special case of a rectangle. There is no particular reason why similarly object-oriented design principles should not be applied to linguistic databases, as soon as sufficiently mature software becomes available.

At present, however, the most striking example of the object-oriented approach applied to textual information is in *hypertext* or *multimedia* systems, that is, systems which allow chunks of text or other objects to be processed as a complex network of nodes, linked together in an essentially arbitrary way. Where true database systems require a formalization of the information content of text, hypertext systems return us to the view of information as an emergent property, resulting from a connection between one piece of discourse and another. Where free text retrieval systems see bodies of texts as huge, but essentially passive, cornucopias of information from which the user must tease out the relevant fruit, hypertext systems generally make explicit several ways of navigating through, and hence making coherent, disparate collections of documents or document fragments.

A typical present-day hypertext system will offer the user a choice of entry points into a network, labyrinth or web of interlinked objects, which may be just a few lines of text (perhaps an explanatory gloss), self-contained gobbets, whole documents or even non-textual objects such as illustrations, video or sound. At any point, the user may be offered a variety of alternative routes, sometimes by the visible presence of a *button* on the screen, often by use of a distinctive typeface or rendering for particular words in the text being displayed. By using a *point and click* device such as a mouse or tracker ball, the user selects the highlighted point in the text, and activates the link associated with it, usually leading to the display of a different object. As well as following pre-set trails of such links, the user can move back to previously visited links, try alternative routes and (in some systems) add his or her own link points, to introduce new objects into the web.

Inevitably, the distinctions between text-oriented, object-oriented and traditional database systems are far from watertight. Increasingly, software vendors see a marketing advantage in grafting the features of one model upon a product of another, whatever the cost in ease of use or good design. Products are already available which combine the relational and text-based models, while many text-based DBMS include hypertextual features or interfaces. Several dedicated software packages with greater or lesser degrees of support for hypertext are also now available as full-scale commercially supported systems (probably the best known being Apple's Hypercard and OWL's Guide), while many research projects have developed prototype systems demonstrating capabilities far beyond the limits of these. Details should be sought in one of the increasing number of survey volumes, such as McAleese (1989a) or Association for Computing Machinery (1989), while Schneiderman and Kearsley (1989) provide a very readable simple introduction. The following discussion will highlight some of the current perceived issues. For details of the use of hypertext in creative writing, see chapter 10 by Williams in this volume.

A basic objective of hypertext systems is to mimic electronically the way in which people tend to use large quantities of paper texts: skimming through different parts of texts in parallel, following cross-references from one text to the other, making notes in a third, and so forth. The comparative ease with which this can be done with electronic texts (which do not slide off the desk and can generally be searched through very rapidly) means that the need for some sort of overview or structure to the process of reading a hypertext is correspondingly greater: people rapidly get disoriented when they can have a hundred or so documents open simultaneously, and lose sight of the thread of argument they thought they were following. Some systems try to solve this problem by providing high-level *maps* of the structure of the hypertext, showing the current whereabouts of its reader; this is, however, only effective for hypertexts which are either already highly structured (such as dictionaries or encyclopaedias) or quite small. In other cases, the best solution to the so-called *lost in hyperspace* problem remains the provision of a record of the track which the current reading of the hypertext has taken.

Creating hypertexts is an expensive and complex affair, partly because it cannot easily be automated. Some of the problems inherent in the collection of electronically tractable texts have already been touched on: selecting and organizing a collection of texts and other objects into a hypertext is an immensely more complex and demanding task than simply creating an anthology, since it also entails deciding on and encoding all the required links between individual components of the hypertext. Many proponents of hypertext have chosen to ignore this problem, generally by elevating into dogma the desirability of being able to add links into an existing hypertext. At a technical level this is clearly important if some of the components of the hypertext are held on read-only media such as CD-ROM. There is also a tendency to walk away from the problem by leaving it to users of a hypertext to create the links they actually want. To use currently fashionable critical jargon, it is argued that hypertexts *empower* the reader, by offering him or her the ability to make explicit associations in support of this or that reading of a text: the infinite plasticity, re-writeability and shareability of electronic text mean that such re-readings can be accumulated with the text in itself in a way which better approximates to our experience of the transmission of written texts over the last few centuries.

At present, hypertext has its most obvious application in the business of education and training: one particularly impressive example is described in Landow (1989). As a way of presenting complex information on a computer screen in a familiar way it has obvious advantages over most other techniques while the pedagogic principles which it encourages (self-paced, exploratory learning based on the use of close-coupled objects of different types and textual explanation) have been at the forefront of educational reformers' priorities since the days of Comenius. For linguists also, hypertext has much to offer. Parallel texts in different languages, or multi-layered linguistic analyses, could be presented hypertextually. Glosses and notes could be linked into a text or dynamically generated from a linked dictionary. A syntactic analysis could be linked to texts exemplifying it. The chief limitations at present seem to be technical and financial ones, imposed by what current hardware can support, rather than any theoretical inadequacy.

Hypertext has been the object of much evangelical fervour of recent years; its critics argue that it is little more than a bundle of useful techiques for improving the management and display of on-line information, while its enthusiasts see it as a revolution of comparable significance to the invention of the printing press. Others have read great social or political implications into the way that the creation of hypertexts dissolves the boundaries between individual documents, even to the point of postulating a great interweaving of all the world's knowledge into a single publicly controlled hypertext (Nelson, 1987). Certainly, much of what is hailed as revolutionary in hypertext (the ability to link texts together by cross-reference, for example) is not in itself particularly novel, having been characteristic of the written word for many centuries; on the other hand, it is only comparatively recently that the technology available to manage texts held in electronic form has begun to be able to match, or even better, the technology used to support such activities in printed texts. In rather the same way that the word-processor has driven out the typewriter, not by doing anything radically different but by doing much the same job rather better, so we may expect to see hypertextual interfaces replacing more conventional ways of interacting with electronic texts over the next few years.

1.7   Rolling your own System

Once upon a time, in the days when computers were huge machines occupying entire air-conditioned basements, attended to by serious people in white coats, everything required of them had to be painstakingly specified as a series of very primitive operations, the semantics of which overlapped very precisely with the machine's physical operation. Instructing a computer required a detailed knowledge of such arcana as memory registers, operation codes, binary arithmetic and other mysteries now relegated to the introductory chapters of textbooks on computer science (or the back pages of electronic fanzines). For most applications, specification at such a level of description rapidly came to be seen as inappropriate and expensive, even by serious people in white coats, and thus began the development of new high-level *programming languages*, which shows no sign of abating.

A programming language is not really a language at all, but a way of stating an algorithm or process in such a way that it can be automatically decomposed (or *translated*) into a series of smaller processes, each of which can be further decomposed, until eventually one reaches the primitives of the machine's instruction set. To use a familiar analogy: my recent decision to make another cup of tea can be compared to my setting in motion the *make tea* algorithm. This involves a number of well-defined sub-tasks (find the kettle, fill it with water, etc.), each of which can be further decomposed into smaller steps (look around the kitchen, compare each object found with my notion of what the kettle is, etc.), and so on, down to whatever level of cognitive or physical science seems appropriate.

In the preceding sections little has been said about the ways in which particular actions are specified for the kinds of program discussed. This is because most computer packages are designed, like other forms of machine, to be controlled at a very high (and highly specialized) level. To pursue the previous analogy, a computer package is like a vending machine: to get my next cup of tea, I need only know how much money to insert, which buttons to press for the right combination of additives, and where the cup is likely to be delivered. Other people, desiring different flavours of hot water, can use the same vending machine and achieve slightly different results. Those who want beverages not anticipated by the makers of the vending machine, however, will still have to go into the kitchen and get busy with the kettle: they will have to learn how to program for themselves.

This task is made considerably easier by the existence of widely available libraries of routines designed for specific, commonly used processes or sub-tasks, which can be combined in a suitable environment. Computers running under the UNIX system are particularly well endowed in this respect, which is one reason for its wide popularity. Libraries of graphical output routines and mathematical functions have been in existence for many years and advice on their use is readily available from your local computer centre. Similar suites of routines for the routine tasks of data input and output also exist, generally highly optimized for specific types of machine. Such routines will, however, only generally be usable from programs written in one of the general purpose programming languages such as Fortran or C, which are not the easiest languages for the beginner to learn. For this reason, particularly in the Humanities, there has been a preference for special-purpose very high-level programming languages, the semantics of which are designed to approximate better to specific tasks (such as string processing or logical analysis) than to general algorithmic processing.

1.7.1 Choosing a Language

Undoubtedly the best way of learning how to program a computer is to do it. This is, however, about the only thing which the process has in common with learning a language. Beginners rapidly discover that there is nothing analogous to the *principle of co-operation* of speech-act theory to be found underlying their interactions with a computer. The prevailing metaphor may be linguistic (we talk of computer *languages*, of *interpreter* and *translators* and even of *human–computer interaction*) but it is a very strange sort of language in which communication is always one-way, one partner being entirely unconcerned about the goals of the other. The disappointment and frustration which many beginners voice, and from which modern software environments seek to distract them, surely has its root in the seductiveness of this misleading metaphor. A better one might be derived from engineering – and indeed, one current trend in the theory of computer science is known as *software engineering*. This seeks to determine principles analogous to the laws of physics, providing mathematical proofs that the behaviour of a given program is determined in the same way as the behaviour of a physical system or machine.

In a sense, a computer program is a machine for managing symbols. The kind of program with which most people are most familiar, a word-processor, demonstrates this clearly: it manages the symbols out of which written language is built. But other kinds of program can equally easily manage other kinds of symbol: database systems, as we have seen, manage representations of objects and relationships; hypertext systems represent ways of interacting with a text; expert systems manage representations of rules and facts; process-control systems manage representations of objects and processes themselves. Perhaps, because human language is to some extent also used for the management of symbols, and may even, by semioticians at least, be described as little more, it is not such a bad metaphor after all.

People generally have very strong views about what is the *right* programming language for a given task (or even for all tasks); such views may well have more to do with what is familiar, or cheap, or well understood (or conversely, with what is novel, expensive or currently fashionable) than with any functional difference. Which is not to underrate the importance of such considerations: once a programming language ceases to be widely used, no matter how excellent it may be, it cannot be recommended to the novice: Algol68, for example, the programming language which I first learned and which I still consider to be in many respects the finest of all, is now as dead as Latin.

Rather than attempt to describe any particular language, therefore, this section attempts to give some general idea of what a computer program is. To learn how to write one, you should consult one (or several) of the available tutorial texts for the language of your choice. If your interest is in the basic notions of programming languages *per se*, you should consult a textbook on programming linguistics such as Gelernter and Jagannathan (1990). Some currently popular languages are described very briefly in section 1.7.3.

1.7.2   What is a Computer Program?

A computer program is a set of symbols which determine the behaviour of an automaton. Even though a computer program can be written to simulate non-deterministic behaviour, it remains a simulation.[3] The symbols managed by all computer programs identify two fundamentally different entities: objects and processes. An object may be something as simple as a numeric value, or an area of storage containing such a value (the distinction is important), or it may be a complex structure of other objects. A process may be a primitive operation such as *add* or a whole sequence of such operations. Management of objects and processes together requires consideration of time (creation and destruction of objects, sequence of actions) and space (allocation of objects and process-descriptions to storage). All programming *languages* can be described in terms of the same basic model of what a computer does when manipulating symbols: data are transferred between objects stored within the program and the outside world, and acted upon by processes. This model applies equally well to the word-processing program I am using to create this text and to the most sophisticated textual analysis system.[4]

Programming languages differ chiefly in the kinds of object which they are designed to manipulate, and in the ways in which processes may be specified. Like real languages, they may differ in their lexica and in their syntax without exhibiting much difference in functional capability. Anything that can be specified algorithmically can be programmed in any language, although some languages may be less helpful than others.

A program, in whatever language, consists of tokens of three kinds: direct representations of values (such as *123* or *CAT*), control words or symbols specific to the particular language (such as IF or PROCEDURE) which have a syntactic function and names of variables, that is, identifiable objects or processes which the program manipulates. In most programming languages, a program may be read as a series of imperative statements, defining a series of actions to be performed. Such actions may be categorized in one of the following ways:

- *Declaration*, that is, the definition of some named object or process.
- *Iteration*, that is, the performance of a sequence of actions until some specified condition is met.
- *Invocation*, that is, the execution of a previously or externally defined process.

At a lower level the kinds of specific operations which most programming languages distinguish include the following:

- *Assignment*, that is, the storing of a value in a particular named location.
- *Evaluation*, that is, the calculation of a result from some combination of symbols representing values and variables.
- *Branching*, that is, the determination of the sequence in which operations defined by the program are to be executed.

As with other complex tasks, programming is best managed in a modular fashion: each operation to be performed should be decomposed into constituent sub-tasks, which can themselves be decomposed, until the level of whatever primitive functions the language in hand supports is reached (in some languages, of course, the primitive operations may in fact be very complex; in others, not). This approach requires analytic skill to identify the sub-processes required and the general operations of which specific tasks are particular variations.

As a trivial example, consider the task of writing a program to print all sentences from a corpus containing the word *harumspice*. This may be divided into two sub-tasks: first, identifying sentences within a corpus; second, determining whether a given sentence contains the word *harumspice* and, if so, printing it. Clearly, identifying individual sentences within a corpus is a task of use in many other applications, while choosing only those containing this particular word is not. If, however, the latter task is redefined as *printing any sentence containing a specific word* – the specific word to be determined when the task is performed – it too will be of general application. Further reflection along the same lines might lead to redefining the way in which the first sub-task is defined: to support different ways of defining exactly what a *sentence* is, for example.

This task of redefinition or *modularization* is crucial to all successful programming. In more recent, so-called *object-oriented* programming languages, this tendency is taken even further. In object-oriented languages such as Smalltalk (Budd, 1987) or even Hypertalk (the comparatively humble programming language for the Macintosh Hypercard system), the familiar distinction between data objects and processes is blurred. Such languages describe the action of a computer in terms of objects and messages: objects contain both information and a specification for how it is, in principle, to be processed; messages control the invocation of object instances. As in object-oriented databases, the definition of an object includes the definition of the processes in which it is involved. This simplifies the programming task: a message can simply state what is required of an object, without being concerned about how that is to be achieved.

As implied earlier, the choice of programming language may often be more influenced by social, political or financial factors than by theoretical considerations. It is also important to consider how the language is implemented on the machine you plan to use, for all languages are not equally well suited to (or necessarily available for) all combinations of hardware and operating system. Programs written in whatever language (*source code*) must always be translated into a lower-level language (*object code*) before they can be executed by the computer. This translation process can be done either by a *compiler* or by an *interpreter*.

A compiler is a program, usually of considerable sophistication, which translates source code input into object code, tightly specified to one particular operating system and one particular machine. The translation process involves checking the validity of the syntax of the input source code and generating object code instructions that will achieve the intended effect, as defined by the language. In most cases, the resulting object code must then combined together with other pieces of object code to form an *executable module*. In many cases, *optimization* is also involved, in which redundant code can be removed and other performance enhancing heuristics applied. The crucial point to note is that the resulting object code resulting from a compiler is a free-standing entity: the compiler is not needed during execution of the program.

An interpreter is a program which makes a computer behave as if it understood the source code directly. The interpreter processes individual statements in the source language as they are submitted to it. This obviously makes simple programs easier to develop and test interactively, but makes large programs generally unacceptably slow. The interpreter must always be present to execute a program; some interpreted languages, such as Snobol, turn this to an advantage by providing syntax for programs to write and then execute other programs.

A good programming environment will include a host of ancillary features to assist in the writing of correct programs. Good screen editors, with word-processor-like facilities, make easier the production of source code; good diagnostic tools, enabling the programmer to trace or step through the execution of a program interactively, inspecting or manipulating the object code in terms of the source code from which it was generated, are almost as essential to the hard-worked programmer as good facilities for the management of object libraries.

1.7.3   A Garland of Programming Languages

This alphabetically ordered list is not exhaustive and contains only cursory information about some widely used programming languages. References are given for introductory textbooks aimed specifically at the non-professional, where these exist.

C is the language in which the UNIX operating sytem was written. It is currently the only serious programming language (apart from Fortran) common to all flavours of computer, (because wherever UNIX goes, there must be a C compiler, of sorts) and probably the language of first choice for the serious software developer. A number of extensions to C have recently been proposed which constitute a new dialect (C++) capable of supporting object-oriented programming.

Cobol is a language still much used in the data processing industry, from which it came. Its syntax and abstract powers are even less ambitious than those of Fortran, but it introduced the notion of complex data objects (records) to the development of programming languages.

Fortran was developed in the late 1950s to demonstrate that computers could be programmed efficiently in something other than machine code. Its syntax is archaic, some of its semantics are abominations, but it shows no sign of succumbing to the death which has been loudly proclaimed as imminent ever since the 1960s. This is partly because it has managed to take on board many of the features of its rivals without shedding any of its own idiosyncrasies, but mainly because its simple design allows for the generation of extremely efficient machine code, which is also why it remains the language of choice for most scientific computer users. You are never far from a Fortran user in a university computer centre.

Icon (Griswold and Griswold, 1990) is an unusual language developed at the University of Arizona by one of the authors of Snobol (see below). It improves on Snobol by introducing modern control structures, and generalizing its symbol management capabilities. It is a language for string processing enthusiasts, with a small but vociferous clan of electronically-linked users worldwide; largely because of its origins it is available at very low cost.

Lisp (Friedman and Felleisen, 1987) is a well-established language designed for the manipulation of symbolic data. It is a *functional* programming language, in which processes and data objects are represented isomorphically, as lists containing either primitive elements or other lists. An understanding of recursion is essential to make the most of Lisp, but its generality and expressive power make it probably the language most widely used in current artificial intelligence research.

Pascal (Ide, 1987a) was one of several languages which would cause Fortran to go the way of the dinosaurs (others included various sorts of Algol, PL/1, Modula-2). It survives chiefly because, for a long time, it was the only alternative to BASIC for those wishing to program the IBM-PC. It is also a very compact and efficient language in which data structures and algorithms are clearly distinguished.

Prolog (Clocksin and Mellish, 1987) is very widely-used in artificial intelligence research. It differs from the others chiefly in being *declarative* rather than *procedural*: a Prolog program simply lists known facts and relationships, from which new facts are inferred at execution time, using a modified version of the predicate calculus.

Snobol (Hockey, 1985) is an unusual programming language developed in the 1960s at Bell Laboratories. It has much to recommend it for the linguist, being easy to learn and containing many built-in string handling features, but suffers from a rather archaic and obscure syntax, which makes proper design and construction needlessly difficult.

As with all other kinds of computer software, languages and their compilers often vary considerably in their availability and even their functionality between different operating systems and different kinds of machine. Inevitably, a middle course must be found between the Scylla of choosing a language limited to one hardware environment and the Charybdis of choosing one best suited to one particular kind of application.

Further Reading

In book form, probably the most useful complete overviews of the general area of computer applications in the humanities disciplines are Lancashire and McCarty (1988) and Lancashire (1991). There are also several earlier but less exhaustive synoptic discussions, for example, Hughes (1987) and Hockey (1980).

For detailed and up-to-date information, the relevant journals, surveys and handbooks should be consulted. Journals and annual conference proceedings are published by the three major professional associations concerned with this area, the Association for Computers and the Humanities (*Computers and the Humanities*); the Association for Literary and Linguistic Computing (*Literary and Linguistic Computing*); and the Association for Computational Linguistics (*Computational Linguistics*). Each of these journals has been in existence for fifteen or more years, and has achieved a corresponding degree of gravitas; the International Computer Archive of Modern English, a loose federation of European corpus linguists, also publishes a very useful bulletin (*ICAME News*), while there are many other perhaps more ephemeral publications of particular interest to the language research community including a Dutch monthly called

Electric Word, newsletters such as the ACL's *Finite String* and the occasional reports put out by particular research projects.

Within the United Kingdom, there is a nationally funded initiative to sponsor the use of computers within undergraduate teaching. This 'Computers in Teaching Initiative' has funded several national centres to provide information and guidance to those wishing to use computers in their teaching, each of which focuses on a particular subject area. For second language instruction, the national centre is at Hull, and for text-based studies in general at Oxford. Each centre produces an occasional newsletter about its activities and employs at least one full-time research officer. Further information may be found in Darby (1990).

For really topical information, or gossip, it is essential to subscribe to one or more of the electronic discussion groups maintained around the world. Electronic mail has proved to be an extrordinarily effective way of improving scholarly communication, in quantity if not always quality. Within the United Kingdom, anyone who has access to a mainframe computer on JANET (the Joint Academic Network, which links all centrally funded computing facilities) has not only the ability to communicate with anyone else on JANET free of charge, but also the ability to send and receive messages on dozens of other similar academic networks world-wide. Such messages may be person-to-person, enabling close collaboration between researchers working at widely different locations, or between individuals and groups. Much traffic of this kind emanates from the many electronic discussion groups or bulletin board systems which now exist. Messages sent by individuals to such systems are automatically redistributed to every subscriber, sometimes directly, but more usually with the mediation of some human editor, who may attempt to impose some decorum on what can as easily become a free-for-all slanging-match as any other open forum.

Most electronic discussion groups have a particular focus and can thus provide a very efficient channel for up-to-date information which can be targeted to exactly those who are (or wish to be) knowledgeable about specific topics, in much the same way as a professional publication. As well as discussion, such groups will often contain announcements of forthcoming events and publications, requests for information, bibliographies, etc., just like conventional journals.

Very similar networks also exist to aid in the dissemination of freely available 'public domain' computer programs or 'shareware'. This is software, often developed in a non-commercial context, the owners of which have chosen to make it widely available, either for nothing or for a small registration fee. As might be expected, much of it is highly idiosyncratic or outmoded. However, a surprisingly large amount of 'shareware' is produced to high professional standards and is used routinely by many thousands of people, despite recent scare stories about computer viruses. In the United Kingdom, there is a national centre for the distribution of such software for popular brands of microcomputer, hosted by the University of Lancaster. A similar archive for software related to the TeX typesetting system is maintained at the University of Aston. NISS, a national information service about these and similar facilities, is jointly implemented by the Universities of Bath and Southampton. To gain access to any of these facilities, you should consult your local computing centre.

Notes

1   That is, a representation in which dark points in the image are stored as one binary value and light points as the other.
2   From 'Conference on Data Systems Languages' the influential standards body which defined it.
3   For a fuller consideration of this philosophical issue, of some importance in what is generally known as *artificial intelligence*, see Boden (1987).
4   It is arguably less relevant to declarative languages such as Prolog.

2 Computers and Natural Language Parsing

Terry Patten

2.1 Introduction

Parsing is the process by which grammatical strings of words are assigned syntactic structure. This structure, in turn, is necessary for many types of text analysis, including the analysis of meaning. This chapter will provide an overview of current computational techniques for parsing and interpreting natural language texts. The emphasis here, as the title suggests, will be on parsing, and much of the discussion of the semantic and pragmatic analyses will concern how these interact with the parser. The sections on higher-level analysis are merely intended to provide some context for the role of parsing in the task of understanding natural language.

Parsing is a critical step in many important applications. First, an early application which is still of major significance is *machine translation* (see chapter 4). Almost as soon as it was understood that computers could manipulate symbols as well as numbers, a rush was on to translate texts automatically from one language to another. This enterprise led to some of the first parsers. Although the enthusiasm of the 1950s and 1960s was later dampened by the realization that sophisticated analysis of meaning was also required, practical systems were produced which helped human translators perform the task more quickly. Despite the difficulty of fully-automatic, high quality translation, the tremendous benefit such systems could provide continues to fuel interest in parsing.

Another motivating application has been the desire to allow people to interact with computer systems in natural language, as opposed to the cryptic or awkward interfaces to which they must currently submit themselves. Natural language interfaces would allow people with no special training or skills to profit from computer interaction. The most attractive form of natural language interface would provide access to the computer through everyday speech. Unfortunately speech understanding introduces additional difficult acoustic and phonological problems which have tended to isolate speech research from parsing. Nevertheless, parsing will be an essential ingredient of spoken language interfaces.

Another application involves skimming a data source for information on a particular topic. Some prototype systems have been constructed that can take input from newswire services, for instance. Here it is probably not practical to attempt to parse all the data – this type of application would involve looking for certain keywords, followed by detailed parsing when appropriate cues have been found. There are many applications of this sort in political and industrial intelligence gathering (Winograd, 1983).

An area of artificial intelligence which could benefit greatly from effective parsing is *computer-aided instruction* (for applications to the learning of languages, see chapter 9). The students are probably having enough trouble learning the subject-matter without having to learn how to use an unnatural computer interface. In addition, natural language answers given by students often provide useful clues, for instance about uncertainty (e.g. through the use of modal hedges). Other types of interfaces, designed to avoid the problem of understanding natural language, restrict the vital channel of communication between the teacher and the student.

Word-processors have made a significant contribution to text preparation, not only through their editing capacities, but also through their access to spelling checkers (see also chapter 10). Parsing may eventually become widely used in word-processors (sentence processors) to find syntactic errors, or perhaps as the first step to finding semantic and pragmatic problems.

Finally, a problem of urgent social and economic concern is parsing the vast databases of texts which are now available. Inexpensive computer storage has made it possible to store the entire text of numerous magazines, newspapers and scientific journals for immediate computer access. The sheer volume of this material makes it infeasible to index it (by topic) manually, and simple keyword searches retrieve only about 20 per cent of the relevant information. It seems clear that automatic indexing will be necessary, and this will involve more than a superficial analysis of the text.

This chapter will outline the computational techniques that have been developed for parsing and analysing natural language texts. It is important to stress the point that parsing is a *process*, not a description, and this discussion will be firmly on the performance side of the competence/performance fence. The grammatical formalism that most elegantly describes linguistic competence is not necessarily also best used to process a language – this should be kept in mind.

The fact that parsing is a process brings another issue to the fore: efficiency. Many of the techniques that will be discussed here are motivated not by the need to infer the correct structure, but by the need to infer that structure in a reasonable amount of time. It may be tempting to think that the speed of today's computers makes efficiency unnecessary, but parsing a large text with a complex grammar can still humble the most powerful modern machines. Efficient parsing techniques have been a major concern in computer science, and some impressive techniques have been developed (occasionally drawing on results from linguistics). These techniques, however, were developed for parsing programming languages that were carefully designed to avoid parsing problems. Although some of these techniques can be applied to natural language, for the most part parsing natural languages must be treated as a separate research problem.

This chapter is divided into three main sections: the first deals with techniques based entirely in syntax; the second examines semantic and pragmatic techniques; and the third looks at how the parsing process can be guided by the semantic and pragmatic analyses. Following the three technical sections, the chapter concludes with a discussion of where parsing stands, and where it might lead as a tool for computational text studies.

2.2 Parsing Techniques

This section outlines some of the key ideas and developments that have had a significant influence on recent parsing systems. The discussion falls into two broad areas. First, a serious difficulty arises even when parsing with simple grammars – the problem of lexical and syntactic ambiguity. The first part of this section will look at basic parsing strategies and techniques that deal with ambiguity. Second, it is one thing to develop grammar that can describe the syntactic complexities of natural language, it is something else to develop grammars that can be used to parse complex constructions. The second part of this section will examine the mechanism and computational properties of some grammatical formalisms that have been used for parsing natural language.

2.2.1 Top-down Processing

There are two basic parsing strategies: top-down and bottom-up. The names reflect the starting point in the constituent tree that the parser must construct. If a sentence is being parsed, at the top of the constituent tree will be a node representing the sentence as a whole, and at the bottom will be the nodes representing the individual lexical items. The parser can easily determine the topmost and bottommost levels of the tree in advance: the trick is to fill the gap in between. It can either start at the top and use the rules of the grammar to suggest the next lower level, or it can start at the bottom and use the rules of the grammar to suggest the next higher level. To illustrate top-down processing (also called *recursive-descent* parsing), suppose the parser is working from the very simple grammar shown in grammar 2.1 (from Allen 1987:67).

1.	S→ NP VP	5.	NP→ ART ADJ NOUN
2.	S→ NP AUX VERB	6.	NP→ ADJ NOUN
3.	S→ NP VERB	7.	VP→ AUX VERB NP
4.	NP→ ART NOUN	8.	VP→ VERB NP

Grammar 2.1

Suppose the parser is attempting to parse *The boy had taken long walks*. The parser begins at the top and starts looking for a sentence. There happen to be three rules describing sentences in this grammar and, since the parser has no basis for choosing one over the other, it will have to try them one at a time, say, in the order in which they appear in the grammar. So the first rule to be tried will be 1, which tells the parser that a sentence can be an NP followed by a VP. The parser will therefore build the next level of the constituent tree, containing nodes for these two constituents (see figure 2.1).

The parser will then start looking for the NP (since English is a left-to-right language the parser looks for the leftmost constituent first). Again, there is a choice of rules for NP, and again let us assume the parser tries the first one, rule 4. Again, it uses this rule to build part of the next level of the constituent tree, containing ART followed by NOUN (see figure 2.1). These can be directly matched to the first two items of the input sentence, and thus *The boy* has been successfully parsed – so far so good. The parser must now go back and try to find the VP, which is in the constituent tree but has not been expanded yet. Again there is a choice, and let us say rule 7 is chosen. The parser adds nodes for AUX, VERB and NP to the tree, finds the AUX and VERB (*had* and *taken* respectively) in the sentence, and begins to look for the NP. Let us say rule 4 is chosen to expand NP. Nodes for an ART and a NOUN are added to the tree.

Until now the parser (by pure luck) has made all the right choices, and has sailed through most of the sentence. But at this point it finds that *long* does not match ART, so something is amiss. The remedy typically employed by top-down parsers is called *backtracking*. The idea is to undo the last decision that was made, and try something else. The last decision made was the choice from the NP rules. This is now undone, with ART and NOUN being removed from the tree, and the parser attempts to parse *long walks* with rule 5. ART, ADJ and NOUN are added to the tree, but *long* still does not match ART. The parser backtracks again and tries rule 6. This time ADJ and NOUN are put in the tree, and the sentence is successfully parsed. If this final NP rule had also failed, it would have been undone, and the parser would have backtracked to

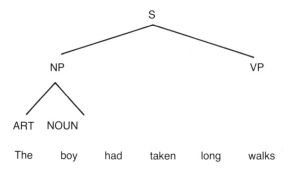

Figure 2.1

the yet earlier decision to use rule 7 for the VP (trying rule 8 instead). If still not successful, the parser would backtrack to the yet earlier decision to use rule 4 for the first NP, and if necessary, backtrack to the very first decision to use rule 1 for the sentence.

There are a few observations that should be made regarding top-down parsing with backtracking. The first is that the backtracking mechanism can eventually try all possible rule combinations. This means that if there is a valid parse, this method will eventually find it. It also means that if it is desirable to return all parses (in the case of ambiguous sentences) the parser can simply be asked to backtrack after saving a successful parse, and it will continue searching for others. Obviously, the parser needs to record where it has been and what it has done to make backtracking possible, but there are simple and efficient techniques for this, which will not be discussed here. Another observation is that this method involves an entirely serial strategy – each choice is taken to its conclusion before other alternatives are considered. It is possible to examine all the different expansions for NP (for instance) at the same time, either literally at the same time using parallel processing hardware, or by having a single processor evenly distribute many small chunks of time among the alternatives. The problem here is that if all the expansions for S are considered in parallel, and for each of these all the expansions of NP are considered in parallel, nine possibilities are already being considered. This kind of geometric progression can easily get out of hand in a large grammar. Most existing top-down parsers use serial search, although the potential for parallelism is increasing with the availability of parallel hardware.

Top-down parsing has both advantages and disadvantages. The advantages are its simplicity (both conceptually and in terms of the ease of writing a computer program), and the fact that it only considers constituents that make sense in the sentence as a whole (the fact that *walks* can be a verb form is never even considered in the above example). The primary disadvantage is that the backtracking mechanism can be wasteful. Consider parsing the sentence *The boy walks*. The parser will try rule 1 first, successfully parse *The boy* as above, but will be unable to find a VP (this grammar requires VPs to contain NPs). It will backtrack (after unsuccessfully trying to find another way to parse the first NP) to the beginning and will try rule 2 for the sentence. Again it will successfully parse the NP, but will be unable to find an AUX. Again it will backtrack (after again trying unsuccessfully to find another NP parse) to the beginning and will try rule 3 for the sentence. It will successfully parse the initial NP (for the third time) but this time it will find the VERB it is looking for. Clearly, parsing the same NP three times is not a wise use of processing resources.

2.2.2 Bottom-up Processing

The basic alternative to top-down parsing is to start with the lexical items and try to build progressively larger constituents, culminating with the sentence. Consider parsing *The small boy was painting the orange blocks* using grammar 2.1.

At the bottom of the constituent tree lie the lexical items *The, small, boy, was, painting, the, orange* and *blocks*. The parser begins by using the lexicon to assign categories to these, and in this case finds the following ambiguous words: *was* (AUX and VERB), *painting* (VERB, NOUN), *orange* (ADJ, NOUN) and *blocks* (VERB and NOUN). A bottom-up parser will try to find constituents that could potentially occupy the next layer up by finding groups of constituents that match the right-hand side of one of the grammar rules. Again, a left-to-right order will be used. First the parser finds that *The* followed by *small* followed by *boy* matches rule 5, and thus form an NP. Constitutents that are found by the parser are stored in a *chart* that keeps track of the constituents found, and which parts of the string they cover. The parser will also find the NPs *small boy* (rule 6), *the orange* (rule 4), *the orange blocks* (rule 5) and *orange blocks* (rule 6); and the VPs *was painting the orange* (rule 7), *was painting the orange blocks* (rule 7), *painting the orange* (rule 8) and *painting the orange blocks* (rule 8) – these are all added to the chart. At this point the parser may notice that it can build the sentences *The small boy was painting* (rule 2), *The small boy was* (rule 3) and *The small boy was painting the orange* (rule 1), as well as the corresponding sentences *small boy was painting* and so on – these are all added to the chart, but do not constitute successful parses because the entire string is not covered. The parser can, however, combine the NP *The small boy* with the VP *was painting the orange blocks* to form a sentence that covers the entire string (by rule 1). The sentence and final chart are shown in figure 2.2.

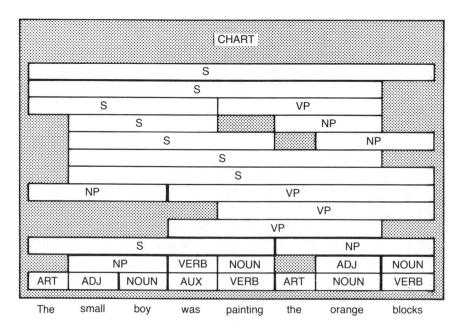

Figure 2.2

One important advantage of this bottom-up parsing is that constituents only have to be built once (unlike the top-down parse with backtracking above); if a constituent is put in the chart, it is never removed. The disadvantage of the bottom-up approach is that many spurious constituents are often built (e.g. all the sentences above that do not start with *The*). The parser does not know what it is looking for; it just combines everything it can, even if it means forming a sentence after an article.

2.2.3   Combining Top-down and Bottom-up Processing

As indicated above, both top-down and bottom-up parsing have advantages and disadvantages. Techniques have been developed that combine the positive aspects of each, but do not suffer from the disadvantages of either. One such technique is to do top-down parsing with backtracking, but any valid constituents found along the way are stored in a chart. Thus any valid constituents that are lost to backtracking will still be available in the chart, and will not have to be reconstructed should they be needed. Recall that when parsing *The boy walks*, the top-down parser described above will parse *The boy* to form an NP three separate times. If this constituent is put in the chart the first time, then when the parser backtracks to try other sentence rules, and it needs an NP at the beginning of the sentence, it can get it from the chart instead of having to reconstruct it repeatedly. But this method avoids the disadvantages of bottom-up parsing, because the top-down strategy only allows potentially useful constituents to be considered.

2.2.4   Looking Ahead

Even when top-down and bottom-up parsing are combined as described above, there is still too much wasted effort on the part of the parser: in particular, there is too much backtracking. Several techniques have been developed that will guide the parser more smoothly to the correct result. These techniques aim at *deterministic* parsing, where there is no guessing at all. Semantic and pragmatic guidance will be discussed in section 2.3, and syntactic techniques will be outlined here. Probably the most important syntactic technique is *lookahead*. The idea is to avoid making a guess (say, between which of several rules to use to expand a NP) by looking ahead a short distance in the text. It may be that the next couple of words eliminate most of the choices from consideration. Suppose the parser is faced with the string *Tammy has* . . . . It must decide whether to treat *has* as the main verb or as an auxiliary. If it just guesses, it could guess wrong and have to backtrack. Suppose it peeks at the next word in the sentence and finds *been*; this determines the choice and solves the problem.

In principle, any choice the parser is faced with can be resolved (with the exception of a genuinely ambiguous sentence) if the lookahead mechanism is allowed to look at the entire sentence. But this type of lookahead is simply parsing by another name, and just begs the question. Typically, lookahead is limited to only a very short distance. Consider the pair of sentences:

1   Have the soldiers given their medals by their sweethearts.
2   Have the soldiers given their medals to their sweethearts?

Here there is a choice to be made at the first word, which can only be determined by looking ahead most of the sentence, and is not resolvable with the limited lookahead typically used. Since *people* have difficulty parsing such sentences, limited lookahead should not be judged too harshly.

Another point that should be made with respect to the mechanism of lookahead is that it will still be beneficial even if it only indicates the correct choice most of the time. Any improvement over making random decisions will have a beneficial effect on the average efficiency of the parser. Lookahead is only one syntactic mechanism for making educated guesses. Others include the notion of *minimal attachment, right association* and *subcategorization*. Minimal attachment is a principle that suggests that, if different rule choices will result in a constituent being placed at different places in the tree, then that one should be chosen which results in the fewest nodes in the tree. That is, don't build any new nodes if a constituent can be attached to an existing one (see Garrett, 1990: 146–7). *Right association* or *late closure* is a principle suggesting that, other things being equal, the parser should choose grammar rules that result in constituents being placed next to the one previously added, rather than attaching them further up the tree. *Subcategorization* allows finer distinctions by dividing traditional categories (NP, PP, NOUN, VERB, etc.) into subgroups. Restrictions can then be placed on which types of VERBS require which types of PPs as arguments, and so on. If the parser finds the verb *put* and later a PP starting with *in, on, at*, etc., it should attach the PP to the *put* phrase, not somewhere else. Now these principles can all lead to wrong decisions, but the point is that they can help the parser make the right decision most of the time, and thereby decrease the time wasted on backtracking.

Thus far the discussion has focused on the problem of ambiguity (lexical and syntactic), pointing out the problems it causes for a parser, and outlining some techniques that help the parser resolve ambiguity efficiently. Only very simple grammars have been presented because ambiguity can occur even in simple grammars, and there was no point in complicating matters. But natural language, of course, requires much more sophisticated grammars to handle its complexities, and the need to process sophisticated grammars is an important issue. Parsing with more sophisticated grammars will be considered in the next four sections.

2.2.5   *Transformational Parsers*

Throughout much of the period when the first major parsing projects were getting underway, transformational grammar was a dominant theoretical framework. Since it was important to have parsers that could handle the more complex aspects of natural language syntax, and since transformational grammar appeared to be successful at describing these phenomena, a transformational parser was a natural idea. In retrospect, the idea of transformational parsers was not very successful, and it is instructive to look at the reasons why.

Transformational grammar consists of a base grammar containing rules of the same form as the simple grammars above, and transformational rules that generate the surface structure through manipulation of the phrase structure trees built by the base grammar (that is, the deep structure). The surface structure is finally passed to the phonological component. Parsing based on reversing transformational grammar runs into several problems. First, notice that the surface trees are not converted into a string form before being passed on. Thus a procedure is required that can take a sentence and produce a surface structure tree. This is a substantial parsing problem in its own right, but is necessary before anything else can be done.

Once the surface structure is available, all that can be done is to reverse the transformations to produce all of the deep structures from which the surface structure could have been generated. It turned out that simply applying transformations in reverse was not feasible: first, if the transformation involved deletions, there may be no reasonable way to recover the deleted item. Second, transformations are often applied in carefully ordered sequences – simply reversing transformations will fail to capture these interactions and may result in an ungrammatical sentence being accepted by the parser. As a result, it was necessary carefully to hand tailor a set of reverse transformations, which could be used for parsing. Designing these reverse transformations was difficult, and even then the parser was still faced with the problem of wading through many possible sequences of reverse transformations.

Despite these problems, there were two major transformational parsers constructed: one at MITRE in the 1960s, and one at IBM in the 1970s (these are discussed in some detail by Grishman, 1986). Nevertheless, these problems were sufficient to prevent transformational parsing from becoming a widely-used parsing framework.

2.2.6 *Augmented Transition Networks*

Probably the most popular grammar formalism for parsing has been the *augmented transition network*, or ATN. This formalism is inherently process-oriented, and is specifically used for parsing, as opposed to elegant linguistic description. Each category (S, NP, PP, etc.) is described as a network, which can be thought of as a map illustrating a network of roads. The map is labelled with a starting point and at least one destination. The goal is to get from the start to one of the destinations. Most of the roads on the map, however, require a toll to be paid, and the toll is a constituent. More precisely, given a sentence, the goal is to get from the start to one of the destinations using the constituents of the sentence in sequential order to pay for the tolls, and to not have any items left over when the destination is reached. The simplest case is shown in figure 2.3. The start (here *a*) will always be on the left of the map, the destinations will be marked with a double circle, and the tolls are indicated on the arcs between the different locations. Given the sentence *The boy threw the ball*, this map only allows one possibility – going from *a* to *b*, costing an NP. The NP *the boy* can be spent leaving *threw the ball* to pay for future moves. Again this simple map only allows moving to *c* at the cost of *threw*, and leaving only *the ball* to spend. This NP must be spent moving to *d*, successfully arriving at the destination with no constituents to spare.

Usually the map will provide more than one way to reach a destination. For instance, the map in figure 2.3 may have a jump arc (an arc that may be taken free of charge) between *c* and *d*. This will allow passage from *a* to *d* with only *The boy laughed* to spend. There may also be arcs that leave a location and loop back to the same location. For instance, if such an arc is placed at location *d* with a PP toll, it will allow any number of PPs to be spent without having to leave the destination. Thus *The boy laughed at the dog on Wednesday* will still allow the parser to finish at *d* with nothing left over (see figure 2.4 for these additions).

Now, one question that needs to be answered here is: when the parser is charged an NP or a PP, how does it know that *The boy* is an NP or that *on Wednesday* is a PP? The answer is that it has similar maps for these as shown in figure 2.4.

If, during the sentence trip, the parser is asked for an NP, it saves its place on the sentence map, and starts on the NP map paying the required tolls as it goes along. Assuming it reaches a destination, it is given a voucher for an NP, which it can use where it left off in the sentence. The constituents it spends on the NP trip form the NP constituent. Notice that the NP network may require the use of the PP network, and the PP network will then require the NP network and so on (*the boy on the horse in the park by the square . . . .*). Here the parser is really working on many different NPs and PPs at the same time, and for each one it must keep track of where it left off, and the words that have not been spent yet. The mechanism used to keep track of all this information is beyond the scope of this chapter. Suffice it to say that computers are good at this kind of bookkeeping.

The grammar as presented so far is called a recursive transition network (RTN) because the networks can invoke each other recursively, as just mentioned. But this sort of grammar cannot handle many of the complexities of

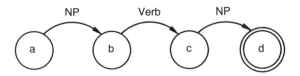

Figure 2.3

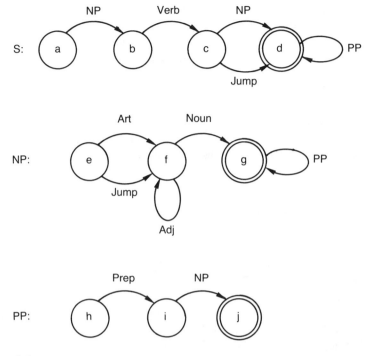

Figure 2.4

natural language (RTNs are equivalent to context-free grammars). For this reason the network formalism is *augmented* (producing the ATN formalism) by allowing the grammar to not only impose tolls, but also to require the parser to do some extra paperwork when traversing the arcs. This paperwork may involve recording some of the properties of the constituent being spent, or checking to see that the constituent being spent meets certain conditions. As a simple illustration, when traversing the arc between *a* and *b* in figure 2.4, the parser may be required to record the *person* and *number* of the NP under the heading of SUBJECT. When paying for the trip between *b* and *c*, the parser will only be allowed to use a verb that agrees with what was recorded under SUBJECT. In general, the formalism allows an arbitrary amount of information to be kept, and arbitrarily complex checking operations to be performed. This allows the ATN formalism to handle anything a transformational grammar can.

The ATN parsing strategy that has been outlined here can be related to the discussion at the beginning of the chapter. The parser starts with the sentence network and tries to find the constituents that are required. This is the top-down strategy described earlier. It is also possible that the parser may have to choose between several paths leaving a location – say, if one arc costs a noun and one arc costs an adjective and the next word to be spent is ambiguous (e.g. try the NP trip with *the orange blocks*). Typically, ATN parsers take the simple approach of trying one possibility at a time and backtracking when necessary.

ATN parsers can also make use of the chart ideas mentioned above, which may tell the parser that the next two words to be spent form an NP (having stored the results of a previous trip that was undone by backtracking) so it does not have to get the NP map out – it can use the same NP to pay the toll as it did last time.

Although ATNs are capable of handling the complexities of natural language, specifying all the required conditions on the arcs can be awkward and cumbersome. Also, because ATNs impose a processing strategy, it can be difficult to integrate newly developed computational techniques. For practical applications, however, ATNs will likely continue to have a large following.

2.2.7   Logic Grammars

An approach that has attracted some attention is parsing with logic grammars, usually within the programming language PROLOG (see Clocksin and Mellish, 1987; and Pereira and Warren, 1986). Here the rules of the grammar are written in terms of logic predicates. The predicates take lists of words as their arguments: one argument is the list containing the entire input string, the other argument is the list that remains once a constituent has been removed from the beginning of the input string. If what has been removed satisfies the definition of the predicate, then the value of the predicate is TRUE, otherwise it is FALSE. For instance, the predicate

np([the,boy,threw,the,ball], [threw,the,ball])

is TRUE because what has been removed is an NP. PROLOG statements can be written to define these predicates, and each statement will correspond straightforwardly to a grammar production rule. In order for these definitions to be general, they must contain variables, which PROLOG requires to be written using upper case. For example:

np(X, Y) :- article(X, Z), noun(Z, Y).

This says that the predicate np is TRUE of an input string X and a remainder Y if the *article* predicate is satisfied by the input string X with remainder Z, and the *noun* predicate is satisfied by the input string Z with remainder Y. This can be stated simply as: There is an NP at the beginning of a sentence X if there is an article at the beginning of sentence X and a noun at the beginning of what follows it; furthermore, the part of the sentence that follows the NP must be the list Y.

Number agreement (for instance) can be checked by adding an extra variable to the predicates. Thus the grammar is then written as a series of PROLOG statements such as:

s(X, Y, NUMBER) :- np(X, Z, NUMBER), vp(Z, Y, NUMBER).
vp(X, Y, NUMBER) :- verb(X, Z, NUMBER), np(Z, Y).
vp(X, Y, NUMBER) :- verb(X, Z, NUMBER), pp(Z, Y).

Of course, many such variables will be needed in practice. While this may not be the most elegant way to write grammar rules, the advantage is that no parser has to be written – PROLOG itself does all the necessary processing. The result is another top-down parser with backtracking.

Notice that the grammars described here are very simple, and that these rules only ask PROLOG to check to see if a sentence can be parsed; the syntactic structures are not saved. The rules of a logic grammar that supports structure building and that can handle complex syntax are not nearly as simple (see Allen, 1987). Logic grammars (especially those written in PROLOG) are an attractive approach to writing small experimental parsers, but it is not clear that this method is the best approach towards an elegant and efficient parser for a large and complex grammar.

2.2.8 Unification

Grammatical formalisms that employ unification have become popular in linguistics lately (see Shieber, 1986; and the introduction to Pollard and Sag, 1987), and unification has some important computational properties that are directly relevant to parsing. The primary computational advantage of unification is that it allows the parser to work with partial descriptions of constituents. The parser can accumulate information about the logical subject (for instance) based on constraints attached to the grammar rules that are used, as well as accumulating information about various NPs based on entries in the lexicon. At any given time this information does not have to be complete – in particular, it may not yet know which NP is the logical subject, and it does not have to guess. Eventually, perhaps much later in the parse, it will become apparent which NP is the logical subject, and the two descriptions can be *unified*. Informally, unification is simply the combination, or merging, of two descriptions to form a more specific description that is still consistent with both. Any operations that could be performed on either of the original descriptions can now be performed on the unified description. Suppose there are two NP descriptions (NP_5 and NP_7 in figure 2.5), one has the article *a* and therefore is singular, and the other has a noun *fish* which leaves the number ambiguous between singular and plural. If it becomes apparent that these are both descriptions of the same NP, then they can be unified (written $\oplus$) to form an NP with the article *a*, the noun *fish*, and the number *singular* (see figure 2.5).

The advantages of unification become most apparent when it is compared to the mechanisms traditionally used in ATNs. When an ATN encounters the first NP in a sentence it is recorded as the logical subject. If the parser later discovers that the sentence is passive, all the information about the logical

NP$_5$:   NP$_7$:   NP$_9$:

  article: a $\oplus$ noun: fish $=$ article: a

  number: singular   number: plural or singular   noun: fish

                                                               number: singular

Figure 2.5

subject will be moved to the logical object instead. This may not seem to be the end of the world, but it adds extra work for the parser, and it poses problems if there are checks being done on the logical subject because the information there may simply be incorrect. Unification avoids this problem because no lexical information is associated with the logical subject until it is determined which NP should in fact fill that role.

This is another example of a general principle that has been discussed before – unification is a technique that allows the parser to avoid making guesses. If it guesses, and guesses wrong, there will be a cost to fix the error. Lookahead and unification allow the parser to continue working without making guesses, thereby make the parsing more efficient.

Unification, or a unification-like mechanism, is a key ingredient of many linguistic formalisms: generalized phrase structure grammar, head-driven phrase structure grammar, lexical-functional grammar, certain categorial grammars, functional unification grammar, systemic grammar and others. Unification allows these grammars to specify constraints on the language without worrying about the order in which the constraints are applied. If ten unifications are required to specify a structure, any permutation of those unifications will produce the same structure. Unification thus allows linguists to specify local grammar operations, without worrying about global ordering of operations. This makes it easier to write and understand complex grammars. Although the theoretical linguists do not use unification for computational reasons, the fact is that it can be, and might as well be, exploited for computational purposes. The computational benefits really stem from the same point: if the order in which grammar operations are performed does not matter, then it is impossible for the parser to try the wrong ordering. Also, the parser will not be forced to make decisions before it is ready, since delaying a decision will not be a problem. Unification, however, does not solve all the computational problems – the parser still must decide which operations are to be performed.

2.2.9   Morphology

The discussions in the previous sections have made the simplifying assumption that all word forms are directly available in the lexicon. An approach that is more flexible, and more economical in terms of storage, is to capture the generalizations in the lexicon in the form of morphological rules. The parser can then use these rules – in effect – to parse words.

There are two broad problems that a morphological analyser faces. First, the analyser must be able to 'undo' the spelling rules for adding affixes, for example. Here the analyser must be able to interpret *moved* as *move* plus *ed*, or *reduction* as *reduce* plus *tion*. Second, the analyser must be able to parse a complicated word to form a constituent tree. Ritchie et al. (1987) describe a morphological representation that involves feature constraints and unification for this kind of word parsing. A detailed treatment of morphological analysis will not be given here, as the basic principles and techniques are similar to those discussed for straightforward sentence parsing.

2.3 Higher-level Processing

This section will outline some of the computational techniques that have been developed for processing above the level of syntax. General discussion of linguistic issues will be avoided here (as these are treated in detail in the linguistics literature); this section will only address issues that have computational significance and for which appropriate computational techniques have been developed. This discussion will be divided into two sections: the first on semantics and reference, the second on pragmatics.

2.3.1 Semantics and Reference

Although the problems of semantic interpretation and resolution of reference have not received as much attention from the computational community as parsing, there are some interesting techniques that have been developed for these tasks. There are also some major problems yet to be solved. Turning to semantic interpretation first, there are two fundamental ideas that serve as the basis for most approaches. One key idea is the *type hierarchy* or *classification hierarchy*. This consists of information about classes and subclasses of objects in the world. Near the top of the hierarchy might be the concept *physical object*. Below this might be the classes *living* and *non-living* with *animate* being a subclass of *living*, and so on. These hierarchies are useful for applying selectional restrictions (e.g. requiring that the argument of *die* be a member of the class of *living* objects). Given a particular concept (say, *dog*), the classes to which it belongs are found by simply following the branches up the hierarchy. This sort of processing can be done very efficiently – in fact, some recent programming languages (the *object-oriented* languages) are specifically designed to facilitate working with classification hierarchies.

Another key concept for semantic processing is the notion of *case roles* or *thematic roles*. The exact set of roles varies slightly but is typified by roles such as

Agent and Instrument. Thematic roles combine with classification hierarchies to enforce selectional restrictions such as a requirement that the Agent for a particular verb must be *animate*. But before the restrictions can be enforced, the roles must be assigned to syntactic constituents based on the syntactic analysis provided by the parser. This can be accomplished through semantic interpretation rules that match syntactic descriptions of constituents and produce partial semantic interpretations for the constituent. For instance, there may be a rule for *put* that matches an active sentence with *put* as the main verb and an *animate* surface subject. The rule would produce a partial semantic description stating that the surface subject fills the Agent role. There will also be interpretation rules for the various articles, prepositions, and so on.

Often syntactic components will (in isolation) have several interpretations, and thus several conflicting semantic rules may match at the same time. A technique useful for resolving these conflicts is *unification*. Unification is used here in much the same way it is used for syntactic analysis. The idea is to produce an interpretation for a constituent by finding a set of interpretations for each of *its* constituents that can be unified. The interpretations can be unified in any order, so the interpreter is not forced to make any particular decision at any particular time; it is able to make local decisions when appropriate, without worrying about any global ordering constraints. Again unification allows the semantic interpreter to avoid making premature guesses about the interpretation, even when there are several possibilities.

A problem that arises when trying to resolve some cases of word-sense ambiguity and definite reference is the problem of finding associations in memory. Consider the following: *I bought a new desk today. The drawer holds files.* There are two problems with interpreting *the drawer* here – first, it is ambiguous; and second, a definite reference usually requires previous mention. Both of these problems, however, can be resolved by noting that a drawer is part of a desk. This is a straightforward association, but in general the associations can be indirect and arbitrary – *files* can be disambiguated by noting that stationery files are often stored in desk drawers. One technique that has been proposed for solving this problem is called *spreading activation*. The idea is to start from the concept in question (e.g. *drawer*) and a database of relations, and find all the entries in the database to which the concept is directly related. If none of these concepts can resolve the ambiguity/reference, then find all the entries related to *them*, and so on until a solution is found. Obviously, finding all these associations can take a long time in a large database. It is very likely that people are good at this sort of associative reasoning because the architecture of the human brain allows the associational paths to be explored in parallel. There is currently considerable interest within the artificial intelligence community in modelling neural networks, and much of this work involves associative memory. Unfortunately, the hardware required to run the associative memory in parallel is not widely available.

Several other problems remain for which no adequate computational treatment is available. These include the interpretation of adjectives, noun–noun modification and quantifier scope. These problems are being addressed, and some progress has been made, but semantic interpretation still has a long way to go.

2.3.2 *Pragmatics*

Pragmatics deals with reasoning about beliefs and intentions. The literature of linguistics and philosophy expresses this reasoning in terms of formal deduction. One approach to automating this reasoning is simply to exploit an automatic theorem prover to perform these deductions in a straightforward manner. This sounds like a good idea, but the general theorem provers required for this task are too inefficient for this to work in any serious application.

One aspect of pragmatics for which computational techniques exist (and these computational techniques may even have an impact on linguistics and philosophy) is the area of intentions with respect to plans. Planning is a major research area in artificial intelligence, and sophisticated treatments of planning problems have been developed. To some extent these results can shed some light on the reasoning about plans that is necessary for understanding natural language. Texts that were produced with some goal in mind, or that describe actions of people, may require reasoning about plans. Computer systems that involve inferring the plans behind texts, and behind the actions of the characters in texts, have been developed by Allen and his colleagues (e.g. Allen and Perrault, 1986) and Wilensky (1981a) respectively. The inference still tends to be inefficient, but at least there are some sophisticated computational ideas being explored.

The key idea behind planning is that there are goals to achieve, and actions – having preconditions and effects – capable of achieving them. To achieve a goal, a plan is constructed which contains an action that has the effect of achieving the goal. The trouble is that the action may have preconditions that are not satisfied. These preconditions are then set as subgoals, and actions (which may themselves have unsatisfied preconditions) must be put into the plan which will achieve them, and so on. Consider the following example (from Wilensky, 1981a):

Willa was hungry. She grabbed the Michelin guide. She got in her car.

In order to understand this set of sentences, it is necessary to interpret them in terms of goals, preconditions and subgoals. First of all, Willa has the goal of satisfying her hunger. This goal can be achieved if she eats out at a restaurant. But eating at a restaurant has the precondition of being at a restaurant. The resulting subgoal of getting there can be achieved by driving, but this, in turn, requires being in the car and knowing how to get to a restaurant. These final two subgoals help to understand the final and penultimate sentences in the example.

Allen and Perrault (1986) looked at the issues involved in understanding and responding to queries at a railway station information counter. They observe that if informative and helpful responses are to be given, it is necessary to understand the client's plan. If someone asks: 'How much is the train to Cleveland?', the system should not simply give the price if all such trains have been cancelled. Similarly, if someone asks: 'What time does the train leave for Cincinnatti?', the system might answer '4 pm from platform 9', since both knowing the time and knowing the location are preconditions of getting to the train.

Only very simple reasoning with plans has been discussed here, but the reasoning can get quite complex. In any case, the artifical intelligence work on planning provides a good understanding of the reasoning involved in planning, the computational representations required for reasoning about plans, and computational techniques for doing this reasoning. The results of this work carry over directly to the problem of reasoning about plans when understanding natural language.

2.4   Guidance from Above

Techniques such as keeping a chart, lookahead and unification, as discussed in section 2.2, allow the parser to produce a syntactic analysis with far less backtracking than a straightforward top-down search. But lexical and syntactic ambiguity often results in the parser having to return with several possible analyses. The number of analyses is not the problem, it is the fact that the parser had to expend the effort to produce them all, when most will be rejected on semantic and pragmatic grounds. The issue becomes most critical when there are multiple ambiguities, producing a geometric progression of possible syntactic analyses. For this reason a considerable amount of work has been devoted to finding techniques where semantics and pragmatics can guide the parser. The interaction between the parser and the higher-level analyses will be the focus here; some methods for performing these analyses have been discussed in section 2.3.

2.4.1   Parsing and the Autonomy of Syntax

Suggesting that the parser may receive semantic and pragmatic guidance raises a important point of contention. On one hand, many linguists hold the belief that, in humans, syntactic analysis is a process independent of semantics and pragmatics (see Garrett, 1990). Since people are very good at parsing, this might suggest that the same approach should be taken when building parsing systems. Within the artificial intelligence community, on the other hand, the potential computational benefits of semantic and pragmatic guidance have motivated a strong tradition in which syntax does not operate independently.

Even on purely computational grounds, however, the issue is by no means simple. The sheer volume of semantic and pragmatic knowledge can make analysis computationally expensive. It may be argued that a lot of effort will be wasted rejecting parses on semantic and pragmatic grounds, which could have been rejected on syntactic grounds at much less expense.

The linguistics community, the psychological evidence and the computational benefits all seem to be split on this issue. For the purposes of this chapter, the autonomy of syntax will be treated as an open issue. There seems to be enough evidence that at least in some cases, to some degree, semantic and pragmatic guidance is advantageous (and psychologically plausible) enough to justify exploring different sources of guidance and how they might interact with the parser.

2.4.2　Semantic Guidance

This section will examine the different approaches that have been taken to providing the parser with semantic guidance. In effect, one technique has already been considered: the case where the semantics is only consulted once a complete sentence has been parsed. This is the minimal amount of guidance possible, and forms one end of the spectrum. At the other end of the spectrum are techniques where the semantic component is in control, and the parser only does what the semantic component tells it to do. The most effective approaches probably lie somewhere in between. This section will present and discuss techniques that represent a broad sample from across this spectrum.

In order to establish the boundaries, the most semantically-oriented techniques will be considered first. Probably the most extensive use of semantically-driven parsing appears in the work of Roger Schank and his students (e.g. Schank, 1986). The approach taken is to identify the main verb of the sentence, and to use the *thematic roles* associated with that verb to provide specific tasks for the parser. If the verb *give* is found to be the main verb, for instance, semantic knowledge indicates that the following roles must be filled: ACTOR (the giver), OBJECT (the thing being given), and TO (the receiver). The semantics will also, for instance, demand that the ACTOR and TO roles be filled by a person or organization. The parser is then given the task of looking through the sentence for suitable constituents. The parser used for this purpose has certain patterns to look for in each case, but typically does not have access to a full grammar of the language. In practice these systems have trouble with complex syntactic constructs, but it may be possible to combine this processing strategy with more sophisticated treatment of grammar.

Another extreme semantically-oriented parsing strategy is to use grammars that are written in terms of semantic categories – these are called *semantic grammars*. This will only be feasible for applications involving a very small domain of discourse, where the set of semantic categories is easily circumscribed. Consider the rules in grammar 2.2 (adapted from Allen, 1987) as part of a hypothetical airline reservation parser.

```
RESERVATION-VP  →  RESERVING RESERVATION-MODIFIERS

RESERVING  →  RESERVE-VERB FLIGHT

RESERVATION-MODIFIERS  →  for PERSON

RESERVATION-MODIFIERS  →  « empty string »
```

Grammar 2.2

These grammars cannot capture syntactic generalizations, and therefore can only reasonably handle a limited set of syntactic forms. They do illustrate an interesting relationship between semantics and syntax, however, as only semantically valid parses are considered.

Given that many interesting applications will require the parser to deal with a wide variety of natural language constructions, this discussion will turn to approaches that involve parsing from a large grammar. In contrast to the semantically-driven approach, these systems typically employ a parser such as those described in section 2.2, but the parser periodically checks with the semantics to make sure it is on the right track. The issue here boils down to how often the parser and semantic analyser interact. If interaction upon completion of a sentence is not enough, a simple alternative is to have the semantics check each constituent as it is parsed. If an NP is found at the beginning of a sentence, but it has no semantic interpretation, then there is no point in continuing to parse the rest of the sentence, as a mistake has apparently been made. This not only saves the parser the effort of completing the faulty analysis, but it also saves the semantic interpeter from examining perhaps several complete (but faulty) parses upon completion. When the NP is rejected, a top-down parser will backtrack (just as if it failed to find an NP) without adding the NP to the chart, to try another alternative. If it is advantageous to catch the parser before it produces a semantically anomalous sentence, why not try to catch it even before it produces a semantically anomalous constituent? Semantic restrictions can be applied every time a grammar rule is invoked. If the parser has constructed a partial NP *the orange thought*, say, when parsing *The man eating the orange thought over the plan*, it can be corrected before it commits the further error of attaching the PP. This example illustrates how semantic processing can save the parser some effort. It also illustrates the possible downside of this approach. Notice that this error can eventually be detected on purely syntactic grounds. The question is whether the parser would have found the error sooner if the semantics had not interrupted. In general, sometimes semantic processing will help, sometimes it will hurt. Ultimately, the decision on whether to impose semantic guidance will depend on the size and efficiency of the two components, whether they must share computational resources (e.g. can they be run on separate processors?) and other issues, which will vary from system to system.

To summarize, the decision as to whether or not to have the parser guided by semantic criteria – assuming no theoretical bias – comes down to the nature of the application at hand. If the texts to be analysed include only a small number of syntactic constructions, and cover only a very limited domain, then a semantic grammar can easily be written to produce an efficient and effective system. If the parser must handle a large subset of English, but efficiency is not critical, then it may not be worth the effort to try to interleave syntax and semantics. If the grammar is large enough that many spurious parses will be produced and efficient semantic analysis can be performed, and efficiency is an issue, then an interleaved system should be considered.

2.4.3 Contextual Guidance

Having seen the potential benefit of semantic guidance of the parser, the question of other possible sources of guidance is raised. The obvious candidate is pragmatics, although this is too broad an area to make any general claims. The traditional domain of pragmatics – reasoning about beliefs and intentions – is certainly required for the understanding of a text, but the inference involved is extremely expensive. The long chains of deductive inferences that characterize traditional pragmatics cannot, as a rule, be computed efficiently; the problem is not deduction itself, but knowing which deduction to make at each step. Thus, traditional pragmatic reasoning during the parsing process is not often a justifiable option. Some techniques have been developed within the computational community, however, which could be construed as non-traditional forms of pragmatic reasoning. It may be possible to use these techniques to guide the parser efficiently. This possibility will be explored in this section.

A technique that introduces a contextual element, but strongly resembles the type of semantic analysis outlined in the previous section, is the use of *sublanguages* (see Grishman and Kittredge, 1986). Here sets of semantic constraints are defined, which are specific to the language used in some restricted domain such as biochemistry or medicine. The common example is that *The polypeptides were washed in hydrochloric acid* is a valid sentence in biochemistry, but *The hydrochloric acid was washed in polypeptides* is not. The necessary constraints can be imposed by a semantic grammar, or interleaved processing as described above.

Pragmatic reasoning is usually discussed as a method for making sense of a text after the fact. But the speaker's beliefs and intentions, if known in advance, can also provide *expectations* about what will be said. These expectations can give the parser some hints about what to look for, and result in more efficient processing. Roger Schank has suggested that language processing can profit from *scripts* of common events, the famous example being a trip to a restaurant. The point is that we all have knowledge about what typically happens at a restaurant, and this knowledge can be used to fill in details that are omitted from a story, for example (see Cullingford, 1986). This knowledge can be stored easily and accessed efficiently.

But some of the expected events will be language events, with meanings and forms that are, at least to some degree, predictable. For instance, after you have put down the menu, you expect the waitress/waiter will ask for your order, and you can predict that an imperative construction will not be used. At least for familiar situations, this type of information can be made available, without having to reason explicitly about the waitress/waiter's beliefs and intentions. The result is that these context-based expectations can help the parser make choices and avoid guessing.

The idea of being able to make specific predictions based on context has been discussed in the sociolinguistics literature under the rubric of *register*. Language use is seen as varying according to a rich set of socio-contextual variables. The language found on postcards from friends on vacation will be influenced by the fact that they are talking about their vacation, the fact that they are friends and the fact that they are writing on a postcard. The language found in the 'experimental design' section of a scientific journal in a particular field will be influenced by the fact that it is describing an experiment in the particular field, by the fact that the description is aimed at experts in this field and by the fact that it is a formal publication (more specific distinctions could be made). Given knowledge of how these variables affect syntactic choices, the parser can be provided with some inexpensive yet valuable guidance. The type of register analysis performed by Halliday (e.g. 1978) results in a hierarchy of situational features. This is useful because even if the details of the situation are not known, the predictions associated with the very general situation classes can still provide some guidance. A project is currently underway at Ohio State University to determine the extent to which Halliday-style register analysis can provide a parser with useful expectations.

2.5   Conclusion

The problem of understanding natural language remains one of the most important, yet most difficult tasks to which computers have been applied. The ability to parse and extract the meaning from texts would be tremendously useful for a wide range of applications. Unfortunately, this ability has not yet been achieved, nor is it likely that the full ability will be achieved in the near future. The current state of the art and the possibilities for the future will be discussed below.

It is currently feasible to build effective and efficient parsers for restricted domains and small grammars. But the general problem of parsing unrestricted text with a large grammar has not been solved. Constructing large grammars is a major problem in its own right, and this has only been attempted by a few, well-funded projects. As a result, the vast majority of parsing research is done using small, experimental grammars. For text studies projects that require a general parser, this means that the parser should be acquired rather than developed. It is likely that available parsers will improve considerably over the next few years. For projects that only require parsing in a restricted domain, or only require a small grammar, it may be currently feasible to construct a parser from scratch.

The current situation is worse for semantics and pragmatics – techniques exist that allow some interesting processing, but only to a very limited extent. Semantic grammars and sublanguage systems, for example, have proved to be effective for analysing texts, but only within a very narrow and predetermined topic area. A good example of the state of the art is described by Hobbs (1986) – the TACITUS system demonstrates sophisticated techniques that handle: some syntactic ambiguity, some noun–noun modifiers, some difficult reference problems and even some instances of metonymy. Most application projects, however, will simply not have the resources to develop this kind of system.

As for the short-term future of natural language parsing and understanding, there are at least two areas in which rapid progress may occur. The first is the area of grammar formalisms. One of the most serious obstacles to progress in computational linguistics has been the gap between the grammars of interest in theoretical linguistics on the one hand, and grammars that could be processed efficiently on the other. Recent interest in unification grammars by the linguistics community offers some hope that theoretical linguistic research will have increasing relevance to computational applications. Returning to the point made at the very beginning of the chapter, there is no reason why theoretical linguists *should* be writing efficient grammars (maintaining the competence/performance distinction), but the fact that the grammars they are developing have some coincidental computational properties will benefit computational linguistics.

A second area that has some promise for the near future is the application of results from research in artificial neural networks (connectionism). As mentioned above, the work on associative memories, in particular, has straightforward application to certain problems in reference and lexical disambiguation. While some are claiming that neural networks will replace traditional artificial intelligence methodology, it appears more likely that neural networks will make an important contribution to certain low-level tasks including memory access, but that processes such as parsing, reasoning about plans and so on, are not at an appropriate level of abstraction for direct neural modelling.

As for the long-term picture, it is hard to say. Progress has been slow but steady for decades, and will probably continue in the same fashion. Breakthroughs will be required from linguistics as well as artificial intelligence, and hopefully there will be an increasing synergy between the two. The picture painted in this chapter may appear bleak, but the fact is that useful text analysis is possible, and the quality of analysis will continue to improve. Automatic understanding of natural language has so many important applications that it should not be dismissed on the basis of its difficulty.

Further Reading

Several general texts describing the processing of natural language have appeared in the past few years. Winograd (1983) provides detailed coverage of syntactic processing. Winograd has gone to considerable effort to make the material in this book accessible to non-programmers. A particular strength of this book is the quality of discussions on the motivations behind the ideas, and the relationship between computational and theoretical linguistics. A smaller but more general text is Grishman (1986). This book covers the whole range of language understanding from syntax to pragmatics and discourse. The section on transformational parsers is particularly good. Grishman assumes readers have some knowledge of programming and data structures, but the text does not require any great degree of computational sophistication. Allen (1987) is another text covering all aspects of language processing, and the topics are covered systematically in considerable detail. The outstanding feature of this book is that consistent notations are used throughout. This greatly facilitates comprehension of how the various processes interact, because the output described in one section will use the same notation as the input described in another. Although Allen claims not to assume a great deal of programming expertise, readers with little computational background may find it difficult to read. Finally, a recent book by Gazdar and Mellish (1989a) takes the most programming-oriented approach of all. This book also provides an overview of computational linguistics from syntax to pragmatics, but actual programming code examples are used throughout the book. The interesting thing about this book is that there are three editions that use three different programming languages: LISP, PROLOG and POP-11.

A very good collection of articles can be found in Grosz, Sparck-Jones and Webber (1986). This collection contains technical papers on many of the topics covered in this chapter: Robinson's article describes a large grammar that has been used in several major natural language projects. One of the original papers on logic grammars (Pereira and Warren), a paper on reasoning about plans (Allen and Perrault) and a description of a script-based system (Cullingford) also appear in this collection.

Some other publications that deserve special mention are: Perrault and Grosz's (1988) survey article of natural language interfaces, which in fact gives a good overview of many issues that are more general than that particular application; and Shieber's (1986) discussion of the different unification-based formalisms and the ideas that bind them together.

3 Computers and Text Generation: Principles and Uses

John A. Bateman and Eduard H. Hovy

3.1 Introduction

The area of study called natural language generation is about twenty-five years old, having started as an offshoot of the discipline natural language processing (also called computational linguistics). It shares interests with a healthy mixture of linguistics, computer science (artificial intelligence), psycholinguistics and, occasionally, philosophy, sociology and neurolinguistics. The central question studied is how one can program computers to produce high-quality text from some computer-internal representation of information. Motivation for this study ranges from the entirely theoretical (linguistic, psycholinguistic) to the entirely practical (to produce output systems for computer programs).

Writing an adequate overview of this subfield is not easy, although a number of admirable general surveys are available: see for example Mann et al. (1981), Kempen (1986) and McKeown and Swartout (1987). No single perspective suffices to cover the majority of existing language generation research. Therefore, in this overview, we maintain three parallel perspectives, organized as three independent dimensions of description. For each major paradigm within this subject space we briefly describe one (or sometimes a few) examples of landmark work. We also give references to the intervening areas, as well as some pointers to the fields beyond. This multi-perspective approach should, we hope, provide a fairly detailed yet easily assimilated overview of the field.

The first organizing dimension, *generator task*, contains three major points (ordered to reflect the history of research):

1 Grammatical realization: how can I say things?
2 Content selection: what shall I say?
3 Motivation for decisions: why should I say it, and why in that way?

The second organizing dimension, *method of generation*, contains four increasingly general points:

1   Canned items: pre-defined fixed sentences or paragraphs are selected and used without modification.
2   Templates: pre-defined items which allow some variation are selected and their spaces are filled in.
3   Cascaded items: initial abstract patterns are selected and then, piece by piece, replaced by successively more detailed patterns, until the cascade bottoms out in the final text.
4   Features: individual features, each controlling one aspect of the desired text, are computed and combined to form a full specification of the desired result, which is then turned into the text.

The final organizing dimension is *register*, as defined in systemic functional linguistics (Halliday, 1978; Patten, 1986). By providing an overall framework for the study of language in general, register enables the rather diverse work in text generation to be related, furnishing a sense of what has been achieved so far and what still remains to be addressed. Register pertains to the generator's sensitivity to (i.e. ability to express suitable locutional variations depending on) the following three aspects of communication:

1   Field: the subject-matter.
2   Tenor: the interlocutors' interpersonal roles and relations.
3   Mode: the situation and means of communication.

This chapter has the following structure: the next section contains a short description of the nature of the three perspectival dimensions we have chosen. Then follows a section describing a number of text generation systems, organized, first, into the three generator tasks, and second, into the four types of generation method. Where relevant, discussions of the register-related aspects of the systems are discussed. The final section points out various promising paths of research and provides pointers to related work in other subfields.

3.2   Perspectives for Describing Text Generators

3.2.1   Generator Task

The study of natural language generation by computer has traditionally focused on the questions of content selection (namely, *what shall I say?*) and grammatical realization (namely, *how can I say it?*). Investigations of the former question have relied for many of their insights on philosophers of language (Grice, 1971; Austin, 1962, etc.); insights for the latter have been provided primarily by grammarians. Traditionally, the field has called the former *text planning* and the latter *realization* (or occasionally, *strategic* and *tactical* aspects). The roots for this separation can be traced back to the hypothesis of autonomous syntax of Chomsky (1965) and others, and though the concept of *message level* (McDonald, Vaughan and Pustejovsky, 1987; Levelt and Schriefers, 1987; Bock, 1982) and similar notions have occasionally been used to denote a level of pre-syntactic sentence specification, the boundaries have never been strictly delineated, and have frequently been called into question; see for example Appelt (1985), Hovy (1988c) and Paris (1988).

Since computational research has focused on the latter (how can I say it?) question, one can, at the current time and using available knowledge, quite easily build a useful (though limited) single-sentence generator program. One cannot, however, as easily build a program that selects material and performs the planning required to organize it into coherent text. In fact, many generators ignore the content selection problem completely. On the other hand, the systems that do attempt to select and organize material tend to skimp when it comes to the *how* question – some simply produce sentence specifications without even trying to make sentences, and many others use canned text (fixed, pre-defined sentences). The unhappy consequence is that intermediate issues, such as sentence delimitation and amalgamation of disparate material, are not properly addressed by either task, and have never been the objects of serious study. Only recently, with the work of Meteer (1990) and Scott and De Souza (1990), has this 'generation gap' (Meteer's term) begun to be addressed.

Recent attempts to increase the expressive power and range of generators have led to a third major question, namely, selecting a particular alternative from a number of options (the *why?* question). This question is more difficult to answer than either the *what* or the *how* questions, and it has to date remained largely unaddressed in natural language processing in general. Understanding these three questions – *how?*, *what?* and *why?* – provides a powerful conceptual framework with which to interpret the issues of language generation.

3.2.2   Generation Method

The second perspective relates not so much to the task of the system being built as to its method of operation. The same methods have been applied to various tasks, with varying degrees of success.

The simplest method of generation appears in every computer program: a common print statement containing a fixed sentence. For example, the computer code in an automated bank teller machine responsible for printing out

Welcome. Please insert your card

(and all the other messages) is a simple text generator. Obviously, the text can be made arbitrarily sophisticated, with as many sentences as required. However, the system has no way of exploiting commonalities across sentences, and hence no way of recombining parts of existing sentences to produce new ones – not even to change

Good morning!

into

Good afternoon!

Canned text systems illustrate how simplicity comes at the expense of power.

The obvious generalization is to create templates instead of canned sentences or paragraphs. Every form letter that contains spaces into which your name and address and the date are automatically entered is a text template. Though enabling some saving of space, template systems by and large suffer from the same lack of combinatory power that hampers canned text systems.

The next level of sophistication is to generalize across all the templates and to extract all the common forms. As discussed below, this approach can result in a phrase structure grammar of the texts produced. Generation is here a process of repeated expansions (most easily explained with single sentences, though it has been performed for paragraphs as well). In English, for example, a form of the NOUN-PHRASE pattern is [DETERMINER ADJECTIVES HEAD-NOUN POST-NOMINAL-MODIFIERS], as in 'the three little pigs from Jupiter', and a SENTENCE pattern is [NOUN-PHRASE VERB-PHRASE]. In order to generate, the system starts with the symbol SENTENCE, which by its rule is expanded into [NOUN-PHRASE VERB-PHRASE], which two symbols are in turn replaced by their patterns, until this cycle of expansion eventually replaces all symbols with words and bottoms out in a sentence. This process has been called cascading or expansion.

Still, however, the cascading method is not completely general – for example, the order of constituents is implicitly captured in the pattern rather than explicitly represented. This can be remedied by generalizing one step further. Just as (going from canned text to templates to cascaded phrase patterns) words are increasingly replaced by classes or by features that identify them, one can go to the limit and define an explicit feature for every possible type of variation the desired text contains: variations of order, tense, mood, type of sentence, and so forth. The generator computes a collection of features that fully specifies a text and then translates those features into the precise text. Such systems we call feature-based.

3.2.3   *Register and Text Generation*

It is well known that language varies according to the language user's geographical and social background – this is called dialectal variation. But there is another kind of linguistic variation as well, one that is more immediately important to computational linguistics: variation according to use, namely *functional variation* (see also Patten's chapter in this volume). A particular functional variety is called a register just as a regional variety is called a dialect. One sees register at work when, for instance, sports commentaries are linguistically different from weather forecasts, fairy tales different from detective stories, air traffic control interactions different from unhurried telephone calls between close friends, etc. This kind of variation is reflected in the relationship between text and context, in the global organization of texts, and in systems of semantics in general.

In order to describe more fully the capabilities of various generators, we make particular use in this chapter of a three-way division of register as defined in systemic functional theory (Halliday, 1978). This division decomposes the communicative function of a text into:

- Field of discourse: the processes, purposes and subject-matter with which the participants are engaged.
- Tenor of discourse: the linguistic and extra-linguistic role relationships of the participants. The linguistic roles are speaker and hearer, initiator and responder, etc. The extra-linguistic roles are the social identities and relationships of participants.
- Mode of discourse: the part that language plays in situations and how it does so. This includes such notions as medium (e.g. written, spoken, typed) and immediacy (e.g. face-to-face or distant).

While human-produced language varies greatly to reflect various registers, some variations can be found in generation systems as well – either accidentally as a by-product of the primary task, or in a controlled way in more sophisticated systems. That is, although different generator designs clearly reflect different concerns and theoretical preferences on the part of their developers, they also reflect the purposes for which texts are to be generated. For example, the generator in a bank teller machine is captured in a fixed client-service role with a very limited area of discussion, and hence requires little overall complexity of design. Different registers of use lead to different kinds of designs of text generators.

While this may be of interest theoretically of itself, the relationship drawn to register has considerably more significant consequences. Registers not only relate context to types of language, they also allow comparisons across types of contexts. That is, the theory of register imposes an organizational classification on situations and context which allows us to relate the seemingly rather diverse properties of language use in differing contexts and, accordingly, also of the text generation systems supporting those diverse language uses. Thus register provides a mechanism for comparing various generators and theories which, taken by themselves, appear incommensurate.

3.3   A Survey of Generation Systems

Table 3.1 summarizes the two dimensions of generator task and method, and provides an outline for the survey:

Table 3.1　The two dimensions of generator task and
method

	How?	*What?*	*Why?*
Canned	canned sentences	canned paragraphs	canned selections
Templates	sentence templates	paragraph schemas	
Cascaded	syntactic phrases	relations, plans	rhetorical goals
Features	grammar features	paragraph features	register features

3.3.1　Grammatical Realization: How can I say it?

The simplest possible generator, a canned text system, is simply a collection of print statements. Its input is usually a number that identifies the particular text desired.

More sophisticated systems are often built using augmented transition networks (ATNs). Since ATNs are simply a method of implementation and not a distinct approach to language generation, we discuss them here. ATNs have been developed and used for both generation and analysis (see Patten's chapter in this book). A network is defined in which each node represents a syntactic class such as NOUN. Directed arcs are used to link nodes; one node is linked to another only if the class of the latter may grammatically follow the class of the former (for example, a noun must follow a determiner, allowing for possible intervening adjectives). Nodes may point back to themselves to allow repeated constituents. When used for generation, the ATN network traversal mechanism is driven by a representation of the information to be conveyed by the text. It hops from node to node, printing at each point an English word for the relevant entity, until it reaches the terminal node. The input provides the content; the ATN provides the grammatical constraints. An excellent description of ATN generation appears in Simmons and Slocum (1972).

For limited applications, canned text systems remain the most easily constructed and prevalent generators today. However, when somewhat more general capabilities are required, more sophisticated techniques must be used. The next step is template-based sentence generation.

Template-based Sentence Construction:　BABEL, KING, etc.　A popular technique for producing single sentences relies on templates, in which slots of a pre-defined template are filled in with appropriate values (usually lexical items; occasionally other templates, filled recursively). As will become clear, the question of lexical selection is the dominant issue in this approach.

Constructing a template generator is simple: you simply write the text and mark the placeholders, as in:

Dear [#1], Congratulations! You may have won $[#2]!!

The most difficult aspect is organizing the templates to minimize redundancy and to facilitate retrieval when appropriate. When the system has only a few templates, they can be stored in a simple list; but otherwise, templates are usually stored in the lexicon, associated with particular lexical items (usually verbs) that cue them. Selecting an appropriate lexical item to give shape to the desired sentence then becomes an important task. The first system to address this problem seriously was BABEL (Goldman, 1975). BABEL performed lexical selection using so-called discrimination trees which were associated with primitive representation items. For example, the item INGEST stood for processes of ingesting food, air, smoke, etc. The desired word sense (and associated template) was determined by a series of stepwise discriminations through INGEST's tree: first *take* was distinguished as ingesting for the purpose of becoming healthier (as in *take an aspirin*), next the ingesting of fluids or objects was distinguished from the ingesting of gases, then *smoke* was distinguished from *inhale* and *breathe*, and so on, until a unique lexical item was found. BABEL's input was a conceptual dependency graph (Schank, 1975), consisting of primitive terms linked together appropriately to represent the meaning of what was to be generated. After finding appropriate lexical item(s), the system filled in the templates associated with the lexemes using an ATN to produce a sentence.

Similar approaches were taken in the phrasal generators TALE-SPIN (Meehan, 1976; discussed later) and KING (Jacobs, 1985). KING was based on the theory that language is constructed entirely out of more or less general phrases, of which the more general ones can be seen as pseudo-syntactic classes (Becker, 1975; Wilensky, 1981b). Jacobs argued for the definition of a number of additional primitive terms under which to classify various expressive phrases. Both BABEL and KING performed lexical selection before grammatical realization in order to take into account the constraints of lexis on sentence structure: since language is phrasal, they argued, and phrases are associated with words, appropriate words must be found before language can be produced.

Not everyone agreed, of course. The opposite approach is taken in the DIOGENES system (Nirenburg et al., 1988), an ambitious generator (still under construction) organized as a set of interdependent modules, each performing a separate function, which communicate by writing the results of their computations on a common area called a blackboard. In DIOGENES, the sentence structure is first built up to conform to the system's input, and then words that can be placed into the structure are found. Here lexical selection is determined not only by the desired meaning (as in the above-mentioned systems) but in addition by the syntactic structure of the sentence – for example, a transitive sentence requires a transitive verb. The lexical selection process is complex, but can be boiled down to the following: the semantic features that must be expressed by some phrase (such as a noun phrase) are presented to the lexical selection module, which then searches the lexicon for the word that expresses most of the features. Remaining features are used to find appropriate modifiers such as adjectives and adverbs (as many as are required to exhaust the remaining features). This algorithm is enhanced by selecting perhaps a less expressive alternative, which allows a satisfactory modifier to handle the remaining features. Another variation of complex lexical selection is exemplified in the WISBER system (Horacek, 1990). Mappings called *zoom schemata* are defined between representation elements (or configurations of them) and lexical items, and the system is capable of applying and composing one or more schemas to express a given input representation in various syntactic forms. A recent study on the computational complexity of such lexical searches and mappings appears in Reiter (1990).

A third approach to the question of lexis and grammar holds that the two processes are not differentiated stratally but are part of the same 'level' of processing and are therefore intertwined. According to systemic-functional theory, for example, lexis and grammar can be integrated into a single unified specification (Halliday, 1978; Matthiessen, 1991). In this interpretation the resources of lexis are simply fine classifications of broad grammatical categories, as embodied for example in the PENMAN system described later.

Cascaded sentence construction: MUMBLE and others   In seeking to generalize the templates in a generator (by creating subtemplates of commonalities, etc.), one gradually builds a hierarchy of increasingly general patterns. Inevitably (the more templates one draws from), these patterns resemble the rules of phrase structure grammars. Taking this approach, one arrives at a straightforward method of building a sentence generator: phrasal substitution of increasing specificity, starting with a general pattern for a sentence and ending with a series of lexical items. This substitution algorithm, named 'cascading' in McDonald (1980), uses one central data structure (a stack, which is simply a list with only one accessible end) and can be summarized as follows:

1   At the beginning, place a suitable general sentence pattern on the stack (e.g. SENTENCE).
2   If the first item on the stack is a syntactic class name, replace it either with a pattern associated with that class (e.g. [NOUN-PHRASE VERB-PHRASE]), or with one (or more) lexical item(s) of that class,
3   otherwise, if the first item is a lexical item, simply print it and remove it from the stack.
4   Repeat from step 2 until the stack is empty and then stop.

McDonald's sentence generator MUMBLE (McDonald, 1980; Meteer et al., 1987) is the most elaborate, extensive and elegant generator of this type, and is one of the landmarks of generator research.

The cascaded method of sentence generation contains an essential drawback, however: the richer the grammar used by the generator (that is, the more syntactic patterns it contains), the more carefully the user has to specify the input to ensure that the program will select the correct alternative when cascading. This can require considerable linguistic expertise of the user – a drawback for a practical computer system. However, in other respects, the cascaded method is easy to understand, produces sentences in left-to-right order, and can provide speedy performance. The generator developed by Danlos (1987) and the realization component of PAULINE (Hovy, 1988a; discussed below) both employ the cascaded method.

A related method called *incremental sentence generation* is described in De Smedt and Kempen (1987) and De Smedt (1990). This method is a computational model of psycholinguistic studies of how people produce sentences. It is based on the assumption that the task of generation can be decomposed into various modules, each with a distinct function, that operate in parallel and interact in various complex ways.

Feature-based sentence construction: PENMAN and others The feature-based paradigm constitutes the most sophisticated method of generation, since in this paradigm each possible grammatical variation is explicitly represented and handled. One defines a unique feature for each type of alternation desired in the text (such as polarity and tense) and provides a distinct value for each possible variant (such as {positive, negative} and {present, past, future}). One then places the features together in a network to capture their interdependencies. This approach affords the generator builder control at the arbitrarily fine levels of linguistic detail. The generation process is then a process of assembling from the network a set of feature values that collectively specify a particular sentence that expresses the desired meaning.

In this paradigm, two basic problems have to be addressed: which features will be used to characterize aspects of the language, and how the features will be represented in the network and combined into a sentence specification.

Addressing the second problem, Kay (1979) developed a notational framework called Functional Unification Grammar (FUG), in which arbitrary features can be represented. An example functional definition for a noun phrase is shown in figure 3.1. A very powerful process called *unification* performs the combination of features from disparate sources in such a way as to respect their combinational requirements. Unification is used primarily for analysis systems (see Patten's chapter, this volume), but recent work has shown its general applicability to generation (Shieber et al., 1989).

Because of their simplicity and easy extensibility, functional unification grammars have been fairly popular in the computational community, with

```
                    CAT  =  NP
                    PATTERN  =  ( ... N ... )

      either:    [ ADJ' = NONE ]
      or:        [ PATTERN = ( ADJ ... )   ]
                 [ ADJ  = [ CAT  = ADJ ]   ]
                 [        [ LEX  = ANY ]   ]

      either:    [ PP  =  NONE ]
      or:        [ PATTERN = ( ... PP )                      ]
                 [ PP  = [ PATTERN = ( PREP NP )   ]  ]
                 [       [ CAT  = PP               ]  ]
                 [       [ PREP  = [ CAT  = PREP ] ]  ]
                 [       [        [ LEX  = ANY ]   ]  ]
                 [       [ NP  = [ CAT  = NP ]     ]  ]
```

Reading from the top, this means: a *NOUN PHRASE* must have a *NOUN*. It need not have adjectives, but if it does, they are *ANY* words of *CAT*egory *ADJ* and precede the noun. The noun phrase need not have any preposition phrases either, but if it does, they are of *CAT*egory *PP* and follow the noun. Here, *PPs* consist of a *PREP*, where the preposition is *ANY* word of *CAT*egory *PREP*, and an *NP*.
From McKeown (1985).

Figure 3.1   Noun phrase definition in FUG

functional and structural approaches alike (since FUG is at heart a framework, one can populate the grammar with features of any type). A FUG was used in the realization components of McKeown (1985) and Appelt (1985), both discussed below, as well as in KING (Jacobs, 1985). In addition, it is also possible to modify the cascading method to handle hierarchically organized FUG-like feature collections instead of phrasal/syntactic patterns. SUTRA (Busemann, 1984) and FREGE (Emele, 1986) are two examples; both contain feature-based grammars of German.

In answer to the first question – which features should be used – a few generators have seriously tried to capture feature-based theories of language in an extensive way. Notable among them, one of the largest (most extensive, and spanning over 25 person-years) generators ever built is PENMAN (Penman, 1989; Mann and Matthiessen, 1983; Matthiessen, 1984).

PENMAN consists of a number of components. The heart of the system is Nigel, the English grammar based on systemic-functional linguistics (Halliday, 1978). Nigel is a network of over 600 choice points called *systems* representing a single minimal grammatical alternation. Rather like an ATN, PENMAN traverses the Nigel network, selecting one of the available features at each system, until it has assembled enough features to fully specify a sentence. Each feature contains zero or more so-called realization operators that instruct the system how to go about assembling the sentence structure and which words to select. On applying the realization operators, PENMAN builds the sentence structure and prints the sentence.

The contents and organization of the Nigel grammar are based on the theories of systemic linguistics. In building a computational system, however, a number of issues arose, which were not addressed by the linguistic theory. The central issue was: how would the grammar traversal mechanism know which choice to make at each system? Though it is possible to control PENMAN by providing a specification of its behaviour at each choice point, a number of auxiliary knowledge sources were developed to simplify the system's input and, where possible, to model additional aspects of systemic theory. One useful construct developed is the so-called Upper Model, a hierarchy of about 200 general types of semantic distinctions made in English. PENMAN's inputs can be written in terms of Upper Model concepts and many of the program's choices are made with reference to the taxonomical organization. Other auxiliary knowledge sources are the program's lexicon, its models of the topic under discussion, and its default settings for choices.

In contrast to the predominance of structural theories in computational parsing, systemic-functional linguistics (Halliday, 1978) has provided the theoretical basis for a surprisingly large number of language generators, including SHRDLU (Winograd, 1972), PROTEUS (Davey, 1979), SLANG (Patten, 1986), COMMUNAL (Fawcett, 1990), and PENMAN.

As with ATNs, systemic grammars contain the structure of the language encoded in a network. Unlike most other approaches, however, systemic grammars seek to address effects of mode and tenor as well. Thus they encode not only 'pure' syntactic information, but also often take into account information from the so-called meta-functional aspects of language: ideational (that is, semantic in the traditional sense), interpersonal and textual (that is, situation-specific and medium-bound). Attempts are made to represent aspects of these phenomena in networks, each on a different layer or stratum, and to connect them so that their mutal interdependencies, and in particular their effects in constraining the grammatical realization, are respected. These are difficult matters to formulate concretely enough to computationalize, and no existing systemics-based program can perform more than a token amount of variation. However, since few other theories of language take these aspects of language into account at all, systemics-based generators hold some promise for growth in these areas. Two interesting attempts at supragrammatical strata in the systemic framework appear in Patten (1986) and Bateman and Paris (1989).

While the task of grammar writing never stops – there are always new aspects to explore – single-sentence realization has become a relatively well-understood problem, to the point where more or less general-purpose systems are being distributed and used by people who have no deep knowledge of linguistics. The area of multi-sentence generation, however, is another matter.

3.3.2   Content Selection and Organization: What shall I say?

This is the second major task of natural language generation. Research on this topic has had a history somewhat similar to that of single-sentence generation, though with a ten-year lag time.

Just as ATNs are a general technique for various approaches of generation, a very general technique of planning was employed in the landmark system KAMP (Appelt, 1985), which planned which content was to be produced. KAMP, one of the most formally precise generation systems ever built, contained a text planner and a FUG sentence realizer. Though it only produced single sentences, KAMP was activated with a number of simultaneous goals to inform the addressee of a set of facts. These goals were achieved by plans to communicate pieces of information; which plans were selected depended on reasoning about the addressee's mental state. Great care was taken in constructing the text by deriving for each part a formal proof that the communicated information would provide exactly and only the desired interpretation by appropriately altering the addressee's mental state. Within the formally-oriented intellectual framework supporting KAMP, it stands as a milestone; however, since the theoretical possibility and practical feasibility of reasoning about human knowledge to the degree required for the formal proofs has not been demonstrated, this approach has not been pursued very actively.

Multi-sentence generators almost all use more or less sophisticated planning techniques to select the material to include and to organize it into a coherent whole. In general, all approaches to this problem employ some type of tree structure, produced or filled in by the planner, to capture the dependencies among and order of the individual clauses.

'Canned' paragraph structure: PROTEUS and others   An example of the closest paragraph-level equivalent to the canned sentence appears in Carcagno and Iordanskaya (1989), who generate paragraphs describing the utilization of a computer. The paragraph is built by pruning out unfilled options from a pre-defined tree-like structure that contains a space for everything the system could potentially communicate. A similar approach is taken in Kittredge et al. (1986) for generating English and French weather forecasts.

In other cases, no text structure is pre-defined, but the results of some other computational processing double as the paragraph structure. Such systems simply assume that the underlying structure of the domain will provide the organization necessary to ensure coherence. An early example is the program TALE-SPIN (Meehan, 1976), which produced paragraphs from stories it made up. Various recent systems, investigating such issues as clause complexes, ellipsis, reference, and so on, take the same approach; see for example EPICURE (Dale, 1990), which generated text from a recipe (the cooking plan was represented as a tree) to illustrate the planning of referring expressions, and the system described in Mellish (1988), in which the tree was a house-building plan. Zukerman and Pearl (1986) used the proof tree of a mathematics solution in a study of the selection of linking expressions, and Weiner (1980) used the hierarchical structure of a tax form.

Perhaps the earliest – and still one of the most impressive – attempts to build a complete text generation system was PROTEUS (Davey, 1979). PROTEUS generated short transcripts describing games of noughts and crosses (tic-tac-toe) played by the system. For example, it generated the following text:

1 The game started with my taking a corner, and you took an adjacent one. I threatened you by taking the middle of the edge opposite that and adjacent to the one which I had just taken but you blocked it and threatened me. I blocked your diagonal and forked you. If you had blocked mine, you would have forked me, but you took the middle of the edge opposite the corner which I took first and the one which you had just taken and so I won by completing my diagonal.

This text illustrates some of the strengths of PROTEUS:

- It can group coherent moves into combinations of clauses, or 'clause complexes'.
- It can discover and signal contrasts ('you would have forked me, but . . . ').
- It can handle fairly complex referring tasks.

PROTEUS generated text in the following way: The input to the program was a list of moves of the game, presented in the order they occurred. From this list, the program picked what moves were to be described in the first sentence and then described them using its systemic grammar. It then returned to the list of moves to design and construct the next sentence, repeating the cycle until it had reached the last move. Moves were grouped into a sentence to reflect 'tactical coherence' in a game – coherence according to the organization of the field of games of noughts and crosses. As with TALE-SPIN and the others, PRO-TEUS used the organization of the game to guide the organization of the text; rhetorically, it depended on and was specific to that game.

Template-based paragraph construction: TEXT and others Paralleling the generalization from canned sentences to templates, a more sophisticated approach to multi-sentence generation that addressed the problems of text structure explicitly was the groundbreaking work of McKeown (1985). Her system TEXT used *schemas*, pre-compiled representations of stereotypical paragraph-length strategies that people employ in communication. Each schema mandates the content and order of the clauses of a single different type of paragraph. McKeown defined the four schemas Identification, Attributive, Constituents and Compare/contrast. (Given the amount of flexibility allowed in schema instantiation, placing McKeown's work at this point in the survey does it some disservice; had additional schemas been provided, the system would have approached the cascaded paradigm. We discuss it here to provide continuity of exposition.)

The following definition was generated by TEXT, where ONR is the Office of Naval Research and DB is the database:

2   [1] A guided projectile is a projectile that is self-propelled. [2] There are two types of guided projectiles in the ONR database: torpedoes and missiles. [3] The missile has a target location in the air or on the earth's surface. [4] The torpedo has an underwater target location. [5] The missile's target location is indicated by the DB attribute DESCRIP-TION and the missile's flight capabilities are provided by the DB attribute ALTITUDE. [6] The torpedo's underwater capabilities are provided by the DB attributes under DEPTH (for example, MAXI-MUM OPERATING DEPTH). [7] The guided projectile has DB attributes TIME TO TARGET & UNITS, HORZ RANGE & UNITS and NAME.

Importantly, the knowledge source of the system was a US navy database which had not been built to support text generation – any attempt to translate directly from the knowledge source would not have produced very good text and certainly not the text above. Considerably more information is necessary in order to create texts such as this.

The schema responsible for the example text above is the Constituency schema, which consists of four basic steps:

1   Identify the item to be described or defined as a member of some generic class or present attributive information about it (sentence [1]).
2   Present the constituents of the item (sentence [2]).
3   Present characteristic information about each constituent (sentences [3] to [6]).
4   Present attributive or analogy information about the item (sentence [7]).

McKeown (1985: 14–15) summarizes her procedure for generating text as follows (assume that the user has asked the system a question such as 'What is guided?'):

1   In response to the input question, database access processes in the system produce a pool of relevant knowledge, consisting of the informa-tion immediately associated with the entity (e.g. its superordinates, sub-types and attributes).
2   A characterization of the question and the information in this pool is then used to select a schema from the schema library.

3   A formal representation of the answer (called a 'message') is constructed by traversing the schema and instantiating information from the pool that matches the requirements.

4   To guide the selection at optional points in the schema, the system uses so-called focusing rules to select the next discourse topic. The three rules, to which McKeown added a fourth, were developed by Sidner (1979).

5   The result of these processes (what McKeown calls the strategic component of the generator) is an ordered list of messages, which are then lexicalized in the dictionary interface.

6   Once lexicalization is complete, surface form realization into English is performed by the so-called tactical component, which uses a functional grammar.

Note that, as in BABEL, lexical selection takes place before the tactical component is entered. In contrast with BABEL, both the dictionary interface and the syntax use the same formalism – functional unification grammar (see above) – a useful simplification.

The texts generated by TEXT were concerned only with objects and their properties – that is, produced registerial variations of field only. In order to generalize somewhat the capabilities of schema-based paragraph construction, Paris (1987) developed methods to provide variation along the registerial dimension of tenor. In her TAILOR system, Paris experimented with tailoring the paragraph content and structure according to the amount of domain expertise the addressee was known to have. She defined a new schema called Process that specified how to communicate causal relations represented in the system's knowledge base. TAILOR was given sensitivity to levels of user expertise and rules to select between combinations of McKeown's Constituency schema and Process, enabling it to generate texts appropriate for experts and novices.

The ROMPER system (McCoy, 1985) similarly defined new rhetorical schemas for a rather different kind of responsiveness, namely to correct the addressee's misconceptions concerning objects and their descriptions. Kukich's generator ANA (Kukich, 1983) contained paragraph-length templates for stock market reports. The text planner SEMTEX (Rösner, 1986) generated paragraphs describing labour market developments, using schema-like structures, and was also part of the German half of a Japanese–German automated language translation effort. The NAOS system (Novak, 1987) generated multi-sentence descriptions of street scenes from input provided by a vision system, using a set of text organizing rules based on visual salience.

Cascaded paragraph construction: RST structuring and others   This section discusses the paragraph-based analogue of cascaded sentence generation. The similarity springs from the fact that both sentence structure and paragraph structure are captured in a tree, and that the source of the tree is a single high-level pattern. By a process of repeated replacement of parts of the pattern by more specific patterns, the initial single source is recursively cascaded to form the eventual tree structure. What differs with the single-sentence case, of course, is the nature of the pattern.

Cascaded text construction has an important benefit over the template method. One of the problems besetting the template method, both for single sentences and paragraphs, is the absence of internal structure within templates. Though templates can be easy to select and use, the system has no resources for reasoning why the template constituents are where they are or what roles they fulfil, and is therefore unable to utilize them in any novel way. In contrast, building paragraph trees out of individual basic patterns provides the system with the requisite information. This approach requires identifying a set of basic patterns that govern coherence in paragraphs, as well as developing a method of assembling them dynamically into paragraphs on demand. While various types of building patterns have been proposed, methods of planning coherent paragraph structure have only been developed in the last five years. We describe here one of the first and most developed approaches.

After conducting a wide-ranging study of hundreds of texts of different types and genres, Mann and Thompson (1988) proposed that a set of approximately twenty-five relations suffice to represent the relations that hold within the texts that normally occur in English. Their theory, called Rhetorical Structure Theory (RST), holds that the relations are used recursively, relating ever smaller blocks of adjacent text, down to the single clause level; it assumes that a paragraph is only coherent if all its parts can eventually be made to fit under one overarching relation. Thus each coherent paragraph can be described by a tree structure that captures the rhetorical dependencies between adjacent clauses and blocks of clauses. Some RST relations are Sequence, Purpose, Elaboration and Concession. Many relations are signalled in text by a characteristic cue word or phrase, which informs the addressee how to relate the adjacent parts; for example Sequence can be signalled by *then* or *next* and Purpose by *in order to*. The RST relations include most of the relations described by Hobbs (1979) or Grimes (1975), and can be assembled into McKeown's schemas.

In order to be of use for computational text planning, RST relations had to be recast in a form which supported an algorithmic treatment. By operationaliz-ing them as plans, Hovy (1988b, 1990) was able to use them in his text structure planner, essentially a cascade mechanism similar to MUMBLE's. The struc-turer was linked to various host systems (such as a data base question-answering system), which supplied it with a collection of facts to communicate and one or more communicative goals. A typical goal could be paraphrased as: 'Make a paragraph using the following facts to ensure that the addressee knows the sequence of events and related other facts associated with X.' It constructed one or more paragraph trees and submitted the leaves of this tree, each a clause-sized piece of material, to PENMAN to be generated. In one applica-tion, the text structurer was given input provided by an expert system, which inspected computer programs and critiqued them for readability and maintainability. An example of an RST-based paragraph tree built from such input, together with the corresponding text, appears in figure 3.2. The boldfaced linking words in the text were inserted by the program based on the RST relations that hold between subportions of the tree.

As initially conceived, the RST structure built coherent paragraphs using input provided by the host system. But very early on, Moore, Paris and Swartout (Moore and Swartout, 1991; Moore, 1989; Paris, 1991) recognized that the same planning method could be used simultaneously to *collect* the material to be generated from a suitably structured collection of information (in their case, from the knowledge underlying an expert system; though data bases would do just as well). Following this avenue of investigation, Moore, Paris and Swartout developed a sophisticated plan language and an extensive library of plans to Justify the actions of the system and to Motivate the user to perform actions. They built a text planner, linked it to PENMAN, and tested their work in a number of domains.

A number of similar investigations are being conducted on various domains with various types of text plans; see Reithinger (1987), Cawsey (1990), Scott and De Souza (1990) and Maybury (1989). Several questions remain to be solved before these ideas can crystallize into a theory. At the current time, no existing system more sophisticated than canned text or templates can produce more than single paragraphs at a time. However, given the amount of work in this area, it is not unreasonable to expect the generation of page-length texts by the end of the decade.

3.3.3 Register Control: Why should I say it like that?

Almost all the early generators, and many current ones, were built with the premise that when they had found a way – any way – to express the given information, they had succeeded. This is a very strong simplification. As soon as it is removed, and the generator is given the capability of expressing the given information in more than one way (and further yet, of selecting to express different subparts of the given information), the generation task becomes significantly more complex. For then the system requires the ability to reason about the communicative effects of variations of content and expression. That is, it needs to know *why* to choose one option over another.

The reasons, obviously, pertain to the interlocutors (generator and addressee) and the communicative environment. These factors influence the entire text generation process: content selection, text organization, referring expressions, lexical selection and grammatical construction can all play a role in the overall communicative effect of the text.

Techniques for reasoning about communicative intent can be implemented to guide the generator's choices with varying degrees of flexibility. Though little work has been done in this area, we identify two principal levels of generator control: *pre-defined* (i.e. canned), once the interpersonal and/or environmental

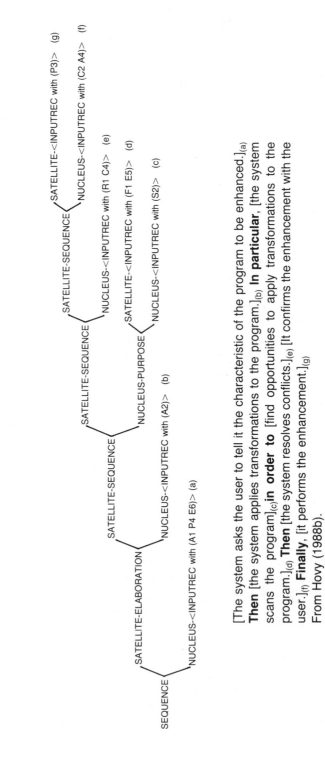

[The system asks the user to tell it the characteristic of the program to be enhanced.]$_{(a)}$ **Then** [the system applies transformations to the program.]$_{(b)}$ **In particular,** [the system scans the program]$_{(c)}$ **in order to** [find opportunities to apply transformations to the program.]$_{(d)}$ **Then** [the system resolves conflicts.]$_{(e)}$ [It confirms the enhancement with the user.]$_{(f)}$ **Finally,** [it performs the enhancement.]$_{(g)}$ From Hovy (1988b).

Figure 3.2 RST-based paragraph structure and text

criteria have been consulted, and *assembled* (roughly, cascaded) through continuous generator requests for guidance.

'Canned' creation of communicative effect: ERMA   In an interesting early investigation of the various processes that are required for language generation, ERMA (Clippinger, 1974) attempted to simulate a patient in a psychoanalytic situation by recreating as closely as possible a paragraph from a natural transcript. ERMA consisted of five modules: CALVIN (collection and censoring of material), MACHIAVELLI (text organization), CICERO (realization), FREUD (monitoring the origins of generator tasks), and LEIBNITZ (the concept definition network). Different parts of the program produced characteristic effects on the text, and the system was constructed so as to produce some of the false starts, hesitations, suppressions, etc., that the patient made. Unfortunately, no further tests of the system were reported, and it is not yet possible to assess all the claims made about the work.

Cascaded creation of communicative effect: IMP and PAULINE   The system IMP (Jameson, 1987) generated answers to questions in an employment scenario, under the goals to slant the text so as to make IMP, acting as the job candidate, appear as attractive as possible. Using a number of rules about the desirabilities of various features (such as family situation, previous job, etc.), a fairly sophisticated reasoning system weighed the costs and benefits of including each piece of information in answer to questions, and assembled a set of suggestions about which aspects to stress and which to elide if possible. These suggestions were then translated into individual English phrases and composed into grammatical sentences.

The first text-generation system to permit interpersonal and environmental aspects of the communication to permeate and influence the generation process across all levels of the linguistic system was PAULINE (Hovy, 1988a). The research question that motivated the construction of PAULINE was: 'Why and how is it that we say the same thing differently to different people, or even to the same person, in different circumstances?' This generator included explicit representations of the system's interpersonal goals, its perceptions of the addressee and of the environment. These goals and perceptions were translated into stylistic, rhetorical and affective goals which controlled decisions, resulting in appropriate variations of the texts produced. In terms of register, PAULINE handled a substantially larger range of tenor relationships than earlier text generation systems.

Representative of the variations that PAULINE was capable of producing are the following paragraphs, which describe a hypothetical US primary election between Carter and Kennedy (Hovy, 1988a: 98–104):

1   Carter and Kennedy were the candidates in a primary in Michigan on 20 February. Carter lost to Kennedy by 1,335 votes. At present, Kennedy has a better chance of getting the nomination than before.

Carter is also closer to getting the nomination than before. Both Carter and Kennedy want to get the nomination.

2   Kennedy diminished Carter's lead by getting all of 21,850 votes in the primary in Michigan. In a similar case, Carter decreased Udall's lead in a primary in 1976, and he easily trounced Udall to be nominated by 2,600 delegates. I am real glad that Kennedy is now closer to getting the nomination than before.

3   ... (*no text*)

These (and other) example texts were generated from the same input material, yet they vary in grammatical form, lexical items and textual organization. What differs is the initial goals supplied to the system: paragraph 1 was generated in a neutral fashion, paragraph 2 was generated trying to slant the addressee towards Kennedy, while paragraph 3 was generated to an antagonistic superior who held Kennedy in low esteem. (In fact, Hovy reports first thinking that paragraph 3 resulted as a bug in the system; only after painstakingly tracing through the generation process did it become clear to him that the various rules combined so as to suppress all text.)

Text differences in IMP were determined directly by considering the effects on the addressee. In contrast, the differences in PAULINE's texts were controlled by a set of twelve so-called *rhetorical goals* which mediated between the system's interpersonal goals and perception of the addressee and conversational situation on the one hand, and the needs for guidance at choice points during generation on the other. These rhetorical goals were found necessary because of the conceptual distance between the abstract concerns of interpersonal goals and situational aspects and the concrete concerns of grammar. This distance resulted in great difficulty in constructing rules to control the generator's decisions. The introduction of rhetorical goals – for example, Formality, Haste, Partiality, Floridity, Simplicity, etc. – provided a mediating point of organization and a place where the language-specific concerns of the abstract concerns could be assembled. Rhetorical goals were appealed to at various stages during the generation process. Importantly, they applied just as well to lexical selection (e.g. in the selection of *trounce* rather than *beat*), grammatical organization, textual organization and selection of content (e.g. in paragraph 2 an additional fact was mentioned to support the statement that Kennedy is significantly closer to gaining the nomination).

As the first generator to be specially designed for producing differing texts for the same underlying knowledge base content according to differential speaker-oriented features of the communicative situation, PAULINE went some way towards multi-register generation. With all the rhetorical goals and the possible values with which they may be assigned, the system could generate an immense number of different texts. A serious problem with the system, however, was the lack of organization among the rhetorical goals and the theoretically unconstrained interaction between them, the text organizer, the grammar, and the lexicon. PAULINE employed a cascaded phrasal grammar/ lexicon consisting of a collection of generation experts that knew which rheotrical goals to query in order to select among possible alternatives. It is difficult to see how generalizations can be drawn and the control of its grammar transported to other generation systems.

3.4 Related Work

Though this survey has covered most of the major contributions to natural language generation, some work has inevitably been omitted. In addition, little reference was made to related fields of study. To the extent that it is general and useful, text generation is only successful because it relies upon the work of grammarians, text linguists, psycholiguists, computational and artificial intelligence researchers, and so forth.

One of the major sources of ideas and information, of course, is the work on grammar performed all around the world. Some of the most influential theories that have not been mentioned are tree adjoining grammars (Joshi, 1987) (used, for example, by MUMBLE), lexical functional grammar (Bresnan, 1978), the functional grammar of Dik (1979a) and the multi-sentence text work of Van Dijk (1985). Grosz (1980) and Sidner (1979) developed ideas on focus and anaphora; they are currently developing a theory of discourse using notions of interlocutor attention and intention (Grosz and Sidner, 1986). In addition to this work, text planning draws on the discourse research of, for example, Kamp (1981), Reichman (1978), Bateman (1985) and Hasan (1978).

Also of relevance is the psycholinguistics work of Levelt and Schriefers (1987) and Bock (1982), and the psychology research on conversational analysis of, for example, Sacks, Schegloff and Jefferson (1974) and Clark and Murphy (1982). For some recent attempts at building generators on so-called connectionist computers, see Kukich (1987) and Ward (1990).

After having played second cousin to the area of computational natural language parsing for almost three decades, the value of studying computational generation in its own right is increasingly being recognized. With its unique perspective on the problems of language, generation identifies and stresses a number of important aspects, not least the necessity for a functional account of language to exercise control over the generator. It is a burgeoning field in which exciting new developments seem to happen every year.

Further Reading

Unfortunately, no textbook of the craft of computational language generation exists today. However, a number of edited collections of conference and workshop papers exist and serve as useful overviews of the various branches of the field. Of these, an outstanding example is Kempen (1987), which contains several papers that summarize important PhD dissertation work and can thus be read as a more extensive overview of the field than this article. The book contains six parts: Pragmatic Aspects, Generation of Connected Discourse, Generator Design, Grammars and Grammatic Formalisms, Stages of Human Sentence Production and Aspects of Lexicalization. Other edited collections are Dale et al. (1990), Paris et al. (1991) and McDonald and Bolc (1988).

Two of the largest and most widely used sentence generators are MUMBLE and PENMAN. Perhaps the most direct impression of these two systems can be gleaned from their documentation, which in both cases contains substantial portions of not overly technical material. The former is best described in Meteer et al. (1987) and the latter in Penman's (1989) documentation. Additional recommended reading on MUMBLE is McDonald et al. (1987) and on PENMAN are Mann and Matthiessen (1983), Matthiessen (1984) and Bateman (1990).

In the area of text planning, McKeown (1985) and Appelt (1985), both reworked versions of PhD dissertations, have been highly influential in the field. McKeown's remains the clearest description of paragraph-length text production using schemas, and the discussion of their implementation is a fine example of the use of ATNs. Appelt's book contains an excellent introduction to the complexities involved in the formal approaches to reasoning about language use. Recommended readings on text structure relations and text planning using these relations are Mann and Thompson (1988) and Moore (1989).

With respect to the future, as generator systems become more complex they will increasingly extend their tenor and mode capabilities. Hovy (1988a) is a readable and interesting description of a system that attempts to address the full problem of generation.

4 Computers and Translation

Derek Lewis

4.1 How Did Machine Translation Start?

Translation of a kind is not an unusual activity for a computer. When a programmer tells the machine to add, say, the numbers 5 and 4, he uses a *language* (such as BASIC) which is more convenient for him than the machine's internal representation of the instruction. In machine language this would be a pattern of 0s and 1s, so that 5 is represented by 101, 4 by 100 and the addition command a similar sequence of binary digits. Likewise letters of the alphabet have number equivalents which, in a word-processing application, are not converted into a form we recognize until they appear on screen or printer. Less trivial instances of translation between what is in the computer and what is more readily comprehensible to human beings are high-level programming languages, query systems for accessing large databases and conversion of digital information into audio or video form. Naturally, substituting numbers for letters in one-to-one correspondence is less complex than, say, checking the syntax of an arithmetical expression (such as $2 + 3 * (9 - 10) / 4$) and performing the operation. Nevertheless it was the principle of switching between information in different codes which initially stimulated interest in using computers to translate from one natural language into another. In the early 1950s this goal seemed attainable within a few years given the sheer speed, memory and processing power of computers. We now appreciate enough of the complexity of the information contained in natural languages to know that FAHQT (fully automatic high quality translation) might never be fully realized. Nevertheless, the term *machine translation* (MT) is still used, despite its dated connotations which reflect that early optimism about the new technology. This chapter presents the principles behind MT today, describes some operational systems and indicates what might yet be achieved.

We begin by describing the main components of typical MT systems.

4.2 Dictionaries

All MT systems use *dictionaries*. Indeed the earliest systems relied almost exclusively on dictionaries in order to translate. They matched each word of the source language (SL) sentence with a target language (TL) equivalent, with predictably poor results.

Nowadays, two types of dictionary are used: monoligual and bilingual. A **monolingual** dictionary is consulted to supply information about the words of the input text (or sentence) before it is further analysed. This information can be morphological, syntactic or semantic, and is attached to individual words to assist in the parsing process which takes place later. A TL monolingual dictionary may also be used to produce TL equivalents from information derived from analysis of the SL. **Bilingual** dictionaries are consulted when the structures, which have been analysed from the SL, are converted into the TL. Seen simply, the SL words and structural units are matched with their TL equivalents. Bilingual dictionaries, therefore, contain SL word entries, grammatical and semantic information about those entries, and appropriate TL words. To take a human analogy, it is as if the (human) translator had first to consult a monolingual dictionary in order to understand the words of the original text before translating them with the aid of a bilingual dictionary. More details on dictionaries in MT appear below. For full discussion of computing in relation to dictionaries, see Meijs's chapter, in this volume.

4.3 The Parser

The second vital component is the *parser*. Parsing in general is discussed by Patten in chapter 2 of this volume. In the present chapter we shall consider parsing specifically in relation to MT. The object of the parser is to identify relationships between SL words and phrases and to build some sort of structural representation of the SL sentence and its subparts. In terms of our human analogy, the translator, having identified the morphemes and words of a sentence, draws these together into coherent units (such as article + adjective + noun, subject + verb + object, coordinated clauses, etc.). A parser thus knows about the permissible distribution of elements and word classes in a sentence or phrase and reconciles this with what the dictionary has told it about the actual input words. For instance, the dictionary may contain the information that the English word *bank* could be either a verb or a noun. The final decision will hinge on further information about the words surrounding *bank*.

Important issues in parsing are the type of parser used (the **parsing strategy**) and the kinds of structure which the parser builds. There is also the question of how much structure the parser should build and what information it should attach to the structure. For example, to translate into a single, closely related TL, the parse could be quite *shallow* since it is unnecessary to build a lot of elaborate structure radically different to the surface SL sentence. If, however, the relationship is more remote, or more than one TL is envisaged, more information may have to be derived from the parse and stored to assist linguistic transfer. The less a translation can be done successfully by word-for-word dictionary look-up, the more significant is the role of the parser.

Identifying the SL words/morphemes and parsing the input text is called the *analysis phase*. For the translation process proper MT systems have components which are not present in other natural language processing applications such as query systems or term banks.

4.4   SL–TL Conversion

Unique to an MT system is the SL–TL *conversion component*. In the earliest systems, this component did little more than consult a bilingual dictionary to find TL equivalents for SL input words (word-for-word substitution). It soon became the focus of research, however, with different strategies emerging which are still being pursued.

The first approach involves direct restructuring of the results of the SL analysis to capture information on words or phrases which will be used later in translation. An example would be the identification of the head-noun in an NP phrase so that its adjective may be pre- or post-posed to conform with the differences between English and French word order. Once the head-noun is identified, either the parser itself could rearrange the elements already at the analysis stage (even before the rest of the sentence is parsed), or a separate conversion component would do it later. If the system is being designed for just one language pair, the first method is feasible: not only may elements be rearranged during the SL parse with the TL in mind, an SL phrase may be fully translated before the rest of the SL sentence has been properly analysed. If, on the other hand, the system is expected to be flexible (e.g. improved or reprogrammed later on), or to handle other language pairs, then the second method is better, because different TLs will all require different conversion procedures. The first method, where the conversion component interleaves with the SL analysis (and may become confused with it), characterizes the *direct translation* approach. The second method illustrates a key feature of the *transfer* and *interlingual* approaches, where processing stages are separated.

4.5   The Interlingual Approach

The basis of the *interlingual* approach is that the *analysis* component transforms the SL text into a highly abstract representation capturing all the essential syntactic and semantic information necessary for translation into several TLs. The interlingual representation aims for universality: it takes no *short-cuts* with a particular TL in mind, nor is there any attempt to convert prematurely into the TL. In theory, an interlingual representation of an SL text should contain all the information conceivably required for translation into any number of possible TLs. If interlingua-TL conversion programs are already available in a system, adding a single SL-interlingua analysis module immediately makes the SL translatable into all the TLs already present – which is economical on effort. Theoretically, the interlingua can be an artificial, formal language (suitable for processing by the machine), Esperanto, or even another natural language such as English. Furthermore, it could be based on semantic, dictionary-type information, or on syntax. The final conversion from interlingua to TL is called *synthesis*.

While attractive in theory, genuine interlinguas proved difficult to construct in practice. One reason for this is that representing an SL text in some abstract metalanguage tempts us to posit the existence of a model of linguistic universals representing all possible aspects of syntax and meaning for all known languages. Such a model has in fact never been devised. When we actually look at the translation process, we see that the human translator deals only with a specific SL–TL pair, mentally mapping equivalents defined for that pair. If, for instance, he has to translate English *wall* into German, he knows that German distinguishes external from internal walls (*Mauer* or *Wand*). The size, shape, materials and purpose of the wall are not relevant (although they might be for translation into another language and the translator might even be aware of them when analysing the German text). The point is that the set of potential features is limitless and a complete *universal* description of English *wall* would have to derive a vast amount of implicit information about the word occurring in a sentence, much of which would be discarded again for a particular TL. The artificiality of the task is reinforced by the fact that no SL explicitly represents all possible real-world information (whatever that is). A further objection to the interlingual approach is that converting an SL message into an interlingua means sooner or later leaving the original text behind as a source of information, relying solely on the picture built up by the interlingua. In practice, of course, the human translator at all stages refers back to the original to check the veracity of his work and revise his own mental version of the SL message. If a computer model has to do the same, it is not clear what the real status of the interlingua is.

4.6   Transfer

The interlingual approach was eventually superseded by the *transfer* model. The essential difference is that, in a transfer system, the component which analyses the SL does not attempt to capture, at the most abstract level, all possible information needed for translation into any language. Instead, the SL is analysed into a so-called SL-*representation* (also called a **normalized intermediate** or **interface** structure or even an **interlingua**) which still follows the SL structure patterns (although the precise level of departure from the SL and the degree of abstraction may vary).

At this point another component, designed for a specific SL–TL pair, converts the SL-representation into a TL-structure from which the translation is derived. This transfer component – a different one for each SL–TL pair – takes the place of the single and language-independent interlingua. While a direct MT system uses a (direct) bilingual dictionary, a transfer module will access its own bilingual dictionary to perform conversion at that level. The transfer module may be pictured as driving the analysis component in such a way that only those questions are asked of the SL which are relevant to the TL.

4.7   Direct vs. Indirect Systems

The interlingua and transfer models are often grouped together as *indirect* systems, in contrast to the first direct MT systems which saw the translation task as a single processing operation on a specific language pair and which stored all data in one bilingual dictionary. In an indirect system each component has access to a number or dictionaries – both monolingual and bilingual – containing the morphological, syntactic and semantic data required for analysis, transfer or synthesis.

The sequence in which we have presented these models reflects the order in which they appeared, i.e. first direct, then interlingua, finally transfer. Earlier direct systems tended to acquire transfer features and became operational (i.e. sold and installed for outside users), while technically more advanced systems have remained experimental. Direct systems include SYSTRAN, METEO, WEIDNER and CULT, while interlinguas initially characterized CETA, METAL, SALAT and DLT. Transfer systems are TAUM-AVIATION, SUSY, LOGOS, GETA-ARIANE and EUROTRA (see appendix).

4.8   Modular Design

Although MT's relatively long gestation has meant that currently operational systems are dominated by techniques developed in the 1960s and early 1970s, some principles of system design are well established. These are: (1) the main analysis, transfer and synthesis components are separated; (2) dictionary information is kept distinct from the (processing) components which use that information; (3) some systems also separate the grammar rules themselves from the algorithms which apply the grammar (as opposed to **bipartite parsers** where the program which does the parsing intermingles both grammar rules and programming statements). The advantage of modular design is that the individual components can be improved without having unforeseen effects on the rest of the system.

4.9   Representations and Linguistic Models

The type of representation in an MT system depends on the level of the linguistic data. One of the first tasks of the analysis component is to identify the words and morphemes (stems and endings) of the SL text. Although there is no standard software to do this, similar approaches are used in different systems. Dictionary items can be stored in stem form, so that inflectional endings do not have to be stored repeatedly for each item. Idioms, on the other hand, may be stored as whole units. Naturally, the morphology of an input text (where some words or endings are ambiguous) may not be fully clarified until after syntactic analysis.

4.9.1   Dictionary Entries

A **monolingual dictionary** entry will typically contain the following information (Lehrberger and Bourbeau, 1988: 60ff):

- Lexical item
- Grammatical category
- Subcategories
- Complementation

A grammatical category may be *noun, verb, determiner,* etc. Subcategories and complementation both specify the types of words which the lexical item can combine with. Complementation generally specifies whether arguments for verbs can take a subject or object (e.g. noun or sentence). Complements for adjectives and nouns include prepositional phrases (e.g. *help for, interest in, equivalent to*). Subcategories define specific features on categories of complements and provide additional semantic information (e.g. a subcategory for the subject of the verb *resemble* is *human*).

A **bilingual dictionary** will contain similar information for one or more equivalents for a single SL lexical item. The grammatical category of the SL lexical item is specified and more advanced systems will define a **context** for the SL entry, which may be a list of SL grammatical constituents, SL words, or even a larger semantic **domain** (e.g. medical, electronics, legal, etc.).

For successful processing, **idioms** and **homographs** must be identified as such in the dictionary. A homograph is a word which can function as more than one part of speech in the SL (e.g. *bank, direct, walk*). Any English verb, for instance, is a potential homograph because forms derived from it can often function as adjectives or gerunds (the *walking man, walking is good for you*). An idiom is a single, multi-word entry which cannot be analysed or translated properly from considering just its individual parts (examples are: *go to the wall, right away, take action, in spite of*). An idiom is entered separately, a key word identified (the least common in the phrase), and its grammatical function as a whole specified (e.g. preposition for *in spite of*, adverb for *right away*). For a bilingual entry, a TL equivalent is given and inflectional data cross-referenced (e.g. *take* is cross-referenced to *handeln* if *sofort handeln* is entered as a German equivalent for *take action*).

Large dictionaries are now handled by software tools called database management systems (see chapter 1 for details). These are programs for storing and accessing large amounts of data and for handling complex relations between data elements. An advantage of DBMSs is that they make the data readily available to other application programs. The move toward DBMSs can be observed in lexical databases generally, not just MT.[1]

4.9.2   *Morphology*

Once a **preprocessor** establishes the individual word boundaries in an SL text a **morphology analyser** breaks the text down into base forms, affixes and compound units. An **inflectional** component (for English) will separate base forms from suffixes (e.g. *unties* → *untie* + *s*). A **derivational** component will establish what new lexical categories are derived from base forms and affixes (e.g. *electric* (NOUN) + *al* → *electrical* (ADJECTIVE), *be* + *calm* (ADJ) → *becalm* (VERB)). A **compositional morphology** component determines what new lexical items are constructed from other, full lexical items (e.g. *by-product, off-white, nationwide, overdose*). To break down an SL sentence into its morphological constituents the MT system will traverse the SL sentence as a *graph*. A graph is a geometrical figure in which points on a plane (nodes) are linked by lines (called arcs or vertices). In figure 4.1 the arrowed lines represent arcs and the nodes word boundaries. The program moves from node to node, segmenting the elements (words) on each arc, and at the same time testing to see if possible base forms can be verified in the dictionary.

Derivational and compositional morphology components are not necessarily present in MT systems, which may rely on items like *becalm, electrical, motor pump* or *solenoid-operated* being entered separately in dictionaries or as idioms. Derivational morphology tends to be idiosyncratic (we say *inflationary* but not *inflational, prettify* and *activate* but not *prettivate* or *actify*), and so may be only partially implemented (e.g. for most English adverbs in -ly and many verbs in re-, such as *reassemble* or even *re-revise*).

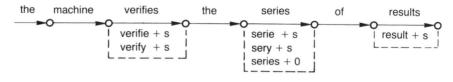

Figure 4.1

4.9.3 Syntax

Syntactic analysis requires more complex representations. It is not strictly necessary to recognize higher-level groupings of constituents in order to parse a sentence. Moving through the sentence, it is possible to recognize a grammatical category for one lexical item, then predict the next with some degree of certainty. If a dead end is reached, the program backtracks to an earlier point and starts with a different prediction. The result is a string of grammatical categories which, if desired, are grouped into higher-level units. This was the strategy adopted by the **Predictive Syntactic Analyser**.[2]

Tree representations of syntactic structure are based on the identification of higher-level units or phrases. A typical **phrase structure tree** is a graph of hierarchically arranged and labelled nodes (figure 4.2).

Grammatical categories at the bottom of the tree are dominated by higher-level constituents closer to the root (S).[3] There are, however, variations to this scheme. In a **dependency model** a word category itself is selected to act as a **governor** or **head** for the group below it (the other words in the phrase). Verbs are natural candidates for heads, acting as centres of **valency**, with variable numbers of satellite constituents, depending on the verb type. A possible dependency tree for the sentence, *The visitors met the president at midday*, is shown in figure 4.3.

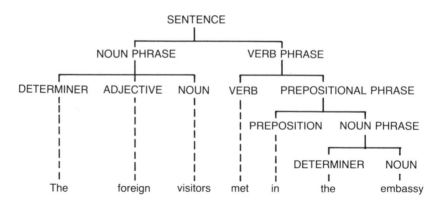

Figure 4.2

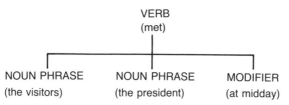

Figure 4.3

Many modern MT systems, such as METAL and the Japanese ATLAS project, extend this approach to **case-frame analysis,** where the verb provides a frame into which semantic case roles are slotted. The attraction is that underlying – perhaps even universal – semantic relationships are captured for mapping onto language-specific surface structures (e.g. active → passive; *to* + noun → dative case noun, etc.; see Hutchins, 1986: 187f).

Given tree representations of this kind, one might expect a close relationship between MT systems and syntactic representations of post-Bloomfieldian structural linguistics. Variations of phrase structure grammars, for instance, were developed by Halliday, Pike and Lamb (Palmer, 1972: 133f). Notably, from 1957 onwards, Chomksy presented his theory of **transformational syntax** which related different surface trees to a single *deep* structure (Chomsky, 1957). In the 1965 version of the model (Chomsky, 1965) all the meaning of a sentence is preserved in a syntax-based, deep structure tree – a useful concept for an MT system, which aims to arrive at just such a representation of an input text for subsequent conversion into an equivalent TL tree. Implemented transformational parsers, however, encountered problems, as already indicated in Patten's chapter (see section 2.2.5). This was mainly because Chomsky's **generative** model derived surface sentences from deep structure trees, not the other way around: it proved difficult to reverse the process and reconstruct *deep* structure information about a sentence from the available surface string. In fact, Chomsky envisaged his model as a **characterization model,** i.e. a way of formally expressing relations between structures, not as a practical method of processing them in a computer (a so-called **production model**).

Linguists proposed several variations of Chomsky's standard transformational model. The **generativists** argued that what was previously deep syntactic structure is really deep semantic structure. **Interpretivists,** on the other hand, retained the distinction and concentrated on refining the operation of transformational rules. In the 1965 version transformational rules were very powerful and often too complex in relation to the linguistic phenomena they described. As a result **government binding theory** prescribed a more general system of language description in which the power and scope of transformations are limited. Transformations are thus not permitted to erase information from a tree, local conditions are specified for their application, and a constituent phrase must have a head (i.e. each verb-phrase has a verb, each noun-phrase a noun, etc.; Wehrli, 1967: 64).

These developments in linguistic theory were not stimulated by the practicalities of implementing standard TG grammars on computers, despite the fact that it has been suggested that GB theory is more appropriate to computational systems, being simpler and less based on generation (as opposed to parsing). GB theory remains essentially a theoretical model, not a practical one for programmers. In other words, an MT programmer might build a parser which (from the outside) behaved as if it conformed to the GB model, but he would find the model little help in devising the rules of the software. In fact most systems designers have evolved their own grammatical models, aside from the major debates of theoretical linguistics. Examples are Hays's **dependency grammar**, Garvin's **fulcrum theory**, Bar-Hillel's **categorial grammar**, Lamb's **stratificational grammar** and, more recently, Gazdar's **generalized phrase structure grammar** and Bresnan's **lexical functional grammar**.

Figure 4.4 illustrates an early example of a **dependency structure** for a parsed input sentence (Hays, 1963: 198). The (unlabelled) nodes are identical to the lexical items and the constituent phrases are nicely continuous (i.e. not split up by others). The tree is called *projective*. This seems to refer to a neat left-to-right order of occurrence of lexical items and the ability to build a tree in which dependency lines do not cross one another and in which the original word order reflects grammatical function (making specification of grammatical class on the tree redundant). English and Russian were felt to be *largely projective* languages.

Garvin describes his **fulcrum approach** as a *common-sense grammatical framework* for MT representations. The object is to identify *pivot words* (fulcra) in a sentence, i.e. those containing most grammatical information. There is a fulcrum for the sentence as a whole, as well as for each of its constituents. Thus for a Russian sentence the fulcrum is its predicate (usually the verb), for a nominal phrase the head-noun. Although Garvin does not refer explicitly to

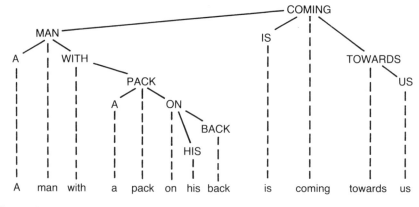

Figure 4.4

phrase structure trees, his system is based on immediate constituent theory and aims, through a series of syntactic passes, to identify and label constituent blocks (e.g. nominal block, prepositional block), governor-modifier structures, subordinate clauses and other *word packages* (Garvin, 1963: 230).

Bar-Hillel's **categorial grammar** is based on two basic syntactic classes, sentence (S) and nominal (N). Other categories are defined by their ability to combine with these classes. Thus an adjective is defined as N/N: the first N is the higher-level nominal which is formed when the adjective combines with an N to its right (/). The notation can be varied, so that the sentence, *Poor John forgets* could be represented as N/[N] + N + S/(N), where [N] means that *John* is a subordinate constituent and (N) that *forgets* is a superordinate one. An advantage of this technique for defining word classes is that phrase structure constituents can be expressed by cancellation. Thus the phrase *highly complex structure* is represented as (N/N)/(N/N) + N/N + N: cancelling out equal elements either side of the / symbol returns a single N (*structure*), which is the head of the phrase.

Sydney Lamb's **stratificational grammar** is a complete theory of language, which is seen as a complex relational network. As much a cognitive as a formal model, it embraces the phonetic to the communicative level and claims to reflect neural connections of the human brain. A stratificational grammar consists of a set of hierarchically organized levels or **strata**. Each stratum contains a set of **tactic rules** for combining elements within that level. **Realization rules** relate one stratum to another. Interesting levels for MT are **lexemic** (words) and **sememic** (meanings and meaningful relations between words). Thus, for instance, the word *big* is a single unit at the lexemic level, but at least two at the sememic level (illustrated by the potential ambiguity of *my big sister*).

Figure 4.5 depicts a sub-tree for a verb + subject constituent structure (Lockwood, 1972: 57). The triangular nodes are downward ANDS, where the upward lines point to an element or a combination and the downward lines the element's components. The downward lines emerge separately from the nodes, meaning that the order of constituents is significant (otherwise they would be joined at the node). The downward facing bracket (also a node) represents a particular class (i.e. sentence). The upward facing brackets (upward unordered ORs) indicate that a distinction is neutralized above those nodes. The diamond labelled Q signifies interrogation. In all, the tree means that a question is realized by reversing the usual subject + verb constituent order. Full trees carry a lot of information about alternative structures and constituents which would be represented by a series of different trees in transformational grammars. Visually, however, they are difficult to interpret (for examples, see Lockwood, 1972).

Lamb's MT system concentrated on identifying lexemes within the broadest possible contexts (including beyond sentence boundaries) as a prelude for finding TL equivalents. Progress was reported, however, on computerizing tactic rules for MT analysis (Hutchins, 1986: 102ff).

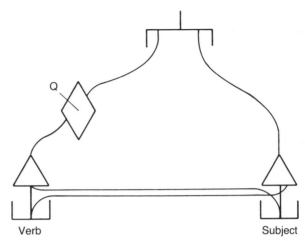

Figure 4.5

Generalized phrase structure grammar (GPSG) and **lexical functional grammar** (LFG) are increasingly used for natural language processing and likely to influence future MT (Gazdar and Mellish, 1987: 234). A GPSG dispenses with transformations and typically attaches **features** to syntactic categories which are carried down the tree (figure 4.6).

Metarules relate particular phrase structure rules to others. Thus, if there is a rule for an active sentence,

R, VP $\longrightarrow$ V + NP + X,

then there is also a correspondence rule for the related passive:

R, VP $\longrightarrow$ V[passive] + X (PP[by]).

R is the rule number relating both structures (E. K. Brown, 1984: 191).

Lexical functional grammar (LFG) evolved from transformational grammar, psycholinguistics and computational linguistics. In an LFG representation there are two levels of syntactic structure. The first, the **constituent-structure** (c-structure), is a conventional phrase structure tree reflecting the surface order of words in a sentence. A c-structure defines syntactic categories, terminal strings (e.g. words), and dominance and precedence relationships. For an illustration, see figure 4.7 (Kaplan and Bresnan, 1982: 173ff).

The corresponding **functional-structure** (f-structure) for this tree is not itself a tree, but a set of **attribute/value pairs** containing grammatical function

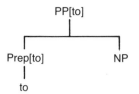

Figure 4.6

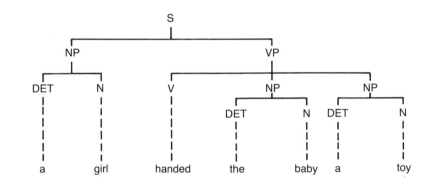

Figure 4.7

names (e.g. subject and predicate), feature symbols and *semantic forms* which are considered purely syntactic. In the above sentence the NP *girl* is the subject, *handed* the semantic predicate, and *baby* and *toy* grammatical objects. An f-structure for this sentence would be as in figure 4.8. The PRED attribute has semantic forms for its values. Written in angled brackets, these provide a list of **logical arguments** (here specifying the agent, theme and goal structure of the sentence) which are the basis for the semantic interpretation of the sentence: they allow semantic functions (and dictionary entries) to be mapped onto the grammatical functions of the f-structure. Differences in surface structure (e.g. *A girl handed a toy to the baby*) are reflected in different f-structures (e.g. PRED 'HAND < (↑ SUBJ) (↑ OBJ) (↑ TO OBJ) >'): in this example a **lexical rule** would indicate that a word in the dictionary with the specifications (↑ OBJ) and (↑ TO OBJ) may appear with the objects rearranged as (↑ OBJ2) for (↑ OBJ) and (↑ OBJ) for (↑ TO OBJ). The up-arrows (↑) indicate slots – here for SUBJ, OBJ etc. – which, when filled, are associated with the PRED 'HAND'. There are no transformations on syntactic trees.

Stratificational and functional grammars tried to capture more information about different layers of information and relationships between phrases (e.g. subject/object, agent/goal, theme/rheme) than purely phrase structure and transformational grammars.

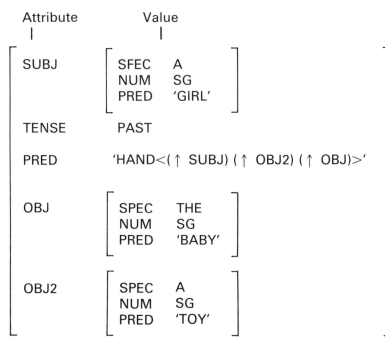

(SPEC =specifier, NUM = number, SG = singular)

Figure 4.8

4.10   Representational Tools

MT systems rely on so-called **software tools** to implement and manipulate the general representations described above.

4.10.1   Charts

Charts were developed in the 1970s by Kay and Kaplan specifically as **data structures** for parsing (Varile, 1983: 73ff). While analysing a sentence, a parser will often have to remember numerous alternative phrase structure trees or sub-trees. Charts are a convenient method of maintaining these alongside each other for as long as they are needed. A chart for the sub-tree in figure 4.9 is shown in figure 4.10, where the numbered circles represent the **nodes** on the tree (nodes 1 and 2 embrace other nodes – see figure 4.11 for the full chart) and the labelling is carried on the paths or **arcs** linking the nodes. The vertical line indicates that the NP constituent dominates the nodes below it (the **dominance** relation); the horizontal line specifies constituents in a linear order

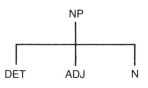

Figure 4.9

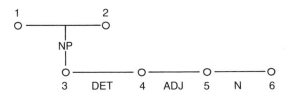

Figure 4.10

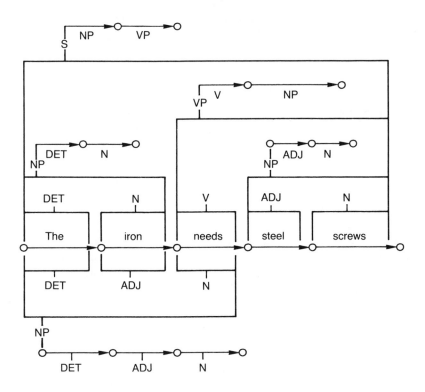

Figure 4.11

(the **precedence** relation). Arcs (also called **edges**) are **inactive** or **active**, depending on whether the parser's hypotheses about current structure are confirmed or unconfirmed).

A possible chart for a parse of the sentence *The iron needs steel screws* is shown in figure 4.11. The main feature of the chart is that, since the alternative partial chart DET + ADJ + N (for *the iron needs*) cannot be included in the S arc along with the other charts, it may be discarded. Legitimately ambiguous sentences, such as *She likes riding horses* (where *riding* is either a gerund or an adjective modifying *horses*), may be represented by alternative full charts, right up to S level. The advantage of charts over previous techniques was that recorded structures are always available: if the parser must backtrack, it does not have to rebuild constituents from scratch. Charts have been used in GETA, SUSY, METAL and EUROTRA. For more on charts in parsing in general, see section 2.2.2 of Patten's chapter, this volume.

Charts and graphs are more than an elaborate notation. Representing and recalling data are key issues in computer science and *remembering* laboriously built information about fragments of natural language is important for computational efficiency. The formal notation for these operations can therefore make all the difference to whether they can be turned into a computer program. Moreover, methods for handling graphs and tree-structures are well developed in mathematics and information processing, so any model which specifies how they apply to natural language is relevant for implementation on a computer (see annotated bibliography).

4.10.2 Tree Transducers

Tree transducers are software tools for changing strings of linguistic data elements (or trees) into other strings (or trees). Let us first consider how a tree may be represented as a data structure in a computer language. A tree consisting of a NP dominating a DET, ADJ and N (figure 4.12) may be represented as the list:

NP (DET, ADJ, N)

which is a data structure signifying that an NP constituent dominates a list comprising a determiner, an adjective and a noun. Bracketed lists are embedded to reflect hierarchical relationships in more complex trees. Thus the tree in figure 4.13 is equivalent to the list in figure 4.14 (the large upward facing

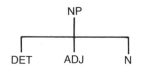

Figure 4.12

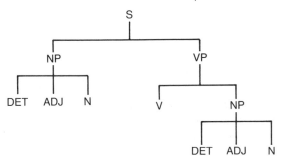

Figure 4.13

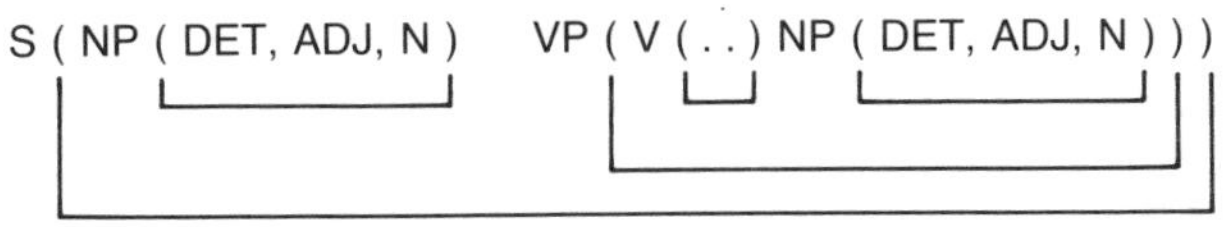

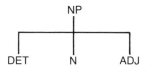

Figure 4.14

square brackets in figure 4.14 are included to make it easier to see which lists are embedded in other lists: symbols immediately to the left of square brackets correspond to parent nodes in the tree).

A transducer simply converts the list into another list. A transducing operation on our NP sub-tree, for example, could be:

NP (DET, ADJ, N) $\longrightarrow$ NP (DET, N, ADJ)

This places the adjective constituent after the noun, giving the new tree in figure 4.15.

Obviously, transducers have direct application in MT systems. Either they can be used to produce deep structure tree representations for an interlingua, or, as part of the transfer component, they can operate on SL-derived phrase structure trees, converting them into new TL-oriented trees. Transducers were first used in TAUM-METEO at Montreal.

Figure 4.15

4.10.3   Q-systems

Q-systems are sophisticated transducers developed by A. Colmerauer and used extensively in TAUM-METEO (Q stands for Quebec). They enable strings of trees to be converted to other strings of trees. A Q-system would act upon the above-mentioned chart for *The iron needs steel screws* as follows. First of all, arcs (sub-trees) would be created spanning the constituents as shown in the chart. Secondly, arcs would be deleted from the chart (a) if they had taken part in a successful match, and (b) if they did not belong to a path from the entry to the exit node of the chart. An example of (b) is the DET + ADJ + NOUN arc for *the iron needs*, which cannot contribute a valid constituent for a parse of the rest of the sentence. Rule (a) would remove all sub-arcs of the successful S arc (marked by +), leaving the overall tree structure as shown under S (figure 4.16).

An example (from Varile, 1983: 84) of a Q-systems-type rule for building one sub-tree from another is:

$$V (X^*) + NP (Y^*) = VP (V (X^*), NP (Y^*))$$

This states that if there is a V constituent followed by a NP constituent, then build a tree in which a new VP constituent dominates the V and NP in linear order (figure 4.17). X^* and Y^* are variables standing for sub-trees already dominated by V and NP respectively. Whatever X^* and Y^* contain is also moved over into the new tree. This is exactly the operation used in the chart above to combine *needs* with *steel screws* into a single VP tree.[4]

4.11   The Semantic Component

An MT system must know more than the basic syntax of a language in order to assign correct SL representations or generate TL forms. In the sentences

1   John drank whisky and soda.
    John drank day and night.

whisky and soda and *day and night* are conjoined nouns. To represent *day and night* as an adverbial modifier of *drank* and not its direct objects, we need to know what **kind** of nouns they are and what kind of nouns are normally the object of *drink*.

2   a hard substance
    a hard problem
    a hard drink
    a hard sell

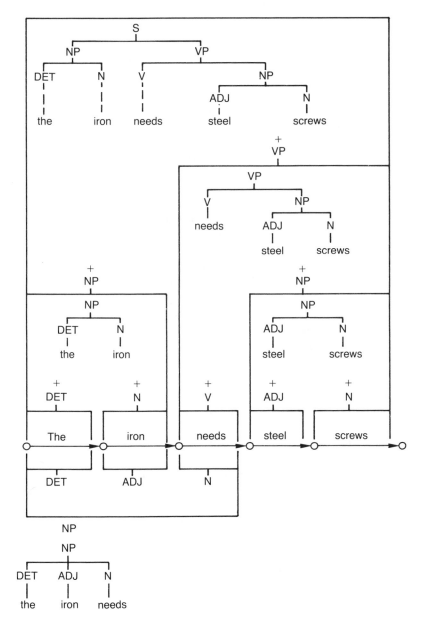

Figure 4.16

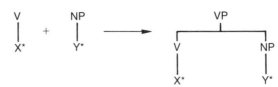

Figure 4.17

Here the adjective *hard* is likely to require different equivalents for each noun in the TL. Either the MT system represents the differences already during SL analysis or it produces the right collocation from dictionary information available during TL generation. Adjectives, nouns and especially prepositions are often polysemic in this way (e.g. *the computer ON the desk, the duty ON wine, run ON petrol, pay ON delivery*).

3   The aircraft missed the runway by the hangar.
    The aircraft missed the runway by 100 metres.

Here the prepositional phrase modifies *runway* in the first example, the verb in the second. Again the translation of *by* depends on semantic knowledge about these items.

4   small car factory
    selector level actuating nut
    automatic current regulator
    compressed air cylinder
    internal combustion engine
    the most eagerly sought after prize
    things we have to do
    all the latest local swimming gala entrants under 14

English compound noun phrases can be notoriously complex. Even if the head-noun is identified, the structure of its modifiers may not be clear without information about the subject area (common sense tells us that it is the *air* not the *cylinder* which is compressed, knowledge of electricity that *automatic current* makes less sense than *automatic regulator*).

5   Rotate disc to lock nut
    Moving parts can kill
    More than half the women interviewed married men with a drinking problem[5]

The structural ambiguity of the examples in (5) can only be resolved by reference to the situation in which they are used.

Virtually no MT system has a separate semantic analysis phase as such, let along a parser which is entirely semantics-based.[6] Semantic information is normally included in dictionary entries as **features**. These features do not define complete word meanings but are used to check **selectional restrictions** between a verb and its arguments, i.e. they assist syntactic disambiguation.

For instance, if the object of the verb *drink* in (1) is restricted to nouns with the feature +liquid, then *day* and *night* will not be selected as an object NP. In principle similar restrictions can be applied between other word classes (e.g. nouns and adjectives, prepositions and nouns). Typical feature classes include:

For nouns:
ABSTRACT: notion, emotion, laziness
ACTION: design, attack, kick
HUMAN: man, engineer, Charles I
MEASURE UNIT: pound, megabyte, microsecond

For adjectives:
QUALITY: genuine, tall, old, intense
DEFECT: bad, defective, malignant
SHAPE: square, hexagonal, amorphous

For verbs:
DEFECT: crack, rust, disintegrate
CAUSATIVE: open, close, kill, move
FACTIVE: know, understand, determine

For prepositions:
LOCATIVE: at, over, beneath
MOVEMENT: between, over, via
TIME: at, before, after

During SL analysis semantic information can be included along with everything else that is discovered about a constituent. The extent of semantic analysis varies, with features for prepositions often too complex for an MT system to implement. Features are most useful in limited subject areas (**domains**), where commonly occurring feature sets enable the system to identify noun sub-classes and interpret the structure of complex nominal phrases.

In figure 4.18, for example, *flight* is the DIRECT OBJECT of *control* and the FUNCTION of *cylinder* is to actuate: *actuating cylinder* is FOR *flight control* (the

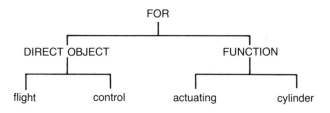

Figure 4.18

domain here is aircraft maintenance, from TAUM-AVIATION (Lehrberger and Bourbeau, 1988: 123).

4.12   Knowledge-based Systems

All current operational MT systems base their SL analysis and TL generation on the representation and manipulation of syntactic categories. Semantic information is used to disambiguate or clarify structure, i.e. as an adjunct to syntax. More advanced semantic models have, however, been proposed. Essentially they are a return to the goal of developing an **interlingua** for representing the meaning of texts, albeit with more powerful linguistic and computational tools. There is no room here to discuss these in detail, but interesting systems for MT applications include MOPTRANS, SALAT and CON³TRA (Shann, 1987: 80ff).

An MOP (memory organization packet) is a higher-level knowledge structure which represents typical events and properties associated with a situation or context (e.g. a visit to a restaurant, a transaction in a shop, etc.). So-called scripts, frames or plans are variations of this approach. If an MT system, for instance, knows about restaurants, it can interpret the sentence *the meal came* as *the meal was served*, which may have to be specified in the TL.

Other systems also aim to refine and extend their base of knowledge beyond conventional features on syntactic classes. SALAT, for example, distinguishes between information that changes and information that remains constant. The first includes the context and situation of the sentence and is derived from the text itself. The second is made up of general world knowledge, and **meaning postulates** (similar to semantic inference rules, e.g. if something is *alpine* then it is also *geographic*). The CON³TRA system (Saarbrücken) likewise separates different kinds of information in a knowledge base which includes purely linguistic data (grammar and lexicon) and general world knowledge. The input text is represented, not just as linguistic structure, but also in terms of its (factual) content. All components interact to pass on as much information as possible for TL generation. Overall it is likely that future knowledge-based machine translation (KBMT) will adopt a similar approach, i.e. logically organized encyclopaedic components will interleave with linguistic ones to provide a fuller representation of the text.

4.13   Current Systems

So far we have looked generally at components, strategies and formalisms in MT. The methods, even goals of individual MT systems, however, vary considerably. Below *three* systems are described, each exemplifying a different approach to MT.

4.13.1 SYSTRAN

Although one of the oldest MT systems, SYSTRAN is commercially the most successful for large computers. It emerged from early direct systems of the 1950s and 1960s and has been used by the USAF, EURATOM, NASA (for Russian and English) and, more recently, by the European Commission principally for French–English and English–Italian (several more pairs are either available or projected).

SYSTRAN's programs implement no formal model of language and do not build trees or taxonomic structure: they *simply run up and down the sentence like a kitten on the keys* (Wheeler, 1987: 193ff). Indeed its developers claim that, despite scepticism in academic circles, it is pragmatic and works. Their declared object has been to provide translation copy, which, however flawed, the user can work with (i.e. for information extraction or post-editing).

SYSTRAN relies heavily on its dictionaries. These are organized as a pyramid, with the simplest at the bottom and the most complex at the top. A text is translated as follows:

1   All the TL words are looked up in the STEM dictionary, which is a straightforward, bilingual, word-for-word dictionary containing basic syntactic and semantic information about each SL and TL entry. Common words are found in a separate High Frequency dictionary and idioms and standard phrases are picked up. A Main Dictionary Look-up routine looks at morphology, storing all possible forms of verbs, adjectives and nouns. The output of this stage is a set of SL sentences with the words, complete with attached dictionary information, in their original order.

2   At the next stage analysis proper begins. Noun groups, together with their head items, are identified and syntactic homographs are resolved.

3   A series of structural passes establishes the syntactic structure of each sentence. Separate passes identify clause boundaries, noun and adjective constructions, prepositional phrases, compound nouns, coordinate conjunctions and enumerations (e.g. *road and bridge construction = construction of roads and of bridges*). Subject and predicate are also parsed.

4   A Conditional Limited Semantics Look-up routine uses semantic information encoded in the dictionary to recognize complex expressions whose elements are not contiguous. Thus, for French *le pilote a noté l'assiette et la direction de vol*, a rule would specify that, if *assiette* precedes a noun such as *vol*, it means *altitude*, not *plate*. The CLS routine also looks at features of noun subjects and objects to identify meanings of verbs and other elements (e.g. *marcher* = function or walk). It should be noted that

some translations will have already been made during the structural passes (a typical feature of direct systems). CLS is used to *tidy up* the translation and make the output resemble a TL original. Awkward or non-standard prepositions are converted after CLS (e.g. English *about* = *au sujet de* after *talk*, not *autour de*).

5   The behaviour of some words (about 115 in English–French) is complicated enough to demand special subroutines for translation. Examples are English *any* or French *il y a* (= *there is, there are, there won't be*, etc.). These routines work by scanning the immediate syntactic context.

6   A synthesis program completes the translation, converting items such as voice, number, person and tense of verbs, articles, inflectional endings and word order.

From this simplified account it is clear that large dictionaries are accessed by a series of *ad hoc* processing routines. Although the programs constitute separate modules for specific tasks, translation is performed as and when available information makes this possible, even before analysis is complete.

4.13.2   *EUROTRA*

Since 1979 the countries of the European Community have been collaborating in the development of a multilingual MT system, EUROTRA. The emphasis is on exploiting the best available techniques to produce an operational system to meet the official translation needs of the nine languages of the community. Although the project is centrally coordinated, researchers in each member state contribute the components for their national languages. This distribution of effort has required the careful design of a common framework for linguistic representations and system modules. Partially completed in 1990 is an operational prototype planned to work with a vocabulary of 2,500 items for each language and within a restricted subject area (information technology). The long-term aim is for a robust, extensible system, eventually with about 20,000 items in each monolingual dictionary producing reasonable to high quality translations (Arnold, 1986).

EUROTRA is basically a transfer system. In figure 4.19 the bottom line shows the levels of representation which the text passes through during processing. The levels are interpreted as follows:

1   **Eurotra morphological structure (EMS)**. The text (sentence) is represented as a string of morphological word forms and lexical categories.

2   **Eurotra configurational structure (ECS)**. From the EMS a tree of constituents is built using context-free phrase structure rules. The tree reflects the surface SL word order.

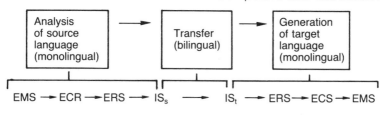

Figure 4.19

3 **Eurotra relational structure (ERS).** Like the ECS, the ERS representation is a tree. However, the surface word order is abandoned and the elements are organized into abstract words with sets of features giving the syntactic category, lexical and inflectional information. Secondly, the ERS tree is *flatter*, i.e. there are fewer higher-level constituents, which makes the tree less complex and easier to manipulate. Thirdly, following the dependency model, certain elements are designated as **governors.** A governor (e.g. verb) has a **frame** comprising a number of **slots** which may be filled by dependent elements called **complements** (for a verb, these will be subject, object, etc.). The governor also commands **modifiers** or **adjuncts** (e.g. prepositional phrases for a verb). In this way the ERS specifies surface syntactic relations.

4 **Interface structure (IS).** The IS is the most abstract level of representation. Case relations are established and some *surface* features (e.g. prepositions and determiners) disappear as structural elements of the tree. There is some uncertainty as to how far ISs should reflect existing ERS syntactic structure and what interlingual semantic information they should formulate which does not correspond to the syntax. Semantic information relevant to European languages includes circumstantial relations (e.g. a single SL preposition expressing a number of different semantic relations, such as *on Monday, on the dole, on time*), time values on sentences (e.g. German *ich arbeite* may be equivalent to English *I work, I am working, I will work*), modality (English and German modal verbs may have other syntactic equivalents in French), and singularity/plurality (German *Nachrichten* (plural) = English *news* (singular)). In any case EUROTRA's designers are attempting to establish only IS semantic categories which are useful to European languages – so-called **euroversals**.

Examples of ECS, ERC and IS structures for a Danish sentence (English: *In 1982 all proposals were passed by the commission*) are given in figures 4.20–4.23 (adapted from Maegaard, 1988). The source language IS (figure 4.22) is the input to the transfer component, which converts it into a corresponding target language IS (figure 4.23).

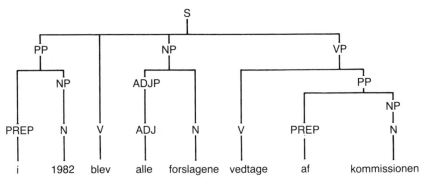

Figure 4.20 ECS for Danish sentence

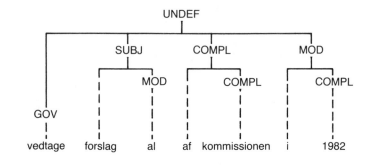

Figure 4.21 ERS for Danish

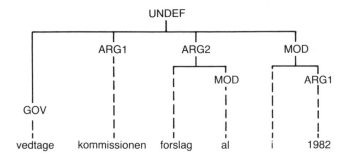

Figure 4.22 IS for Danish

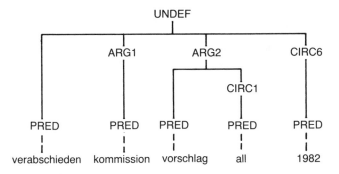

Figure 4.23   IS for German

Transfer is as simple as possible. In the above example it involves merely replacing Danish lexical items by German ones. Consider, however, mapping the German *Anna redet gerne* (= verb + adverb) onto the English *Anna likes talking* (verb + gerund). Since there is no one-to-one correspondence of syntactic elements, any IS representation of the German involves establishing quite abstract categories for a simple transfer to operate upon. The alternative is make the German–English transfer component just complex enough to handle these cases (manipulating tree nodes and lexical items accordingly). As a rule EUROTRA's designers aim to reduce the complexity of transfer, so that the main descriptive burden falls on the monolingual components (analysis is performed without reference to the TL – the same goes for generation with respect to the SL). Once the target language IS has left the transfer module, it moves through the ERS, ECS and EMS stages to final translation.

Apart from being the largest and most ambitious MT project ever mounted, EUROTRA is interesting for producing representations which are accessible to linguists and which can be altered in the light of experience or the properties of a particular language.

4.13.3   Weidner's MicroCAT

Weidner's MicroCAT is a relatively low-cost MT system implemented for a stand-alone personal computer. The specifications are for IBM PC/XT or compatible with 640 RAM and at least 3.5 MB hard disk memory. The assumption is that the PC is dedicated to MT, since some modules depend on special hardware which may be incompatible with other applications. Nevertheless, the MicroCAT brings MT capability into the small business or even the classroom. Like SYSTRAN, it is widely operational, uses no apparent linguistic theory and owes much to older direct translation techniques. Post-editing is essential for high quality.

Integrated into the MicroCAT is a **word-processor,** including simultaneous split-screen editing of source and target texts. The **bilingual dictionary** is the heart of the system, providing a menu-driven scheme for entering information about homographs, idioms and single-entry lexical items. There is limited provision for specifying semantic features (e.g. time, manner, place on adverbs; human, group, body part, etc., on nouns), although it is not clear how this information affects performance. Only one meaning per part of speech may be entered into the dictionary, so that different translations for, say, the noun *report* (= German *Bericht* or *Knall*) must appear in separate subdictionaries (which the translation module accesses in the order specified by the user). The user can create virtually any number of subdictionaries for particular subject fields, ensuring consistency of terminology.

Apart from pre- or post-editing, the user may improve performance only by modifying SL–TL dictionary entries. There is no monolingual dictionary and no means of entering information to improve SL analysis directly. Analysis operates locally on constituents and does not build a representation of the whole sentence. Linguistic rules are inaccessible for modification or inspection and the user enters semantic and other features on dictionary items only from a fixed menu list (what effect such information has on the translation is often difficult to track). The system always aims to return a result, although it has predictable limitations in handling subordinate and complex structures and can occasionally produce bizarre results (e.g. deleting all words in a list). If the system *hangs up* it is impossible to ascertain why. On the whole, however, the raw output in a specific domain is comprehensible enough to be post-edited by a translator or skilled monolingual operator. The rate of translation is claimed to be 1,600 words per hour.

4.14   Classification of Systems

The MicroCAT is a **machine-assisted translation (MAT) system** whose strengths lie, not in its analysis or transfer components, but its support for the translating environment (i.e. word-processing, dictionaries, batch operation and communication with other computers). These **interactive** systems rely heavily on the user (translator) to improve their output, usually by pre- or post-editing texts or creating suitable dictionaries. Similar systems to Weidner are LOGOS (not implemented for PC), PC-Translator and the Globalink Translation System (GTS) – these last two being possibly the cheapest MT systems of all (around £1000). PC-Translator is recommended for *highly repetitive, non-literary documents* by its suppliers. Another system, ALPS, allows the user to interact with the linguistic processing component itself, asking him during translation to choose between lexical equivalents and resolve ambiguities or problems of syntactic analysis. ATLAS is also reported to depend on interaction during analysis (Hutchins, 1986: 318).

Interactive systems are generally contrasted with fully automatic ones, although no system can provide FAHQT for all types of text. Even a highly automatic system such as METEO relies on working within a limited domain (the language of weather forecasts) for a single language pair (English to French) to achieve 80 per cent success. It is also unlikely that METEO could ever be extended to wider applications, even within meteorology. We can therefore say that all MT systems are interactive in as much as their input is strictly controlled or their output needs some sort of human revision – even if this takes the form of mental scanning to extract information or to decide if translation by a human being is warranted.

The fact is that, despite their achievements, current operational systems are not linguistically sophisticated. The most promising immediate prospect is full implementations of transfer or quasi-interlingua systems (such as EUROTRA) with the flexibility to handle wider ranges of text and allow users to adapt linguistic rules and lexical data. They should also have a higher ceiling of improvement in response to feedback from their users.

4.15   Evaluation

Because MT is not fully developed for universal application, the potential user needs a clear model of **evaluation** in order to decide if a particular system will meet his own specifications.

Before considering how MT systems are evaluated, we should observe that MT is part of a complex **translation market** influenced by a number of factors. These are the nature of typical clients (national and international organizations, research centres, industry and media, etc.) as well as the subject areas (commerce, technology, science and law) and text types (correspondence, circulars and scientific articles) which are most commonly translated. The biggest language services are maintained by supranational organizations and official bureaucracies, a prime example being the European Community. An interesting feature is that the traditional dominance of the English language as an international *lingua franca* is counterbalanced by a growing commercial demand on the part of end users for product descriptions written in the language where the item will be sold: this means that, although passive knowledge of a foreign language such as English is increasing, the demand for good translations is expected to rise. Translators themselves are a heterogenous group with an unclear professional identity and widely differing qualifications, productivity levels and pricing policies (there is also a significant *twilight zone* of casual or part-time translators). A final factor is the so-called *latent market* of translations which are desired but not carried out because of cost, time, lack of translators, etc. (For a discussion of the translation market and its implications for MT, see Blatt et al. (1985) and Kingscott (1989).)

In 1979 the Commission of the European Community instituted a study of the translation market with a view to using MT (Slype et al., 1981), reported in Blatt et al., 1985). According to this survey, only 30 per cent of translators were familiar with MT-produced texts, with almost half happy with the results. Eighty per cent of companies who used external translation services felt that raw MT was adequate for conveying the basic informational content of texts, while only 65 per cent of language service departments and 40 per cent of independent translation agencies thought MT useful. Translators themselves tended to regard updating dictionaries and post-editing recurring basic errors in MT output as tedious and demotivating (although still preferable to the drudgery of manually translating the language of weather reports, as shown by the TAUM-METEO system, whose introduction reduced the high turnover of staff for that particular field).

Apart from the reactions of both client organizations and translators to the quality and usefulness of MT, cost is a key factor. According to the EC survey there was no doubt that, disregarding the often considerable cost of purchasing and maintaining the hardware and software, an MT system which can provide raw output for pure information extraction is much faster and up to four times cheaper than human translation. Predictably, when output has to be post-edited to improve its quality, the cost differential narrows, although a revised version can still be about 25 per cent cheaper.

These are only guidelines, however. To be really useful, a model of evaluation must consider a number of factors in detail, not all of which are straightforward (for descriptions of such models, see Blatt et al., 1985; Lehrberger and Bourbeau, 1988; and Rasborg, 1989). Quality of translation is the factor most often referred to, although this depends on text type, subject area and who will read the translation for what purpose. Thus a scientist scanning output to see if the original is worth translating by a human being will judge MT output very differently from a technician relying on clear instructions to install an item of equipment safely. Although quality in MT is probably more concerned with utility and less with good linguistic style than other types of translation, we should not forget that all translation is about words and cannot avoid handling language competently if it is to be successful.

Criteria for assessing MT **quality** are:

- Intelligibility
- Fidelity
- Usability
- Acceptability
- Linguistic characteristics.

Intelligibility may be rated on scales of *clear* to *totally unintelligible*, or measured by comparing the time taken to read and understand the MT output with that for a conventional translation. Cloze tests can also be applied to MT texts to assess their level of readability (which is equated with intelligibility). **Fidelity** measures the amount of information in the SL which is repeated in the TL and requires a direct comparison of the original text with its translation.

Both fidelity and intelligibility rely on subjective judgements on the part of the assessors and are therefore open to question.

Since both **usability** and **acceptability** depend on the user's individual requirements, they are assessed in joint consultation between the system supplier and the user. Clearly they are influenced by intelligibility and fidelity, and the consultation process may specifically include tests for these. Other methods include asking users what they think of samples of MT output (inviting them to weight errors or deficiencies), preparing and comparing summaries of MT-derived and conventional translations, or getting a TL speaker to carry out a set of translated instructions to establish their effectiveness. It is difficult to draw up any general scheme for measuring usability or acceptability since they are always oriented to specific users.

While intelligibility and fidelity are content- or information-oriented (and directly involve the end user), **linguistic characteristics** are more specifically concerned with details of lexical and grammatical coherence (e.g. measuring and comparing the number or correct/incorrect lexical equivalents, sentence or clause constructions). Thus statements about the proportion of correctly translated morphological units, noun phrases, subject–object relations or embedded structures are useful for system designers and for identifying which components to improve (e.g. dictionaries or processing modules). Knowles (1979) provides an illustration of this kind of evaluation for SYSTRAN.

At an *economic* level, criteria for evaluation include:

- The time taken to input text and translate it.
- The time taken to correct/post-edit the translation.
- The time required to read the translation and understand it.

Other economic factors are the cost of:

- Acquiring (purchasing or leasing), installing and maintaining the hardware and software.
- Training staff to use the system.
- Setting up and updating dictionaries.
- Post-editing and revising output.
- Improving and extending the system (e.g. to other subject areas, text types or language pairs).

The user should also be able to relate the volume of text to be translated to the operational cost of the system (as a rule, the larger the volume of texts of a uniform type, the more economical is the system). Training should take account of the standard of documentation for the system, and its overall *ease of use* or ergonomy. Improvability should include the likelihood of degradation of performance after dictionaries reach a certain size or contain a large number of idioms.

A potential user of MT will weight the above factors according to individual needs. Speed, for instance, may be more important than quality, or the need to have translations may outweigh their actual cost.

The literature on MT contains numerous informed reactions to operational systems and partial evaluations of their performance (these are provided by users, developers or interested individuals). So far the fullest professional evaluations of MT systems in practical use over a significant period have been carried out for SYSTRAN and TAUM (for summaries see Hutchins, 1986: 216ff, 229ff, 232f) and the conclusion seems to be that, for a large organization handling large amounts of text in restricted linguistic domains (which is what many translators do already), MT is commercially viable. On the other hand, MT is still a relatively new and evolving product in an already diverse market and has yet to establish its final position. The competitive situation is also sharpened by the emergence of new commercial computer aids to translation, notably integrated word-processor termbanks.

4.16   Termbanks

The 1980s saw a major expansion in the performance of personal computers (PCs) and data storage techniques (especially the compact disk or CD, which can hold the equivalent of 340,000 pages of closely typed text). At the same time a new type of PC-based MAT system emerged offering the user word-processing (for manual translation) with computerized on-line dictionary look-up (including cut and paste facilities at the screen cursor location). Since they make no attempt to generate automatically a TL translation from an SL text, such packages do not perform MT at all. They are, however, relatively inexpensive and avoid the pitfalls of user expectations traditionally associated with MT. Termbanks in fact owe little to the built-in dictionaries of earlier MT systems. While MT dictionaries contain a lot of morphological, grammatical and semantic data for access by a computer program, a termbank typically displays definitions and information about usage directly to the translator. For this reason an on-line termbank is organized as a text database and employs quite different storage techniques.

An example of an integrated word-processing/dictionary translation aid is TERMEX^{TM}, which appeared in the mid-1980s. The system allows the translator, from within a TL text, to call up (and paste directly into the text) entries from standard off-the-peg dictionaries or from data files the translator has already compiled. Dictionaries can have up to one million entries, with entry access times of up to 3 seconds claimed. Each entry (**record**) is free format (i.e. it contains any text up to 900 characters) and consists of a **term** (a head word or phrase up to 50 characters) plus a **data area** with any number of **fields** of varying length.

Figure 4.24 illustrates a possible (English) entry for the German term *Bildschirm*. The **term** ([*Bildschirm*] is the **record** keyword which the system looks up. The characters in curly brackets are **field** names (kept short for easy pasting in). For each field there is a **data area**, which contains the information. If the translator enters a field name, the contents of the data area for that field are inserted into his text. In the above entry the dictionary compiler has included notes on the different senses of *Bildschirm* and the final field {code} refers to reference sources, compiler's name, etc. (the field layout does not have to be the same for each record). The first seven fields are visible at the bottom of the screen, otherwise the translator scrolls across a maximum sixteen lines. It is also possible to create subsets of dictionaries (e.g. create a dictionary subset of all records ending in *communication*) or to chain blocks of fields (according to field name) so that fields in other records are automatically consulted.

Apart from general dictionaries, precompiled glossaries in TERMEX™ are currently supplied for aeronautics, computer science, mechanical engineering and business/finance, with automobile industry, iron and steel, medicine and political science in preparation. So-called **background dictionaries** are supplied read-only (they range from 2,000 to 3,500 terms and can be used in a local area network), while **foreground glossaries** are direct-access files to which new terms can be added or existing ones modified (from 100 to 1,200 terms). The **computerized dictionary manager** is the basic software tool for handling the database and integrating it with a standard word-processor. The suppliers of TERMEX™ estimate a world-wide distribution of up to 3,000 installed systems, with approximately 1,000 in Germany, 500 in France and 100 in the United Kingdom (in 1990). Whereas the MicroCAT was supplied at approximately £8,000 for a single language pair in 1986, a TERMEX system could be assembled for under £500 in 1990.

A similar package to TERMEX is MULTITERM (available from 1990), which claims to offer totally free text entry. Since there are no data fields for entries, text is input as in a word-processor via a window which can be set to full screen size. An entry may include lists and tables (with indentations) and can be up to 4 Kb in size (or two typewritten pages). The total number of entries is limited only by the computer hardware. The user classifies terms and their

```
─────── Term: [Bildschirm] ──────────────────────
{t1}   VDU
{a1}   short for: video display unit
{t2}   screen
{a2}   synonymous with VDU
{t3}   monitor
{a3}   in this sense a VDU to display the status of a system
{code}   sources, references, translator
```

Figure 4.24

translations by means of **attributes** which come pre-defined or can be created from scratch. An attribute is a straightforward (ASCII) character code such as word class, date of entry, author, subject field, etc., and is used to access information. Thus, specifying <mathematics>, <functions>, <noun> and <brown> (= author's name) would display the data associated with these attribute names. The system is potentially multilingual, allowing terms in any number of languages to be cross-referenced. Translations can be pasted directly into a text being run on a standard word-processor.

SUPERLEX and INK TextTools are both marketed as terminology management support systems. With the TextTools package, the user can construct his own dictionaries and consult terms on-line during translation. TextTools' main components are TEXAN and LOOKUP. TEXAN (TEXt ANalyzer) carries out a linguistic analysis of a source text (English only), displaying the stem forms, the contexts and the frequencies of terms it has encountered (TEXAN performs its own morphological reduction, filtering out articles, prepositions, conjunctions, etc., and recognizing the base forms of inflected words). On the basis of the terms found the user can either set up new dictionaries or update existing ones. The LOOKUP program allows the bilingual dictionaries to be accessed on-line (i.e. during translation) and terms to be directly pasted in. Small English to Dutch, French, German and Spanish dictionaries are supplied – for each language pair there are 2,000 term general business dictionaries and 500 term dictionaries of basic computer vocabulary.

TERMDOK, assembled by the Swedish Centre for Technical Terminology (TNC), claims to be one of the largest multilingual termbanks accessible from a PC. Unlike the previous systems, TERMDOK is permanently stored on CD-ROM and cannot be modified by the user. It comprises over 225,000 technical terms (with translations, definitions, synonyms and related concepts) held in seven dictionaries on CD-ROM. The dictionaries, which may be handled separately or as a single database, are as follows (the county of origin of the termbank is given in brackets and multilingual generally denotes English, French, German and Russian):

- AFNOR-Normaterm: 47,000 French–English terms (France);
- Termium: 100,000 English–French terms (Canada);
- TNC: 28,000 terms; Swedish/multilingual (Sweden);
- TNC excerpts: 6,000 terms from magazines, journals, reports, etc. (Sweden);
- Swedish Standards: 17,000 terms (Sweden);
- RTT: 25,000 terms; Norwegian/multilingual (Norway);
- TEPA: 9,000 terms; Finnish/multilingual (Finland).

TERMDOK can be run alone or from within a word-processor. Words are called according to their context, language or field. Entries are classified under main term, synonym, definition or foreign language equivalent and can be accessed by term, definition or translation. Entries contain the Swedish main term, grammatical information, abbreviated and related forms, synonyms, references, applications and context, as well as translation equivalents (although these are not given for every term). For each entry there is also a reference number (for source document) and a classification code. It is reported as being most useful for Swedish, English and French, with coverage of other languages (especially Russian) less comprehensive (Davies, 1989).

Integrated word-processor termbanks are a development of a basic translator's aid, the (electronic) dictionary, as traditionally compiled and maintained by national terminology centres or similar organizations. Large electronic dictionaries from the 1960s onwards include EURODICAUTOM, the terminology database of the European Commission, and the facilities of the Bundes-sprachenamt for translating technical texts for the German Ministry of Defence. Remote users typically access the system by dialling up a telephone computer link or requesting information on paper or microfiche (see Arthern, 1979; Goetschalckx, 1979, for descriptions of these systems and their mode of operation; also Ahmad et al. for references to similar termbanks). The fact that such facilities can now be brought directly onto the translator's word-processor screen is likely to have major commercial implications. Unlike true MT, integrated termbanks are flexible in application, computationally straightforward and do not require radical changes to current working practices. All of these factors are bound to make them more readily acceptable to the translating fraternity.

Further Reading

General surveys of the history and development of MT in the mid-1980s are contained in Hutchins (1986), Slocum (1987) and King (1987). The style is clear, jargon-free and accessible to linguists. The work by Hutchins is possibly the most detailed and extensive survey of MT ever produced and can be used as a reference guide for more detailed descriptions of individual operational systems and research projects. Nirenburg (1987) covers more technical aspects of MT and natural language processing (NLP), while Billing (1987) critically assesses the latest systems under development, especially in Japan.

The material on linguistic representations and software tools can present difficulties to the interested amateur or applied linguist unfamiliar with current computational models. Older but still standard introductory works which avoid mystification are King (1983) and Winograd (1983). The reader who is really keen to get to grips with computational linguistics and natural language processing (NLP) is advised to study Gazdar and Mellish (1989), which describes the basic approaches and techniques of NLP (including parse strategies and charts, etc.); topics are illustrated with listings in the PROLOG programming language, although the reader will need to be fairly adept at PROLOG in order to follow the programs and possibly rewrite them so that they work on a particular implementation of the language. Allen (1987) also introduces the essentials of NLP and includes appendices on symbolic notations and programming constructs (although these can be difficult to follow in the text). Simmons (1984) gives clear descriptions and illustrations of how procedural logic can be used to represent linguistic information. Worth mentioning here is Crookes (1988), who combines a lucid introduction to a subset of PROLOG (i.e. one which really is for the beginner) with a small model program for translation which uses tree structures and what might even be regarded as a primitive interlingua. The best introduction to core PRO-LOG, including its facilities for NLP, remains Clocksin and Mellish (1987).

Apart from describing the functions of the different linguistic components of MT systems, Lehrberger and Bourbeau (1988) provides the most detailed model for MT evaluation produced so far. Observations on the current translation market in Europe and the place and prospects of MT are included in Kingscott (1989), Blatt et al. (1985) and Slype et al. (1981). Users' experiences of a number of operational systems (in particular Logos, Weidner and Systran) are collected in Lawson (1985); see also Ananiadou (1987). For a discussion of the programming languages and software tools involved in implementing the EUROTRA model, see Johnson, King and des Tombe (1985), Johnson and Varile (1986), Rosner and Petitpierre (1986). Rasborg (1989) gives a general description of EUROTRA and applies a model of evaluation to the system so far.

Snell (1983) is recommended as an excellent short introduction to terminological data banks (type, function, compilation and use, etc.). For promotional material on current integrated word-processor dictionary systems for personal computer, see the list of software suppliers below. Melby (1987a, 1987b) discusses general requirements and issues in a computer-assisted translation environment.

The journal *LT Electric Word* (formerly *Language Technology*), which reports on anything to do with language processing, is useful for descriptions and reviews of current products, especially for small computers. Academic periodicals in which research and review articles on MT appear include *Literary and Linguistic Computing* (the journal of the Association of Literary and Linguistic Computing) and *Computational Linguistics* (published by the MIT Press for the Association for Computational Linguistics). The new journal *Applied Computer Translation* is also of interest. For a comprehensive list of general sources for documentation on MT and major conferences see Kingscott, 1989: 43–6).

Notes

1   Examples are the German ADIMENS system of text processing and terminology (Schmitt, 1987) and those listed in Ahmad et al. (1987). For further information on DBMS generally, see Becker (1988: 98ff, 508).

2   The PSA originated in the mid-1950s at the National Bureau of Standards (USA) and was further developed at Harvard. It was the precursor of the Augmented

Transition Network (ATN) Parser, which was widely used in natural language processing from the 1970s.

3   Trees are usually drawn with the **root** at the top. Seen from the so-called leaf nodes (the words of the sentence), the **higher level** or more abstract constituents lie **deeper** in the tree. However, a parse can work either from the root (S) or the leaves (words). The first method is termed **top-down** and the second **bottom-up**. Whereas linguists equate higher-level constituents such as NOUN PHRASE or VERB PHRASE with depth (greater abstraction), in a top-down parse, the deeper nodes are those furthest from the starting point, i.e. closest to the leaves.

4   For a more technical description and evaluation of Q-systems, see Whitelock and Kilby (1983: B-3ff).

5   Examples from Lehrberger and Bourbeau (1988: 98ff) and Köller (1979: 36).

6   Except, possibly, Wilks' preferential semantic parser, which claimed to have no explicit syntactic information at all. For a brief description and discussion of the issues, see Ritchie (1983) and Wilks (1983). For further detail, see Whitelock and Kilby (1983: F-1ff).

Appendix 4.1   MT Systems Mentioned

System	When developed	Where developed	Language-pairs
SYSTRAN	1964–	California, Munich, Luxemburg	Russian–English French–English English–French/Spanish/Italian (more projected)
CETA	1961–71	Grenoble	Russian–French (started: German–French, Japanese–French)
TAUM-AVIATION/ METEO	1965–81	Montreal	English–French
SUSY	1967–	Saarbrücken	Russian–German (modules for German, Russian, French, Esperanto)
CULT	1969–	Hong Kong	Chinese–English
METAL (LITRAS)	1970–5 1978–	Texas (Linguistics Research Centre), West Germany	German–English
LOGOS	1968–78 1982–	United States	English–Vietnamese German–English English–German/French

continued overleaf

Appendix 4.1 continued

System	When developed	Where developed	Language-pairs
GETA-ARIANE	1971–	Grenoble	Russian–French (many other projects, including German–French French–English)
SALAT	1973–	Heidelberg	Modules for English, German, French
WEIDNER (MicroCAT)	1977–	Chicago	English–French/German/ Spanish/Italian/ Portuguese French–English Spanish–English
EUROTRA	1978–	European Community	All EC languages
DLT (Distributed Language Translation)	1979–	Utrecht	Esperanto as interlingua
ALPS (Automatic Language Processor)	1980–	Provo, Utah	English–French/German Italian/Spanish
ATLAS	1981–	Japan (Fujitsu) and Stuttgart	English–Japanese Japanese–English/German
MOPTRANS	1978–	Yale	Spanish–English French–English
PC-TRANSLATOR	1983–	Houston, Texas	English–Spanish Spanish–English French–English English–Danish Danish–English English–Swedish Swedish–English
GLOBALINK TRANSLATION SYSTEM (GTS)	1985–*	Washington USA	English–Spanish/ French/German/Russian (and vice-versa) Chinese–English

*Originally based on research at Georgetown University undertaken in the 1950s.

Appendix 4.2   Software Suppliers (Selected List)

GLOBALINK Translation System, Nestor, PO Box 63, Essex Street, Newbury, Berks RG14 6BR.

LOGOS Computer Systems Deutschland GmbH, Lyonerstrasse 11, 6000 Frankfurt-am-Main 71, Germany.

METAL, Siemens Aktiengesellschaft, Germany; Symbolics, St John's Court, Easton Street, High Wycombe, Buckinghamshire, HP11 1JX.

MULTITERM, Trados GmbH, Rotebühlstrasse 87, 7000 Stuttgart, Germany.

PC-Translator, Linguistic Products, Houston, TX, USA; Multi Lingua, 61 Chiswick Staithe, London, W4 3TP.

SUPERLEX, Salford Translations Ltd, UK. Tel. 061-236 3568.

TERMEX™, Multi Lingua, 61 Chiswick Staithe, London W4 3TP.

TERMDOK, Walters Lexicon Co., Södermalmstorg 8, 17800 Stockholm, Sweden; Multi Lingua, 61 Chiswick Staithe, London W4 3TP.

INK International, Prins Hendriklaan 52, 1075 BE Amsterdam, Netherlands.

Weidner's MicroCAT, (until 1990) ESC (South), Fryern House, 125 Winchester Road, Chandler's Ford, Southampton SO5 2DR.

5 Computers and Corpus Analysis

Geoffrey Leech and Steven Fligelstone

It is difficult to write on the subject of this chapter, simply because the field of computer corpus research is growing and changing so quickly. Up to five years ago, the compilation and analysis of computer corpora was a minority interest, quite marginal to the mainstream of natural language processing. The few who indulged in this arduous pastime were mainly humanities scholars, interested in the use of the computer in stuyding literary and linguistic texts for their own sake. Recently, however, this field has attracted strong interest from those working in information technology: for example, in the development of speech recognizers or machine translation systems. The future importance of corpus-based research looks assured. So why has this change come about? Later in the chapter we will try to answer this question.

But first, some more basic questions need to be answered: questions such as 'What is a computer corpus?' 'What are such corpora for?' 'What can one do with them?' and 'What is the history of their development up to now?'

5.1 What is a Computer Corpus?

Computer corpora are, essentially, bodies of natural language material (whole texts, samples from texts, or sometimes just unconnected sentences), which are stored in machine-readable form. They may be stored by means of various storage devices, of which, at present, hard disks, diskettes, magnetic tapes and CD-ROM are the most readily available. The fact that they are composed electronically, and stored in machine-readable form, means that they can be accessed by a computer user, automatically searched, copied, transferred to another computer, and so on. Programs can also be written to manipulate them in various ways. These capabilities make a computer corpus a powerful resource for linguistic research and its applications in software development.

It should be added that computer corpora are rarely haphazard collections of textual material: they are generally assembled with particular purposes in mind, and are often assumed to be (informally speaking) **representative** of some language or text type. This has implications for the uses of corpora (see section 5.5 below), both for purposes of linguistic research, and for the pursuit of statistical approaches to 'natural language processing'.

Finally, as we shall see, a corpus may contain more than just words. A usual requirement for a corpus is in-built indexing of some kind, such as line or sentence reference numbers. But additionally a corpus may contain information (of a grammatical nature, for example) about the words and phrases which make up the text in the corpus (see section 5.6).

5.2   How are Computer Corpora Created?

Computer corpora are created by inputting textual material into a computer via some input channel such as an electronic keyboard. The input may be performed either manually or automatically. In the early days of the 1960s and 1970s, text[1] was input manually by cumbersome devices such as a card punch. Nowadays, manual input takes place on a massive scale by means of the keyboards of terminals, workstations or microcomputers: word-processing has become such an all-pervasive activity that, on a world scale, this kind of input must produce millions of machine-readable text words per minute. The task for the corpus compiler is in part that of inputting the text, but also, more and more frequently, that of 'capturing' machine-readable text which already exists in great abundance, as a result of word-processing. Modern technology even enables data capture, e.g. of machine-readable press agency reports, to take place by satellite.

As for automatic input of text, this has become feasible in the past 10 to 15 years through the development of optical character readers (OCRs) such as the Kurzweil Data Entry Machine (KDEM). These machines are capable of deciphering the visual image of a page of printed or typewritten material, in a wide variety of typesizes and fonts, so that whole books can be read into the computer far quicker than a human typist could input them via a keyboard. Such OCRs require 'training', and 'misread' the text in ways that may require subsequent correction. But they are fast becoming cheaper and more effective (see also chapter 1).

We mentioned briefly in section 5.1 that other types of information may be included in the corpus. Such information cannot, as a rule, be 'captured', but must be included expressly. Some ways in which this can be achieved, and the types of information typically involved, are mentioned in sections 5.6 and 5.7.

5.3 What Computer Corpora Exist?

A computer corpus can consist of anything from a few thousand words of text typed into a PC by its owner, to hundreds of millions of words of text acquired through 'data capture' by a large-scale research institution. Such is the proliferation of machine-readable text at the present time, that documentation of corpora lags far behind their creation, so that it is impossible to give anything more than a fragmentary list of what computer corpora exist in various languages.[2]

Since English is the language most widely 'computerized', however, it may be useful to describe some of the more notable English language corpora or corpus types in existence. Corpora in other languages are less adequately documented, but we shall end this section with a few words about them (see section 5.3.5).

5.3.1 *Corpora of Written English*

We begin by mentioning two corpora which have been around for a comparatively long time, and have been used by researchers worldwide.

The Brown Corpus   Compiled by Nelson Francis and Henry Kučera at Brown University, (USA), in 1961–4, the Brown Corpus is, effectively, the first computer corpus of English to be compiled. (Notice our use of the present tense, since the Brown Corpus still exists, and can be copied and used more effectively today than it could when it was first compiled. Computer corpora are eminently **re-usable** resources.) The Brown Corpus, officially known as 'a Standard Sample of Present-Day Edited American English for Use with Digital Computers,' consists of some one million words, subdivided into 500 text samples of about 2,000 words each, randomly sampled with fifteen text-type categories (or **genres**) from material published in 1961. (See Kučera and Francis, 1967; Francis and Kučera, 1979, 1982).

The Lancaster-Oslo/Bergen Corpus   This corpus was designed to be, as far as practicable, an exact match of the Brown Corpus, except that the material consists of British rather than American English (see Johansson et al., 1978; Hofland and Johansson, 1982; Johansson and Hofland, 1989).

Other corpora of written English   The Brown and LOB Corpora were assembled primarily for linguistic research purposes, and have been distributed and employed in a wide range of research contexts.[3] However, in terms of size, they now look rather small in comparison with more recent corpora which have been 'captured' rather than laboriously compiled. As already mentioned, technological advances over the past few years have brought about an enormous explosion in the creation and proliferation of machine-readable text. Corpora have grown up for reasons totally unconnected with research. Examples are the corpus of the American Printing House for the Blind (many millions of words) and the Gill Corpus (a smaller corresponding British Corpus) developed for the automatic conversion of texts into braille. Other corpora, such as the Associated Press corpus, are spin-offs from modern computerized communication systems – in this case, that of press agency reports. (The existence of such corpora does not, unfortunately, mean that they are freely available for anyone to use – see section 5.4.)

Sheer quantity of text-words is no longer of particular significance in itself. Of greater interest to many is the extent to which a corpus covers a wide-ranging variety of text types, or (on the contrary) aims at representing a limited text type, such as press reports. The Brown and LOB Corpora were assembled to be 'representative' of a core of common written English text types (hence the term 'Standard Sample'). On the other hand, some corpora are intentionally restricted: for example, in China, two corpora of specialized English have been assembled (for English language teaching purposes): a million-word corpus of scientific and technological English (Yang, 1985), and a smaller corpus of the English of the oil industry (Zhu, 1985). There is scope and potential demand for many specialized corpora such as these.

5.3.2 Corpora of Spoken English

In comparison with written language, there is a great shortage of machine-readable spoken language data. For practical purposes, a spoken text can be converted into machine-readable form only if it undergoes a more or less laborious process of transcription.

The London-Lund Corpus   One such corpus, which has been widely used for research, is the *c.*500,000-word London-Lund Corpus (= LLC) of British English speech, consisting of the spoken half of the Survey of English Usage Corpus. This corpus was originally compiled and transcribed in London under the direction of Randolph Quirk, and was later computerized by Jan Svartvik and his team at Lund in Sweden (see Svartvik, 1990). The text is transcribed in considerable detail, by means of a prosodic notation showing features such as stress and intonation. The brief extract in figure 5.1 illustrates the transcription conventions of the corpus.

The IBM/Lancaster Spoken English Corpus (= SEC)   This is another corpus of spoken English, much smaller than the London-Lund Corpus (*c.*50,000 words). Its particular strength is that it exists in various versions: for example, orthographically transcribed, prosodically transcribed, and grammatically tagged versions (see Knowles and Lawrence, 1987; see also section 5.6), as well as in the original sound-recorded version.

```
well ^very nice of you to ((come and)) _spare the
!t\/ime and#
^come and !t\alk# -
^tell me a´bout the - !pr\oblems#
and ^incid\entally# .
^I [@:] ^do ^do t\ell me#
^anything you ´want about the :college in
"!g\eneral#
I ^mean it !doesn`t "!h\ave to be {con^f\ined#}#
to the ^problems of !\English# .
[@: @:] and the ^horrors of :living in :this ´part
of the c/ollege#
or ^anything like th/at#
*( - laugh)*
```

Figure 5.1

Speech Corpora   What are generally described as 'speech corpora' are relatively small collections of data, in terms of words, which nevertheless provide a great deal of phonic detail for speech technologists working in such research areas as speech synthesis and speech recognition. These, like the Spoken English Corpus, exist in the form of high quality audio recordings, as well as in the form of transcribed text (with various levels of 'labelling' or annotation). For English, notable examples are TIMIT (American English) and SCRIBE (British English – still under development) (see Moore, 1990). Unlike other corpora we have discussed, speech corpora generally contain artificial material: e.g. decontextualized sentences, chosen to represent particular combinations of sounds.

Other corpora of spoken English   At the other end of the scale of corpus size, there are corpora which are machine-readable transcripts of official proceedings. Examples are the Canadian Hansard (the official record of the proceedings of the Canadian House of Commons) (ongoing and over 60 million words in length), and the Sizewell Corpus (13 million words) (see Sinclair, 1987: 21–2), the proceedings of an official public inquiry into the siting of a British nuclear power station. These clearly represent a very special and untypical kind of spoken discourse – close, because of its formality, to written language.

5.3.3   Corpora of Both Spoken and Written English

A corpus which claims, in some sense, to represent the English language obviously has to contain both spoken and written material. The Birmingham Collection of English Text (see Sinclair, 1987) is a corpus which contains both, albeit in different proportions. It consists of more than 20 million words, including more than one million words of spoken material. This is the first major corpus to be built largely through the use of OCR technology (see section 5.2).

The Birmingham Collection was developed mainly for lexicographical purposes, with the support of the publisher Collins, and led to the publication of the Collins Cobuild Dictionary (Sinclair et al., 1987). The Cobuild Dictionary was a breakthrough in the use of computer corpora as a data source for lexicography, and this trend is now being followed by two other major British publishers, Longman Group and Oxford University Press. Longman is undertaking a 50 million-word English corpus entitled the Longman-Lancaster Corpus, and Oxford University Press is leading a number of collaborators (including Longman) in a proposal for a National Corpus of British English, to amount to 100 million words. Both these corpus projects will involve spoken as well as written text, since such a combination is clearly essential for general lexicographic purposes.

Another corpus being planned at the moment is an International Corpus of English (Greenbaum, 1990), to consist of closely corresponding one million-word constituent corpora (both of speech and of writing) from a dozen or so major countries of the world in which English is a first or second language.

5.3.4 Corpora vs. Collections

The mention of the 'Birmingham Collection' above is a reminder that the concept of a closed corpus, such as the Brown Corpus, is no longer particularly appropriate now that OCR input and electronic data capture are leading to a vast increase in the availability of machine-readable text. 'Collection' is a looser word, suggesting that acquiring textual material is rather more like opportunistically building up an archive, as a diffuse and ongoing repository of data. In the United Kingdom, the Oxford Text Archive (Oxford University Computing Service, 1983) has already set this trend. On a worldwide scale, two new initiatives which are heading in the same direction are the Association for Computational Linguistics' Data Collection Initiative (ACL/DCI) and the Text Encoding Initiative (TEI), both based in the United States, but with an international remit (see Liberman, 1989; Ide and Sperberg-McQueen, 1990; and Burnard, this volume). These are projects aiming to make electronic text material available, in a standard format, in large quantity, and in sufficient variety, for purposes of research and development.

5.3.5 Corpora for Other Languages

By focusing on English, we have been able to enlarge on the amount and variety of computer corpora which have been coming into being over the past thirty years. But in one respect, our account has been misleading. Equivalent corpus-building activities have been going on, to a lesser extent, with other languages. A recent survey[4] of corpora in Europe shows that machine-readable corpora have been, or are being, compiled in sixteen different languages (excluding English). To mention a few: the survey shows existing corpora of 190 million words of French (chiefly consisting of the monumental historical corpus of the Trésor de la Langue Française), 27.5 million words of German, 60 million words of Dutch, 30 million words of Italian and 12 million words of Serbo-Croat.

5.4   How Far are these Corpora Available?

Regrettably, there is a huge gulf between the amount of computer corpus material in existence, and the amount which is available for use in any realistic sense. Textual material is subject to copyright law and the law of confidentiality. These two factors alone effectively bar the use of the vast majority of corpora from the vast majority of potential users. It is difficult to negotiate more than limited access to the use of corpus material: for example, for some corpora it is possible (with permission) to make use of concordance material, as opposed to the original material. For four of the corpora mentioned above (Brown, LOB, LLC and SEC) it is possible to obtain a copy, for academic research purposes only. These and other corpora are available through ICAME (International Computer Archive of Modern English), publishers of the *ICAME Journal*.[5] The Oxford Text Archive makes available considerable quantities of textual material under similar conditions (see chapter 1). Corpora developed under commercial funding arrangements will normally be subject to even tighter restrictions, if available at all. With new initiatives such as the ACL/DCI and the British National Corpus, it is intended to seek more favourable conditions for the research use of corpora, in the hope that machine-readable text holdings will come to be recognized as a public research resource to some extent analogous to the holdings of a national copyright library. But there is a long way to go before anything like such a situation is reached.

5.5   What are Computer Corpora for?

We have noted above the striking difference in size between one type of corpus and another. What is needed for some purposes, especially those of speech science and technology, is a corpus which, although small in terms of words, is extremely detailed in the kinds of information it gives about the spoken signal. At the other end of the size spectrum, a corpus of 50 million words or more is desirable for some areas of computer lexicography (e.g. collocation analysis), and a corpus of 500 million words or more may be desirable for some aspects of the statistical training of language models (see section 5.7.4). In fact, all other things being equal, for the last two applications, the more corpus data the better.

In the following sections we outline some of the most important uses to which corpora are put.

5.5.1   Speech Science and Speech Technology

Apart from a purely scientific interest in phonetics, the applications here are mainly in the areas of **speech synthesis** (devising machines which will simulate human speech production), and **speech recognition** (devising machines to simulate the opposite process of speech understanding or transcription). For most purposes, speech synthesis is a matter of automatically converting text into speech, whereas speech recognition (more difficult) is a matter of automatically converting speech into text.[6]

5.5.2   Linguistics and Natural Language Processing

Under this heading, as under the previous one, the uses of corpora are in part purely a matter of exploiting the evidence of corpora for descriptive and theoretical purposes. There is a growing breed of 'corpus linguists'[7] who regard the computer corpus as a major, or even indispensable, tool of their trade. The concept of 'consulting a corpus' to test hypotheses, or to provide evidence, in linguistic research is becoming more established, and the range of research in this area can be seen in the bibliography assembled by Altenberg (1991). Further, for computer applications in natural language processing (e.g. building better parsers), corpora are beginning to be seen as an essential resource, because they lend themselves to the building of robust, probabilistic computer systems, which require 'training' over a large body of data, as well as the providing of a 'testbed' for evaluating the performance of non-probabilistic systems. In a nutshell, corpora represent 'uncensored', unrestricted language data, providing the challenge of 'total accountability' which successful language processing systems are going to need in many applications. For example, a successful speech recognizer will have to face up to the need to process whatever its user may decide to say – which, in most contexts, is open-ended and cannot be predicted in advance. It has been forcefully argued (e.g. Sampson, 1987) that only probabilistic systems, trained on corpus data, can cope with the open-endedness, the messy profusion, of real discourse.

To say that a corpus is 'representative' of a (type of) language does raise difficult questions of a methodological or even philosophical nature, but it is worth reflecting on the fact that unless an assumption of some kind of representativeness **is** made, the idea of 'training' a language analyser would be irrational.

5.5.3 *The Overlap between Speech and Natural Language Processing*

Although the applications in speech (section 5.5.1) and natural language (section 5.5.2) research have been listed above as if they were distinct, in fact they overlap considerably. This is already suggested by the discussion of speech recognition in section 5.5.2. In fact, as Geoffrey Sampson has pointed out,[8] the distinction between the two is really a conflation of two different dimensions: (a) the processing of a spoken vs. written data, and (b) the processing of small ('micro') vs. large ('macro') units of text. In keeping with the 'micro' focus of most speech technology research, speech corpora have been designed mainly to help in the processing of small phonetic segments below the level of the word. Yet 'macro' analysis, such as syntactic parsing, is also of importance in speech processing: the syntactic structure of a sentence helps to determine, for example, its prosodic features such as pauses and tone group boundaries. Similarly, grammatical analysis is needed to determine (say) whether a word pronounced /led/ should be written *lead*, or vice versa.

5.5.4 *Lexicography*

The advantages of using corpora in the making and revising of dictionaries (see Meijs, this volume) have become obvious, now that corpora of the size of the Birmingham Collection and the Longman-Lancaster Corpus have become feasible. In a sense, while dictionary publishing continues to prosper, the notion of a printed dictionary made of paper is being overtaken by the notion of a dictionary as a lexical database, stored in machine-readable form, and capable of being searched and updated by computer. A corpus which interfaces with the database is again something that can be updated and automatically searched, so that information can be transferred from one to the other. (See Sampson (1989) on the testing of a lexicon or dictionary against a corpus.) Printed dictionaries are not so much primary products of this process as secondary products ('spin offs') of the computational 'lexicon development environment' (Boguraev and Briscoe, 1989). The lexical database can be adapted for both humans and machines as users: a lexicon which is capable of parsing unrestricted natural language text is bound to need an extremely detailed lexicon, which itself has to draw upon corpus data as an authoritative warranty for its definitions, its sense distinctions, its ordering of senses by frequency, and other types of lexical information.

5.5.5 *Other Applications of Corpus Research*

Among other applications of machine-readable corpora are:

1 Machine translation (see Lewis, this volume; see also Brown et al. 1990 for one line of corpus research in this area, making use of the Canadian Hansard Corpus as a bilingual – French/English – corpus).

2   Text checkers (see Atwell and Elliott, 1987), i.e. computer systems which attempt to evaluate a person's writing – including spelling and grammar – and where appropriate to suggest remedies in the form of spelling corrections, etc.
3   Educational applications (see Last, this volume): e.g. the use of concordances for CALL (computer-assisted language learning) – see especially Tribble and Jones (1990).

Further applications with educational connections are:

1   The use of error corpora, and corpora of learners' language,[9] to identify learners' areas of difficulty in learning a language; and
2   The use of multilingual corpora (with parallel texts which translate one another) for purposes of studying contrastive analysis and translation.[10]

5.6   What Sorts of Information may be Held in a Corpus?

We have so far considered the corpus only as a collection of 'raw text', that is, words and (possibly) punctuation. However, as with most objects which are collections of some kind, it is often useful to impose some structure on the whole. In a corpus which contains, for example, text samples dating from a range of periods,[11] it may be useful to include the information about the date of origin (or, indeed, other information such as authorship, title of work, nationality of author, and so on) within the body of the corpus. Such information about its contents can then be used to extract data selectively from the corpus. For example, one might extract, or perform operations on, a small sample of literature from each of the periods, or on all of the text samples from just one or two periods.

To many linguists, what counts as 'useful information' goes far beyond such headings. For some purposes, it is useful to be able to get at information about individual sentences, words and even sub-word units. Although, in principle, one could attempt to extract such information from raw text, using appropriately programmed tools, it is often better, in practice, to analyse the corpus in advance, and encode the analysis along with the text, making the information retrieval a relatively trivial rask. Corpora which contain such additional layers of information can be termed 'annotated corpora'. As will become clear in section 5.7.2, what information one should put into a corpus depends on what one wants to get out of it. For now, we simply introduce some of the types of information whose use is becoming widespread.

5.6.1   *Word-tags*

Although there is nothing new in the idea of assigning individual words to a particular word-class, it is no trivial task to do this with every word in a body of text. But there are considerable benefits to having a corpus in which every word is accompanied by a label which indicates what type of word it is. (Some practical advantages of this are illustrated in section 5.7.2.) One problem is that what class a word belongs to turns out in many cases to be very difficult to decide.

A further (related) problem is that there is no universally accepted set of grammatical categories for all the words in a language. These difficulties notwithstanding, several corpus builders have underaken the task of adding word-tags to corpora. Often, there is sufficient overlap between the various schemes or 'tagsets' used to make them acceptable and useful, if not ideal, to other users. LOB and Brown are both available in a tagged format which has been widely used in research.[12]

A more obvious problem, perhaps, is the sheer size of the task of tagging a large corpus accurately. In fact, it is now possible to tag text automatically with a relatively high degree of accuracy, reducing the human task mainly to manageable manual correction procedures. One means of such automatic tagging is described in section 5.7.2.

Figure 5.2 shows samples of 'tagged text' from the LOB Corpus:

```
hospitality_NN is_BEZ an_AT excellent_JJ virtue_NN ,_,
but_CC  not_XNOT  when_WRB  the_ATI  guests_NNS  have_HV
to_TO  sleep_VB  in_IN  rows_NNS  in_IN  the_ATI  cellar_NN
!_!
```

```
the_ATI  lovers_NNS  ,_,  whose_WP$  chief_JJB  scene_NN
was_BEDZ  cut_VBN  at_IN  the_ATI  last_AP  moment_NN  ,_,
had_HVD comparatively_RB little_AP to_TO sing_VB
```

```
´_´ he_PP3A stole_VBD my_PP$ wallet_NN !_! ´_´
roared_VBD Rollinson_NP ._.
```

Figure 5.2

5.6.2 Syntactic Annotation

If word-tags are useful, then syntactic labelling is potentially even more so, as discussion in section 5.7.2 will show. If one adopts a straightforward phrase-structure model of syntax, it is possible to represent linguistic structures as 'trees'. It is further possible to convert such trees into labelled bracketing, so that a sentence annotated as in figure 5.3 tells us the same things about the

```
[S[NP[D The_ART D][N house_NL1 N]NP][VP[V has_VH3 V]
[NP[A blue_ADJ A][N walls_NN2 N]NP]VP]S]
```

Figure 5.3

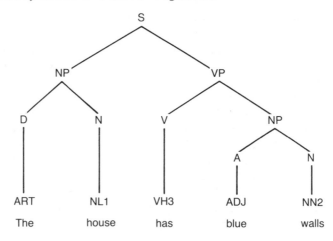

Figure 5.4

sentence's structure as the more familiar tree diagram (figure 5.4). Predictably, annotating a corpus in this way is more arduous than merely adding word-tags, but several such projects have been or are being undertaken (see Leech and Garside, 1991).

One such scheme, in which we have been involved, entails undertaking a 'skeleton parse', i.e. indicating a sentence's structure in terms of a limited set of major constituents. Figure 5.5 is from the parsed SEC corpus.

```
[S[N Nemo_NP1 ,_, [N the_AT killer_NN1 whale_NN1 N] ,_,
[Fr [N who_PNQS N][V 'd_VHD grown_VVN [J too_RG big_JJ
[P for_IF [N his_APP$ pool_NN1 [P on_II [N Clacton_NP1
Pier_NNL1 N]P]N]P]J]V]Fr]N] ,_, [V has_VHZ arrived_VVN
safely_RR [P at_II [N his_APP$ new_JJ home_NN1 [P in_II
[N Windsor_NP1 [ safari_NN1 park_NNL1 ]N]P]N]P]V]._.S]
```

Figure 5.5

5.6.3   Other Kinds of Annotation

Before leaving the subject of annotated corpora, we should emphasize that grammatical tagging and parsing are not the only types of annotation to consider. Currently, for example, a considerable effort in annotation is taking place in speech technology, including broader and narrower types of phonetic labelling. At a far more abstract level, annotation is also beginning in the area of discourse analysis. Little has so far been done in the area of semantic annotation, but the need for such annotation is likely to become a matter of priority in the future. In such areas as semantics and pragmatics, the besetting human problem of annotation becomes more evident: the difficulty of deciding on a system of annotation which will command 'consensual' support from linguists.

5.7 What can be done with Computer Corpora? Four Types of Corpus Processing

Although in principle one could sit at a computer terminal all day and simply read a corpus like a book, this way of proceeding would utterly fail to make use of the strengths of the corpus as an information source. Before a computer corpus can become fully exploitable by a user, some kind of automatic processing of the text data must take place. In this section, we shall present four kinds of automatic processing in an order which reflects the logic of their development.

5.7.1 Linguistic Data Retrieval: Concordancing

The simplest and most familiar kind of processing a corpus has to undergo is that of **linguistic data retrieval** (see Burnard, this volume). If a corpus is to be useful, we obviously need to be able to search it quickly and automatically to find examples of a particular linguistic phenomenon (say, a word), to sort the set of examples as required, and to present the resulting list to the user. The kind of program which performs these tasks is a **concordancer**, and the output it produces is known as a **concordance**. A concordance is a list of all the examples of the **target item** (the linguistic phenomenon being searched for), normally accompanied by enough context to enable a human being to study the item's occurrence in detail. The list can be ordered alphabetically according to the context, or on some other principle. The best-known kind of concordance output is known as a **KWIC concordance** (= Key Word In Context), which appears in a convenient form – see figure 5.6. – with each example consisting of

```
                  party conferences │round the world, there
         ly on their showing last time │round and smaller parties general
ts chances of success in the next │round of applications for North Sea
  Augusta.   Leading into the final │round, he fell victim to one of the
  46th year, fashioned an emotional │round of 65 to snatch the green jacke
    Norman's course-equalling second │round 63 was the turning point.  My
  Aintree fall with a winning clear │round last spring.  Pat Eddery took
nocking out Tim Witherspoon in one │round earlier this month.  But for the
   preferred,  Lloyd who?).  But by │round 6 of a remarkable contest, they
      a big cat, with his tail curled │round his front paws as good as gold.
the biggest boy, Jack Tall, turned │round and ran and ran and ran. He nev
    and now the white cistus.  In a │round bush it grows, this cistus of
illage near the front line. I came │round a bend in the road and there wa
      were ways and means of getting │round these things.   Was it like
      they'd love just sort of sitting │round and chatting and bringing cu
              "With the country all │round me, I would stand
```

Figure 5.6

a separate line of text, and with the target item displayed in the middle of the page or screen. This kind of display is obviously of use to (for example) a lexicographer. In fact, KWIC concordances were the means by which the Birmingham Collection was used for compiling the Cobuild Dictionary (see section 5.3.3; also chapter 6).

There are many possible variations on a computer-generated concordance. The target item does not have to be a word: it can be a sequence of words (e.g. an idiom such as *over the moon*), or a part of a word (e.g. the suffix *-less*), or a sequence containing gaps – e.g. the target item *ke∗p∗ ∗ nose∗ to the grindstone*, with ∗ (the so-called wildcard symbol) representing an unknown number of letters, including zero, would match with, and hence retrieve, all examples from this list:

Keep his nose to the grindstone
Kept their noses to the grindstone
Keeping Peter's nose to the grindstone
Keeps everyone's nose to the grindstone
etc.

There are many other possible embellishments of the basic concordancer. Some widely used concordancers or text retrieval packages are the Oxford Concordance Program (OCP – Hockey and Martin, 1988), WordCruncher (Jones, 1987), KAYE (Kaye, 1989) and CLAN (MacWhinney and Snow, 1990).

An additional trivial facility which can be built into a concordancer is a count of the number of occurrences of the target item in the corpus as a whole, or in various sections of it. From this it is easy to go one stage further, and to generate word frequency lists (sorted alphabetically or in rank order). A number of such frequency lists have been published, and have been found useful both for research and for educational applications.[13]

From word frequency lists various other statistical results can be derived: e.g. type-token ratio distributions for various corpora (see Carroll, 1971); comparison of corpora in terms of significantly different frequency patterns (see the comparisons of the Brown and LOB Corpora in Hofland and Johansson, 1982: 471–544). More interesting, for most users, is a frequency list of word-combinations, or collocations (see Beale, 1989), although for this purpose a very large corpus (say, of more than 25 million words) is ideally required. Such a collocation frequency list is unmanageably and uninformatively vast, unless the program filters out unwanted combinations (e.g. those occurring only once in the corpus) and homes in on the more significant collocations. The best way to do this is to employ a statistical measure of the 'bondedness' of two or more items, setting a threshold to capture only those word combinations which occur significantly more frequently than one would predict on the basis of chance. This measure is known as 'mutual information'.

The recent availability of computer corpora such as the Brown, LOB and LLC corpora has led to an exploitation of corpus data retrieval in many linguistic studies: not only in lexicography but in grammar, semantics, pragmatics, sociolinguistics, and discourse analysis (to mention a few fields).[14] In this context, the computer corpus can be thought of as, in the main, a resource to be systematically consulted by the scholar. Formerly, linguistic scholars (e.g. Jespersen, 1909–49) pursued their studies by collecting together their own corpora, and through alert reading finding their own examples, which they would then store on paper in filing cabinets, or other pre-electronic storage devices. The modern computer can supply, almost at the touch of a button, more examples of the target item than a traditional researcher might collect in many months. It is important to note that target items need not be restricted to words orthographically defined, but can include other symbols, such as punctuation in a written corpus, stress and intonation markers in a spoken corpus. Hence computer corpora have provided a rich source of evidence for studies of English punctuation (see Meyer, 1987) and English prosodics (see Altenberg, 1987).

The role of the computer in such researches should not, however, be overvalued. In the cases we have discussed, the data-retrieval processing performed by the computer is intellectually trivial: all the interesting intellectual work is still performed by the human analysis. The computer's task becomes much more significant when we come to the development and use of annotated corpora (see section 5.6).

5.7.2   The Linguistic Annotation of Corpora

We recognize the need for corpus annotation through asking: What is it that cannot be achieved through the computer's data retrieval work, as so far discussed? What limits our ability to retrieve data is the absence of linguistic information, apart from that which is immediately available in the 'raw corpus' – spelling, punctuation, and so on. For example, someone using a corpus for research on English grammar might have any of the following three data retrieval requirements:

1   Find all and only the examples of the semi-auxiliary *HAVE TO*.
2   Find all and only the examples of noun–noun sequences (such as *cable car*).
3   Find all and only the examples of relative clauses (including relative clauses which have a zero relative pronoun, as in *the books **I have read***).

None of these would be easy to find unless we had an annotated corpus as described in section 5.6. Thus, with respect to (1), if we specify a target item *have to*, this will be insufficient: we will need to make separate request for *had to*, *has to* and *having to*, in order to retrieve all forms of the lexeme *HAVE*. Even then, we may mistakenly retrieve examples with *to* as a preposition, rather than as an infinitive marker, as in *She gave what she **had to** the poor*. As for (2), the notion of a noun–noun sequence is impossible to specify in terms of spelling and punctuation; however, if a grammatically tagged version of the corpus were created, it would be possible to ask for a list of all such sequences. Suppose, for example, that *cable car* appears in the corpus as *cable*__NN1 *car*__NN1(where NN1 signifies 'singular noun'). Then a concordance request which asked for the target item *__NN1 *__NN1 (where again * is a 'wildcard' symbol for a number of characters – excluding space) would find *cable car* and all such sequences. In the case of (3), there is not even any way of specifying the classes of words which make up the target item, since even if we could locate all relative pronouns in the corpus, this would not help us to find the zero relative clauses which lack such pronouns. Here, then, a tagged corpus is not enough: we require a **parsed** corpus, in order to be able to identify automatically where relative clauses occur. (On parsing, see Patten, this volume).

These three examples show how, in specifying more sophisticated data retrieval requests, we need to specify abstract linguistic information (structures, patterns, categories) of various kinds. Hence we have to build linguistic information **into** the corpus, by adding the required linguistic annotations.

Grammatical tagging of corpora   In many ways, grammatical tagging – the procedure which adds a grammatical category label to each word in the corpus – is the most manageable and immediately useful kind of corpus annotation to undertake. Some of the corpora already mentioned are annotated by means of similar systems of tags (see Francis, 1980; Garside et al., 1987: 170–9). Among spoken corpora, the SEC and some parts of the LLC have also been grammatically tagged (see section 5.3.2).

Once a corpus has been tagged (or otherwise annotated), it is possible to use a concordancer to retrieve data on the basis of a target item which includes annotations. For example, with the CLAWS2 tagset used for the SEC Corpus, the semi-auxiliary *HAVE TO* can be targeted by means of the search specification *__VH* *__TO (once again we are using * as a wildcard – note that in this tagset, VH0, VHD, VHG, VHN, and VHZ represent forms of the verb *HAVE*, while TO represents *to* as an inifinitive marker). To find examples of noun–noun sequences like *cable car*, we could simply specify our target item as *__N* *__N*, which asks for any word with a tag beginning with N – in fact, for any noun. If we wanted to be more specific, and to restrict our search to common nouns (excluding sequences of proper nouns such as *George Washington*), we would simply add a second N to each tag: *__NN* *__NN*.

For example (3), as already noted, we would need a corpus which had undergone a syntactic analysis of higher constituents such as phrases and clauses – in short, a parsed corpus, or (as it is sometimes called) a **treebank** (see Leech and Garside, 1991). To search this treebank for relative clauses, all we need is to identify the beginnings and ends of constituents labelled with the symbol for relative clauses (in the case of our skeleton treebank, Fr – see the example in figure 5.5). A standard sort of concordance should be able to use such labelled brackets as its target item, and to search for them just as it could search for a single word. However, since a treebank is, in effect, a set of parse trees, it is more satisfactory to use a different kind of concordance program, which converts the linear, one-dimensional nature of the bracketed text into a two-dimensional tree structure (a program of this kind is the Treeconc program developed by Taylor, 1988). In fact, the more one adds abstract levels of structure, such as syntactic and semantic analyses, to the corpus, the more the text data retrieval facility needs to shift towards non-linear methods of display and storage, such as those represented by a parse tree.[15]

Automatic annotation Tagged and parsed corpora have many applications in addition to that of handling grammar-based data retrieval requirements. For the present, however, let us turn from the annotated corpora themselves – as end products – to the process whereby the annotations are made.

In principle, there is no reason why annotation, such as grammatical tagging, should not be done by hand – such a method was adopted, for example, by Ellegård (1978) in his grammatical analysis of part of the Brown Corpus. But in practice, manual annotation is slow, labour-intensive and liable to error and inconsistency. Hence it is preferable to develop, if possible, automatic annotation programs even though such programs will probably have a significant error rate, and require extensive post-editing of the corpus material.

An example of an automatic annotation system is CLAWS, the tagging system developed for tagging the LOB Corpus, and since used on other corpora (see Garside et al., 1987, chs 3 and 4). CLAWS manages to tag between 96 and 97 per cent of the words in a corpus correctly. It is worth spending a little time, focusing on CLAWS, to consider the actual structure of the automatic word-tagging system itself. Various approaches to automatic tagging can be taken, but the most successful appears to be one which employs a probabilistic method (technically, an elaboration of a Markov process model).

A probabilistic word-tagging system makes use of a type of statistical language model (a Hidden Markov Model – see Poritz, 1988), which calculates two types of probability, marked p and q in Figure 5.7, where w . . . . represents a sequence of words, and t . . . . represents the sequence of grammatical tags (word class labels) which may be associated with them.

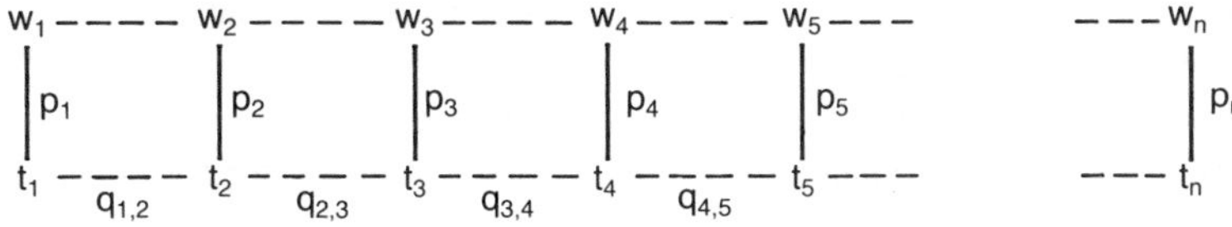

Figure 5.7

The first type of probability (p) is the probability that, if a word tag t_i occurs, the word in question will be w_i. The second type of probability (q), a *transitional* probability, is the probability that if t_i occurs, the following tag will be t_{i+1}. In a language like English, where many words are grammatically ambiguous (the word *round* has five possible word classes), there are obviously many different sequences of tags which could, in principle, be chosen. For example, in the sequence *cut down on smoking*, *cut* could be a noun or a verb, *down* could be a preposition, a prepositional adverb, a noun or an adjective, *on* could be a preposition or a prepositional adverb, and *smoking* could be a verb (present participle), a noun or an adjective. The correct sequence in this case is shown in figure 5.8. But, in principle, the sequence given in figure 5.9 (and many others) would also be possible.

Figure 5.8

Figure 5.9

Figure 5.9 does not make grammatical sense: it will be found to be highly improbable, both because of the unlikelihood in English of certain transitions (e.g. NOUN–ADJECTIVE), and also because of the unlikelihood of certain tags occurring with particular words (*down* occurs as an adjective only in limited expressions such *the down train*). Hence the calculation of the total probability of the word sequence and its tag sequence will show (a) to be very much more likely than (b). In fact, if the tagging system is successful, it will choose (a) as the most likely of all sequences – and this is the sequence that will be output.

The probabilistic tagging system clearly does not make use of sophisticated linguistic knowledge, such as a human being uses in decoding a word sequence. Nevertheless, using statistics and a very simple grammar (a probabilistic finite state grammar) it achieves a remarkable degree of success. How does it do this? The hidden ingredient, in fact, is that the tagging system must have access to reliable probability estimates, and these in turn have to be derived from an already tagged corpus (see section 5.7.3).

Different methodologies of annotation The above example of automatic tagging is not quite as automatic as it appears: the machine does most of the work, but human intervention is also a crucial component, since the output has then to be checked and corrected manually, by a human analyst. In fact, successful corpus annotation always involves a partnership between human and machine: but the partnership can be of at least three different kinds (1) **automatic processing with post-editing,** (2) **interactive processing,** (3) **machine-aided manual input.**

We can illustrate these three methodologies with reference to the task of producing treebanks: that is, of corpus parsing. If we remember the special difficulty of dealing with unrestricted text data – the challenge with which the computer corpus confronts us – it is perhaps not surprising that no one has so far succeeded in developing an effective corpus parser. As with word-tagging, it is likely that probabilistic methods, because of their **robustness,** will be most successful. But so far, the complexity of the task of parsing even an average-length sentence can prove baffling, and can tax the resources of the largest computer.

(1) *Automatic processing with post-editing* A successful, fully-fledged corpus parser will be required to assign a syntactic analysis to any arbitrary sentence from a corpus, with close to 100 per cent success. Such a parser is urgently needed – but no one has yet succeeded in building one. It is reasonable, however, to suppose that we may apply the same basic methodology as was described for grammatical tagging to this higher-order task. This would mean that automatic parsing would take place to a reasonable degree of success, and that errors would be subsequently corrected in a manual post-editing phase. (A semi-successful experiment in corpus parsing on this model is described in Garside et al., 1987: ch. 6).

(2) *Interactive processing* Whereas methodology (1) involves an automatic processing stage followed by a manual processing stage, methodology (2) involves an intermittent interaction process, whereby the human analyst, sitting at a terminal, can intervene during the course of parsing, and edit the automatic parsing output as required on-line. (An example of this method is that of Aarts and van den Heuvel, 1985).

(3) *Machine-aided manual input* Methodology (3) looks like a step back into the past, for it requires a human 'grammarian' to sit at a terminal and humanly parse each sentence as it appears on the screen. But, particularly with regard to probabilistic parsing, this seems to be the best track to go along for the present. The method involves adopting a fairly simplified form of phrase-structure parsing known as 'skeleton parsing'. The grammarians who input sentences can achieve an impressive speed of input (more than one sentence per minute at the optimum), and a high degree of accuracy and consistency can

also be achieved. The 'machine-aided' part of the process is crucial: a special fast input program (the EPICS program written by Roger Garside at Lancaster – see Leech and Garside, 1991) builds a stack of currently unclosed constituents, so that the well-formedness of the parse can be automatically verified, and parsing can be accomplished with a minimum of key depressions.

This methodology seems to be the most effective for the moment, because a prerequisite for a sufficiently robust corpus parser is a previously (accurately) analysed treebank of sufficient size to provide exemplars of all grammatical rules and (where required) adequate data on the frequency of these rules. However, this leads on to the topic of our next section.

5.7.3   Induction of Datastructures from a Corpus

The next kind of corpus processing is **inductive** in the sense of deriving from one corpus generalized information which can then be used in the analysis of another. Induction, the deriving of generalizations from individual instances, is essentially a statistical process. The objects which we generate from a corpus by induction may be given the general term of **datastructures**. In the simplest case, that of a 'raw', unannotated corpus, they include word frequency lists and collocation lists as discussed in section 5.7.1.

With a tagged corpus, two important datastructures can be derived: (1) a tagged frequency lexicon (a sorted list of word-tag pairs, with their observed frequencies); and (2) frequency list of observed tag sequences (in particular, of tag–tag pairs). Figure 5.10 gives very brief extracts from such lists (data from Johansson and Hofland, 1989).

```
i.    planned_JJ          6    (adjective)
      planned_VBD         7    (past tense)
      planned_VBN        30    (past participle)
      planners_NNS        3    (plural noun)
      planning_NN        53    (singular noun)
      planning_VBG       14    (-ing verb)


ii.   IN   ATI        35500    (preposition + neutral article)
      IN   NN         16679    (preposition + singular common noun)
      IN   AT          9706    (preposition + singular article)
      IN   NP          8145    (preposition + singular proper noun)
      IN   PP$         7856    (preposition + possessive determiner)
      IN   JJ          7317    (preposition + adjective)
```

Figure 5.10

As it happens, the lists in figure 5.10 contain precisely the kinds of data needed to provide estimated probabilities for a grammatical tagging system based on a Hidden Markov Process model. Thus the frequency information induced from one corpus furnishes a tagging system with estimated probabilities needed to tag another corpus. (Naturally how good those estimates are depends, among other things, on the size of the corpus analysed.) The Hidden Markov Process model is, in fact, a simplified model of how language works: it has a probabilistic lexicon ((1) above) and a probabilistic finite state grammar ((2) above).

We can now see that inducing data structures such as lexicons and grammars from an annotated corpus is an essential stage in a cyclic development of corpus analysis methodology. The first step is to obtain a corpus and to annotate it (if required) by any method – by hand or by machine or both – which will enable rough frequency data to be derived. The next step is to induce frequency datastructures such as a lexicon and a grammar. The third step is to use the frequency information in these datastructures to 'drive' a corpus analysing tool, such as a tagger or a parser. Step 4 is to use this tool to annotate a new corpus: this step is analogous to Step 1, except that the tool now has a basis for enhanced performance, in the improved frequency data obtained. So a second cycle of development has now begun. The manual correction of the tagging of this step enables a more reliable set of frequency statistics to be obtained by Step 5 (= Step 2), and so the cycle proceeds, as indicated by the following table:

Annotate new corpus data	Step 1	Step 4	Step 7
Induce datastructures	Step 2	Step 5	Step 8
Update corpus annotating tool	Step 3	Step 6	Step 9

(and so on)

If we move from tagging to the more advanced task of parsing, the same cycle applies. In this case, the datastructures induced include:

1   A lexicon specifying the grammatical categories of words (including syntactically important information such as the complementation types of verbs – transitive, intransitive, and so forth).
2   A grammar specifying the observed frequency with which rules are instantiated in the corpus. Assuming the simple model of a context-free phrase structure grammar, what this means is that each minimal subtree (consisting of a mother node and its daughter node(s)) observed in a treebank adds one to the count of a corresponding rule in the grammar.

A frequency figure is associated with each rule (x and y in figure 5.11) to give it an estimated probability weighting. From such frequency data, it is possible to

Example of minimal subtrees, and the associated CF PSG rules:

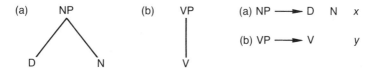

Figure 5.11

calculate the probability of each rule, and on that basis to calculate a 'figure of merit' for each parse of a sentence, the parse with the highest figure being designated as the best (= most likely) parse.

Looking back to section 5.7.2, we see that the different methodologies employed in tagging and in parsing are reasonable interpretations of the stages these two processes have currently reached in their cycle of development. In tagging, research teams have reached Stage 5 or beyond; but in parsing they are still at Stage 1 – that of collecting enough data to be able to get a probabilistic parser off the ground in a rough-and-ready way.

Viewed in this light, corpus processing has a very long way to go. Corpus parsing (in comparison with semantic annotation, for example) is a well-understood procedure. But it suffers from simplified models and an inadequacy of analysed data. A context-free phrase structure grammar is manifestly too weak a model for good results, and one direction of progress is in developing more sophisticated models, such as a probabilistic unification grammar. (On unification, see Patten, this volume.) Another direction in which to advance is to integrate a corpus parser within a grander scheme for corpus analysis, including semantic analysis. It has often been claimed that in natural language processing, syntax cannot be reasonably separated from semantics, and this may yet prove the case in corpus analysis.

5.7.4   Self-organizing Methodology: Training corpora

The final method of corpus processing is known as a **self-organizing** method, because it entails that the computer itself learn how to analyse corpora more successfully, by iterative progression towards optimal performance.

It has been seen that the cycle of corpus processing development (as described in section 5.7.3) is itself an iterative procedure. But there is a practical impediment in this procedure, in that at each stage of the cycle where a new corpus is annotated, the output from the analytic system has to be manually corrected. Otherwise no progress would be made in obtaining more reliable frequency data to enhance the accuracy of the system.

There are, however, ingenious modern statistical methods to avoid this stage of manual intervention (see Bahl et al., 1983; Jelinek, 1985b). Although it would be out of place here, and beyond our competence, to explain these methods in detail, the general approach is not too difficult to understand. The basis of the self-organizing methodology is a type of procedure known as an EM (estimation-maximization) algorithm.

Suppose we have a grammatical tagging system incorporating a Hidden Markov Model, as in section 5.7.2, and suppose we use this tagging system to assign tags to a new corpus. The idea of an EM algorithm is to adjust the parameters of the model so as to maximize the likelihood of the tags occurring as they do according to the analysis of the corpus. It might be supposed that this is a totally vacuous procedure. Surely, according to the Hidden Markov Model, the tags which have been assigned to words are precisely those which are found to have the greatest likelihood of occurring? However, this likelihood is based on the immediate context of each example. If the probabilities are re-estimated for the whole corpus, and adjusted to attain the closest 'fit' with the data, the result will be an improved probabilistic model. This re-estimation procedure can be iterated until no further improvement emerges.

We have discussed the EM technique with reference to grammatical tagging, but it may be applied to other kinds of language models, such as probabilistic grammars.

The process of adjusting the parameters of the model to a new corpus is known as 'training', and the corpus used for this purpose is known as a 'training corpus', as opposed to a 'test corpus', which is used to test out the performance of the model as demonstrated in an analytic system such as a tagger or a parser. Not surprisingly, the procedure of training natural language processing software in this way is extremely demanding in terms of computer resources. It forms a natural conclusion of the journey we have taken from discussing the intellectually simple process of data retrieval in section 5.7.1 to discussing the complex task of building systems which adapt to the corpus data they encounter in section 5.7.4.

Conclusion

In this chapter, after presenting a picture of the current state of computer corpus resources, we have discussed the applications of computer corpora, and the various ways in which corpora can be processed and analysed.

We believe that in the next few years computer corpora will take a position of growing importance in natural language processing and linguistic research. As this chapter has made clear, such research progresses slowly and cumulatively, and there are many areas in which we are not close to achieving success. Yet in the past two or three years a remarkable upsurge of interest in corpus linguistics has taken place. So far corpus work has been largely restricted to those who have access to powerful hardware, capable of handling the large amounts of text which it often involves. But as hardware becomes both cheaper and more powerful, this will change, and we may expect corpus resources to become more readily available for use, not only for academic and industrial research, but also for educational applications.

Summary

In this chapter we have:

- Explained what is meant by a 'corpus', and mentioned ways in which corpora are created.

- Pointed to a recent growth of interest in language corpora, and given examples of corpora currently in use.
- Pointed out that **spoken** English is under-represented among current corpora.
- Indicated some of the main areas in which corpora are used, including lexicography, linguistic research, natural language processing, language teaching and speech recognition.
- Shown that in addition to 'raw text', various kinds of information can be held in a corpus.
- Described ways in which corpora can be processed, with particular emphasis on (1) information retrieval, (2) corpus annotation, manual and automatic, (3) induction of datastructures with applications to automatic, probabilistic corpus analysis.
- Predicted a further increase in the availability of, and interest in, computer corpus resources.

Further Reading

The *ICAME Journal* currently appears once a year and gives an excellent insight into current corpus-based activities. It typically contains a report (with abstracts) of the most recent ICAME Conference, as well as news, reviews and longer articles. For a wide-ranging selection of papers concerned with the creation and exploitation of computer corpora, the reader is referred to a series of books published by Rodopi: Aarts and Meijs (1984, 1986), Meijs (1987), Kytö, Ihalainen and Rissanen (1988) and Aarts and Meijs (1990). Johansson and Stenström (1991) is a similar kind of book, but in addition to the papers, it contains a reference section consisting of Bengt Altenberg's *ICAME Bibliography*, and a survey of English-language computer corpora (Taylor, Leech and Fligelstone, 1991). Both of these documents can also be obtained in machine-readable form from ICAME (see note 5). For detailed accounts of work associated with a couple of the most important corpora, see Sinclair (1987) which describes the COBUILD Project, and Svartvik (1990) which deals with the London-Lund corpus of spoken English. Johansson and Hofland (1989) is a recent example of a corpus-derived word frequency listing. In this case the corpus used was LOB. The particular strengths of this listing are that it takes word and grammatical tag combinations (rather than simply morphological forms) as its basic unit of analysis, and that it deals extensively with collocation frequencies. For those interested in exploring the application of corpora to the development of probabilistic language analysis techniques, the collection of research reports in Garside, Leech and Sampson (1987) is a useful, though 'gentle' introduction. For those to whom mathematical formulae are not something of a deterrent, Bahl et al. (1983) is a good place to start; it cites results of experimental work by IBM, which has been substantially built upon in recent years.

Notes

1   Text is used here as an uncountable noun: a reflection on the way computers are turning electronic text into a mass commodity.
2   Recent surveys include: Taylor et al. (1991), and a thorough analytical survey of European corpus resources which was presented by A. Zampolli at the SALT Workshop on Corpus Resources, Wadham College, Oxford, January 1990. Much of the information presented by Zampolli (but not the narrative) is included in SALT (1990). A database about archives and corpora and related projects is now being maintained by the Center for Text and Technology at Georgetown University. Contact: Dr Michael Neuman, Georgetown Center for Text and Technology, Reiss Science Building, Room 238, Georgetown University, Washington, DC 20057.
3   See the *ICAME Bibliography* by Bengt Altenberg, which appeared in *ICAME News*, No. 10 (1986). In this bibliography, items which refer to or make use of the Brown, LOB and London-Lund Corpora are indicated. An updated and much enlarged version can be obtained in machine-readable form from ICAME (see note 5), and is included in Johansson and Stenström (1991).
4   By A. Zampolli – see note 2.
5   Their address is:

> ICAME,
> The Norwegian Computing Centre for the Humanities,
> PO Box 53,
> Universitetet,
> N–5027 Bergen,
> Norway.

6   See Fallside and Woods (1985) for a good overview of speech processing. See also Bahl et al. (1983) and Jelinek (1985a) on probabilistic approaches to speech recognition.
7   See the *ICAME Journal*, which includes reports of the annual ICAME Conference. See also Aarts and Meijs (1984, 1986, 1990) and Meijs (1987) for a wide range of contributions to this field.
8   In a background paper for the SALT Workshop on Corpus Resources, Wadham College, Oxford, February 1990. (See SALT, 1990, 13–15).
9   One example of a corpus of learners' English is the **PIF Corpus** assembled by Claus Faerch at Copenhagen. A more recent corpus of learners' English (with the focus on errors) is the **Longman/Birkbeck Corpus of Learners' English**, which is being compiled by the publishers Longman in association with Paul Meara, Birkbeck College, University of London. Other projects of learners' language are planned.
10   Examples of multilingual corpora are the **Canadian Hansard** corpus (see section 5.5.5 above), with parallel texts in English and French, **FELSI** and the **Danish–English–French Corpus in Contract Law** (see Taylor et al., 1991).
11   Examples of corpora dealing with historical periods of the English Language are the **Helsinki Corpus of English Texts (diachronic part)** (see Kytö and Rissanen, 1988; Kytö, 1989) and the **Century of Prose Corpus** assembled by Louis Milic at Cleveland State University (see Milic, 1990).

12   The tagged LOB and Brown Corpora can be obtained from ICAME, at the address given in note 5 above. The Manual of the tagged LOB Corpus (Johansson et al., 1986) can be obtained from the same source.

13   Frequency lists of the untagged Brown and LOB Corpora are published in Kučera and Francis (1967) and Hofland and Johansson (1982) respectively. There are also more recent publications with frequency lists based on the tagged corpora: Francis and Kučera (1982) for the tagged Brown Corpus, and Johansson and Hofland (1989) for the tagged LOB Corpus.

14   A longer and more exhaustive list of applications is provided by Svartvik (1986): 'lexicography, lexicology, syntax, semantics, word-formation, parsing, question-answer synthesis, software development, spelling checkers, speech synthesis and recognition, text-to-speech conversion, pragmatics, text linguistics, language teaching and learning, stylistics, machine translation, child language, psycholinguistics, sociolinguistics, theoretical linguistics, corpus clones in other languages such as Arabic and Spanish – well, even language and sex.' Anyone who believes this list is an exaggeration (although some latitude must be allowed for the nature of the occasion – a speech in honour of Nelson Francis!) should work through Altenberg's recent bibliography (see note 3), which gives the lie to any suggestion that corpus linguistics is a narrow, inward-looking field.

15   This is not to say that such facilities are necessarily more difficult to use, as the simple-to-use Treeconc program demonstrates. The complexity of retrieval devices to the user is more a function of their ability to deal with various kinds of input material. The in-house program Treeconc only accepts input in a particular format, whereas a program like OCP can be set to work on virtually any kind of material – but its user must learn how to do this. There is a growing need for powerful **corpus-handling tools** (see SALT, 1990), and it is arguable that one significant means of containing the complexity of the *corpus-user interface* would be to adopt a standard text encoding format – see Burnard, this volume.

6 Computers and Dictionaries

Willem Meijs

6.1 Introduction

One could say that the connection between computers and dictionaries first arose in the 1970s, when computers began to enter the printing and publishing world on a large scale, and the production and typesetting of dictionaries, like that of most other kinds of books, came to include a computerized stage, i.e. a stage in which all or most of the contents was available in so-called 'machine-readable form'. It is this feature of machine-readability that has given rise to what by now has become the conventional name for a computerized dictionary, viz. 'machine-readable dictionary'.

I shall bow to convention, and use this name – or rather the generally accepted abbreviation for it: MRD – in this chapter, but not without first pointing out that it is not very accurate as a descriptive label for most recent MRDs, in which the computer involvement covers much more than just machine-readability as one of the stages in the production of a dictionary. In fact, dictionary-making nowadays is almost inconceivable without intense interaction between computers and lexicographers at all stages, from inception to final production.

In this chapter, after a brief discussion of the kinds of information typically present in good dictionaries (section 6.2), I shall first show how the use of computers in dictionary-making has gradually expanded in the past twelve years or so, on the basis of a discussion of three roughly comparable MRDs in which the new possibilities were explored and developed (section 6.3). Section 6.4 discusses in some more detail how the computer has changed the art of lexicography. Specific kinds of information (on such things as spelling, hyphenation and synonyms) which could be easily extracted from MRDs soon found their way into widely used practical application programs, such as word-processors, while the rise of the CD-ROM promises to make on-line dictionary access a standard feature for ordinary PC owners in the near future (section 6.5). When MRDs gradually came to be more widely available this gave rise to a range of research activities devoted to the possible utilization of MRD-derived data in various NLP (natural language processing)[1] tasks.

However, opening up the full range of MRD data turned out to be a quite formidable task in itself, as is illustrated in section 6.6. Section 6.7 discusses some central themes in research based on MRD data, presenting some emerging results of this kind of research within a larger NLP context. Finally, section 6.8 contains some suggestions for further reading.

My aim in this chapter is, on the one hand, to survey the developments in the field, and on the other hand, to present a few specific instances in sufficient detail to give the reader some idea of the complexities involved. Most of these more detailed instances are taken from research work that I am directly involved in or closely acquainted with. I have tried to avoid overlap with Boguraev and Briscoe (1989), to which I refer the reader for more detailed information about some of the British and American work mentioned.

6.2 Dictionary Information

Before embarking on a discussion of particular MRDs, it may be useful first to present a brief overview of the kinds of information dictionaries typically provide. Obviously, the range and variety of the information in any particular dictionary will depend on such things as degree of coverage, intended readership, specific purpose – monolingual or bilingual, etymological, 'common core' or specialized in a particular area like law or technology – etc. Still, we can say that an entry in a reasonably sophisticated monolingual dictionary will typically contain information like the following:

1 Form of the headword, possibly with spelling variants.
2 Part of speech: noun, verb, adjective, etc.
3 Further grammatical information on such things as countability, transitivity, restricted attributive use, etc.
4 Inflectional variants: plurals, past tense, participles, irregular forms, etc.
5 Pronunciation and stress in some standard notation.
6 One or more sense indications (meaning definitions, or a cross-reference to a synonym).
7 Examples illustrating the use of the word in the different senses.
8 Expressions and collocations in which the headword commonly occurs.
9 Derivations, compounds, etc.
10 Usage notes, special uses, etc.

In addition there may be information on such things as etymology, semantic field, synonyms and antonyms, register (formal, colloquial, etc.), regional variation (American English, Scots, etc.), subcategorization, etc. Good bilingual dictionaries usually contain a similar range of information-types for the 'target language', in combination, naturally, with links to words and phrases in the 'source language'.

Dictionaries differ widely in the ways in which they present all this information, in how they structure an entry internally, and in what will count as one entry. Thus some take form as the decisive criterion for an entry, irrespective of grammatical category, resulting, for instance, in one entry which covers both noun and verb uses of the same form (cf. *work* as noun and as verb), while others will turn these into two separate entries. Similarly, whether different meanings going with one and the same form (cf. *seal* as a kind of stamp and *seal* as a kind of animal) will result in one or more entries may depend on the policy adopted with respect to polysemy: sometimes words develop widely different meanings which are nevertheless historically related, and a dictionary which uses such historical principles may still group them together under one headword, while another dictionary may decide to make them into separate entries. Again, some dictionaries group derivations as 'run-ons' under the headword from which they are derived, while others present them as separate entries, and some in fact use both methods.

Whatever the policy in such matters, it is clear that every dictionary faces the problem of giving its entries a reasonably clear hierarchical structure. Usually the more general information is given first, with the implication that it applies to everything that follows, while more specific information is given at the level to which it applies. Thus spelling, pronunciation and overall part-of-speech category are usually given first because they apply across the board. However, a noun that is normally countable, but non-countable in one of its meanings, should contain that information at the appropriate sub-level. Similarly, if a verb can function in a number of different (subcategorization) patterns, those patterns should be indicated at the level of the senses to which they apply.

All this may sound reasonably straightforward. However, given the sheer bulk of a dictionary, the fact that usually many different people contribute to it, and the complexity of the entries, it is clearly very difficult to produce a dictionary that is completely systematic in every detail. Hence in practice one can often come across inconsistencies in these respects. Even then, as far as the human user for which the dictionary is intended is concerned there is mostly no great harm done: s/he can usually figure out what is meant to apply where. Computers require a much more rigorous level of consistency. Fortunately, as the next section will show, they are also invaluable in achieving such a high consistency level.

6.3   Three Stages in MRD Development

The gradual expansion of the use of computers in dictionary-making is nicely illustrated by the first machine-readable versions of three quality dictionaries produced in Great Britain: the OALD, the *Oxford Advanced Learner's Dictionary* (Hornby, 1974), LDOCE, the *Longman Dictionary of Contemporary English* (Procter, 1978), and Cobuild, the *Collins Cobuild English Language Dictionary*

(Sinclair et al., 1987). They are comparable in that all three are intended for (advanced) learners, and in that they all provide detailed information of the kind discussed in the previous section, but they differ widely in the amount of computer involvement that went into their production, and they can thus be regarded as typical of three successive stages in this development.[2]

In the late 1970s the OALD was one of the first British dictionaries to become available in machine-readable form.[3] This was a true MRD in the strict sense of the word. It thus included everything needed to turn it into a printed book, such as typesetting instructions, font changes, special symbols, etc. Here the computer had thus not played any role in the actual lexicographical preparation of the dictionary.

On the other hand, the computer-tape of the LDOCE, which became available soon afterwards, is not only machine-readable, it is also computer-assisted, i.e. the computer contributed in other ways as well as just by making it ready for printing. In the case of LDOCE the computer was actively employed in the actual making of the dictionary. Computer programs were used to check overall consistency, for instance, to make sure that only words from the controlled vocabulary were employed in the definitions.[4] The computer was also used to register additional information not meant for inclusion in the book in its printed form. Thus there are markings to be found for (semantic) subject fields, register, regional origin, etc. on the tape, but not in the book. (I shall return to this in the next section.)

To give an idea of the differences between the OALD and LDOCE tapes, figures 6.1 and 6.2 show what part of the entry for *fault* looks like on the OALD and LDOCE tapes respectively.

As one can see from figures 6.1 and 6.2, the OALD tape is basically in the form of unstructured lines of text, interspersed with number codes for font changes, etc., which makes it rather difficult to identify the different kinds of information. The LDOCE tape, by contrast, has separate records for each different type of information (headword, spelling information, pronunciation, part of speech, definitions, etc.). Moreover, the fields all have identification markers in front of them in the form of numerical codes, which makes it possible, using fairly simple search procedures, to spot like information. The

---

(fault) 2/fclt/ 3n 81 6[C] 4sth that makes a person, thing, etc imperfect; defect; blemish; flaw: 3She loves me in spite of all my @s. Her only @ is Qexcessive shyness. There is a @ in the electrical system. 7at @, 4in the wrong , at a loss; in a puzzled or ignorant state: 3My memory was at @. 7to a @, 4excessively: 3She is generous to a @. 7find @ (with), 4complain (about): 3I Qhave no @ to find with your work. He's always finding @.

Figure 6.1   Part of the entry for fault on the OALD tape

```
12221501<F0029700<fault
12221602<01< <
12221703<fC:lt
12221805<n<
12221907<0100<< < T
12222008<a mistake or imperfection:% There are several
     faults in that page of
12222118<figures. ! a small electrical fault in the motor
12222207<0200<< < T Y
12222308<a bad point, but not of a serious moral kind, in
     someone's character:% Your
12222418<only fault is that you won't do what you're
     told. ! I love her for her
12222518<faults as well as for herh VIRTUEi%s
12222607<0300<<GOZL< K N VY
12222708<%tech# (in the science of the earth
     =hGEOLOGYi) a crack in the earth's
12222818<surface, where one band of rock has slid
     against another
12222907<0400<<NTZT< T
12223008<(in games like tennis) a mistake in a service,
     which may lose a point
```

Figure 6.2   Part of the entry for fault on the LDOCE tape

angular brackets within the fields are used to separate specific types of data further, and blanks (or nothing) between such brackets explicitly indicate their absence.

Cobuild, finally, constitutes an example of a dictionary which involved the computer in all of the four stages distinguished in Zgusta's *Manual of Lexicography* (Zgusta, 1970): data-collecting, entry-selection, entry-construction and entry-arrangement. First a very large corpus of language data was collected from a number of sources and stored in a database. The actual lexicographical work – assigning word-class, pronunciation, inflectional behaviour, writing definitions, etc. – was also computationally 'monitored' by the use of standardized dictionary 'slips', which prompted for particular types and formats for each kind of information. Easy access to the corpus allowed the entry writers to draw on the concordanced data to help the process of sense-discrimination, to detect collocational patterns, to provide example sentences, etc. And again various procedures were used to ensure consistency and completeness in the final product.[5]

Summarizing this brief overview of the increasing use of the computer in dictionary-making, we can say that the development was one from aiding the printing process, via consistency-checking, to almost all-embracing data-gathering and production-monitoring. If the OALD could be called the first strictly computer-readable MRD, and LDOCE the first computer-assisted MRD, then Cobuild might best be described as the first computer-designed MRD.

6.4 The Computer's Contribution

Talking about the use of 'the computer' as such is not very revealing, of course. Basically the computer is a dumb machine, which does not do anything by itself. Its strength is that it can store huge amounts of data, and that it can manipulate and relate these data swiftly and effectively in ways and quantities which would take humans a lifetime to emulate manually (and probably in a very error-prone fashion at that). But it is only via clever programming (in combination, of course, with the ever-expanding hardware facilities) that computers can perform these tasks in ways that constitute real enhancements of, and improvements on, how humans could do them. In the final analysis it is the human lexicographer that is in control, and it is her/his creative insight into what the dumb machine can be made to do, that determines the scope of the computer's involvement in the lexicographer's task. The following lists various ways in which the computer is nowadays used to facilitate and enhance dictionary-making, showing for each application the respective contributions of man and machine.

6.4.1 Corpus Data

The computer has helped to revive, and in fact revolutionize, an activity that used to be part and parcel of the linguistic discipline until the rise of transformational generative grammar in the 1960s: corpus data collecting. The great traditional grammarians (Poutsma, Kruisinga, Jespersen) were ardent data-gatherers, as their voluminous grammars amply demonstrate. While the transformationalists' simple substitution of linguistic intuition for data-collection went to the other extreme, they did have a point in their criticism of the traditional form of data-collection as being flawed by a bias for the unusual, the irregular: in the traditionalists' search for special, 'interesting' phenomena the larger generalities were all too often overlooked. Computer-aided corpus linguistics has made it possible to overcome this traditional bias towards the extraordinary, and develop a more balanced view of the 'spread' of linguistic phenomena – lexical as well as syntactic ones – and their relative contributions to the language as a whole. (See chapter 5, this volume; also Aarts and Meijs, 1984, 1986, 1990; Meijs, 1982, 1984, 1987).

Thus some iron laws concerning corpus size in relation to lexical coverage have emerged (cf. for instance, Francis, 1982). The most important, and to some extent the most discouraging, one could be termed the law of diminishing lexical returns. As the size of a corpus increases, the average incidence of word-types decreases. Thus while the one million-word LOB corpus yields about 50,000 different word types, the 7.3 million-word Birmingham Main Corpus (compiled for the Cobuild Dictionary) contains only 132,000 different word-types. In other words, while the size of the corpus has increased sevenfold, the number of word-types has not even trebled. Even then, many of the newly occurring word-types will be *hapax legomena* ('singletons') and may therefore not provide sufficient (contextual) information to be lexicographically useful. As Renouf (1987a: 121) explains: 'in any corpus of natural running text, approximately half the word types will occur once only, and the majority of the remainder will occur fewer than ten times.' She proposes the useful notion of 'lexical resolution' by analogy with the field of photography. From a lexicographical point of view the really common words are not problematic: any corpus will contain lots of examples to get illustrative material. Uncommon words are not very problematic either: they either do not occur at all, or they will be *hapax legomena*. Either way, they will usually not make it to the (general) dictionary. It is for the inbetween range of words – the not very common but not quite uncommon ones – that one needs a large corpus, for only a large (and balanced) corpus will yield a sufficient number of examples to provide useful lexicographical material.

6.4.2 Data Selection

Although lexicographers – as distinct from linguists generally – have, of course, always been collecting and selecting items, it is no exaggeration to claim that the computerized collection of corpus data has added a whole new dimension to the art of dictionary-making. Given a sufficiently robust analytical and statistical apparatus, computerized corpus data can provide the lexicographer with reliable information on words (and expressions) in context. Statistical information on their relative frequency can be an important indicator as to which items to include in the dictionary. Inspection of actual occurrences found in their original contexts can help the lexicographer to decide what and how many senses to distinguish. And when the selection process is over, the same set of data can be used as a rich source of life-like examples-in-context to model the example sentences on.

Nowadays nearly all printed texts will have passed through a machine-readable phase at some stage. However, collecting and storing just anything and everything that is available in machine-readable form clearly will not do. The selection of corpus data to constitute the reservoir from which dictionary items are to be taken is obviously determined by such criteria as availability, size, coverage, up-to-dateness, generality, representativeness, etc.

Thus the data for the Cobuild dictionary are derived from a corpus of 20 million words of text (including about 1.3 million words of spoken English), which were processed over a number of years from about 1980, some by keyboarding, but most by means of optical scanning. The composition of the corpus was designed to produce a cross-section of the language that could be characterized as in some sense representative of standard, general (not too technical), natural, adult use of the English language.[6]

Apart from theoretical considerations there are all kinds of practical aspects that play a role in the data-collecting process. Thus there is the question of copyright, storage capacity, how to deal with different punctuation and spelling conventions, errors, etc. – many of them by no means trivial matters (cf. Renouf, 1987b, for information on such aspects).

6.4.3   The Lexicographer's Electronic Workbench

Having large quantities of language materials on disk in itself is of course not enough. One must also have the means of retrieving and relating them economically and efficiently. One of the most common ways of doing this is via a so-called KWIC (Key Word in Context) concordance program. A KWIC-concordance program scans the corpus for occurrences of specific items and produces files (or screen-displays) in which all occurrences found are presented with a bit of (preceding and following) context – usually 5–10 words before and after. Such surveys are obviously very useful to suggest different shades of meaning (possibly resulting in different senses), illustrative examples, etc. Ultimately it is, of course, up to the lexicographer to decide how many and what shades of meaning are to be represented by different senses, which corpus-sentences exemplify these most accurately, etc.

Concordancing and indexing of the corpus data thus lead to the construction of lists of words referenced for their occurrence in the corpus, which, on the basis of various criteria, such as frequency considerations, target lists for foreign learners and general lexicographical principles, results in the definitive database of words to be included in the dictionary.

The tremendous advantage of a suitably equipped computerized environment – the lexicographer's electronic workbench as it has been called – is the much greater ease with which data can be inspected, related and manipulated, the much wider range that can be covered, and the much greater consistency that can be achieved. Thus the system can be arranged so that (for instance) items below a certain frequency threshold are automatically excluded; it can be menu-driven in such a way that for any item to be accepted, certain kinds of information (part-of-speech category, translation-equivalent, etc.) must always be present, entering this information can be in the form of simply mouse-clicking on one of a fixed set of choices offered on the screen, etc. In short, a computerized environment can relieve the lexicographer of a great deal of the drudgery, allowing her/him to concentrate on the real lexicographical work, while at the same time ensuring that the lexicographical decision-making – which may be shared over a large number of individuals – will be consistent within pre-defined options and boundaries.

This kind of highly computerized, database-centred environment is characteristic of how good dictionaries are made nowadays. The Cobuild dictionary is the first British example of a (monolingual) dictionary produced with such massive computer involvement. A comparable multilingual environment is that built up around a range of bilingual dictionaries being produced in Holland by the Van Dale publishing house.

Like the Cobuild dictionary, the Van Dale dictionaries have been produced on the basis of a database derived from a corpus. The first dictionary produced was a monolingual dictionary of Dutch (van Sterkenburg and Pijnenburg, 1984). In addition to the usual definitions this dictionary also contains so-called 'meaning summaries' for specific senses. These are brief characterizations of those senses, usually in terms of a slightly wider category. Thus one of the meaning definitions of the word *organ* might be prefixed by the label 'musical instrument', another by the label 'body part', another by the label 'communication channel', etc.

In production of the bilingual dictionaries from Dutch into a foreign language (Dutch–English, Dutch-French, Dutch–German, etc.), these same labels (automatically retrieved from the monolingual database) have been used with rigorous systematicity to introduce the various translation equivalents. The underlying assumption here is that a Dutch learner of English, German, etc. is familiar with the various senses that a given Dutch word can have (as indicated by the meaning summaries), so that the labels are an automatic guide to the right translation, since s/he knows which of the senses of the Dutch word applies in a given context. In the derived databases developed for the various 'Dutch into some foreign language' dictionaries, the relations between the Dutch words and their translation equivalents are thus not direct, but indirect (and therefore much more refined), via the meaning summaries. Semi-automatic utilization of these derived databases in turn significantly eased the subsequent production of the corresponding 'foreign-language into Dutch' dictionaries, although, as Al (1988) explains, simply 'inverting' them (automatically producing, for instance, an English–Dutch dictionary from the corresponding Dutch–English one) is not feasible. However, the availability of the derived databases in combination with the original monolingual database opens up even wider perspectives, such as a very considerable facilitation of various 'foreign-language into foreign-language' dictionaries (French–English, English–German, etc.).

6.5 Practical Applications

From the early 1980s on there has been a steadily expanding flow of research and development work directed towards exploring and exploiting the wealth of lexical information available in MRDs. Some of this was limited to the relatively modest aim of extracting only one or two easily identifiable types of information for a specific purpose, while other, more ambitious undertakings have attempted to analyse and chart the dictionary material as fully as possible, including the less tractable aspects. I shall deal with some of the latter kinds of endeavour in some detail later, but first I shall discuss some aspects of the former kind of utilization, one which has in fact had very substantial and concrete effects on what for most computer users at home and in office environments has become one of the most common and most practical software applications: word-processing.

6.5.1   Word-processors and On-line Word-lists

The rise of the personal computer in the past ten years or so has led to the production of user-friendly software packages in which on-line word-lists have become a common feature (see also Williams, this volume). While many of these lists were originally hand-built and limited, some have been considerably expanded and enhanced by the incorporation of MRD-derived information for a large common-core vocabulary.

Thus most word-processor systems nowadays have a spelling-checker. This usually incorporates an extensive list of words stored in a format which allows fast look-up, pattern-matching procedures, 'filters' which can spot common typing errors, impossible letter combinations, etc. When the user invokes the spelling-checker, the words in the text are compared with those in the list, and when a word is encountered that is not in the list the form is highlighted and the user is prompted for a decision. Depending on the system concerned, of course, this may mean that the user can ignore the warning and go on, adding the word to the list if s/he so desires, or select one of the alternative spellings suggested by the system.

Most word-processor systems also have automatic hyphenation procedures in combination with a 'line-wrap' option. This means that the system will attempt to break off long words automatically at appropriate junctures within a fixed or user-definable 'hyphenation-zone' of a certain number of character positions at the end of the lines. In some cases the basic information for such hyphenation procedures has been derived from MRDs in which the entry-words have special markers (like the raised dots in OALD and LDOCE) to indicate possible 'break-up points'.

Some word-processors have a thesaurus attached to them, and once again in some cases this has been derived from MRD sources. The user who is unhappy about a particular word because s/he feels it does not quite express what s/he has in mind, or because it is not quite stylistically appropriate, or simply because s/he wants some variation, can focus on the word in the text and prompt the thesaurus for suggestions. Usually these suggestions are in the form of lists of synonyms (and in some systems antonyms as well), arranged according to part-of-speech, and within part-of-speech, in subgroups according to different senses. The more sophisticated systems allow iterative application, i.e. when the first round of suggestions does not yield a satisfactory substitute for the text-word, one can focus on one of the suggestions (provided that is itself a key-word) and see what *its* synonyms and antonyms are, and so on *ad infinitum*.

On-line bilingual word-lists have not yet become a common feature of most word-processors. But some specialized software houses (for instance INK International) have developed translation packages incorporating MRD-derived data which can be used in combination with most standard word-processing systems (see also Lewis, this volume). These consist of software rather similar in organization to that of a thesaurus, except that the suggestions provided by the system are words or phrases in a target language, supplied by an on-line translation word-list for that language integrated in, or loaded in combination with, the system. Often such systems allow the user to compile and consult their own additional translation-lists for specialized technical terms, as well as options to mark particular words for purely automatic translation (i.e. without any subsequent user intervention).

6.5.2 Programming Aspects

The more sophisticated features of on-line word-lists like the above, and of the surrounding techniques and procedures, are not without intrinsic linguistic interest, and some of these features, as we shall see, are relevant also for the exploration and utilization of fully-fledged MRDs. Thus a spelling-checker would be no good – a nuisance, in fact – if it could only recognize word-stems, and would hence stop at all inflected and conjugated forms (plurals, tenses, participles, etc.). Therefore, if (as is likely) its basic word-list consists of word-stems plus all irregular plurals, past tenses, etc., it will need some kind of amplification to make it recognize and 'pass' well-formed regular inflections and conjugations. One way of bringing this about would be to create such regularly derived forms automatically from the stems and then add them to the list. This would be rather costly in terms of storage, and not very clever, since it would fail to make optimal use of the linguistic insight needed to create the derived forms (*worked* from *work*, *gazed* from *gaze*, *copied* from *copy*, *referring* from *refer*, *altering* from *alter*, *sticks* from *stick*, *matches* from *match* etc. – notice the variation!). Since the linguistic insight is needed anyway, it would be better to use it analytically rather than synthetically, i.e. to incorporate it in the procedure which tries to relate a text-word to the stem-entries in the word-list (i.e. directly or via 'decomposition').

Similar procedures could be used to make the spelling-checker accept derivational prefixation and suffixation and compounding. Most spelling-checkers that I am familiar with do not bother about these, and probably correctly so in view of the diminishing returns involved, except for a simple overall procedure which accepts input consisting of words consisting of two entry-words connected by a hyphen. Apparently the spelling-checker going with the word-processor I am using to prepare this manuscript roughly follows these principles. Thus it accepts *non-smiler* and *sub-categorization*, but not *nonsmiler* and *subcategorization* (without hyphens). Similarly, it accepts *bookmark*, *book-mark* and *book-match*, but not *bookmatch* (which shows that *bookmark* is in its basic list, while *bookmatch* isn't). The fact that it accepts *recognizer*, but rejects *anticipater* (suggesting *anticipator* instead as a possible correct spelling) may serve as a final demonstration of its relatively high degree of sophistication: specific information takes precedence over more general rules, where applicable.

6.5.3   New Horizons: Dictionaries on CD-ROM

With the advent of the CD-ROM ('read-only-memory compact disk') and the possibility of linking a compact-disk player to a computer, access to detailed dictionary information is now fast becoming 'democratized' as a commodity within reach of ordinary PC owners. The storage capacity of a CD-ROM (some 600 MegaBytes) is such that it can cope with multi-volume encyclopedias, dictionaries, the bible, Shakespeare's complete works, *Who's Who?*, the telephone directory, etc.

A recent British example which speaks to the imagination is the twelve-volume Oxford English Dictionary, which has been produced by Oxford University Press on a single compact disk (plus two floppy disks with the software for efficient access). In Holland, Van Dale have likewise marketed a CD-ROM entitled 'Lexitron' based on their 'Grand Monolingual Dictionary'. The accompanying software allows the user to search the lexicon in various modes. Thus one can consult Lexitron orthographically or in a thesaurus-like fashion. It is possible even, if one does not know the spelling of the word one is looking for, to access the information via a fancy sound representation. Thus typing in *kornètbief* (which is roughly how Dutch speakers pronounce *corned beef*, with stress on the second syllable) would still lead the user to the correct entry.

Concluding this section it seems appropriate to speculate that the astounding expansion of storage capacity, coupled with the increasing commercial availability to the general public of computerized dictionary information, probably signal the imminent demise of the dictionary as a book. In a decade or so, on-line dictionaries on disk or CD-ROM will no doubt be the norm rather than the exception. With systematic link-ups with up-to-date corpus data (from newspapers and periodicals, for instance) properly institutionalized, dictionaries will become a dynamic service rather than a static source of information. Users first procure a 'starter' monolingual or multilingual dictionary, and they will then, from time to time, receive 'updates' (just as they do with other kinds of software packages, such as word-processors), reflecting changes and additions to the language.

6.6   Opening up MRD Information

As I have pointed out, the word-lists mentioned in the preceding section are restricted to just one or two kinds of information, having been compiled or extracted for a particular, limited purpose (spelling-check, hyphenation, synonym-search, etc.). The same goes for another kind of use, not in the normal word-processor sphere, to which MRD data have been put: providing lists of words with their stress-patterns and pronunciation in some standard phonetic transcription. Such lists have proved to be useful in research concerned with speech-recognition and speech-synthesis (cf. Briscoe, 1985; Carter, 1989, and the references given there). However, with this kind of application we are entering the wider area of natural language processing, and it is more appropriate, therefore, now to look at efforts to open up as much as possible the full range of MRD data, rendering it amenable to further investigation and utilization.

The lexical component always used to be a very weak point in work on NLP. The average speaker of the language commands an active vocabulary of at least 20,000 words. Compiling word-lists that came anywhere near this in size, coverage and depth of detail was something that went far beyond the usual resources available to research – both financially and in terms of time and manpower. Hence most research undertakings in the NLP area character-istically ended up with very small 'sample' or 'toy' lexicons with fewer than thirty entries (cf. Whitelock et al., 1987, cited in Boguraev and Briscoe, 1989: 10). Since these were usually hand-made and custom-built, they would normally seem to fit the bill (i.e. the requirements of the particular system or application for which they were specially designed) rather nicely, and thus obscure the problems that would crop up if one were to expand them to a realistic lexicon approaching that of actual speakers of the language in size and complexity.

It was only when MRDs gradually became available to the research community that the incorporation of fully-fledged, realistic lexicons in NLP contexts began to look like a viable proposition. The various projects that were subsequently set up to explore and exploit MRDs opened up new possibilities which had hitherto been largely unsuspected. For English, most of this research – some of which I shall discuss in the next sections – has been based on LDOCE. This is mainly because the MRD version of LDOCE, as pointed out in a previous section, came in a form that was already quite well structured to begin with, and because it is characterized by a combination of special features lacking in most other MRDs, such as special semantic markers, and the use of a limited controlled vocabulary used in its definitions and examples.

Researchers that have worked on 'opening up' data contained in the LDOCE MRD are, among others, Moulin and Michiels (Liège), Alshawi, Briscoe and Boguraev (Cambridge), Wilks, Fass and others (New Mexico), Meijs, Akker-man, Vossen and others (Amsterdam). Undoubtedly on a 'global' scale this means that there has been a considerable amount of overlap and duplication in the efforts of these various research terms. On the other hand, there were important differences in the aims and emphases in these different research settings. Thus the Liège team concentrated on the internal consistency of the grammatical system embodied in the dictionary, the Cambridge researchers' emphasis was on making the dictionary optimally compatible with on-line access, the New Mexico team focused especially on computational semantic aspects, while Amsterdam's first concern was with making the material available for use in semi-automatic syntactic analysis of corpus-texts.

I shall now discuss in some more detail certain aspects of the work performed in the 'ASCOT' project, reported on in Akkerman et al. (1985, 1988), to show the complexity of what has come to be called the 'restructuring' of an MRD. This description can be seen as an illustration of the kind of nitty-gritty problems facing any researcher(s) trying to make even a highly structured MRD like LDOCE amenable to NLP tasks.

6.6.1 Coming to Grips with the MRD: the Nitty-gritty

Even if the MRD is quite well-structured, as in the case of LDOCE, systematic identification and extraction of the various different types of information contained in it is a quite formidable job, due to the size and complexity of the material. Obviously MRDs contain a wealth of data on many different aspects of words: spelling, pronunciation, morphology, syntax, semantics, collocational behaviour, register, usage, etc. (cf. the outline of the kinds of information typically present in dictionary entries). Reliable extraction of any of these information-types crucially depends on (1) sufficiently systematic organization of the MRD entries, (2) sufficiently formalized – or at least formalizable – information, and (3) adequate automatic software programs and procedures to single out and retrieve the particular type of information required. While there are, of course, many interesting theoretical aspects involved here (some of which will be the focus of a later section), establishing whether (1) and (2) are the case and (3) can be achieved for a particular MRD is mostly a fairly sobering, down-to-earth matter, involving quite a lot of nitty-gritty.

Thus in spite of the highly structured and systematic nature of the LDOCE material, it soon became apparent in the ASCOT project, as in similar research undertakings, that making it amenable for utilization in NLP contexts still required a lot of further processing. Essentially this involved making the computer explicitly do the kind of 'silent' amplification and restoration that human users of the dictionary presumably perform almost unwittingly when they make use of information that in itself is incomplete or implicit in one way or another. Most of this could be done semi-automatically, i.e. by means of specially developed software programs, but there was still a fair amount of manual checking and correction involved as well, such as:

- The creation of separate entries for words with more than one wordclass in the same entry. For example, the entry *depilatory* adj,n [Wa5;C;U] resulted in the two entries *depilatory* adj with the codes Wa5 and B (default code for ordinary adjectives) and *depilatory* n with the codes C and U.

- The creation of new entries for so-called 'also-words' and American English variants, e.g.: *creativity* also *creativeness* /. . . ./ n [U]; *colour*, AmE *color* v 1 [T1;X(1),7] (...) 2 [IO] (. . . .), etc.

- The decomposition of complex LDOCE codes, e.g.: *desire* v 1 [T1,3,5c;V3]; *break off* v 1 [T1,4;IO: (with)]; *see* 2 [Wv6;T15a,6a;V2,3 (fml & only pass.),4,8].

- The creation of full forms of derivations of which only the suffix is given. In LDOCE, a tilde or a dash is used to denote the kind of abbreviation that is used. In case of a tilde, the abbreviated form can be added to the headword, as in *daydream* v (. . . .) ~er n. When a dash is used, part of the headword must be replaced by the given abbreviated form. Examples are: *defensible* adj (...) -*bly* adv; *dishonour*, AmE -*or* v (. . . .).

- Error-correction. Since the restructuring program contained many procedures that read each line of the dictionary, expecting the correct information in each code position, a side effect was that many imperfections were detected.

For further details see Akkerman et al. (1988: 43–72). Other researchers who have worked on restructuring LDOCE have also commented on the complexity of the task. Cf. e.g. Alshawi et al. (1985: 172): 'The development of the restructuring programs is a non-trivial task because the organization of information on the typesetting tape presupposes its visual presentation, and the ability of human users to apply common sense, utilize basic morphological knowledge, ignore minor notational inconsistencies, and so forth', and 'the code is geared more towards visual presentation than formal precision'.

6.6.2 Standardizing Dictionary Access

Now that more and more MRDs are becoming available, efforts are being made to coordinate and standardize the research into these rich resources of lexical knowledge. A central goal in these efforts is the development of a generalized and standardized 'computational lexical entry' model (Tompa, 1986; Gonnet and Tompa, 1987), which ideally should result in a situation in which any MRD could be converted to a standard format that systematically accommodates any of the kinds of information characteristically present in dictionaries. In addition, there is a tendency to make new computer versions of dictionaries adhere to standards that are being developed for any kind of computerized textual material, such as SGML (Standard Generalized Markup Language; cf. Amsler and Tompa, 1989; also Burnard, this volume). Thus a recent edition of the *Oxford Advanced Learner's Dictionary* has been produced in SGML format.

An important effect of this kind of standardization is that (given sufficiently powerful storage and retrieval facilities) it will allow systematic access and comparison of different MRD sources. One set-up which already allows such multiple MRD exploration is the WordSmith system developed by the Lexical

Systems group at IBM Yorktown Heights (cf. Byrd et al., 1987), in which LDOCE, various Collins dictionaries, and Webster's Seventh Collegiate Dictionary can be accessed simultaneously.

A European counterpart of this is being developed in 'ACQUILEX' ('Acquisition of Lexical Knowledge for Natural Language Processing Systems'), an ESPRIT-project subsidized by the European Economic Community (cf. Boguraev et al., 1989). In this project, in which researchers from Amsterdam, Barcelona, Cambridge, Dublin and Pisa cooperate, a number of monolingual and bilingual MRDs (among them LDOCE, Collins bilingual Italian–English and English–Italian, Van Dale monolingual Dutch and bilingual Dutch–English dictionaries) are first 'processed' and then transformed to a standard format based on a particular conception of how a computational lexical entry should be organized. Once that has been done, specific types of information will be systematically studied. For instance, using one of the bilingual dictionaries as a 'bridge', it will be possible to compare the conceptual organization of a particular semantic area in two completely independent monolingual dictionaries. In principle it might also be possible to 'enrich' one dictionary which happens to have little or no information of a certain kind (subcategorization, say), using data from another one which does have ample information in the relevant area. The idea is not that this will be done on any kind of massive scale. Rather, the project has the character of a feasibility study which should yield a reasonable insight into what is in principle possible, especially with a view to NLP applications.

6.7   Research Applications: Using MRD Information for NLP purposes

Natural language processing is concerned with the analysis and generation of natural language in all its aspects: phonological, morphological, syntactic, semantic, etc. As we have seen, good dictionaries provide useful information on all such aspects, hence a lot of work on MRDs has concentrated on making the relevant kind(s) of information computationally available to specific NLP contexts. I shall deal with two kinds of utilization in some detail: syntactic and semantic utilization.

6.7.1   Syntactic Utilization

Most NLP contexts require syntactic parsers that can analyse natural language input. Many different parsers have been developed, from many different theoretical angles: functional grammar, lexical functional grammar, government and binding, generalized phrase structure grammar, etc. (for further details see Patten, this volume). Whatever their theoretical orientation, it has invariably become clear that in order for such parsers to handle actual natural language with some level of success, part-of-speech information alone is not sufficient. Essentially what is needed in addition to syntactic category is context-sensitive subcategorization information. Since LDOCE is one MRD in which detailed information of that kind is available in a consistent and formalized format, a lot of work on the LDOCE MRD has thus been concerned with the extraction and systematic exploitation of it in parsing-systems of one kind or another.

Thus the ASCOT system, mentioned above, was specifically designed to provide this kind of rich lexical information for a sister project at Nijmegen University, called TOSCA (Aarts and van den Heuvel, 1985). After all the nitty-gritty problems mentioned in section 6.6.1 had been overcome, the resulting files containing only the corrected and refined syntactic data were turned into an easily accessible database in so-called 'L-tree' format (Skolnik, 1980), which can be used on-line to attach any (or all) of the various types of information automatically to words in an input-file (which may be a list of words or free text).

In the TOSCA system the words in a corpus of texts are first provided with their major part-of-speech category codes by means of the 'CLAWS' tagging program developed at Lancaster University (Garside et al., 1987; see also Leech and Fligelstone, this volume). A run through the ASCOT system then provides the additional subcategory information essential for adequate opera-tion of the 'extended affix grammar' embodied in the TOSCA system. Basically the context-sensitive information from the ASCOT lexicon is used to provide the 'affixes' needed to fill the 'attribute-slots' attached to the nodes in the parse-trees being developed. The grammar checks the consistency of such attributes and eliminates inconsistent values. In this way the grammar can check, for instance, whether the subject noun phrase agrees in number with the finite verb, taking into account such complexities as singular nouns that can take plural or singular verbs (*team*, *cabinet*), or plural only (*police*). Similarly, it can use information on the possible verb-patterns of main verbs, or the fact that a particular adjective can only function attributively, to favour a particular analysis and rule out rival ones.

The output of the TOSCA system is in the form of a corpus of fully syntactically analysed sentences, which, like its pilot predecessor, the CCPP corpus (Keulen, 1986), will be stored in an 'LDB' (Linguistic Data Base – Van Halteren, 1984) shell, specially geared to linguistic investigation.

6.7.2   Semantic Utilization

Semantic features and predicate-argument structure   Nowadays analysis does not stop at syntax, however. Over the past few years a lot of energy and resources have been invested in attempts to also extend NLP research to that most intractable area of the linguistic spectrum: semantics. And here again MRD-based research has gained an ever more important role.

Closely allied to syntactic subcategorization is what, depending on one's theoretical stance, may be variously denoted as valency, predicate-argument structure, case roles, theta roles, etc. Most characteristically this involves the functional-semantic roles (Agent, Theme, Instrument, Location, etc.) which certain major clause-elements – especially noun phrases – play *vis-à-vis* the verbs with which they occur. Very few dictionaries, if any, give clear, formal(izable) information in this respect, although sometimes definitions contain indirect clues on such aspects. Thus sometimes the definition states that the object of a particular verb-entry must denote a person, or a thing (or either), or there may be information on the subject – often in the form of a bracketed phrase: (*of a person*), (*said of animals in the mating season*), etc.

   Again the LDOCE MRD is exceptional in that it has a quite elaborate system of so-called 'box-codes', in terms of a feature hierarchy involving well-known distinctions like 'Concrete', 'Abstract', 'Animate', 'Human', etc. These box-codes are only present on the computer-tape; they do not occur in the book. They are given for nouns, adjectives and verbs: for nouns they help to narrow down the conceptual class to which the entry-word applies; with adjectives they indicate the class of nominal concepts they can be used to qualify, and for verbs they explicitly indicate restrictions on their first, second and possibly third arguments. Although this does not yet add up to a complete Case role programme, it is none the less extremely useful information for any NLP system which tries to cover semantic aspects as well as syntactic ones. Not surprisingly, therefore, researchers have tried to incorporate this kind of information from the LDOCE MRD in various NLP contexts. Voogt-van Zutphen (1987, 1989) reports on one such attempt, undertaken from the perspective of Functional Grammar (Dik, 1978, 1989a). As the name suggests, Functional Grammar (FG for short) is a theory which tries to give functional semantic aspects their due. It uses a system of Case-like Argument Roles based on a hierarchy in terms of 'activity potential', in which distinctions such as those indicated by the LDOCE box-codes are central ('Humans' are typically 'active', 'Inanimate' objects typically 'inactive', for instance). Voogt-van Zutphen shows that in most cases the box-code information provided with verbs, for instance, is not quite sufficient unambiguously to settle the functional role of the associated noun phrase arguments. Thus the subject NP in *Peter delivered a blow* and in *Peter suffered a blow* is 'Human' in both cases, but the case-role is 'Agent' in the former, and 'Experiencer' in the latter. Voogt-van Zutphen therefore concludes that, although the LDOCE box-codes do provide very useful basic information, automatic conversion into FG-like predicate-argument frames is not generally possible. She points out, however, that such conversion would perhaps be possible if further information also present in the MRD material – specifically in the so-called 'subject-field codes' and in the definitions – is taken into account. Here we enter another area on which there has been quite a lot of research, some of which will be reviewed in the remaining sections.

Semantic fields, taxonomies, lexical knowledge   We may regard a good monolingual dictionary as a linear, alphabetically ordered representation of the passive and active vocabulary of normal, educated speakers of the language.

There is, of course, ample evidence (including empirical evidence based on psycholinguistic experiments concerning lexical access) to suggest that a language user's mental lexicon is not, or not primarily, organized in this way, as a long list of isolated elements. Rather, the mental lexicon forms a coherent, tightly-knit whole, whose elements are somehow intricately related to one another along a number of different dimensions: phonological, morphological, orthographical, etc. One of the most basic organizing dimensions, no doubt, is the semantic-conceptual one, as witness word-association and semantic priming tests: words activate, 'call up', other words that are related to them in meaning. A dictionary in machine-readable form in principle allows one to waive the alphabetical ordering of the printed book, and study its inherent semantic-conceptual organization. And this is exactly what a lot of research on MRDs has tried to do.

Some of the obvious questions to ask in this connection are: which words 'belong together'; how can we characterize the groupings that emerge; what is the nature of the links that connect them? The answers resulting from investigations of these questions are coined in terms of the various ways in which man's attempts to classify the world around and within him can be described: thesauruses, taxonomies, semantic fields, hierarchies, networks, graphs, etc. Not many dictionaries indicate semantic relations of this kind explicitly and systematically. Once again the LDOCE MRD is an exception in this respect. Its 'subject-field codes' (not present in the printed version) indicate the semantic field to which the senses of a lexical item belong: zoology, botany, sports, religion, architecture, etc. Although there is a sub-field layer for most main fields, the codes taken together do not form a clear hierarchical structure, and they have been rather unevenly and not very consistently applied. Still, as Janssen (1990) shows, they provide very valuable information which, especially in certain specific domains – law, sports, food, for instance – can be used to guide automatic semantic disambiguation procedures.

Where explicit semantic-field markers are absent, taxonomic structure has to be derived from information that is implicit in other parts of the dictionary entries, especially the definitions. Amsler's two texts (1980, 1981) constitute pioneering enterprises to lay bare, in a semi-automatic fashion, the taxonomic hierarchies implicit in the Merriam-Webster New Pocket Dictionary. One of Amsler's important findings is that the taxonomies that emerge from his investigation are not so neat and strictly hierarchical; hence he calls them 'tangled hierarchies'. In the 'LINKS' project (Meijs, 1986, 1988, 1989; Vossen et al., 1988, 1989), similarly tangled relationships were found to obtain in the top nodes of the noun taxonomies emerging from a study of the definitions in LDOCE. Cf. figure 6.3, from Vossen (1990a).

Vossen points out that there are some striking inconsistencies in these LDOCE-derived networks:

1   There are some 'islands' in the network of concepts which are circularly defined and are not related to the main network, e.g. 'creature' and 'animal'; 'vessel', 'boat' and 'ship'.

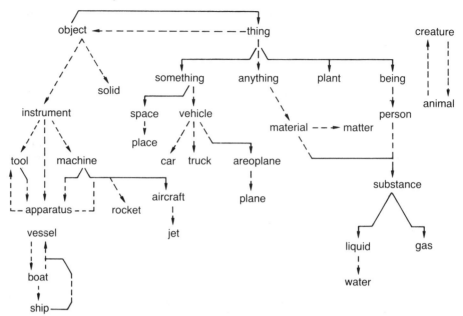

Figure 6.3   Top-level taxonomies in LDOCE (from Vossen, 1990a)

2   Some concepts which one might expect to be closely related are not. According to LDOCE 'person' is more closely related to 'plant' than to 'animal'. Something similar holds for 'aeroplane' and 'plane' on the one hand, and 'rocket', 'aircraft' and 'jet' on the other.

3   Because more or less the same concept is sometimes paraphrased in different ways (e.g. 'material', 'matter' and 'substance', or 'aeroplane', 'plane' and 'aircraft'), some apparent relations between words in the network may in reality be redundant.

Vossen suggests that the problem may be not all that serious, because most of the inconsistencies occur towards the top of the hierarchies, which means that they can be amended manually in a relatively simple way.

Taxonomic and hierarchical relationships are very important for the development of reliable logico-semantic interpretation procedures in NLP. A key notion here is that of 'hyponymy'. Clarity about hyponymy relations is important for handling things like entailment, inferences, etc. Dik (1989b) develops a truth-conditional approach to what he calls relational reasoning in Functional Logic in which hyponymy plays a central role. Dik distinguishes three kinds of hyponymy:

a   Lexical hyponymy   (rose)(flower)
b   Hyponymy through predicate formation   (tea rose)(rose)
c   Hyponymy through term formation   (red rose)(rose)

As far as MRDs are concerned, (a) is of course central. Still, (b) and (c) are also relevant: compounding occurs both in dictionary entries and in definitions. Dik points out that relative adjectives (*big, small, long*, etc.) need special attention. Thus *I saw a big flea* entails *I saw a flea*, but not *I saw something big*: relative adjectives require reference to some norm, which must somehow be coded in the lexicon. (Presumably the LDOCE definition, which refers to 'more than **average** size' for *big* is not very helpful here.)

Another important aspect is the nature of the relationship: (in)transitive, (a)symmetrical, etc. Thus verbs like *precede, follow*, etc., which must be marked for 'order' in the lexicon, denote a transitive relation: if A precedes B and B precedes C, then it follows that A precedes C. Words in this class may have a converse relation with each other, with logical consequences: if A precedes B, then B follows A.

Everyday language does not always adhere too strictly to such truth-conditional logicalities, however. Thus one can say *the two cars were chasing each other at full speed*, without meaning to imply that car A chased B *and* that car B chased car A. Similarly, one can say *the explosions followed each other in quick succession*, without meaning to suggest that each explosion followed every other explosion. As Sanford (1987) points out, everyday logic ('common-sense reasoning') will sometimes fall short of the standards of logic in the truth-conditional sense.

This aspect of normal language use is given special prominence in the so-called 'naive semantics' approach to knowledge representation (Dahlgren, 1988; Dahlgren and McDowell, 1989). The concepts and categories that people use are often vague, gradient and intermingled; they are not like scientific concepts, and hence often not truth-conditional in the usual sense. That communication between speakers of the same language is by and large successful is due to the fact that they are 'anchored in the real world', in which there are some real, stable classes of objects, states, events, etc.

Apart from the usual things, word-meanings in this approach are also associated with a large number of characteristics along various dimensions, such as typical behaviour, social status and function, characteristic tools, instruments and other paraphernalia (books, briefcases, gowns and wigs for lawyers, judges, etc.), as well as common assumptions about character traits, such as ambition, articulateness, cleverness, educational background, etc.

Knowledge representation in the naive semantics framework thus does not aim to reduce everything to abstract primitives, but tries to represent the intertwined conceptualizations and categorizations people associate with word meanings. The cognitive model developed along these lines is based on empirical observation of constraints governing selection restrictions in the use of a large number of verbs, psychological studies of classification, and philosophical studies of epistemology. The result, which is claimed to reflect 'the naive ontology embodied in English', is a so-called directed acyclic graph rather than a binary tree, which means that its nodes can have more than two subordinate nodes, and that it allows cross-classification. Apart from more traditional distinctions, this ontology gives prominence to notions such as

SENTIENT, NATURAL, SOCIAL, SELF-MOVING, GOAL, ACHIEVE-MENT, etc. The naive semantic relations and taxonomies proposed by Dahlgren are thus not as neat and ordered as most theories assume: they are more like the 'tangled hierarchies' from Amsler (1980) and Vossen (1990a).

Essentially, the approach developed by Fass (1989), as embodied in his Meta5 grammar, is an attempt to utilize the full range of semantic relations connecting the sense descriptions in the lexicon, by means of 'collation' (combination) procedures which can trace these connections via the genus and differentiae information stored in the lexical entries. The sense frames are in the form of PROLOG list structures associated with word senses, pairing arcs and nodes: the arcs contain the genus information, and the nodes the differentiae, and both of these themselves again comprise (combinations of) word senses, with their own associated sense frames, so that by tracing these links in the collating process, one can traverse the semantic network of senses. The nodes further contain information to guide the semantic disambiguation process, such as functional and structural information for nouns, preferences and assertions for adjectives and adverbs, and case-frames for verbs. Figures 6.4a–c are examples of sense frames for an adjective, a noun and a verb from Fass (1989).[7]

Via the collating procedures, the Meta5 grammar attempts to find the best sense-matches for the words that are being combined syntactically. The Meta5 framework is especially interesting in that, in addition to 'normal readings', the grammar also allows various metonymic readings, such as Producer for Product (*He bought a Ford*), Controller for Controlled (*Nixon bombed Hanoi*), and Object

```
sf(male1,                          sf(crook1,
   [[arcs,                            [[arcs,
     [[superproperty, sex1],            [[supertype, criminal1]]],
      [property, male1]]],             [node0,
    [node1,                            [[it1, steal1, valuables1]]]]).
     [[preference, organism1],
      [assertion,
       [[sex1, male1]]]]]]]).
```

Figure 6.4a   Figure 6.4b

```
sf(eat1,
   [[arcs,
     [[supertype,[ingest1, expend1]]]],
    [node2,
     [[agent,
       [preference, animal1]],
      [object,
       [preference, drink1]]]]]]).
```

Figure 6.4c

for User (*The buses are on strike*) – for details see the article, which describes in some detail how the system decided on the most likely reading of the sentence *Mary drank the glasses*. Metonymy is something that is also represented to some extent in the LDOCE material, albeit indirectly, by (sometimes fairly systematic) sequences of literal and extended senses within entries. Wilks et al. (1989) point out that for a full-scale lexicon of this kind, the LDOCE material would have to be analysed in a way that would yield clear genus and differentiae information, something which, they assert, is as yet 'beyond the abilities of the best current extraction techniques'.[8]

The redundancy rules in Dik's (1989c) model of a computational FG lexicon are somewhat similar in effect to Fass's collating rules. Thus their application to *sailor* and *kick* results in frames like the following, which can be regarded as statements of selection restrictions for the words concerned:

1   predn([sailor, [hum,masc,anim,concr,vert]]).
2   predv([kick,[act,dyn,contr],
        [[[anim],t,[ag]],[[concr],t,[go]]]]).

Dik claims that restrictions such as these will allow (3a) and (3b), while excluding (4a) and (4b):

3a   The sailor kicked the boy.
3b   The sailor kicked the book.
4a   *The sailor kicked the city. (city not concrete)
4b   *The book kicked the boy. (book not animate)

It is doubtful, actually, whether LDOCE-derived information would be helpful to reject (4a), since the first sense of *city* is in fact concrete ('a usu. large and important group of houses, buildings, etc. . . . .'), while the second is animate and collective ('all the people who live in such a place'). An even more important complicating factor however (but one which any serious attempt to use realistic lexical data would have to face), is the fact that every word may have a number of senses. Thus there are six senses for *boy*, seven senses for *kick*, and two senses for *city* in LDOCE, bringing the number of theoretically possible readings for *the boy kicked the city* (or *the city kicked the boy*) to $6 \times 7 \times 2 = 84$!

Clearly, then, to make use of the networks of semantic relations that are hidden in the interconnections between word-senses in dictionaries, disambiguation of the words used in the definitions is essential, i.e. it must be unambiguously clear in which sense any word is being used in a dictionary definition. For LDOCE various researchers are working on this kind of disambiguation (cf. Wilks et al., 1989; Vossen, 1990a). Given the daunting amounts of data to be dealt with, such disambiguation is a formidable job.[9] However, as Vossen (1990a) points out, a number of heuristic strategies may be employed to do this semi-automatically.[10]

In the 'LINKS' project[11] this disambiguation has now been completed manually for the most central and most frequently used words, and the results have been incorporated in 'DEVIL', a prototype 'chain-scanning' system which can relate definitions upwards and downwards in the semantic network (cf. Vossen and Serail, 1990), while taking account of the further complications caused by 'linker' and 'shunter' structures ('PART OF' relations, cross-category references (N>V, A>N, etc.) via nominalizations, etc. – cf. Vossen, 1989, 1990b; Vossen et al., 1989). Once this definition disambiguation process has been completed, it will be possible, for example, to extend Fass's kind of 'collative semantic analysis' – which so far works only for a limited 'toy' lexicon containing 460 word senses – to one of a more realistic size by the incorporation of systematized dictionary-data.

Further Reading

Zgusta (1970) provides a comprehensive account of what lexicography traditionally involves. Sinclair (1987) gives a detailed description of dictionary-making in the computer age, on the basis of the Collins Cobuild project. The Aarts and Meijs volumes (1984, 1986, 1990), along with Meijs (1987) and Garside et al. (1987), provide information about corpus linguistics (see also Leech and Fligelstone, this volume), which has come to play such an important role in modern, computer-based dictionary-making. Boguraev and Briscoe (1989) present an overview of research in which MRDs are explored for NLP purposes.

Notes

1   I use NLP as a cover term for natural language processing of all kinds, including computational linguistics, text-to-speech processing, (semi-)automatic translation, language-oriented artificial intelligence etc. See also Patten, and Bateman and Hovy, this volume.
2   Notice that my remarks about the OALD, LDOCE and Cobuild refer to their *first* machine-readable versions, as these best illustrate the successive stages discussed in the text. Both OALD and LDOCE have since produced new editions with more computer involvement. Also, my remarks about these dictionaries are not to be taken as judgements about the substantive contents of these dictionaries in any kind of evaluative way – that has been done by others, cf. e.g. Akkerman (1989) and Lemmens and Wekker (1986).
3   In the United States the first computer-readable dictionary, the *American Heritage Dictionary* was produced as early as 1970.
4   At least the editors *claim* that they machine-checked the definitions in this way (p. ix). In the LINKS project we found that some non-controlled vocabulary words slipped through all the same.
5   For more details cf. various contributions in Sinclair (1987), particularly those by Jeremy Clear, Ramesh Krishnamurthy, Rosamund Moon and Patrick Hanks.

6   For details about the compilation, processing and correction of the corpus material (which, among other things, involved a division into a main and a reserve corpus) see Renouf (1987b).

7   Why the entry for *eat* should have *drink* as preferred object is not clear to me. Perhaps there is an error here, and figure 6.4c is in fact meant to be the sense frame for the verb *drink*.

8   Developments in MRD-research are moving at an accelerating pace, however. The 'LINKS' project has meanwhile yielded syntactic parses for all noun, verb and adjective definitions in LDOCE, which may well be able to supply the kind of information Wilks et al. (1989) require.

9   The task is alleviated somewhat by the fact that LDOCE uses a controlled vocabulary for its definitions and examples. However, since these are all common words, they are also ones that tend to have relatively many senses. The job is further complicated by the fact that the defining vocabulary also contains many complex words derived from the controlled vocabulary.

10   Similar suggestions are made in Copestake (1990), in the context of the Cambridge contribution to the ACQUILEX project.

11   The basic methodology for the LINKS project was as follows: first an appropriate grammatical coding was applied to the words of the restricted vocabulary and their inflected forms. This coding was then automatically inserted in all of the meaning descriptions, the outcome being a grammatically coded 'corpus of meaning descriptions'. Subsequently, a syntactic typology was developed for the structures of the meaning descriptions of each of the major parts of speech (POS), nouns, verbs, and adjectives, resulting in parser-grammars for each of them. Applying these grammars to the corpus then resulted in syntactically analysed meaning descriptions in which it is possible systematically to identify pre-modifiers, kernels, post-modifiers, etc. (for details see Vossen et al., 1988, 1989).

7 Computers and the Study of Literature

John F. Burrows

7.1 Introduction

'They order ... this matter better in France': and, in this matter, Sterne's elusive ironies have no place. Through its emphasis on ranking and ordering and, by implication, on the logic of classification, the French term *l'ordinateur* points to deeper and more general truths than are encompassed by the strictly numerical connotations of our term, 'computer'. The semantic difference is obvious but, as we shall see, its ramifications are immense. On a lesser point, the French term may also seem less alarming to those, too common among students of literature, who still believe that mechanical calculators cannot help us to answer the questions that really **count**.

Without overriding some genuine differences, the concept of *ordonnance* embraces genuine affinities between the methodological bases of literary studies and the computer-assisted collection and analysis of data. Let us work, first, towards a sketch of these affinities and differences and afterwards give it substance by considering a range of procedures and results.

Literary texts, like all other artefacts and many natural phenomena, are repositories of meaning. Meaning, as the information scientists have taught us, lies in patterns discernible amidst the circumambient noise.[1] 'Noise' is everything that conspires against the transmission of meaning by confusing its patterns: it may – to take a bare handful of examples – be the actual noise of electrical interference on a telephone line; the quirks of the genetic code that obscure a specimen's membership of a class; the missing fragments of a broken statue or the additions to a painting by an incompetent restorer; the marks of an author's failure to convey an intended meaning or the effects of a reader's failure to attend to what the text is saying.

If words like 'meaning', 'pattern' and 'noise' are to be usefully applied across so wide a range, some important distinctions must be acknowledged. The differences between what is lacking of a broken statue and what may have been added to a painting call for quite different interpretative procedures. The question of a restorer's possible incompetence points towards problems of value judgement: these scarcely arise in the case of electrical interference (save in the impoverished but not trivial sense that degrees of interference, the cost of overcoming them and the desirability of doing so can be accurately assessed). The matter of 'intention', of some concern in literary studies, where the concept of authorship is open to debate but the existence of authors is undeniable, has a different force in the case of the genetic code, where meaningful patterns can be recognized but where those whose concern is with the intentions of a putative designer must proceed by faith and inference.

In the matter of 'reception', there is another difference between the study of natural phenomena and the study of artefacts. Students of the genetic code or of such phenomena as the growth-rings in trees may be regarded, though not in a pejorative sense, as eavesdroppers: the messages are *there*, no doubt, but no one would argue that they were addressed to the scientists who decipher them. In the study of artefacts, on the other hand, meaning seeks us whenever (as by opening a book or looking at a painting) we allow it to do so. And yet, though some intellectual disciplines are necessarily more interventionist than others, the analysis of patterns always entails a degree of intervention and distortion. Even when no microscopes, telescopes or spectacles are used, the eye of the beholder is never a transparent medium. This point is reinforced and the difference between the study of natural phenomena and that of artefacts is lessened by the recognition that, using the word in a duly liberal sense, 'noise' is actually polysemous. When two separate telephone conversations are garbled by a crossed line, the two pairs of participants form opposite opinions of what is message and what is merely noise. So also when a scientist or student of literature chooses to focus attention either on those features that distinguish a particular specimen from its fellows or on those that unite it with them. Either the idiosyncratic or the common features will, for the immediate purpose, be set aside as 'noise'.

Provided we remain alert to the potency of differences like those so briefly illustrated, the underlying idea of an opposition between pattern and noise makes a theoretical model of great generality. Within its framework, a number of procedures and constraints unite those disciplines where computer assistance has come to be recognized as indispensable and those, like literary studies, where it is only beginning to make its mark.

In literary studies, as elsewhere, we examine and compare patterns. They may be sets of taxonomic differentiae, uniting certain texts in a genre or sub-genre or as moments in the evolution of a tradition or a school. They may be signs of individual authorship or of the larger cultural forces that inscribe themselves in and through the writings of individual authors. They may be large thematic patterns, established less often on the basis of direct statements in the text than by such inferences as underlie those readings of *King Lear* which emphasize the parallels between the main plot and the Gloucester sub-plot. They may lie in the juxtaposition of characters or the modulations of a narrative. They may, at their most concrete, consist in sequences of images, sets of tropes, poetic rhythms, shifts of semantic register, or even (as I shall go on to argue) the frequency patterns of very common words. They may also, though it is not fashionable to say so, help clarify our understanding of what we value and so contribute to the assessment of artistic excellence or inadequacy.

Across this wide range and in the many cases not mentioned, some principles hold good. Although they are usually (and no doubt should always be) firmly grounded in the realities of a text or set of texts, our patterns, like those of our colleagues the scientists, are not the original objects in the fullness of their own being but selections, abstractions, interpretations and misinterpretations. The personal and cultural distance between any author and any reader, as between any speaker and any listener, prevents us from attaining the ideals of unambiguous communication and exact representation. To acknowledge this, however, is not to rejoice in that dark victory or to think it absolute. Without denying our limitations, we do well to admit the importance of differences of degree, to study our texts as observantly as we are able and to represent them as accurately as we can.

Interpretation is, above all, an act of judgement: the better informed the judgement, the greater the likelihood that an interpretation will deserve acceptance. The recent tendency, especially in the humanities and social sciences, to emphasize the interventionist aspect of interpretation, to insist that such-and-such is an ideological construct, and to play down the importance of any inherent patterning in the phenomena owes much to theorists like Foucault. We should certainly heed the reminder that interpretations are constructs and that the acceptance they may gain need not testify to their truth. But it does not necessarily follow, as e.g. Foucault (1967) would claim, that their acceptance chiefly testifies to shared prejudices like a preoccupation with the advantage of the majority or an undue deference for the authority of the 'establishment'. As is evident whenever we are persuaded by an uncongenial argument, their acceptance may rest, rather, on their validity.

What is this 'validity'? Another set of constructs, of course. But these are constructs so formal that, like a rough trigonometry of meaning, they go far towards ideological neutrality. The recognition of similarity and dissimilarity is fundamental to the operation of these formal constructs. The requirement of completeness is met by the inclusion of all like cases. The requirement of relevance is met by the exclusion of unlike cases. Concomitance, sequentiality and recurrence are only extensions of the same ideas. The major literary fallacies, circularity and unfalsifiability, are tautologies in disguise.

Other less precise criteria straddle the boundary between the territory of formal validity and that of ideologically-based approval or disapproval. When we speak, for example, of the 'depth' and 'subtlety' of an interpretation, we do not always – but may legitimately – refer only to the acumen shown in dis-tinguishing like from unlike. (Theobald's famous emendation, 'a babbled of greene fields', where early editions of Shakespeare's *Henry V* had 'a Table of greene fields', epitomizes my point. While Theobald's reading now has the support of palaeographers, it presumably originated in a recognition that *a babld* – that is, *he babbled* – was better suited than *a Table* to its context.) 'Superficiality' and 'inconsistency' may likewise refer only to failures in observing a likeness or unlikeness. 'Significance' ranges across a whole spectrum of meaning, from its application in statistical analysis as an exact measure of probability to its broad evaluative area of reference in the humanities. Even so complex a criterion as 'originality' rests upon the comparison, usually an implicit comparison, of interpretations: especially in simple cases, like that of plagiarism, such comparisons can sometimes be exact.

So far as the validity of any interpretation rests upon considerations like these, there is no obvious disjunction between the basic processes of literary scholarship and those of computer-assisted analysis. Like the notes we take and the card indexes we make, computers serve most immediately as instruments of observation and memory. Their enhancement of those powers is evident in the speed with which they scan a text, the accuracy with which they gather every instance of any given phenomenon, and the flexibility with which they can arrange and rearrange a set of data.

The computer also surpasses our capacity for carrying out those forms of classification in which membership of a class is defined by the presence, the absence, or the markedly different incidence of certain explicit features. It has long been recognized that, unlike his sister Sarah, Henry Fielding often used the already archaic form *hath*. Without computer assistance, it would be unwise to claim that this differentia operates, without exception, in a large body of material. In 75,553 words, from eight of his narratives, *hath* occurs ninety-seven times and is to be found in every text: in 75,892 words, from eight of her narratives, it does not occur at all. Such claims can now be made with as much certainty as the accuracy of the texts and the efficiency of the computer programs permit. Computers are of less obvious use to literary scholars in those other forms of classification where class-membership is defined by differentiae that do not figure explicitly and unambiguously in a given set of texts. It seems inconceivable, for example, that a psychological effect like the 'catharsis' that Aristotle attributes to tragedy is consistently evoked or even accompanied by explicit stylistic signals. For all his empirical impulse, Aristotle's genres rest on differentiae too unempirical for a computer and his generalizations soar beyond its powers. And yet, as it stands, my contrast between explicit and inexplicit grounds of classification is too simply framed. Without indulging the anthropomorphic hopes or fears that lie behind many popular accounts of 'artificial intelligence' and virtually mysticize the machine, we must recognize that a number of existing computer programs, one of which is described by John B. Smith (1985), make it possible to unite classes in super-classes, to form categories of categories with an increasing degree of generality.

The computer, finally, is unlikely ever to encompass the vague immensities of human memory. The rapidly increasing capacity and availability of data-stores like CD−ROM may well foretell a time when computers will enable us to range swiftly and accurately across the field of recorded knowledge. But much of the knowledge on which students of literature draw is not likely to be recorded. There is what Trilling calls 'a culture's hum and buzz of implication . . . the whole evanescent context in which its explicit statements are made' (1961: 206), a context much like what Hirsch (1987) sees as the very basis of cultural literacy. There is also what one might call the Aunt Gertrude factor, where a worthwhile literary insight grows from the unexpected recollection of some small personal experience: 'Just like Aunt Gertrude,' we say, and pursue the analogy sometimes to valuable ends. But (save in the unlikely event that we set in the tables of its memory all trivial fond records, the records in an average lifetime of more than 20,000 Bloomsdays) what computer will ever store poor Gertie's little deeds and sayings and those of all her kind?

7.2 Authorship Attribution

Computers have been widely used in attempts to establish the authorship of anonymous or doubtful texts. One consequence is that statistical analysis, properly so called, has displaced the mere counting of idiosyncratic features. In illustrating the range of methods used in this form of literary statistics, one should first glance back to the analyses conducted by scholars like Udney Yule and Williams before computer assistance was available. Udney Yule (1944) worked, with great subtlety, on the distribution of content-words, an approach that has not borne more recent fruit. Yule (1939) and C. B. Williams (1940) also examined characteristic differences in sentence length, an approach limited but not entirely frustrated by inconsistencies of punctuation and by the need to distinguish between the mere lengths and the actual shapes of sentences. For more recent work in this area, see Oppenheim (1988) and Burrows (1987a: 213–16). Making rather more use of computer assistance, especially in the statistical phase of their work, and paying particular attention to the incidence of chosen function-words, Ellegård (1962) showed that, among the known candidates, Sir Philip Francis is the most likely author of the Junius Letters, while Mosteller and Wallace (1964) showed that Madison is much more likely than Hamilton to have written the disputed *Federalist* papers.

Although his object was not so much to distinguish Swift's 'signature' as to analyse his style for interpretative purposes, Milic (1967) gave another early lead in studies of attribution, the first in which the capacities of the computer were put to use throughout.[2] In view of the diverse achievements of more recent scholars, it may seem strange to say, more than twenty years later, that we still know too little about the probabilistic side of the language. My point of departure is that, ever since that time, the quest for linguistic universals, associated especially with the work of Chomsky, has been a dominant force in linguistics; and, accordingly, the 'surface grammar' of Fries, though never superseded, has been set aside. Yet work like that of Fries, of which Milic took advantage, is altogether more congenial to a quantitative approach. The essential difference can be seen whenever, as often happens in the study of so complex a system as language, an exception is encountered. For Chomsky and his followers, the exception, if 'grammatical', rightly calls for a revision of whatever 'rule' it breaks. For students of the probabilistic aspect of grammar, treating of the Friesian 'surface', the exception is allowed to bear such weight as its frequency of occurrence requires. Thus, when Milic seeks to distinguish Swift's writings from those of his contemporaries, he need not confine himself to absolute marks of difference: within proper statistical constraints, it is sufficient to show (as he does) that Swift is more or less given to the use of certain forms of expression. Probabilistic rules, that is to say, lie in the realm of 'fuzzy logic': unlike the rules of a universal grammar, they can treat of what is almost always, or usually, or not often, or only seldom the case. A probabilistic grammar of English, in which rules of that kind were enunciated, would much enhance our understanding of what is to be expected, grammatically, in writings of a given era, genre or author. It would supply a firmer basis for comparison than the little samples offered by Milic and his successors (myself included). And, above all, it would provide a more appropriate basis than the calculation of chance in assessing the weight of data where the operation of chance is a peripheral rather than a central factor. As may be inferred from the comments of Johansson (1985), collections like the Brown and LOB corpora would greatly assist in such developments: but a probabilistic grammar would be a much subtler instrument than a dictionary of frequencies.

Under proper constraints, the claim that a given outcome is upheld, though not ensured, by the knowledge that heavy odds obtain against its having come about by chance is a reputable feature of statistical method. Beyond the accuracy of data, the best recognized constraints bear chiefly on the homogeneity and size of 'populations' and on the need either to confine any conclusions to the population analysed or else to set about the more difficult task of statistical prediction by ensuring a valid range of samples.[3] In the field of literary statistics, these constraints are most easily breached by a poor choice of texts used as 'controls'; by employing most statistical techniques when (as in short poems) the frequencies of the phenomena are low; or by failing to recognize that, even if a certain text has more in common, say, with Shakespeare's writings than with those of any of his known contemporaries, it may yet be the work of an unknown hand. With due forethought, these constraints can all be met.

Another difficulty is that the odds obtaining against chance outcomes are greatly reduced when, through the operation of non-chance factors, all outcomes are not equally probable. If a bag containing 1,000 marbles, 50 red and the remainder of various other colours, were emptied on a carpet, any of the marbles might fall anywhere. One outcome, highly unlikely but no less likely than any other, would show all the red marbles lying together; in many other outcomes, each equally unlikely, the red marbles would be scattered; and, in others again, they would consistently lie close to the marbles of certain other colours. Now, in most passages of 1,000 words of ordinary English prose, we could expect to find between 30 and 70 instances of *the*: the number would tend to run high in disquisitory prose, low in intimate dialogue. But, provided that it was intelligible prose, there is no chance whatever that all or even most of the instances of *the* would lie close together. Wherever they lay, they would have nouns lying nearby and many of them would have instances of *by*, *of* and *in* lying next to them. In passages of dialogue, the many instances of *I* would also be widely distributed and would tend to be accompanied by instances of *you* and *me*. Without any further multiplication of examples, it is clearly unreasonable to press an argument based on such grammatically and contextually interdependent variables by treating them as if they were independent variables like marbles.

Although these methodological problems are not confined to the field of attribution, they arise there with unusual force. In this form of scholarship, perhaps, there is more need to strive for certainty than there is in literary interpretation: certainly there are more signs of such striving. Among the many tests of authorship enunciated by Morton, those treating of word-strings and frequency ratios (1978) do not allow enough for the difference between dependent and independent variables. Morton rightly argues that we are able to distinguish confidently between two people even though they resemble each other in many ways: the purpose is met if there is a sufficient number of differences or even a single unequivocal difference. He applies the analogy by studying the incidence, in different authors, of strings like *of the*, *in the* and *to the* and ratios like that of *a/an*. Where a statistically significant discrepancy (marked by a probability of less than one chance in twenty) is observed, he regards that particular test as a valid discriminator. Where there is little discrepancy, the test is discarded because authors need not differ in every stylistic particular. So far, so good. Then, in a manner justified only when the various tests are independent of each other, he proceeds to compound the odds ($1/20 \times 1/20 \times 1/20 \ldots$) and rapidly arrives at very long odds against the possibility that mere chance is distinguishing between his authors. But these are not independent tests. In texts where any of the common prepositions occurs unusually often, the others are also likely to do so: they all run high, for example, in formal styles where post-modification is common; and, when they do so, the frequency of *the* rises with them. The ratio of *an* to *a* is also high in formal styles because *an* commonly precedes the nouns and adjectives of a Latinate vocabulary, which often begin with prefixes like *in-* and *un-*. In compounding his odds as if these phenomena were independent of each other, Morton is acting as if (to extend his own analogy) red hair, blue eyes, pale skin and freckles were independent personal differentiae. And his calculation of 'degrees of freedom' is not a sufficient precaution when many of the tests are so closely interlocked.

Despite these and other statistical deficiencies,[4] Morton's tests can yield results consonant with those of other scholars. In a notable case, Farringdon worked beside (but independently of) Battestin, one of the most eminent of Fielding scholars, in establishing which essays in *The Craftsman* (1734–9) could be attributed to Henry Fielding. From traditional forms of internal evidence, Battestin concluded that thirty-one of the essays could be attributed, with some confidence, to Fielding while ten others stood on less firm ground. Using a modified version of Morton's tests (in which much appropriate preparatory work was undertaken and after which the results of the various tests were not compounded but only summed), Farringdon was able to offer unreserved support for twenty-seven of Battestin's thirty-one confident attributions and scarcely reserved support for another three. The remaining essay is so different in genre that it presented special stylistic features.[5]

What is to be made of the paradox in which such convincing results flow from the use of tests whose deficiencies attract persistent criticism from competent statisticians like M. W. A. Smith, Stevenson and Thomson? After allowing something for Farringdon's cautious procedures, I can only suppose that the manner in which stylistic differentiae are interlocked enables them to register even on defective instruments. We do not need keen vision to distinguish, at sight, between most Scandinavians and most Greeks: the various particulars reflect one general difference. That explanation is supported by the fact that many disparate methods of stylistic analysis, shortly to be sketched, have yielded plausible (though not all equally plausible) distinctions between the writings of different authors. Here, too, a myriad of seemingly discrete particulars reflect the quiddity of an authorial style.

If that is a fair resolution of the paradox, it does not follow, as Morton (1989) would have it in a recent piece in the *Times Literary Supplement*, that we should rejoice in statistical primitivism and not attempt to develop better methods than his own. We need rather to work patiently towards better methods, towards a clearer explanation of our procedures and results, and towards a better understanding of the probabilistic patterns of the language generally. In pursuing those ends, we need also to match a natural desire to work on celebrated cases like *Henry VIII* and *The Revenger's Tragedy* with a more sober, though less immediately rewarding, concern for testing our methods thoroughly on cases where the true answers are not in any doubt.

Among many other approaches, there is a successful attempt to distinguish Donne from Jonson in poetic metre and so to assign a doubtful poem to the latter author (Greenblatt, 1973). There is a subtle analysis of authorial differences in the distribution of alphabetic characters in ancient Greek texts (Ledger, 1985). The identity and the location of *hapax legomena*, word-types that each occur only once in a given text, have long been regarded as a test of authorship, a test to which computers should bring a new exactitude. Morton (1986) offers a test of this kind; but his procedures have been challenged by M. W. A. Smith (1987a). There is also a promising but inadequately tested line of inquiry into the changing incidence of 'word-links' (or co-occurrences) in Shakespearean and possibly Shakespearean texts (Slater, 1975a, 1975b, 1977, 1978, 1982, 1983; but see M. W. A. Smith, 1986). The postulate is that, where two texts share an uncommonly high proportion of word-types, they are likely to come from the same phase of Shakespeare's literary career and that, where there is little or none of this sharing, the texts may come from different phases or even from different authors. The test needs further work because too little is known about this aspect of authorial homogeneity.

Other scholars treat of Muller curves, expressions of the diminishing rate at which new words accrue as more texts are added to a homogeneous set. When a sudden increase in that rate follows the inclusion of a new text, it is taken to reflect a different lexical repertoire, perhaps that of a different author. The most sustained contribution to work of this kind is that of Ule (1977, 1982). Drawing on a not dissimilar model developed by Fisher for use in zoological research, Efron and Thisted (1976) made a study of Shakespeare's vocabulary and later used it in a little test of authorship (1987). Since other factors than a change of authorship – a change of genre, for example – may influence these rates of change, tests of this kind have yet to be developed as thoroughly as they deserve.

As a sequel to his searching criticism of other work in the field of attribution, M. W. A. Smith (1987b, 1988, 1989) offers a new battery of tests treating of the first words of speeches, of the incidences of other common words, and of collocations like Morton's. Although these last variables are not independent of each other, Smith makes more thorough tests than Morton, uses a wider range of appropriate 'controls', and assesses his results with far more caution. Yet another recent model (B. J. R. Bailey, 1990) is designed to treat of sequentiality and transitional probabilities in the common function words. What, for example, is the probability of observing the next word as an article provided that the currently observed word is not an article?

My own attempts at attribution (Burrows and Hassall, 1988; Burrows, 1989a) have arisen as a by-product of work whose main emphasis is on literary interpretation. Here, as in that larger field, I have proceeded by analysing the frequency patterns of **whatever** words occur most often in a given set of texts. The number of word-types included is governed only by the length of the texts themselves: the more the better until the point where the frequencies begin to fall too low for sensible comparisons. (That point is usually reached before any but the most common of undeniably lexical words have entered the list.) After the frequencies with which the word-types appear in the several texts have been tabulated, the Pearson product-moment method of correlation is used to establish a matrix showing the varying degrees of mutual relationship among the word-types. While a careful inspection of the matrix shows which word-types interrelate most (and least) closely with which others, the overall pattern of relationships is made more intelligible by using any of the statistical methods that extract the 'principal components' of such matrices. (My own practice is to employ 'eigen analysis', using the MINITAB package.) The most powerful of the components are then shown as the axes of graphs like graph 7.1. In a final statistical step, the 'eigen matrix' is multiplied through the original table of frequencies for each text. The results are then shown in graphs like graph 7.2.

The lists of authors and of word frequencies for this pair of graphs are shown in tables 7.1 and 7.2. The statistical procedure is set out in an appendix. But the

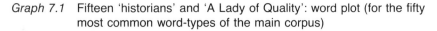

Graph 7.1 Fifteen 'historians' and 'A Lady of Quality': word plot (for the fifty most common word-types of the main corpus)

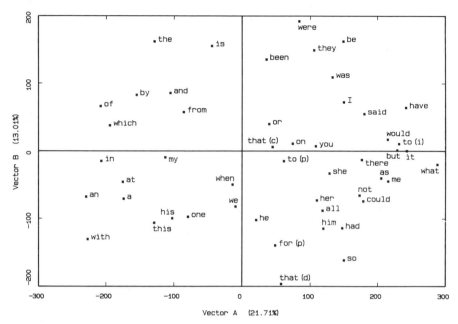

Graph 7.2 Fifteen 'historians' and 'A Lady of Quality' (based on the fifty most common word-types of the main corpus)

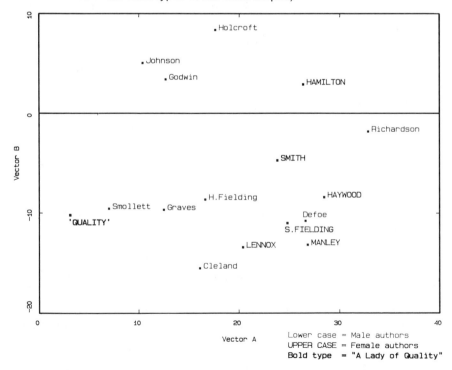

Table 7.1 Main set of forty authors

Alphabetical list		*Chronological list*	
A	Jane Austen (1775–1817)	G	Daniel Defoe (1660–1731)
B	Anne Brontë (1820–49)	ZA	Mary de la Riviere Manley (1663–1724)
C	Charlotte Brontë (1816–55)	ZH	Samuel Richardson (1689–1761)
D	Emily Brontë (1818–48)	U	Eliza Haywood (1693?–1756)
E	John Cleland (1709–89)	L	Henry Fielding (1707–54)
F	Wilkie Collins (1824–89)	E	John Cleland (1709–89)
G	Daniel Defoe (1660–1731)	X	Samuel Johnson (1709–84)
H	Charles Dickens (1812–70)	M	Sarah Fielding (1710–68)
I	E. L. Doctorow (1931– :US)	Q	Richard Graves (1715–1804)
J	Maria Edgeworth (1767–1849)	Y	Charlotte Lennox (1720–1804)
K	George Eliot (1819–80)	ZL	Tobias Smollett (1721–71)
L	Henry Fielding (1707–54)	V	Thomas Holcroft (1745–1809)
M	Sarah Fielding (1710–68)	ZK	Charlotte Smith (1749–1806)
N	Miles Franklin (1879–1954: Aust.)	P	William Godwin (1756–1836)
O	Elizabeth Gaskell (1810–65)	S	Elizabeth Hamilton (1758–1816)
P	William Godwin (1756–1836)	ZG	Ann Radcliffe (1764–1823)
Q	Richard Graves (1715–1804)	J	Maria Edgeworth (1767–1849)
R	Kate Grenville (1950– : Aust.)	ZI	Walter Scott (1771–1832)
S	Elizabeth Hamilton (1758–1816)	A	Jane Austen (1775–1817)
T	Thomas Hardy (1840–1928)	ZC	C. R. Maturin (1782–1824)
U	Eliza Haywood (1693?–1756)	ZJ	Mary Shelley (1797–1851)
V	Thomas Holcroft (1745–1809)	O	Elizabeth Gaskell (1810–65)
W	Henry James (1843–1916: US)	H	Charles Dickens (1812–70)
X	Samuel Johnson (1709–84)	C	Charlotte Brontë (1816–55)
Y	Charlotte Lennox (1720–1804)	D	Emily Brontë (1818–48)
Z	Alison Lurie (1926– : US)	K	George Eliot (1819–80)
ZA	Mary de la Riviere Manley (1663–1724)	B	Anne Brontë (1820–49)
ZB	Katherine Mansfield (1888–1923: NZ)	F	Wilkie Collins (1824–89)
ZC	C. R. Maturin (1782–1824)	T	Thomas Hardy (1840–1928)
ZD	Iris Murdoch (1919–)	W	Henry James (1843–1916)
ZE	Vance Palmer (1885–1959: Aust.)	ZN	Edith Wharton (1862–1937)
ZF	Hal Porter (1911–84: Aust.)	ZM	H. G. Wells (1866–1946)
ZG	Ann Radcliffe (1764–1823)	N	Miles Franklin (1879–1954)
ZH	Samuel Richardson (1689–1761)	ZE	Vance Palmer (1885–1959)
ZI	Walter Scott (1771–1832)	ZB	Katherine Mansfield (1888–1923)
ZJ	Mary Shelley (1797–1851)	ZF	Hal Porter (1911–84)
ZK	Charlotte Smith (1749–1806)	ZD	Iris Murdoch (1919–)
ZL	Tobias Smollett (1721–71)	Z	Alison Lurie (1926–)
ZM	H. G. Wells (1866–1946)	I	E. L. Doctorow (1931–)
ZN	Edith Wharton (1862–1937: US)	R	Kate Grenville (1950–)

Table 7.2   The Fifty Most Common Word-types of the Main Corpus: Incidences for Fifteen Eighteenth-century Authors and 'A Lady of Quality'. (Incidences shown as text-percentages)

	E	G	L	M	P	Q	S	U	V	X	Y	ZA	ZH	ZK	ZL	Qual
1 the	4.86	4.42	4.55	3.98	6.07	4.48	5.05	4.49	6.02	4.78	3.74	3.69	4.15	4.32	5.52	4.16
2 and	3.29	4.10	2.65	3.08	3.42	3.23	2.92	2.44	3.72	3.94	2.83	2.66	3.39	3.38	3.52	3.57
3 I	2.32	3.59	3.44	3.07	3.53	2.86	3.35	4.11	3.24	2.77	3.19	2.59	3.80	3.97	2.45	3.49
4 of	4.25	2.68	3.09	3.21	4.56	3.43	3.43	3.17	3.47	4.12	2.89	3.38	2.56	3.17	3.81	3.55
5 a	1.92	2.01	2.08	1.48	2.04	2.67	2.02	1.86	1.76	1.77	2.15	1.85	1.90	1.67	2.42	2.00
6 was	1.51	1.89	1.64	2.00	1.95	1.65	2.00	1.86	2.01	1.63	1.73	1.91	1.70	1.98	1.60	1.94
7 to(i)	1.82	2.11	1.79	2.60	1.61	2.04	2.38	2.18	1.90	2.27	2.25	2.23	2.36	2.45	1.70	1.81
8 in(p)	1.77	1.39	1.69	1.82	2.12	2.20	1.80	1.69	1.46	1.66	1.61	1.52	1.77	1.48	1.93	2.19
9 my	1.92	1.37	2.07	2.21	2.40	1.81	2.41	2.32	1.64	2.05	2.43	1.98	2.07	1.83	2.11	3.08
10 to(p)	1.58	1.33	1.52	1.39	1.60	1.49	1.62	1.55	1.47	1.17	1.56	1.46	1.83	1.56	1.52	1.55
11 he	0.99	1.61	1.20	1.26	1.02	0.68	0.57	1.48	1.35	0.68	1.22	1.58	0.73	1.16	1.52	1.50
12 had	1.29	1.39	1.13	1.24	1.36	1.21	1.09	1.31	0.84	0.67	1.17	1.19	1.05	1.28	0.92	0.95
13 it	1.17	1.28	0.88	0.90	0.91	0.54	1.05	1.05	1.15	0.36	0.89	0.95	0.98	0.92	0.45	0.37
14 her	1.29	0.32	0.86	0.89	0.41	1.76	1.37	0.51	0.14	0.67	1.83	1.47	2.32	0.97	0.49	0.23
15 me	1.19	1.53	1.28	1.13	1.34	0.97	1.23	1.95	1.10	1.01	1.59	1.38	1.26	1.47	0.88	1.02
16 with	1.04	0.99	1.13	1.06	0.92	1.32	0.80	1.00	0.89	1.20	1.38	1.08	0.92	0.91	1.43	1.45
17 his	1.06	0.76	0.88	1.50	0.96	0.53	0.50	0.68	1.02	0.70	1.24	1.44	0.72	0.95	1.61	1.70
18 as	0.97	1.32	0.92	1.12	0.72	1.12	0.93	1.00	0.82	0.68	0.66	0.78	1.36	0.98	0.76	0.63
19 not	0.96	0.86	0.77	0.70	0.66	0.56	0.61	0.88	0.83	0.80	0.76	1.11	0.96	0.77	0.72	0.63
20 she	0.64	0.30	0.61	0.61	0.31	1.06	1.32	0.49	0.16	0.44	1.11	0.77	1.07	0.68	0.27	0.13
21 that(c)	0.79	1.09	0.79	0.97	0.91	0.72	1.04	1.01	0.66	1.14	1.05	0.81	0.81	0.99	0.85	1.00
22 but	0.58	1.04	0.64	0.79	0.49	0.74	0.98	0.97	0.74	0.68	0.64	0.87	0.73	0.68	0.57	0.62
23 at	0.82	0.70	0.81	0.62	0.63	0.66	0.67	0.71	0.75	0.74	0.75	0.60	0.59	0.62	0.70	0.80

24 for(p)	0.95	0.70	0.58	0.71	0.57	0.61	0.72	0.69	0.43	0.74	0.71	0.74	0.73	0.62	0.67	0.65
25 on(p)	0.51	0.35	0.54	0.58	0.28	0.21	0.53	0.62	0.39	0.30	0.28	0.07	0.36	0.45	0.43	0.30
26 which(rp)	0.91	0.67	1.12	0.55	0.76	0.83	0.70	0.79	1.04	0.82	0.82	0.37	0.53	0.84	0.80	0.97
27 him	0.39	0.84	0.48	1.15	0.41	0.34	0.24	0.72	0.56	0.26	0.67	1.06	0.34	0.54	0.57	0.69
28 have	0.32	0.37	0.51	0.63	0.43	0.33	0.48	0.52	0.46	0.40	0.38	0.58	0.53	0.52	0.32	0.35
29 by(p)	0.68	0.44	0.51	0.64	0.52	0.51	0.75	0.48	0.67	0.96	0.60	0.56	0.56	0.52	0.64	0.84
30 all	0.60	0.59	0.51	0.62	0.31	0.17	0.61	0.51	0.35	0.37	0.38	0.50	0.39	0.30	0.43	0.51
31 be	0.34	0.44	0.43	0.60	0.44	0.45	0.56	0.55	0.67	0.70	0.46	0.70	0.71	0.52	0.42	0.38
32 this	0.63	0.64	0.77	0.60	0.76	0.65	0.40	0.67	0.51	0.24	0.70	0.24	0.47	0.46	0.73	0.77
33 from	0.50	0.28	0.52	0.51	0.50	0.44	0.52	0.44	0.41	0.55	0.42	0.55	0.31	0.60	0.42	0.46
34 were	0.22	0.45	0.30	0.37	0.54	0.28	0.40	0.38	0.63	0.34	0.23	0.34	0.40	0.37	0.28	0.35
35 that(d)	0.37	0.43	0.36	0.31	0.20	0.34	0.09	0.43	0.29	0.13	0.39	0.37	0.24	0.31	0.35	0.29
36 could	0.49	0.44	0.31	0.57	0.26	0.26	0.26	0.41	0.32	0.43	0.31	0.41	0.38	0.49	0.29	0.29
37 would	0.23	0.28	0.19	0.43	0.30	0.17	0.32	0.35	0.32	0.21	0.38	0.48	0.40	0.40	0.27	0.29
38 you	0.10	0.04	0.56	0.09	0.20	0.22	0.24	0.50	0.19	0.22	0.25	0.34	0.44	0.31	0.26	0.02
39 they	0.17	0.55	0.20	0.30	0.31	0.17	0.37	0.16	0.46	0.53	0.13	0.36	0.51	0.21	0.21	0.15
40 said	0.01	0.22	0.19	0.13	0.24	0.16	0.47	0.33	0.15	0.06	0.39	0.25	0.52	0.22	0.14	0.06
41 when	0.26	0.35	0.34	0.33	0.22	0.27	0.26	0.21	0.21	0.41	0.28	0.11	0.35	0.28	0.29	0.34
42 an	0.37	0.29	0.37	0.31	0.42	0.52	0.25	0.27	0.35	0.32	0.35	0.32	0.31	0.37	0.44	0.44
43 or	0.33	0.52	0.23	0.24	0.22	0.38	0.16	0.27	0.31	0.54	0.09	0.40	0.30	0.33	0.18	0.15
44 is	0.15	0.13	0.36	0.20	0.36	0.24	0.20	0.17	0.52	0.40	0.19	0.27	0.30	0.14	0.20	0.18
45 we	0.22	0.74	0.43	0.30	0.23	0.49	0.14	0.30	0.05	0.32	0.07	0.26	0.09	0.15	0.12	0.35
46 so(av.d)	0.65	0.38	0.40	0.49	0.24	0.38	0.43	0.36	0.27	0.22	0.55	0.52	0.49	0.36	0.30	0.27
47 one	0.27	0.29	0.27	0.22	0.26	0.29	0.16	0.23	0.19	0.23	0.20	0.21	0.29	0.24	0.25	0.27
48 there	0.20	0.29	0.10	0.10	0.17	0.16	0.15	0.18	0.18	0.09	0.10	0.19	0.20	0.17	0.13	0.08
49 been	0.22	0.22	0.24	0.23	0.44	0.26	0.34	0.30	0.32	0.16	0.24	0.19	0.23	0.30	0.20	0.21
50 what	0.23	0.22	0.24	0.30	0.18	0.22	0.27	0.34	0.26	0.11	0.22	0.34	0.33	0.24	0.13	0.10

NB. For author-codes at head of columns, see Table 7.1. Word-types where homographs have been separated are marked by part of speech. All contracted forms, like *can't* and *I've*, have been expanded and counted as two words; in an extension of this process, *cannot* has also been counted as two words.

graphs are the heart of the matter. Graph 7.2 shows an entry for Smollett lying to the west of a set of entries for the work of fourteen other novelists of the first half of the eighteenth century. Beside the Smollett entry is one representing 'The Memoirs of a Lady of Quality', a text whose authorship has been disputed. These memoirs, which run to more than 44,000 words, give a sympathetic account of the notorious career of Lady Vane and were included by Smollett in *Peregrine Pickle*. They were thought by some to be her own work but are now generally regarded as Smollett's.[6] Like all of the other works incorporated in this graph, they give a retrospective first-person narrative of events in the speaker's life, a literary form known in the eighteenth century as the 'history'.

A graph like this does not prove that Smollett wrote the 'Memoirs', but it does attest that fourteen of his contemporaries (none of whom is associated with the authorship of the 'Memoirs') are less likely candidates than he. A more direct form of evidence, known specimens of the writing of Lady Vane, is not available. But the possibility that she happened to write more like Smollett than did any of the other fourteen is lessened by the main configuration of this graph. Counting Smollett, all seven of the formally educated male writers lie to the west of the six female writers and far to the west of Richardson and Defoe, the two men who had a less formal education than their fellows and who are well known for their vernacularity. To resemble Smollett as closely as the graph suggests, Lady Vane would have needed, for example, to write even more formally than Mrs Lennox, whose wit and erudition led Dr Johnson to admit that not all women were incapable of writing well.

For a closer understanding of graph 7.2, it should be thought of as transparent and overlaid on graph 7.1, from which its patterns derive. Those word-types whose frequencies run high in Smollett and his more immediate neighbours lie to the west. Those that run low among them and high among the other writers lie to the east. Those that contribute little to this pattern of differentiations lie around the middle of the graph. The association, at the western end, of prepositions, articles and *which* – *who* is not among the fifty most common word-types – is in keeping with my earlier remarks about 'formal' styles. The dearth of phrasal connectives towards the east and the presence there of *but*, and most personal pronouns and auxiliary verbs marks a less closely wrought syntax, a more personal emphasis, and (taken with *said*) a stronger tendency to report the remarks of others. The impersonal generalizations of Johnson and Godwin, a strong presence even in their retrospective narratives, are marked by the location of *the* and *is* in their north-western territory. In this particular graph, *my* and *his* stand apart from the other personal pronouns largely because the Lady of Quality has so much to say about 'my lover', 'my lord' and 'his lordship': *her* is not similarly affected because she has almost nothing to say about any other ladyship than herself. Among the writers whose work I have studied (as later graphs will show), high incidences of *this* are characteristic of the 'Augustan' style of eighteenth-century men and, compared to their successors, of the eighteenth-century writers as a group. By virtue of its reference to something syntactically (and not merely deictically) near at hand, the word marks their tendency to write exactly. That inference is supported by the high incidence of vaguer referentials in the work of most eighteenth-century women writers and many more recent writers. In these other writers, moreover, *it* and *there* are often used as mere 'place-holders' in expressions like 'It is a far, far better thing' and 'There is a happy land'.

Thus graph 7.1 shows which words behave most like and most unlike each other in the present set of texts. The intervals marked along the edges of the graph measure relative, not 'real' distances and express the degrees of resemblance among the correlation coefficients for the various word frequencies. The interrelationships among the coefficients, that is to say, show which words do (and do not) run concomitantly to high and low frequencies of occurrence in these texts. By arraying the words, relative to each other, in a sequence (or 'vector') of comparative resemblance, the process of eigen analysis enables the words to be entered in the graph as neighbours or non-neighbours. The percentage values shown beside 'Vector A' and 'Vector B' in graph 7.1 indicate the extent to which these first two (of fifty) vectors express the interrelationships of the correlation matrix. Over a fifth of the information in the matrix, the whole complex of frequency relationships, is taken up in the east–west sequence of word-types in Vector A, and another eighth in the north–south sequence of Vector B. The remaining two-thirds of the information, dissipated among the many lesser vectors, has to do with less pervasive features: with particular points of resemblance between two writers who have few points in common; with the sorts of difference that enable good readers to distinguish between Smollett and Fielding though they write much like each other and are fairly close neighbours in graph 7.2; and with a myriad of other small (but certainly not uninteresting) departures from a systematic regularity. By allowing the word-types to choose themselves and by analysing their frequency patterns in such a way as to let them tell us which of these writers most resemble which others in the groundwork of their language, we gain some useful new insights. That claim is not at odds with other approaches to literature and language: to the extent, indeed, that the language is systematic, different approaches should yield complementary results.

The possibility that Smollett took up and revised a version of her affairs written by Lady Vane should also be entertained. In an article (Burrows, 1989a) treating of texts where revision by a second hand was possible, I showed that, if the word-list was progressively truncated from the bottom and the remaining patterns were re-analysed, the doubtful texts gradually moved into the territory of the putative author. I took this evidence to suggest that the processes of revision are more likely to alter the most visible aspects of another writer's work than to affect the no less idiosyncratic frequencies of *the* or *and* or *of*. In the present case, a similar series of analyses leaves the entry for the 'Memoirs' beside Smollett's own entry from first to last, and thus reduces the likelihood that Lady Vane made any substantial contribution to the writing of her tale.

Before turning to the less widely publicized field of computer-assisted literary criticism, we should consider what emerges from the foregoing discussion of methods of attribution. Although the many tests described are capable of further development and should continue to be subjected to the scrutiny of competent statisticians (just as the results should be assessed by literary scholars), none, in my view, deserves only to be discarded. The success obtained, in varying degrees, by such a diversity of procedures points once more to the profoundly systematic nature of the language. Since computers make it easy to apply a number of different tests to any given problem, the notion of working with a single form of test seems unlikely to survive the present developmental phase. Kenny (1978, 1986) and M. W. A. Smith (1987b, 1988, 1989) are notable among those who have already begun to test one question in several ways.

Notwithstanding its importance and the attention it has been given, the establishment of authorship is not a central activity in literary studies. The number of doubtful texts, though large, is not unlimited. And, though plagiarism and fraudulence offer useful applications for reliable tests of authorship, they seem unlikely to present new kinds of problem and so yield conceptual advances. (It seems likely that more work goes on in this area than is reported in academic journals. In my experience, on which I, too, am free to comment only in the broadest terms, the narrow linguistic repertoires of ordinary people make their 'stylistic signatures' easier to distinguish than those of more gifted writers.) Yet, beyond its immediate uses, evidence of authorial individuality is of particular value at a time when literary theorists are inclined to disregard the author's role. Whether because their interest is in literature as a reflection of larger social forces, in the aesthetic properties of literary works, or in the ways in which readers 'construct' literary texts, they are clearly entitled to let the matter of authorship alone. But, even on present evidence, they are not entitled to deny that literary works are marked by the particular stylistic habits and, by a not unreasonable inference, the intellectual propensities of their authors.

7.3   Computer-assisted Literary Criticism

Two radical objections to the quantitative analysis of literary texts bear more directly on interpretative work than on attempts to establish authorship. The objections themselves and my reasons for believing that neither can be sustained should be assessed in the light of the ensuing account of work that has actually been going on. Fish's claim (1980) that stylistics – an acceptable umbrella term for an area of literary studies in which quantitative methods are now prominent – is necessarily circular deserves the crude riposte that much else in literary scholarship is open to that charge. Fish is blurring the distinction between experiment and exploration, and requiring that stylistics be more strictly experimental than any other form of literary inquiry. His claim is also open to the better rejoinder that stylistics need not be circular and is often demonstrably not so. The circle is broken whenever exploratory analysis leads to an unforeseen conclusion or requires a major change in method; and there is no trace of circularity in some of the experimental work that will be mentioned in due course. Van Peer's argument (1989) that it is inappropriate to 'reify' the words of an ongoing text by plucking them out of context and setting them in tables has more force. In many but not in all respects, a word or phrase is certainly most meaningful when it is seen in context: the question (on which we shall see strong affirmative evidence) is whether anything further can be learnt by taking a word away for a time from its contextual neighbours and setting it among its semantic or grammatical kinsfolk, other specimens of its own type. In its strength but also in this limitation, Van Peer's argument applies more generally than he concedes to all scientific inquiry into the constituents of living organisms and dynamic systems; and, in stylistics at least, the guinea-pigs survive the experiment, are liberated, and return unblemished to their proper habitat.

In a notable essay, John B. Smith (1978) drew close comparisons between the main forms of computer-assisted literary criticism and those of 'conventional' critical practice. Given the background of most of those who have taken up literary computing and given their belief that their scholarly aims remain essentially unchanged, such a conjunction was to be expected. Yet there is an attitudinal gap. It is easy and not unjust to blame some of our colleagues for their reluctance even to assess our wares. On being shown that quantitative analysis supports a known truth (and might therefore be thought useful in doubtful cases), they will comment, loftily, that everybody knows that. When the analysis yields a result that displeases them, they will cheerfully declare that all statisticians are Cretans. Easy, not unjust, but only half the story. Literary statistics is often damaged by the extravagant claims of some of its practitioners. There is also a tendency, among the ablest statisticians, to lose sight of the literary substance of their argument and the literary audience to whom, ultimately, it needs to be addressed. It may be that arguments based on a sophisticated use of quantitative evidence should be presented in two forms: a technical account for publication in the specialized journals and assessment by an expert readership; and, for publication in the literary journals, an account in which the conclusions are fully addressed and the details of statistical method are relegated to an appendix.

In an important area some way from most others, computer-assisted studies of prosody and poetic phonology have yielded sophisticated results. An innovative article by Bratley and Ross (1981) makes an empirical approach to prosody, employing the Fast Fourier Transform, a method of assessing any signs of patterning in change. While this technique, like other forms of time-series analysis, is obviously well-suited to the study of prosody, it may also, as they argue, lead towards a better understanding of the language in its dynamic aspect, an aspect inaccessible to most other statistical techniques. Two other articles, one by Dilligan and Lynn (1972–3) and one by Logan (1982), draw on an established prosodic theory. A later article by Logan (1985) treats of phonology. In all four articles, procedures are clearly set out, results are carefully assessed, and shortcomings are recognized. Dilligan and Lynn developed programs consonant with the linguistically based Halle-Keyser theory of prosodic stress and applied them to specimens of iambic pentameter taken chiefly from Chaucer and Hopkins. The results show a high level of accord between the computer's assessment of 'metricality' and the Halle-Keyser measurement of stress. Most cases of discord between theory and results form intelligible groups, suggesting possible refinements of the program. Logan's programs are based on a modified version of the Halle-Keyser theory. He shows how, in a succession of 'passes' across a machine-readable text, the computer improves on the doggerel-rhythm assigned at its first attempt. He compares his results with the findings of traditional prosodists and carefully explores his failures. But his greatest advance lies in his development of an index of 'metrical complexity', which relates the patterns of metre to the underlying linguistic patterns of normal stress and which thereby admits comparisons between the work of different poets or the methods of different prosodists. Logan's more recent article on phonology faces 'the problems of identifying the significant literary arrangements of individual sounds, describing them, and relating these sounds to meanings' (Logan, 1985: 213). The argument is too intricate to summarize here but, as with his concept of metrical complexity, his interpretation of the data yields valuable insights in the territory of stylistics and literary criticism.

The comparison of an author's revisions, from version to version of a work, is a traditional scholarly and critical activity to which the computer brings obvious benefits. These are evident in studies ranging from Guinn's small but perceptive account (1980) of Crane's revisions of *The Red Badge of Courage* to massive projects like Gabler's new edition of Joyce's *Ulysses* (1984). Computer assistance may not, in principle, be essential for the establishment of a 'synoptic' text like Gabler's: but it makes it a far more feasible enterprise and so facilitates the testing of those new theories of textual provenance that are associated, especially in Shakespeare studies, with the idea of the synoptic.

In some of the most accessible forms of computer-assisted criticism, the computer is employed only for the initial gathering of data, which are then brought to bear on the sorts of question that literary critics customarily investigate. Sabol (1989) addresses the problems of narrative reliability in Ford Madox Ford's *The Good Soldier*. (For further critical uses of rather similar data, see Sabol (1982), and Bender and Briggum (1982).) A computer-based concordance to the novel supplies her with all the instances of *that* and so helps her to locate the propositions in which Dowell, the narrator, affirms his knowledge and manifests his doubts. (Sabol does not mention the loss of instances that might flow from the deletion of *that*, as in 'I know he was there': but, in a brief foray into the text, I found no such deletions and accept that Ford was not much given to them.) Within the terms she proposes, her scrutiny of these propositions sustains Sabol's conclusion that Dowell is a more reliable informant than most critics of the novel have held. But she does not entertain the idea that an assessment of Dowell's reliability, in so subtly organized a narrative, might also take account of the ostensibly artless sequence in which his knowledge is disclosed to the reader. Not until the second last page of the novel, two pages after announcing, 'Well, that is the end of the story', does Dowell declare: 'It suddenly occurs to me that I have forgotten to say how Edward met his death.' A study of the sequential relationship between Dowell's discoveries and his disclosures would add a dimension to arguments like Sabol's.

Considerations of sequence come to the fore when Waggoner (1989) turns from the differentiation to the development of character in Milton's *Samson Agonistes*. Waggoner treats of clearly marked syntactic forms – like questions, imperatives and negatives – and uses the computer to assign them to their speakers and to locate them in the sequence of the text. While the study fulfils its objects in defining an aspect of Milton's dramatic art, investigations along such lines will benefit from advances in the probabilistic analysis of syntax. Merideth (1989) uses much the same syntactic forms to show differences between male and female characters in three of Henry James's novels.

The programs used by Waggoner and Merideth were designed by Potter for her own studies of syntactic forms in the plays of Bernard Shaw and other modern dramatists. Much of her work has to do with relationships among dramatic characters within plays and with comparisons between plays, as registered by syntactic markers of such attitudes as dominance and submission (Potter, 1980, 1989b, 1989c). But, in a more unusual facet, her work points towards 'reception theory' and 'reader-response criticism'. Potter (1982) had a mixed group of people read the first acts of twenty-one plays then answer a questionnaire about their responses to the attitudes of the characters. In a careful statistical exercise, their responses were correlated with her own analyses of the character's syntax. Especially in the matter of dominance, the two sets of findings showed a close correspondence. As a potential instrument of reception theory, such experiments deserve to be extended.

The fact that 'thematics' has figured more prominently in French studies than in English may owe something to the wider historical range, in French, of frequency dictionaries, which supply an invaluable basis for statistical comparisons of the changing incidence of lexical words. This form of criticism is well illustrated by the work of Goldfield and Fortier. By addressing a wider range of texts than Riffaterre had done and by using quantitative methods to good effect, Goldfield (1989) sets out to test and is then able to modify Riffaterre's perceptive but impressionistic ideas on the subject of 'tic words' – verbal mannerisms – in the fiction of de Gobineau. Fortier (1989a) treats of more prominent thematic features – semantic fields like *happiness*, *confinement* and *night* – and arrives at suggestive and sometimes unexpected contrasts among four modern French novels. Both here and in a broader, more reflective piece (1989b), he explains his methods very clearly and also shows how the computer can enforce a modification of preconceived ideas.

Like Fortier's semantic fields, the image-clusters studied by Ide (1987b, 1989a, 1989b) and John B. Smith (1980) are not abstractions, but accumulations of just such revealing particulars as any New Critic would have approved.

And, as in the work of the New Critics, the particulars examined by these newer critics are not treated as stable entities. They are regarded, rather, as gathering meaning by mutual association, by their changing roles in the forward movement of a text, and by the shape they derive from and help to confer upon it. Ide and Smith also resemble their predecessors when their attempts to find clear boundaries for their concepts of an 'image' lead them on to uneasy ground. (Smith, however, is at an advantage over most other image-gatherers in so far as almost everything in Joyce's *Portrait* – unlike *Ulysses* – is mediated through Stephen's eyes and can well be seen as an aspect of his 'imaging' of himself, of Dublin, and of 'a world elsewhere'.) When these critics take leave of their predecessors, it is not so much because they use computers but because they analyse their data with uncommon statistical sophistication. Except in the appendices, Smith's book gives less explicit evidence of its quantitative foundations than do Ide's articles. Most of her work has been concentrated on the imagery of a single extremely complex poem, Blake's *The Four Zoas*. In grappling with its shapes and patterns, she has become as engrossed with her methods of analysis as with the results they yield. By offering a model of how to use techniques like cluster analysis and Fourier analysis to determine the density and the periodicity of patterns, her work, accordingly, may well prove more valuable to other literary statisticians than to students of Blake's verse.

At its best, as in the work of Brower (1951), the attention paid by the New Critics to 'close reading' as they sought to catch the precise 'note' of a particular work remains entirely admirable. There is something of a fashion nowadays for condescending to their narrowness of vision and their humanistic pieties. And yet, as Johnson said of the Metaphysical poets, to write on their plan it was at least necessary to read and think. Those virtues prevail in Milic's book on Swift (1967), referred to earlier, and in Burton's book on Shakespeare (1973). In her emphasis on grammatical matters, her attempt to develop a formal theory of style, and her unobtrusive use of statistical methods, Burton stands apart from the New Critics. But her concentration upon the plays, her observation of subtle recurrences and changes, and her elegant exposition of difficult material set her work with theirs.

The emphasis placed by the New Critics on the intrinsic properties of literary works contributed to the overthrow, more than forty years ago, of author-oriented studies like the *English Men of Letters* series. In studies of that kind, firm distinctions between literary criticism and literary biography were rarely sought: the putative 'mind of the author' had a central place; and the literary works themselves were treated as moments in the growth of such a 'mind'. It would be hard to find a modern critic or biographer who believes that Pope's heroic couplets show a constricted imagination, that *The Tempest* is best interpreted as Shakespeare's farewell to the theatre, or that the psychological simplifications and the naive progressivism characteristic of that older school of thought deserve to be revived. And yet, by a pretty paradox, it is in the intrinsic properties of literary works that recent scholars identify authorial 'signatures' and find quantitative evidence of change within an authorial style. Enough has been said of the identifiability of signatures. In the matter of stylistic change, Brainerd (1980), treating only of the changing incidence of personal pronouns, is able to establish a chronological grouping of Shakespeare's plays. Butler (1981) studies features of the language of Sylvia Plath's four volumes of poetry and finds strong evidence of movement from a more formal and ornate to an ostensibly plainer but more subtly charged style. Burrows (1987a, 1987b) finds evidence, in both the dialogue and the narrative of Jane Austen's novels, of movement from a more 'Augustan' to a more fluid style. None of these studies takes airy leaps from the stylistic evidence to the authorial mind. None offers Whiggish metaphors of progress. But within the writings of these authors, they all show consistent changes, in definable directions, over a period of time. If he were able to see such evidence and to conquer his presumable distaste for quantitative procedures, a biographical critic of the older school might feel that the whirligig of time had brought him a small measure of revenge. But when, as can now be foreseen, quantitative stylistics allies itself with cognitive science, the manner in which styles and minds are linked should prove too rigorous to appease such ghosts.

The foregoing pages of this section bear out John B. Smith's forecasts, from 1978, of emerging resemblances between computer-assisted and 'conventional' criticism, each in its many kinds (but with a special affinity in work of a 'formal' or stylistic cast). He also drew attention, however, to broad resemblances between computer-assisted and structuralist criticism, notably in their shared emphasis on the patterning and the relativism of meaning. With the advantage of hindsight, it is possible to see why, in spite of those shared emphases, no marriage actually took place when structuralism was still potent. At a time when the programs available for literary computing could treat only of particulars, the structuralists roamed at large across the world of ideas. Now that this practical difference has less force, some differences of principle are more visible. A single example may suffice: the marking of firm boundaries, especially in binary schemes of categorization, is characteristic of structuralism; the registering of small differences of degree across an unbroken spectrum is characteristic of statistical method and, hence, of the chief forms of computer-assisted criticism.

From the vantage-point of 1991 (itself so soon to become a subject for the wisdom of hindsight), other developments can be conjectured. If, in future, computer-assisted criticism does draw on the legacy of structuralism, it seems likely to gain more from its forerunners, especially the Russian Formalists, than from the French and American structuralists themselves. If, in the second place, the post-structuralist enterprise continues to outlive structuralism, this newer wave of theorists may find advantage in the capacity of the computer to go over the ground in different ways, deconstructing one classificatory model and resolving it into another and yet another. In either event, computer-assisted criticism seems likely to become an ever stronger force in literary studies. With the growth of large stores of machine-readable texts, like the Oxford Archive (see also chapter 1), and with the dissemination of sophisticated programs, critics who seek computer assistance will be relieved of most preparatory work and left free to concentrate on their essential goals. Their goals, one may hope, will include a greater emphasis than ours on the theoretical implications of their work. They should benefit from our limitations and mistakes and they will begin with a better understanding of what computers can and cannot do.

Most of the examples so far given of computer-assisted criticism have testified, among other things, to a concentration upon comparatively narrow topics. With the growth of suitable archives, the most compelling objection to the conduct of wider-ranging studies will be met. If the computer is to contribute as much as it might in literary studies, the wider-ranging studies of the future will need to include much more work than has yet been done on genre differences and on historical changes in the language of literature.

The few existing computer-assisted treatments of those larger topics tend to be succinct, mathematically advanced and based on small samples. These are not discrete characteristics. There is still a dearth of really wide-ranging sets of machine-readable texts within given genres or across any long historical range. Only scholars of genuine statistical skill are equipped to follow Fisher in the analysis of small samples. Since these methods do not lend themselves to simple exposition in plain language, those who are capable of using them tend to publish brief technical accounts of their procedures accompanied by terse statements of their findings. Among the best examples of this highly technical work are Brainerd's studies of Shakespearean genres (1979) and of chronological relations among Shakespeare's plays (1980), and Martindale's several studies of evolutionary trends in the language of English poetry (1973, 1981, 1984).

As distinct from the more exploratory work that prevails in computer-assisted (and 'conventional') literary studies, these are experimental analyses in a strictly scientific sense. The results are among the most compelling in the field and deserve to be known, if not fully understood, by a larger literary audience. How can we meet the acute problem of communication between the highly numerate few, the merely numerate minority, and the more or less innumerate majority of literary scholars? It is too optimistic to suppose that, as literary computing advances, we can look forward to so great an advance in numeracy among literary scholars as the proper comprehension of work at this level would entail. The important role played by Cherry (1957) and Campbell (1983) in making the work of Shannon and Weaver (1949) more accessible to innumerate readers suggests a second path, a framing in words of the gist of a mathematical argument. A third but arduous path lies in the establishment of sufficiently large databases to admit the use of simpler and more easily elucidated forms of statistical analysis in those areas of literary history and taxonomy where only the most sophisticated work now flourishes. As the scope of machine-readable archives increases and as optical character-scanners (see chapter 1) become capable of accurate work on the hand-set typefaces of older texts, this third path will become less arduous, less time-consuming and less expensive.

The most thorough quantitative account of the history of the language of English literature produced before the advent of computers is that of Miles

(1964). Her astonishing labours treated of the main classes of content-word (nouns, verbs and adjectives) in 1,000-line samples of the poetry of 200 poets ranging across six centuries. Her suggestive but primitive ways of presenting the data are complemented by a more searching reassessment by Ross (1977). Ross's little study has the further merit of sketching the problems of definition that arise from the interpenetration of three sorts of differentiae. As we have seen, authorial styles can be distinguished from each other with increasing confidence. The differences that arise when an author changes genres can also be assessed. But differences between authors of different eras and changes, over time, within a given genre are coloured by more general chronological changes in the language of literature and presumably in the language as a whole. Yet a study of those more general changes must treat of them as they manifest themselves in the writings of particular authors working in stagnant or evolving genres. A proper analysis, that is to say, must somehow steer through powerful cross-currents. There is yet another difficulty: when 'genres are defined empirically, on the basis of underlying linguistic and stylistic patterns . . . they do not necessarily follow labelled genres – the odes by Keats are different from poems with the same label by Wordsworth' (Ross, 1977: 53).

The data shown in graphs 7.3 and 7.4 represent an attempt to meet these difficulties. The present selection from a somewhat larger corpus of specimens amounts to over a million word-tokens by forty authors ranging from Defoe to the present day, as listed in table 7.1. (Delays in being granted some copyright permissions require the omission, from the present discussion, of further twentieth-century authors.) The smallest authorial sets comprise around 8,500

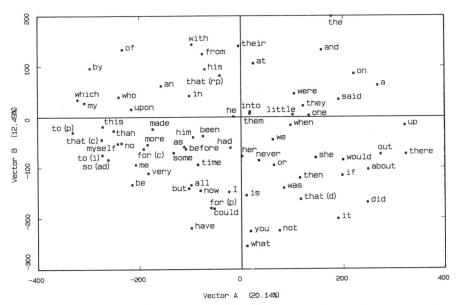

Graph 7.3   Forty 'historians': word-plot (for the seventy-five most common word-types of the corpus)

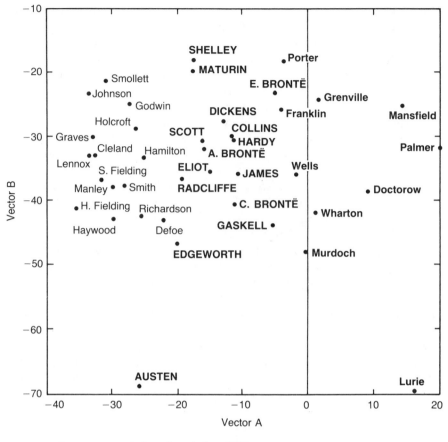

Lower case = Authors born before 1760
UPPER CASE = Authors born between 1760 and 1850
Lower case = Authors born after 1850

Graph 7.4   Forty 'historians' (based on the seventy-five most common
word-types of the corpus)

word-tokens; the largest, around 75,000. The texts are all retrospective
fictional narratives, couched in the first person and treating of the narrator's
supposed experiences or observations. Only the narrator's own words are
incorporated in the analysis. Most of the narratives are embedded in larger
works of fiction: but in some of the more recent texts, the outer narrative frame
is only lightly sketched; and in a few texts, like Defoe's, there is none. The
composition of the corpus was not carefully designed save for a conscious
attempt to keep the number of male and female writers roughly equal and,
ultimately, to fill any large gaps in the historical sequence. The whole set of data
was subjected to the same form of analysis as was described earlier, when
Smollett was being examined. The results of correlating the seventy-five most

common word-types, well over half of all the word-tokens in each text, are shown in graphs 7.3 and 7.4.

The most striking feature of graph 7.4 is its grouping of authors by era in the roughly continuous line of chronological change shown on the horizontal axis, the most powerful vector deriving from the matrix. Among the few noteworthy anachronisms, Defoe, Richardson and Mrs Gaskell are all 'ahead of their time'. My marking of boundaries at 1760 and 1850 is neither arbitrary nor premediatated but an empirical response to the evidence as it emerged. Within this 'population' (as also in some preliminary trials on personal letters of that period), the former boundary seems to mark a large change in the language of writers born after 1760, who began to publish around the turn of the century. Those born in the 1760s and 1770s (Mrs Radcliffe, Maria Edgeworth, Sir Walter Scott and Jane Austen) all lie along the line of demarcation, separated even from their nearest predecessors.

The latter boundary, set at 1850, falls in a period during which the 'history' was out of fashion: few notable writers of these first-person narratives were born between Collins in 1824 and the end of the century. Yet my evidence suggests that, while the 'history' lay dormant, the language of English fiction (like the English language generally?) continued its passage towards modern vernacularity. The highly vernacular first-person narratives of Mrs Gaskell, who was born in 1810, set her almost at the edge of the modern cluster. The comparatively formal styles of some more recent writers carry them back towards the nineteenth-century cluster. But neither in the cases shown here nor among the others I have more tentatively examined does even a single member of the nineteenth century or the modern cluster intrude into the other territory. Thus the evidence, overall, is not of an abrupt transition in the language like that which seems to have occurred in the latter part of the eighteenth century, but of slower processes of change.

Graph 7.3 illustrates these processes. The word-types lying at the western, or eighteenth-century, end of the spectrum include the relative pronouns *who* and *which*, the conjunction *that*, most of the common prepositions, and several common intensifiers. Those lying towards the eastern, or modern extremity include *and*, *then*, such adverbial particles as *up*, *out*, and *about*, and (as was noted earlier) *it* and *there*, which often serve as 'place-holders'. The decreasing incidence, over three centuries, of those two relative pronouns (used chiefly in embedded adjectival clauses) and the major prepositions (often used for the post-modification of nouns, as in 'a man of sense' rather than 'a sensible man') gives evidence of a change from a more complex to a less highly wrought syntax. The idea is upheld by the increasing incidence of *and* and *then* and also by the likelihood that *that* declines in frequency because it is so often deleted nowadays. The increasing use of particles marks a change from latinate verbs like *exclude* and *surrender* to two-part verbs like *leave out* and *give up*. The decreasing use of specific intensifiers (like *very*, *more* and *so*) seems to mark a change from a small set of fixed forms like these to a much larger set, individually less common, of vogue-words like *absolutely*, *completely*, *perfectly* and *totally*.

When the first-person narrative revives, there is some evidence of a subtle change in genre. The wide separation between *I* and *me/myself/my* in graph 7.3 is in keeping with my impression as a reader that, in its modern form, the 'history' no longer treats so much of 'what happened to me' as of 'what I saw'. The easterly location of *the* and *a* (but not of *an*, for a reason given earlier) supports my impression: 'what I saw' often treats of *things* rather than persons observed whereas, in the earlier texts, 'what happened to me' often emphasizes 'what he did to me' and treats of real or threatened sorts of personal exploitation. In the latter part of the nineteenth century, 'what I saw' commonly deals in experiences of the supernatural and the fantastic. But, in our own century and especially recently, first-person narrative seems to have re-entered the literary mainstream. Very often, however, these new 'histories' present their own narrators ironically and explicitly project themselves as fictive.

The vertical axis of graph 7.4, representing the second most powerful vector, distinguishes between the most 'monologic' and the most 'dialogic' of the narratives. The contrast, naturally, is clearest in the extreme cases. Jane Austen's Brandon, Willoughby and Mrs Smith recount their 'histories' to very active interlocutors. In the texts by Mary Shelley and Charles Robert Maturin, on the other hand, the narrators, once in motion, continue almost uninter-rupted to the end. Even though the analysis treats only of the words of the narrator, the presence of an active interlocutor is marked by a high incidence of 'response-words' like *what* and *you* and *not*, as shown by their locations at the southern extremity of graph 7.3.

Graph 7.4 suggests interesting possibilities for further inquiry. The modern writers shown here (like the dozen others whose work has been examined but cannot yet be included) differ more sharply from each other than the eighteenth- or nineteenth-century writers (except Jane Austen) differ from their contemporaries. The five Antipodean writers form a little cluster in the top corner. The American writers so far studied differ more sharply from earlier writers and from each other than do the twentieth-century British. And, finally, the lack of any consistent separation of male from female writers in the modern set is something not merely to be registered in its own right. Their indistinguishability in gender and their scattering in other respects act as forces powerful enough to obliterate the clear differences between their male and female predecssors, which were shown in graph 7.2 and which, with two notable exceptions in Emily Brontë and Mary Shelley, could also be shown in the nineteenth-century set.

These last few reflections on the overall shape of graph 7.4 are in keeping, I should suppose, with what most good readers of fiction would say, for example, of the comparative homogeneity of eighteenth-century prose and the comparat-ive diversity of national, regional and personal styles in our own time. There is no reason to suppose that those readers would expect such a picture to emerge from a statistical analysis of the most colourless word-types in the language. The point that deserves a closing emphasis is that, in this method of analysis, the word-types are allowed to 'choose' themselves, to interrelate at their 'choice', and to show up **whatever** mutual patterning is most influential as an expression of resemblances and differences within a given set of texts. Graph 7.3, in short, is not a set of discrete entry-points but a closely woven network of meaning of a kind which we have scarcely begun to understand and which no one could have hoped to examine systematically before the advent of computers in literary studies.

Further Reading

In a growing and varied discipline like literary computing, no single work commands the central ground. Two admirable books (Hockey, 1980; Oakman, 1980/1984) and a substantial article (Butler, 1985a), all now a little out of date, survey the field as a whole. A recent collection of essays (Potter, 1989a) focuses on literary criticism. All of these give extensive references. Together with two journals, *Computers and the Humanities* and *Literary and Linguistic Computing*, they constitute a valuable guide to further reading.

Appendix 7.1   Annotated List of 'Minitab' Commands

As applied to Table 7.2, the following set of MINITAB commands will produce a close approximation of Graphs 7.1 and 7.2 (but not an exact replica because – for compact presentation – the percentages shown in Table 7.2 have been rounded to two decimal places.)

```
MTB>   oh 0                      # allow continuous scrolling through loops
MTB>   outfile 'table.out'       # name output file
MTB>   read 'table.doc' c1–c16   # read word frequency data into columns
MTB>   let k1 = no. of rows      # i.e. no. of word-types in 'table.doc'
MTB>   let k2 = no. of columns   #i.e. no. of 'texts', authors, etc. in 'table.doc'
MTB>   execute 'rowprop.mtb'     # use first stored loop described below to
                                 # convert text-percentages of 'table.doc'. to
                                 # decimal fractions of the total of entries in row.

MTB>   let k4 = 400 + k1         # prerequisite for executing 'eigenloop.mtb'
MTB>   set c204                  # set labels for word-types: e.g. 1:50
MTB>   set c304                  # set labels for authors or texts: e.g. 1:16
MTB>   set c305                  # set further group-labels: e.g. male/female
MTB>   execute 'eigenloop.mtb'   # use second stored loop described below to
                                 # perform processes of correlation and eigen
                                 # analysis
                                 # and to make rough line-plots of results
MTB>   stop                      # (unless making use of following optional step)
# OPTIONAL EXTRA STEP: to precede 'stop'.
# To facilitate direct comparisions between graphs, it is often useful to rotate
# a graph upon either or both of its axes. (Graphs 7.1 and 7.2 were rotated vertically.)
```

```
MTB>   let c201 = −1 * c201      # rotate horizontal axis of 'word plot'
MTB>   let c301 = −1 * c301      # rotate horizontal axis of 'text plot'
                                 # likewise c202 and c302 for vertical rotation
```

COMMANDS IN FIRST STORED LOOP: 'rowprop.mtb'

The functions of this loop are: to standardize 'text-percentages' like those of Table 2 by converting them into decimal fractions of the sum of each row; and to transpose the rows and columns so that data for word-types, not texts, can be correlated. The simpler process of correlating text-columns was used in Burrows 1987a.

```
rsum c1-ck2 c100             # calculate divisor for use in conversion
copy c1-ck2 m1
transpose m1 m2
copy m2 c1-ck1               # columns and rows are now transposed
let k3 = 1
noecho
store
let ck3 = ck3/c100(k3)       # convert the first column to decimal fractions
let k3 = k3 + 1              # allow progress to second and later columns
end
print k3
execute the commands k1 times
echo
print c1 ck1                 # show that the procedure is complete
```

COMMANDS IN SECOND STORED LOOP: 'eigenloop.mtb'

The functions of this loop are: to derive a Pearson product-moment correlation matrix from the data; to extract, scale, and compound the principal components of the matrix; and to print rough plots of the results and prepare them for more accurate plotting.

```
echo
copy c1-ck1 m3               # data-table now shown as m3, for later use
correlate c1-ck1 m4          # correlation matrix now in m4
eigen m4 c151 m5             # eigenvectors now in m5, eigenvalues in c151
let k10 = sum(c151)
let c152 = c151/k10
let c153 = 100*c152
let c153 = 100*c153
round c153 c153
let c153 = c153/100
write c151, c153             # eigenvalues now percentages of sum of eigenvalues
copy m5 c401-ck4             # tabulate data in eigenmatrix to allow arithmetic
copy c401-c403 c201-c203
erase c401-ck4
print c153
```

```
let c201 = c201*k1*c153(1)      # weight first eigenvector with its own eigenvalue
                                # and scale results by multiplying by k1 (number of
                                # word-types). This prevents the number of word-
                                # types from acting as an artificial variable.
let c202 = c202*k1*c153(2)      # likewise for second eigenvector
let c203 = c203*k1*c153(3)      # likewise for third eigenvector
write c201-c204                 # print vectors and their word-type labels
lplot c202 c201, c204           # make word-plot for first two vectors: cf. Graph 7.1
lplot c203 c201, c204           # make similar plots for other combinations of vectors
lplot c203 c202, c204
mult m3 m5 m6                    # compound two earlier matrices to give new matrix
                                # in which data for texts are fitted to word-data

copy m6 c401-ck4
copy c401-c403 c301-c303
erase c401-ck4
print k1
print c153
let c301 = c301*k2*10           # scale values of first new vector by multiplying by
                                # k2 (number of texts: cf. corresponding step above);
                                # and by multiplying results by 10 for pure
                                # convenience
let c302 = c302*k2*10           # likewise for second new vector
let c303 = c303*k2*10           # likewise for third new vector
write c301-c305                 # print new vectors and their author- or text-labels
lplot c302 c301, c304           # make text-
lplot c302 c301, c305           plot for first two new vectors: cf. Graph 7.2
lplot c303 c301, c304
lplot c303 c301, c305
lplot c303 c302, c304
lplot c303 c302, c305
```

'HISTORIES' BY FORTY AUTHORS: LIST OF TEXTS AND COPY-RIGHT ACKNOWLEDGEMENTS

Note: the characters named are the narrators of their 'histories'. Extracts marked 'Clr' are taken from the public domain. Those marked 'OUP' are included by permission of Oxford University Press and those marked 'Gld' by permission of Garland Publishing Inc. Others are as specified below.

JANE AUSTEN (1755–1817)

OUP Col. Brandon   *Sense and Sensibility* (1811): ed. Chapman, London, OUP, 1923/1960, pp. 204–11.

OUP Willoughby   *Sense and Sensibility* (1811): ibid., 1923/1960, pp. 319–32.

OUP Mrs Smith   *Persuasion* (1817): ibid., 1923/1959, pp. 198–211.

ANNE BRONTË (1820–49)

Clr   Agnes   *Agnes Grey* (1847): Haworth edn, NY, Harper, 1899–1903, iii.355–87.

Clr   Helen   *The Tenant of Wildfell Hall* (1848): ibid., v.132–65.
Clr   Markham   *The Tenant of Wildfell Hall* (1848): ibid.,
                     vi.471–502.

CHARLOTTE BRONTË (1816–55)

Clr   Crimsworth   *The Professor* (1857): Haworth edn, NY, Harper,
                     1899–1903, v.15–39.
Clr   Louis Moore   *Shirley* (1849): ibid., ii.643–50.
Clr   Robert Moore   *Shirley* (1849): ibid., ii.471–502
Clr   Lucy Snowe   *Villette* (1853): ibid., iii.46–54.
OUP   Rochester   *Jane Eyre* (1847): ed. Smith, London, OUP, 1973,
                     pp. 309–20.

EMILY BRONTË (1818–48)

OUP   Isabella   *Wuthering Heights* (1847): ed. Marsden & Jack,
                     Oxford, Clarendon Press, 1976, pp. 209–25.
OUP   Lockwood   *Wuthering Heights* (1847): ibid., pp. 3–39.
OUP   Nellie   *Wuthering Heights* (1847): ibid., pp. 43–76.

JOHN CLELAND (1709–89)

Gld   Bernard   *Memoirs of a Coxcomb* (1751): New York, Garland,
                     1974, pp. 366–85.
Gld   Coxcomb   *Memoirs of a Coxcomb* (1751): ibid., pp. 100–16.
Clr   Three whores   *Woman of Pleasure* (1748–9): ed. Wagner,
                     Harmondsworth, Penguin, 1985, pp. 134–48.

WILKIE COLLINS (1824–89)

Clr   Betteredge   *The Moonstone* (1868): New York, Random House,
                     nd, pp. 11–32.
OUP   Fairlie   *The Woman in White* (1860): ed. Sucksmith,
                     London, OUP, 1975, pp. 309–27.
OUP   Gilmore   *The Woman in White* (1860): ibid. pp. 113–44.
OUP   Miss Halcombe *The Woman in White* (1860): ibid., pp. 161–203.
OUP   Hartright   *The Woman in White* (1860): ibid., pp. 21–60.
OUP   Mrs Michelson *The Woman in White* (1860): ibid., pp. 327–66.

DANIEL DEFOE (1660–1731)

OUP   Cavalier   *Memoirs of a Cavalier* (1720): ed. Boulton, London,
                     OUP, 1972, pp. 204–18.
OUP   Crusoe 1   *Robinson Crusoe* (1719): ed. Gowley, London,
                     OUP, 1972, pp. 40–53.
OUP   Crusoe 2   *Robinson Crusoe* (1719): ibid., pp. 200–9.
OUP   Moll 1   *Moll Flanders* (1722): ed. Starr, London, OUP,
                     1971, pp. 18–42.
OUP   Moll 2   *Moll Flanders* (1722): ibid., pp. 206–24.
OUP   Roxana   *Roxana* (1724): ed. Jane Jack, OUP, 1964, pp.
                     54–82.

CHARLES DICKENS (1812–70)

OUP   Convict   *Pickwick Papers* (1837): Illustrated edn., London,
                     OUP, 1948, pp. 74–81.

OUP	Stroller	*Pickwick Papers* (1837): ibid., pp. 35–40.
OUP	Miss Wade	*Little Dorrit* (1855–7): ed. Sucksmith, OUP, 1979, pp. 644–51.

E. L. DOCTOROW (1931–)

	Blue	*Welcome to Hard Times* (1961): London, Pan Books, 1977, pp. 135–55: by permission of André Deutsch Ltd.
	Daniel	*The Book of Daniel* (1972): London, Pan Books, 1982, pp. 31–44: by permission of Macmillan Ltd.
	Paterson	*Loon Lake* (1979): London, Pan Books, 1981, pp. 225–35: by permission of Macmillan Ltd.

MARIA EDGEWORTH (1767–1849)

Clr	Thady	*Castle Rackrent* (1800): London, Macmillan, 1895, pp. 1–24.
Clr	Lady Davenant	*Helen* (1834): London, Macmillan, 1896, pp. 62–88.
Clr	Lady Delacour	*Belinda* (1801): London, Baldwin & Cradock, 1833, i.43–90.
	Moriarty	*Ormond* (1817): ed. Jeffares, Shannon, IUP, 1972, pp. 368–75: by permission of Irish Academic Press.

GEORGE ELIOT (1819–80)

Clr	Hetty	*Adam Bede* (1859): Standard edn, Edinburgh, Blackwood, nd, ii.247–52.
Clr	Latimer	'The Lifted Veil' (1859): in *Silas Marner* etc., ibid., pp. 280–341.
Clr	Mirah	*Daniel Deronda* (1874–6): ibid., ii.13–37.

HENRY FIELDING (1707–54)

	Man of Hill	*Tom Jones* (1749): ed. Battestin & Bowers, Wesleyan edn, 1975, pp. 451–80; and
	Mrs Fitzptr'k	*Tom Jones* (1749): ibid., pp. 581–601: extracts by permission of University Press of New England.
Clr	Mrs Heartfree	*Jonathan Wild* (1743): ed. Henley, New York, Barnes & Noble, nd, ii.165–88.
Clr	Julian	*A Journey* (1743): ibid., ii.252–81.
OUP	Wilson	*Joseph Andrews* (1742): ed. Battestin, Oxford, Clarendon Press, 1967, pp. 201–25.
OUP	Capt. Booth	*Amelia* (1751): ed. Battestin, Oxford, Clarendon Press, 1983, i.66–150.
OUP	Miss Mathews	*Amelia* (1751): ibid., i.47–60.
OUP	Mrs Bennet	*Amelia* (1751): ibid., ii.268–303.

SARAH FIELDING (1710–68)

Clr	Camilla	*David Simple* (1st edn 1744): i.253–78, ii.1–52.
Clr	Cynthia	*David Simple* (1st edn 1744): i.188–227.
Clr	Daniel	*David Simple* (1st edn 1744): ii.283–93.

Clr   Isabelle   *David Simple* (1st edn 1744): ii.100–208.
Gld   Cleopatra   *Cleopatra & Octavia* (1757): New York, Garland, 1974, pp. 7–176.
Gld   Octavia   *Cleopatra & Octavia* (1957): ibid., pp. 177–219.

MILES FRANKLIN (1879–1954)

Sybylla 1   *My Brilliant Career* (1901): Sydney, Angus & Robertson, 1980, pp. 42–58; and
Sybylla 2   *My Brilliant Career* (1901): ibid., pp. 126–41; and
Budgery   *Prelude to Waking* (1950): Sydney, Angus & Robertson, 1950, pp. 47–62: extracts by permission of Collins Angus & Robertson.
Sybylla 3   *My Career Goes Bung*, Melbourne, Georgian House, 1946, pp. 114–63: by permission of Georgian House Ltd.

ELIZABETH GASKELL (1810–65)

Clr   Cynthia   *Wives and Daughters* (1866): Knutsford edn, London, Smith Elder, 1906, pp. 542–52.
Clr   Half brother   *My Lady Ludlow* etc. (1858): ibid., pp. 391–404.
Clr   Job   *Mary Barton* (1848): ibid., pp. 114–24.
Clr   Lady Ludlow   *My Lady Ludlow* (1858): ibid., pp. 60–124.
Clr   Matty   *Cranford & Other Tales* (1853): ibid., pp. 60–71.
Clr   Middleton   *Cranford & Other Tales* (1853): ibid., pp. 384–409.
Clr   Nurse   *Cranford & Other Tales* (1853): ibid., pp. 422–45.
Clr   Sally   *Ruth* (1853): ibid., pp. 163–9.

WILLIAM GODWIN (1756–1836)

OUP Caleb   *Caleb Williams* (1794): ed. McCracken, London, OUP, 1970, pp. 288–303.
Gld   Ruffigny   *Fleetwood* (1805): New York, Garland, 1979, i.210–300, ii.1–73.
Gld   Scarborough   *Fleetwood* (1805): ibid., iii.286–325.

RICHARD GRAVES (1715–1804)

OUP Miss Townsend *The Spiritual Quixote* (1773): ed. Tracy, London, OUP, 1967, pp. 79–98.
OUP Graham   *The Spiritual Quixote* (1773): ibid., pp. 131–5.
OUP Mrs Booby   *The Spiritual Quixote* (1773): ibid., pp. 149–54.
OUP Rivers   *The Spiritual Quixote* (1773): ibid., pp. 187–223.
OUP Johnson   *The Spiritual Quixote* (1773): ibid., pp. 286–93.

KATE GRENVILLE (1950–)

Lilian 1   *Lilian's Story*, Sydney, Allen & Unwin, 1985, pp. 114–22; and
Lilian 2   *Lilian's Story*, ibid., pp. 177–83: extracts by permission of George Allen & Unwin Ltd.
Louise   *Dreamhouse*, Brisbane, University of Queensland Press, 1986, pp. 54–68; and

	Joan	*Joan Makes History*, Brisbane, University of Queensland Press, 1988, pp. 249–62: extracts by permission of University of Queensland Press.

ELIZABETH HAMILTON (1758–1816)

Gld	Delmond	*Modern Philosophers* (1800): ed. Luria, New York, Garland, 1974, i.118–51.
Gld	Bridgetina	*Modern Philosophers* (1800): ibid., ii.80–97.
Gld	Julia	*Modern Philosophers* (1800): ibid., iii.306–26.
Gld	Mrs Mason	*Cottagers of Glenburnie* (1808): ed. Luria, New York, Garland, 1974, pp. 24–115.
Gld	Mary Stewart	*Cottagers of Glenburnie* (1808): ibid., pp. 298–320.

THOMAS HARDY (1840–1928)

Clr	Lady Icenway	*Noble Dames* (1891): Library edn., London, Macmillan, 1952–60, pp. 137–74.
Clr	Lady Petrick	*Noble Dames* (1891): ibid., pp. 153–63.
Clr	Manston	*Desperate Remedies* (1871): ibid., pp. 432–8.
Clr	Pierston	*The Well-Beloved* (1897): ibid., pp. 33–8.
Clr	Selby	*Wessex Tales* (1888): ibid., pp. 33–41.

ELIZA HAYWOOD (1693?–1756)

Gld	Miss Forward	*Betsy Thoughtless* (1751): New York, Garland, 1979, i.144–79.
Gld	Mrs M.	*Jemmy & Jenny Jessamy* (1755): New York, Garland, 1974, i.260–83.
Gld	Mrs Welby 1	*Jemmy & Jenny Jessamy* (1755): ibid., ii.109–42.
Gld	Celia	*Jemmy & Jenny Jessamy* (1755): ibid., ii.241–56.
Gld	Sophia	*Jemmy & Jenny Jessamy* (1755): ibid., iii.132–73.
Gld	Mrs Welby 2	*Jemmy & Jenny Jessamy* (1755): ibid., iii.290–304.
	Eunuch	*Philidore & Placentia* (1727): in *Four Before Richardson*, ed. McBurney, Lincoln, U. of Nebraska, 1963, pp. 195–208; and
	Placentia	*Philidore & Placentia* (1727): ibid., pp. 213–20: extracts by permission of University of Nebraska Press.

THOMAS HOLCROFT (1745–1809)

OUP	Henley	*Anna St Ives* (1792): ed. Faulkner, London, OUP, 1970, pp. 443–64.
OUP	Miss Wilmot	*Hugh Trevor* (1794): ed. Deane, London, OUP, 1973, pp. 192–208.
OUP	Wilmot	*Hugh Trevor* (1794): ibid., pp. 231–51.

HENRY JAMES (1843–1916)

Clr	Mrs Bread	*The American* (1st edn 1877): London, Macmillan, 1883, ii. 136–49.
Clr	Lady Emma	'Maud-Evelyn' (1900): *The Complete Tales*, ed. Edel, London, Hart-Davis, 1962–4, xi.44–75.

Clr Godfather   'Last of the Valerii' (1874): ibid., iii.89–122.
Clr Governess   'Master Eustace' (1871): ibid., ii.341–73.
Clr Painter   'The Special Type' (1900): ibid., xi.171–92.

SAMUEL JOHNSON (1709–84)

Clr Hymenaeus   *The Rambler*, Nos 113, 115: *Works*, 12 vols,
                         London, 1810, v.265–71, 278–84.
Clr Misella   *The Rambler*, Nos 170–1: ibid., vi.175–88.
Clr Captator   *The Rambler*, Nos 197–8: ibid., vi.327–38.
Clr Betty Broom   *The Idler*, Nos 26, 29: ibid., vii.101–4, 113–16.
OUP Imlac   *Rasselas* (1759): ed. Tillotson & Jenkins, London,
                         OUP, 1971, pp. 20–37.
OUP Pekuah   *Rasselas* (1759): ibid., pp. 97–106.

CHARLOTTE LENNOX (1720–1804)

OUP Sir George   *The Female Quixote* (1752): ed. Dalziel, London,
                         OUP, 1970, pp. 209–52.
OUP Cynecia   *The Female Quixote* (1752): ibid., pp. 343–7.
Gld Henrietta   *Henrietta* (1758): New York, Garland, 1974, pp.
                         41–170.

ALISON LURIE (1926–   )

     Garrett   *The Truth about Lorin Jones* (1988): London,
                         Sphere Books, 1988, pp. 91–124; and
     Mumpson   *Foreign Affairs* (1984): London, Sphere Books,
                         1986, pp. 70–1, 119–26, 155–7, 165–8, 172–5;
                         and
     Zimmern   *Imaginary Friends* (1967): Harmondsworth,
                         Penguin, 1978, pp. 7–29:
                         UK rights for extracts by permission of A. P. Watt
                         Ltd, on behalf of the author; US rights by
                         permission of the Melanie Jackson Agency, New
                         York.

MARY DE LA RIVIERE MANLEY (1663–1724)

Gld Baroness   *New Atalantis* (1709): New York, Garland, 1972,
                         i.133–41.
Gld Elonora   *New Atalantis* (1709): ibid., ii.61–109.
Gld Delia   *New Atalantis* (1709): ibid., ii.181–91.
Gld Lovemore   *Adventures of Rivella* (1714): New York, Garland,
                         1972, pp. 16–31.

KATHERINE MANSFIELD (1888–1923)

                         'Poison', in *The Stories of Katherine Mansfield*, ed.
                         Alpers, Auckland, OUP, 1984, pp. 377–82; and
                         'The Lady's Maid', ibid., pp. 382–6; and
                         'Epilogue I-III', ibid., pp. 137–50; and
                         'An Indiscreet Journey', ibid., pp. 179–91: extracts
                         within public domain in UK; US rights applied
                         for.

C. R. MATURIN (1782–1824)

Clr	Annibal	*The Fatal Revenge* (1807): New York, Arno Press facsimile, 1974, ii.250–74.
Clr	Ildefonsa	*The Fatal Revenge* (1807): ibid., iii.169–77.
OUP	Alonzo	*Melmoth the Wanderer* (1820): ed. Grant, London, OUP, 1968, pp. 73–118.
OUP	Guzman	*Melmoth the Wanderer* (1820): ibid., pp. 399–434.
OUP	Stanton	*Melmoth the Wanderer* (1820): ibid., pp. 28–60.

IRIS MURDOCH (1919–   )

Julius	*A Fairly Honourable Defeat*, London, Chatto & Windus, 1970, pp. 361–7; and
Jake	*Under the Net*, London, Chatto & Windus, 1954, pp. 31–54; and
Hilary 1	*A Word Child*, London, Chatto & Windus, 1975, pp. 17–24; and
Hilary 2	*A Word Child*, ibid., pp. 111–25; and
Crystal	*A Word Child*, ibid., pp. 248–54: extracts by permission of Chatto & Windus Ltd.

VANCE PALMER (1885–1959)

Boy	'Mathieson's Wife', in *Let the Birds Fly*, Sydney, Angus & Robertson, 1955, pp. 3–21; and
Young Blue	'The Red Truck', ibid., pp. 36–52; and
Foreigner	'The Search', ibid., pp. 53–61: extracts by permission of Collins Angus & Robertson.

HAL PORTER (1911–84)

Hal-pal	'Party Forty-Two and Mrs Brewer', in *Selected Stories*, Sydney, Angus & Robertson, 1971, pp. 132–45; and
Dulling	'Princess Jasmine-Flower', ibid., pp. 157–68; and
Only son	'Francis Silver', ibid., pp. 210–20; and
Marcus	'Gretel', ibid., pp. 233–46: extracts by permission of Collins Angus & Robertson.

ANN RADCLIFFE (1764–1823)

Clr	Louisa	*A Sicilian Romance* (1790): New York, Arno Press facsimile, 1972, i.64–79.
Clr	Cornelia	*A Sicilian Romance* (1790): ibid., ii.32–45.
Clr	Adeline	*The Romance of the Forest* (1791): New York, Arno Press facsimile, 1974, i.78–96.
OUP	Dorothée	*The Mysteries of Udolpho* (1794): ed. Dobrée, London, OUP, 1966, pp. 523–35.
OUP	Ludovico	*The Mysteries of Udolpho* (1794): ibid., pp. 631–6.

SAMUEL RICHARDSON (1689–1761)

OUP	Grandison	*Sir Charles Grandison* (1753–4): ed. Harris, London, OUP, 1972, iii.116–31.

Mr B. 1   *Pamela* (1740–41): London, Dent, nd, ii.102–19; and

Mr B. 2   *Pamela* (1740–41): ibid., ii.325–32; and

Clarissa   *Clarissa* (1747–8): London, Dent, nd, iii.353–72: extracts by permission of J. M. Dent and Everyman's Library.

WALTER SCOTT (1771–1832)

OUP Elspeth   *The Antiquary* (1816): London, Henry Frowde, OUP, 1912, pp. 362–72.

OUP Hermione   *Fortunes of Nigel* (1822): ibid., pp. 289–302.

OUP Holdenough   *Woodstock* (1826): ibid., pp. 252–62.

OUP Wand'ng Willie   *Redgauntlet* (1824): ibid., pp. 123–46.

OUP Maxwell   *Redgauntlet* (1824): ibid., pp. 295–301.

OUP Nanty Ewart   *Redgauntlet* (1824): ibid., pp. 337–43.

OUP Lilias   *Redgauntlet* (1824): ibid., pp. 393–409.

OUP Menteith   *A Legend of Montrose* (1819): ibid., pp. 39–47.

OUP Staunton   *The Heart of Midlothian* (1818): ibid., pp. 389–99.

MARY SHELLEY (1797–1851)

OUP Frankenstein   *Frankenstein* (1818): ed. Joseph, London, OUP, 1969, pp. 31–49.

OUP Monster   *Frankenstein* (1818): ibid., pp. 102–44.

'The Sisters of Albano' (1828): *Collected Tales and Stories*, ed. Robinson, Baltimore, Johns Hopkins, 1976, pp. 51–64; and

'The Mourner' (1829): ibid., pp. 81–99; and

'Transformation' (1831): ibid., pp. 121–35: extracts by permission of Johns Hopkins University Press.

CHARLOTTE SMITH (1749–1806)

OUP Adelina   *Emmeline* (1788): ed. Ehrenpreis, London, OUP, 1971, pp. 206–25.

OUP Monimia   *The Old Manor House* (1793): ibid., pp. 470–89.

Gld Medora   *The Young Philosophers* (1798): New York, Garland, 1974, iv.203–315.

TOBIAS SMOLLETT (1721–71)

OUP Miss Williams   *Roderick Random* (1748): ed. Boucé, London, OUP, 1979, pp. 117–36.

OUP Melopoyn   *Roderick Random* (1748): ibid., pp. 379–96.

OUP Cadwallader   *Peregrine Pickle* (1751): ed. Clifford, London, OUP, 1979, pp. 383–7.

OUP L. of Quality   *Peregrine Pickle* (1751): ibid., 1979, pp. 432–538.

OUP McKercher   *Peregrine Pickle* (1751): ibid., 1979, pp. 692–732.

OUP Clarke   *Sir Launcelot Greaves* (1762): ed. Evans, London, OUP, 1979, pp. 18–50.

OUP Zelos　　　　　　　*Ferdinand Count Fathom* (1753): ed. Grant, London, OUP, 1979, pp. 110–26.

　　H. G. WELLS (1866–1946)

　　Wallace　　　　　'The Door in the Wall', *The Short Stories of H. G. Wells*, London, Benn: OUP, Melb., nd, pp. 144–61; and

　　Lieutenant　　　'The Flying Man', ibid., pp. 245–51; and

　　Clayton　　　　'The Inexperienced Ghost', ibid., pp. 899–912; and

　　Jimmy　　　　　'Jimmy Goggles the God', ibid., pp. 913–26: extracts by permission of A. P. Watt Ltd., on behalf of the Literary Executors of the Estate of H. G. Wells.

　　EDITH WHARTON (1862–1937)

Clr　Old Man　　　'The Duchess at Prayer', *Crucial Instances*, New York, Scribner, 1901, pp. 8–32.

Clr　Curator　　　'The Rembrandt', ibid., pp. 123–49.

Clr　Culwin　　　'The Eyes', *The Ghost Stories of Edith Wharton*, London, Constable, nd, pp. 28–46.

Clr　Cora　　　　'The Looking Glass', ibid., pp. 232–50.

Acknowledgements

My research could not have been conducted without generous support from the Australian Research Council and the University of Newcastle, New South Wales. The computer package employed for the analysis forms part of MINITAB (University of Pennsylvania). I owe more personal debts to several colleagues, especially Alexis Antonia, David Hoole, Sandra Britz and Nicole Cox for their work in the preparation and analysis of the texts. N. M. McLaren of Cambridge University, N. Collis-George of the University of Sydney, and C. S. Wallace of Monash University have given valuable statistical advice at different times. The responsibility for any errors and misjudgements remains my own.

Notes

1　The seminal text is Shannon and Weaver (1949). For an early account of the linguistic applications of the model, see Cherry (1957) and for an account of many recent applications, see Campbell (1983).

2　In a notable departure from the consensus of praise for Milic's book, Fish (1980) takes it as a signal example of the failings of stylistics. But Milic (1985) convincingly defends himself and the methods of stylistics.

3　For two succinct appraisals, see Stevenson (1989) and Thomson (1989). For admirably lucid introductions to statistical method, listed in order of increasing difficulty, see Kenny (1982), Butler (1985b) and Brainerd (1974).

4   Morton's methods, as represented in his own work and in that of Merriam (1982), have been severely criticized for their statistical shortcomings, notably by M. W. A. Smith (1985). See also Merriam (1986); Stevenson (1989) and Thomson (1989).

5   *New Essays by Henry Fielding*, ed. Martin C. Battestin, with a stylometric analysis by Michael G. Farringdon (1989). Compare Battestin's Table of Contents, pp. vii-viii, with Farringdon's summary of his results, pp. 561–2. For some reason, Farringdon also expresses reservations about two further essays, which are not among Battestin's set of confident attributions.

6   For an authoritative comment and further references, see *Peregrine Pickle*, ed. James L. Clifford (1964), pp. xvi–xviii, xxxii, 793–801.

8 Computers and Textual Editing

Wilhelm Ott

Reliable editions of literary texts are the basis without which scholarly research in the text-based disciplines would be impossible. History of language, historical lexicography, metrical studies, stylistic analysis, interpretations of literary/philosophical/theological works rely on them and on the exactness, precision and completeness of text and apparatus they offer. It is no wonder, therefore, that – though they range among the most expensive undertakings in the humanities – many editing projects are being undertaken: for German texts dating from the eighth to the sixteenth century alone, *Germanistik* 31 (1990) 234–42 lists 335 current edition projects.

For the same reason, the possibility of mechanizing single steps necessary in the course of preparing a critical edition was being discussed even before computers capable of handling textual data were available. The Hinman Collator, an opto-mechanical device developed in the 1940s by Charlton Hinman (see Hinman, 1947), and used by him for the internal collation of more than eighty volumes of the First Folio Edition of Shakespeare's works, is perhaps the best-known example of such mechanical aids.

In the meantime, electronic data processing has revolutionized not only the sciences, but with some delay also research in the humanities. With the help of computers, not only so-called internal collation, the purpose of which was to detect variations in different copies of the same printing, but also the collation of different versions of the same text became feasible. The pioneer in this field was Vinton A. Dearing, who since 1962 has used computer programs to collate (manually pre-sorted) corresponding lines of up to 99 different versions of a text.

It is not the purpose of this chapter to give a detailed history of computer applications to textual editing, especially since good overviews are available (see Love, 1971; Oakman, 1975; Hockey, 1980, Butler, 1985c, 1990; additional information may be found in the reports on various conferences on this subject: CNRS, 1979; Catach, 1988; Schwob, Kranich-Hofbauer and Suntinger, 1989; for the first two decades of computer-aided textual criticism, see also the bibliography by Ott, 1980, covering the period until March 1983; a more recent systematic approach is found in Shillingsburg, 1986). I therefore prefer to concentrate on the methodological and technical aspects of computer applications to the preparation of critical editions and to do this against the background of the experiences of my group at the University of Tübingen and of the tools we have developed here.

Of course, every edition has its own special problems, depending on the genre of the text and on the time in which it was written. There are fundamental differences between the methods required for editing an ancient text, where the oldest surviving manuscripts are younger, perhaps by several centuries, than the lost autograph of the author, and the methods applied when editing texts of the nineteenth or twentieth century, where the first printed editions and the author's manuscripts are both available. Despite these differences, there are many technical problems which are common to every editorial project. At least since Helmut Praschek published *Die Technifizierung der Edition – Möglichkeiten und Grenzen* (Mechanization of the Edition – Possibilities and Limits) in 1965, it has become common in discussions like this one to break up the editing process itself into several successive and logical distinct steps and to consider the ways in which the computer may be able to help at each stage (cf. Love, 1971; Ott, 1973ff; Howard-Hill, 1973; Hockey, 1980; Oakman, 1980; Butler, 1985c, 1990). In Ott, Gabler and Sappler (1982), we distinguished the following eight steps in the preparation of a critical edition:

1　Collection and preliminary listing of the witnesses (manuscripts, early quotations; for more modern texts: drafts, autographs, early editions).
2　Collation of the texts to discover variants.
3　Evaluation of the results of collation (genealogy; final listing of witnesses to be considered for the edition; selection of variants to be included in the apparatus).
4　Constitution of the copy text.
5　Compilation of the critical and historical apparatuses.
6　Preparation of indexes.
7　Preparation of the printer's copy from the results of 4, 5 and 6.
8　Publication of text, apparatuses, indexes.

For Praschek, these steps have to be preceded by the definition and elaboration of the editorial principles valid for the current project. Laying down, first of all, the principles and requirements of the work is, of course, necessary not only for editions, but for all kinds of scholarly work. The fact that it may be necessary to refine or revise them during the progress of the work is no objection to this basic rule – which sometimes seems to be forgotten when a project relies essentially on computer applications. The starting point should not be what it is possible for the computer to do, but what is required by the discipline. The computer can supply neither the relevant questions nor the methods; nor can it take over the responsibility for the results. Professional scholarship in the humanities profits most from the computer when it takes it seriously in its role as a tool and does not misuse it as a problem-supplying and problem-solving device. The tool, however, should be mastered.

Fortunately enough, in the preparation of a critical edition, there are a lot of technical tasks and problems to be carried out which can be substantially supported by approved computer methods and existing software.

8.1 Publishing

Let us start with the last of the eight steps listed above, the publication of the results of the editorial effort of often a whole team of scholars over a period of many years. In the not too distant past, a 'manuscript' or typescript of the edition (preface, text, apparatuses, indexes) had to be given to the publishing company. There, a new transcription had to be made on some keyboard, if single letter typesetting was not used. New errors similar to those which had been eliminated by the editor's efforts over years were likely to be introduced in this new copy.

Typesetting errors were unavoidable not only in critical editions, and well-established procedures were followed in order to eliminate them before printing. For critical editions, more care and effort is required for this step than for 'ordinary' books like novels or scholarly monographs, where the redundancy of natural language is able to make up for many a misprint without real loss of information. The main purpose of a critical edition is to present the exact wording of the text as intended by the author, or as existing at a given time, and to provide reliable documentation of the variants of its transmission or of the different forms the text showed during its genesis. Even subtleties like differences in punctuation or the replacement of a single letter, perhaps changing indicative mood to subjunctive, are essential. The worth and usefulness of a critical edition depend entirely on the reliability and correctness of the text and apparatus.

8.1.1 *Electronic typesetting*

The development of technology in the past twenty-five years has made it possible for this last step in the preparation of an edition to lose much of its drudgery. Since the mid-1960s, typesetting can be done automatically from a 'manuscript' recorded by computer on paper tape (for hot metal TTS typesetting machines which were available since the 1930s) or on a magnetic data carrier (tape, disk) for third-generation phototypesetting machines, which also eliminated the – still possible – risks of mechanical errors of paper-tape-driven equipment. No wonder therefore that Harold Love, in 1970, spoke of a 'revolutionary element', of an area where the computer was not only 'streamlining old methods', but in which the editing process itself was beginning to 'show fundamental modifications', when he discussed the possibility – at that time, according to his knowledge, untested by an editor – of 'the text being assembled on magnetic tape and set by the computer itself' (Love, 1971: 55). Shillingsburg repeats this view: 'at its best, it has the potential to revolutionize scholarly editing and publishing' (Shillingsburg, 1986: 138).

It is interesting to look also at the possible disadvantages which both authors saw: according to Love, 'the only drawback is that one would not in the present state of printing technology end up with quite so handsome a piece of book-production' (p. 56) – a fear that has been realized to an extent he perhaps did not foresee. The reason today is, however, not the current state of printing technology, but the 'do-it-yourself' attitude of hobby homeworkers among humanities scholars (supported by the relevant advertising of the desk-top-publishing industry) who believe that they can do not only without professional typesetting equipment but also without typographic training and experience. It is one of the merits of Shillingsburg's book to have drawn attention to the necessity of involving 'craftsmanship and design and the ability to attend to the details of the typesetting and book-designing trades' (p. 148). These are the problems that will remain even when the rest of the technical problems (like incompatibilities between the computer of the editor and that of the publishing house, and between the corresponding software packages, which Shillingsburg (pp. 150ff) mentions) have become obsolete.

8.1.2   Page Make-up

In addition to the absolute requirement that a critical edition must not contain misprints, typesetting critical editions poses technical problems which other scholarly publications do not have. And since the setting of critical editions is normally not the daily bread-and-butter business of composing firms, this may – at least at present – still lead to problems.

One of the problems when typesetting editions is the pagination and the setting of the apparatuses, of which often more than one is found at the bottom of the page – sometimes in addition to normal footnotes. Unlike normal footnotes, apparatuses cannot be broken into lines before pagination. Critical apparatuses are traditionally printed not like footnotes in scholarly monographs, where each footnote starts on a new line, but as blocks of text with justified right margins, leaving a bit more blank space between the single notes within the line. It is done that way because the single entries are, in comparison with normal footnotes, usually rather short: they often fill only a quarter or half of a line. Setting them in single lines would not only look ugly, but would consume a lot of space. Editions which show many variant readings in the apparatus would become significantly more voluminous and more expensive.

A further peculiarity of critical apparatuses for prose texts is that the single annotations are keyed to the relevant text words not by reference numbers printed in the text and repeated at the bottom of the page, but by counting the lines on every page and prefixing the critical annotation with the number of the line of text in which the annotated text word is found. This means that the content of the single lines itself depends on the pagination (which itself depends on the number of critical notes necessary for the single pages).

These technical peculiarities are the reason why, in conventional hot metal typesetting, not line-casting machines but Monotype machines, with single letter composition, were employed for critical editions. This allowed one to move not only whole lines to a new place, but also parts of lines, and to exchange single characters easily without leaving visible traces of these manipulations. In the output of photocomposers, which consists of photographic paper or film, this flexibility has been lost: parts of this material are moveable only with the aid of scissors and paste; when text spans which are not whole lines are moved in this way, this will almost inevitably leave some tracks of uneven spacing or missing alignment on the page.

Manually paginating photocomposed critical editions with the aid of scissors and paste is therefore almost impossible. A solution to this problem which has sometimes been chosen is to set the apparatuses not as blocks of texts, but in two columns of short entries, each starting with a new line. Arranging apparatuses the old way with commercially available photocomposing systems normally requires interactive work at a display terminal and new setting of at least the apparatuses after a preliminary manual pagination, a procedure which bears a similar risk of error to that of the conventional techniques.

The advantage of computer composition for critical editions depends to a large extent on the question of whether the pagination too can be included in the automatic procedure. Therefore, the typesetting program which is part of TUSTEP, the 'TUebingen System of TExt analysing and processing Programs' has as a standard feature automatic pagination, without human intervention at a terminal, of texts containing not only footnotes, but, since 1974, in addition, up to nine different apparatuses at the bottom of the page (cf. Ott, 1979b: 32; a more complete description is contained in Ott, 1975, 1976). Those critical annotations may not refer to the text only, but also to the footnotes which may be original to the text to be edited. The program relies on careful markup contained in the text which allows it to run in batch mode, to make its own decisions on line ends and page breaks in accordance with typographic rules, and to insert footnotes, apparatuses, marginal settings, running heads, and the like.

This batch-processing approach may look antiquated in the time of WYSIWYG (what you see is what you get) and interactive working, but it has some serious advantages over an interactive approach, where everything that has to be done by human intervention must be repeated when the same step is executed a second time. These advantages have been recognized in the meantime also by other typesetting programs relying on markup (like TeX), and are the reason that standards like SGML, the 'Standard Generalized Markup Language' (ISO 8879, 1986), are evolving and are increasingly being applied also in the typesetting industry (see also chapter 1 above).

But the advantage of automatic pagination lies not only or even primarily in saving some time and money. Consistently applied, it may really revolutionize the method of organizing an editing project, as the following example shows.

When, in 1980, vol. III of series VI of the complete works of Gottfried Wilhelm Leibniz (*Philosophische Schriften*. Hrsg. v. d. Leibniz-Forschungsstelle der Universität Münster. 3. Band: 1672–1676. Berlin: Akademie-Verlag) had been finished, which contains in chronological order more than 100 documents of very different length, the editors had found that with this procedure they could, without catastrophic financial consequences, change not only single pages, but even the whole arrangement of the single pieces contained in this volume. They had done this only a few weeks before the final printing of the volume, after having checked everything in page proofs on the basis of some preliminary arrangement. As a consequence of this experience, the editor decided, for future volumes, not to wait five years until all the material for a full volume was prepared, dated and commented, but to print a small volume of about 200 pages every year *ad usum collegialem*. This 'Vorausedition' shows text and apparatuses in the same typographical form as provided for the final edition, only with a different page width and depth and in smaller type; it not only serves as a report on the progress of the work, but also makes available the hitherto unpublished material to colleagues all over the world. In this way, the critical remarks and suggestions of other scholars interested in this work are stimulated and can be taken into account for the selection of the pieces to be contained in the next volume, for their chronological arrangement and for final corrections, before the volume in question is published. To date, eight volumes of the 'Vorausedition' have been printed. As Schepers says in the preface to the eighth volume (October 1989; cf. also Schepers, 1981), a further essential advantage of this procedure lies in the strict time schedule for every step to be carried out periodically every year.

8.1.3   Special Characters and Fonts

A further problem for composing critical editions used to be the availability of characters beyond those used in the everyday business of composing and printing firms. One should bear in mind that about 90 per cent of what is composed is newspaper material; for this there exist other problems than for setting books with multilingual quotations or containing texts written in ancient European dialects with odd diacritics and with special symbols for the critical annotations.

Also in the past, not every typesetting firm had available all the fonts and characters required for such books. Firms had to be employed that were accustomed to doing work of this kind. But in the age of electronic composition, the availability of special characters should theoretically no longer present any problems, since one no longer uses hardware (like the matrices of linotype or monotype machines) for storing the character images; character images are stored electronically, in digital form, as numerical values representing the start and stop points of cathode ray strokes or as values defining the outline of a character for pixel-oriented devices; the number of different characters which can be held in this form is virtually unlimited. The fast spread of hardware-independent page-description languages like POSTSCRIPT, for which a great variety of font libraries are available on the market, will further remove the obstacles which one is still likely to meet in today's practical work. In the TUSTEP environment, we did not have difficulties in this respect, since the DIGISET photocomposing machine of which we have used different versions since 1969 allowed us to define our own characters easily and to load them from the tape, which also contained the text to be composed. Many of the requirements of the editions which we have prepared up to now could not have been met otherwise.

However, not every composing firm has the knowledge or experience to modify the programs or the character fonts of the composing equipment. And many manufacturers of photocomposers do not provide the documentation on the definition of existing fonts which would be necessary to create single additional characters which would show the same typographic details as the other characters of the same font. The lack of interest of the manufacturers in providing the pertinent information is at least understandable against the background that the aesthetic quality of the available fonts has traditionally been a major argument for the selection of composing equipment from a certain manufacturer.

8.2 Preparing the Manuscript (Printer's Copy)

Concerning the preparation of an (electronic) manuscript and computerized typesetting, there is no fundamental difference between the preparation of an edition and the preparation of any other publication, apart from the special requirements just mentioned. The fact that a text which is stored in a computer need never be retyped even when large numbers of corrections are made is appreciated in the meantime in any environment where texts are to be handled. The relevant techniques have been ubiquitous for years and are commonly associated with the terms 'word processing' and 'computer-aided publishing'. This possibility of preserving over many phases of subsequent revisions the state of correctness reached in previous steps is the more essential the more effort needs to be applied to exactness and correctness. Therefore, it no longer makes sense for an edition not to apply computer-aided composition from electronically stored 'manuscripts'.

However, if word-processing and computer-aided typesetting were all that computers could contribute to scholarly editing, this would not merit a chapter in the present volume. In editing projects, electonic data processing can – and should – do more than support typing, correcting and typesetting. These more technical steps are not at all special to critical editing or to scholarly work in general.

Data processing becomes a specific tool for scholarly research on the basis of further functions which the computer offers beyond its capability of storing and printing data:

1   Information stored in a computer can be retrieved according to manifold search strategies; they range from the simple coincidence of a string of characters used as a search string with a corresponding string in the stored text, and extend to sophisticated pattern-matching algorithms based on regular expressions, allowing the user to retrieve parts of a text (words, strings) corresponding to each other and to the search pattern in certain aspects (such as: same ending, same stem, same phonetic pattern of orthographically different words).

2   Stored information (texts) can be decomposed into its elements (words, parts of sentences); from these elements, those with certain properties can be selected; they can be arranged e.g. in alphabetic order, in the order of their phonetic transcription, in the order of a 'normalized' orthography, or according to their frequency or to other non-alphabetic information.

3   Different versions of the same text can be collated; the differences found can be shown in a form suitable for visual inspection (on the screen or on a printer); they can be supplemented with additional information (such as manuscript code and location in the text) and written to a file in a form which allows further automatic handling, e.g. sorting them in order to get an index of typical replacements made by a copyist, or grouping them into entries for critical apparatuses.

4   Stored information (texts) can not only be changed at single locations (when correcting typing errors or revising a chapter using a word-processor or an on-line editor), but can also be altered automatically, using algorithms like searching and replacing character strings or patterns by other strings, or omitting or relocating parts of text according to user-defined rules; these rules may be of any complexity as long as they are unequivocal.

5   Stored information (texts) can be transformed into numerical values (e.g. the frequency of the different variant readings); with these numerical values, numerical calculations can be carried out.

These functions, which the computer offers beyond word-processing, support not only the more clerical tasks of typing, correcting and printing, but also the scholarly part of editorial work itself which corresponds to steps 2–6 in the above schema of editorial tasks. Automatically collecting the variant readings or the differences in subsequent stages during the development of a text; safely administrating and evaluating them – in editions of antique texts, including questions of stemmatic relationship; gaining a complete and exact overview of the usage of words and spellings, of prepositions and other syntactic features, of orthographic peculiarities of single manuscripts; getting persistent control over the editor's own decisions and the alterations made in the course of the editing process to the text and apparatus; exploiting the text with indexes, comments, references to sources and cross-references to similar passages: those functions which are beyond mere word processing may add new qualities to editorial work by replacing 'impressionism and the random instance' (Love, 1971: 54) by a systematic approach based on the complete material.

Not all of these steps are of equal weight for every edition; their importance depends on many factors. When the autograph of the text to be edited is available, then methods for determining the genealogy of the witnesses, for reconstructing an archetype and for constituting an 'original' text, which are essential for editions of classical Greek and Latin texts, are without meaning. However, the tools which are used to determine the variants present in the different versions of a text as a result of its tradition by manual transcription through centuries, may be used also for detecting and recording the differences in a work which has developed to its final stage through different phases of corrections, additions and revisions.

The application of the particular tools presupposes some basic familiarity with their usage. It cannot be the task of this short article to make up for a comprehensive introduction or to examine how the methodology to be applied in the different steps can be supported in detail by computer application. I will concentrate on one of these tools only, namely automatic collation, which is especially relevant for the preparation of critical editions, also beyond the task of collecting variants. For other, more 'standard' procedures and programs, some hints must suffice.

8.2.1   Indexes, Word-lists, Concordances

Apart from word-processing software, which allows the entering, correction, editing, formatting and printing of texts, the most commonly available types of software for handling textual data are indexing programs. They decompose a text into its components (e.g. single word-forms, single phrases or whole paragraphs), record the exact location of these constituents (e.g. adding codes for the source text and references like page- and line-numbers) and sort them according to rules to be defined by the user (see also chapter 1 of this volume). This offers the possibility of having available, in any stage of the editorial work and for every state of elaboration of the text, concordances and word-lists arranged alphabetically, or according to their endings, or to the frequency with which they occur, and to consult them when working on the text and the corresponding annotations. Updated versions of these lists are easily available when required by the progress of the work.

The invaluable contribution which the availability of these lists can make to the editorial work, especially for step 4, has been stressed ever since the role of the computer for the preparation of editions has been discussed (cf. e.g. Praschek, 1965: 134f). In fact, we have found that editions which have been prepared in the conventional way, without computers, have revised their text just before final printing, when, due to the fact that the text had been transcribed on a computer for photocomposition, a KWIC (keyword in context) concordance was available at almost no cost except for some computer time and the printer output.

For certain purposes it may prove useful to extract from a text only words which have been specially marked (e.g. proper names, quotations or text passages which need further consideration). This can be done by the same programs which are used for generating word-lists or for sorting bibliographies. The same procedures can be used again for preparing the indexes which are to be published as an appendix to the edition (step 6 in the above schema) or in a separate volume. Significant differences may however be found in the fleixibility and functionality of different programs. Some of them have been developed for the office environment, and sometimes do not meet the requirements of scholarly work (foreign alphabets, diacritics, sorting according to normalized forms without changing the wording of the index entry, etc.).

8.2.2   *Numerical Computation, Statistical Evaluation*

The functions which gave the computer its name, involving calculation with numerical values, take part also in the generation of word indexes, when absolute and relative frequencies are to be given for each entry. For the preparation of an edition, especially of ancient texts, numerical calculation plays a further role. If more than two manuscripts are available which offer different versions of the text, it may be useful to start from a list of variants (found by conventional eye collation and subsequent recording of the variants in a file, or by computer collation of the different extant versions entered as full texts) and to calculate the relative proximity or distance of the different witnesses on the basis of the number of variant readings they have in common.

The application of methods of mathematical statistics, including cluster analysis and other specially designed methods of computer-aided solution of questions of stemmatological relations, has been for more than two decades the subject of a large number of publications, for which Jacques Froger's book *La Critique des textes et son automatisation* is one of the early and prominent examples. Since the pertinent discussions seem to have ceased more or less at the beginning of the 1980s, most of the relevant titles can be found in the bibliography mentioned earlier, which I published in 1983.

Indeed, after much initial enthusiasm, no great progress seems to have been achieved in the last twenty years, at least as far as the application of numerical methods to questions of manuscript affiliation and stemmatology is concerned. As witness to this, consider the fact that K. Aland decided to publish in 1987 all of the material for ninety-eight completely collated 'Teststellen', text passages selected for this purpose, from the Catholic Letters of the New Testament in a form which had been principally developed before 1972 (cf. Ott, 1973), leaving aside some of the more statistically-oriented tabulations, and decided to do this after 'many experiments . . . in which both the statistical method hitherto applied and the cluster analysis turned out to be not ideal for the goals which we had in mind' (Aland, 1987: VII, my translation; cf. also Benduhn-Mertz, 1985). The programs developed for the New Testament material were used later by Adolf M. Ritter for an attempt to analyse stemmatically the Corpus Dionysia-cum Areopagiticum. On the results, see his report in Ritter (1980). And the initial enthusiasm has given way to a certain scepticism, as expressed by R. H. Pierce:

> The use of computers and spreadsheets makes it possible to include a very large number of ms. and readings in a data set, e.g. those representing an entire Gospel. If this is done, any hope of assessing the material directly will be gone: and investigators will be obliged to place their trust in the methods they employ. This they ought to be unwilling to do unless they have already satisfied themselves about their reliability by testing them on material which they are satisfied they can evaluate without their aid. (Pierce, 1988: 41)

Also P. M. W. Robinson, who at first glance seems to be more optimistic regarding statistical methods, prefers to rely (apart from automatically generat-ing 'manuscript profiles', showing for each MS the number of readings it has in common with every other manuscript) on putting his material into a database and on using it for 'speedy development and testing of hypotheses concerning manuscript relations' (Robinson, 1989: 174).

Here, I cannot resist the temptation to quote the last sentences of my 1973 article:

> In conclusion, I need not emphasize that my attempts to use the computer to help with the problems of textual editing are very far from automatic textual criticism or textual editing in its philological phase. There are tasks which should be wholly left to computers, such as the final printing. For the rest, the best that can be done to help the textual critic is to supply him with a firm basis for his work. (Ott, 1973: 206)

8.2.3 Text Collation

Apart from the attempts to solve stemmatological problems with the aid of the computer, collecting and recording variant readings was the second field for which computational help was sought early on, especially when preparing a variorum edition of ancient texts. Apart from the work of Dearing mentioned above, one of the first relevant publications is Jacques Froger's article entitled 'La collation des manuscrits à la machine électronique' (Froger, 1964–5); from the same time, compare also Praschek (1965).

'The exuberance with which bibliographical and textual scholars have begun to tinker with computerized collation has produced claims so large and enthusiasm so infectious that there is a danger of forgetting that so far they are only experimenting', so writes Robert L. Oakman (1972: 333), where however he reports only on the work of William M. Gibson and George R. Petty undertaken in 1970, and that of Margaret S. Cabaniss dating from the same year. In his 1975 article, which no longer covers collation alone, Oakman quotes more than thirty relevant publications, more than twenty of them having appeared before 1972.

Collating is a basic requirement for all editions for which more than one 'witness' containing the text or one of its preliminary stages is to be evaluated, irrespective of whether it is the edition of an ancient text, whose principal purpose is the reconstruction of a lost original version of the text and the presentation of the history of its transmission in a critical apparatus, or the edition of a modern or contemporary text, where – beyond the elimination of possible printer's errors in the existing printed editions – the development of the work to its final form is to be revealed and presented in a 'genetic apparatus'. On the result of this first step all further editorial steps are founded; on the exactness with which it has been carried through depends the reliability of the whole edition. Therefore, the increase in exactness, completeness and reliability which can be achieved by computer application is more important for this step than the possible savings in time and money.

The same argument had been used by Fabian and Kranz (1971) for internal collation using the Hinman Collator, which enables 'only a significantly faster internal collation of two copies' (p. 391, my translation), but is, at the same time, 'a tool whose importance goes far beyond mere simplification of laborious collations of texts', because it allows us 'to establish a basic text which is definitive regarding its reliability' (p. 399, my translation). For 'internal' collation, computer-aided collation of texts, previously entered by manually transcribing them on a terminal or by optical scanning seems to be less efficient: the necessity of previously entering and storing the texts in the form of strings of characters not only means additional effort; by the same procedure, one loses information which is important for the internal collation, such as the size of inter-word spaces, line distances, the form of single letters, etc.

But, beyond collecting and recording variant readings, automatic collation has other fields of application, two of which are especially relevant for textual editing: it can be a more economic replacement for proofreading and manually correcting texts in any case where absolute exactness of transcription is essential (as, e.g., when entering the text to which all the other witnesses are to be collated manually or automatically); and it can serve as an accurate, fast and reliable tool for checking (and keeping track of) the results of any manual or automatic operation performed on the text.

The potentiality of automatic collation, its usefulness and importance for scholarly work in the humanities in general and in textual editing in particular, is seriously underestimated not only by many users, but also by designers of the programs. It may therefore be useful to have a closer look at automatic collation and its application.

Of course, 'rationalizing' and 'increased reliability of the results' are often only two sides of the same coin; in many cases, the rationalization of certain steps by computer application is the precondition for their being carried out at all.

Now, reliable textual collation is so basic for critical editions that any help by computer programs is valuable. But in order to make it a tool which will be consistently applied in everyday work, a computer program must meet some additional requirements beyond reliability.

For automatic collation, these basic requirements can be summarized as follows (for a more explicit examination of these requirements cf. Ott, 1979a, 1989a):

1 Collation must be really automatic; it must not rely on manual intervention.
2 For the task of collecting variant readings, collation must be possible for an indefinite number of versions.
3 The results of collation must not only be made visible for inspection by the scholar's eye, but must also be available in a form which allows their further processing by other programs.

What does 'automatic collation' mean?

Realignment of the versions after encountering variant readings In the first publications on automatic collation, a major role was assigned to the problem of automatic realignment of the texts after variants have been encountered (cf. the detailed report in Oakman (1975). This problem has been taken up again by Robinson (1989) who describes in detail his solution to it.)

In contrast, many PC-based collation programs advertised nowadays for collecting variants rely on manual intervention, as does the program COLLA-TIO, which was first described in 1986 by Gabler and Kreitmair, or the program URICA! ('User Response Interactive Collation Assistant'), described by Cannon and Oakman (1989): 'The system performs a word-for-word comparison, locking the keyboard as soon as a word in the master text no longer matches a typed word in the second text. The user then enters the variant text at the keyboard until a point of match is reestablished' (p. 470); or, when working on two files stored on disk, 'when a mismatch is found, the machine beeps and pauses for the user to determine why the mismatch occurred' (p. 471). This procedure responds to what Praschek proposed in 1965 (p. 131), and is a modern reanimation of the punched card verifier used in the 1960s: one fed a pile of pre-punched cards containing the data to be verified into it and re-keyed the data from the manuscript. As soon as a keystroke did not match the holes recorded on the cards, the keyboard blocked; if the current keystroke was wrong, it could be corrected by the operator; if the data in the card were wrong, the card was marked with a half-circle hole in the margin above the relevant column and could be corrected in a second step. Kreitmair's and Oakman's program adds the possibility of recording the variants which have been classified by the user as 'insertions', 'deletions' or 'changes' in a file of variants, together with their reference, according to the third of the above-mentioned requirements.

An interactive approach like this prevents many possible applications of computer-aided collation: if collation by computer is not really automatic, it will never be used for consistently checking the results of the single steps of interactive or rule-based work on a text, or for repeating the collation if for some reason the collation basis changes during the editing process (e.g. when in the edition of an ancient text, the edition text has been constituted on the basis of the evaluation of the previously collected variant readings).

Of course, for some cases, there are practical limits to really fully automatic realignment; there will always be a compromise between this requirement and the expense in computing time necessary to achieve it.

In order to overcome problems with different spellings or other typical replacements, a not too simple collation program will contain some rules for determining if two words are variants of one another; in addition, provision will be made that these rules may be supplemented by parameters or tables which depend on the language of the text and on other factors, and which therefore are supplied by the user (cf. those described in Robinson, 1989: 103; for the TUSTEP program VERGLEICHE, see TUSTEP, 1989: 454–5).

But when there are extensive insertions or deletions in the texts to be collated, little help is given by these rules and other provisions which serve only for identifying different but similar words or phrases as such. When at a single location an insertion or a deletion extends over more than about two typewritten pages, even the program VERGLEICHE contained in TUSTEP requires help by the user. The reason is that the longer a mismatch is, the more words (which may show 'minor' differences) must be recognized as 'basically identical' or corresponding to each other before the texts can be realigned. The exponentially increasing computing time necessary for this procedure provides the limits. The help the program requires can, however, be given in advance, in the form of pairs of references indicating for each of the two text versions the passages which the program is required to collate. It is wise also to omit from automatic collation insertions or omissions which are less extensive (e.g. of the length of half a page, which the program has *per se* no difficulty in identifying), when they can easily be found by a scholar who has some knowledge of a text. Of course, the program will record which passages have been included at all in the collation.

Delimiting variant readings   Apart from the problem of automatic realignment (which the interactive programs avoid), there is a further problem, namely the subdivision of the mismatching pairs of strings or word sequences into meaningful pairs of variant readings. No program can provide subdivisions meaningful in every instance. Therefore, it would have been a chance for programs relying on interactive work to provide means for the user to group adjacent differing words into meaningful units of variant readings. This could have added a quality which programs working automatically cannot provide. But even this chance has been missed: in URICA!, which (at least in the version described in Cannon and Oakman, 1989) relies on human intervention in every case of mismatch, 'in the case of replacements, it is necessary to move through each text until the position of rematch is found' (p. 471).

This is even less than can be achieved by a fully automatic approach which tries, as TUSTEP does, to group the pairs of variant readings as 'atomistically' as possible, on a word-by-word basis. As long as the program recognizes two varying words as being 'principally' the same, they are treated as pairs of variant readings, no matter whether the following pair of words also shows differences or not.

Of course, this grouping cannot be made on the basis of merely counting the words; an omission or insertion of a single word within such a sequence would lead to totally unrelated groupings. Also here, the program must recognize the words it treats as variants of each other as 'basically' the same, be it on the basis of the characters the words consist of (and which, for the purpose of collation, have eventually been transformed according to the above-mentioned rules supplied by the user), or because the surrounding words are recognized as variants of each other.

However, the result of this procedure often does not make sense. So, the grouping of the pair of variant readings 'Der Knabe] Des Knaben' would be far more adequate than the 'atomistic' approach of subdividing them into two pairs of variant readings: 'Der] Des' and 'Knabe] Knaben'. It does not, however, seem feasible to provide language-independent algorithms which could identify meaningful larger units of sense. Compared to possible unsatisfying algorithms, the 'atomistic' approach at least has the advantage of regularity.

On the other hand, all material collected automatically normally must be subject to revision by the scholar's intelligence in order to be used in a scholarly way, e.g. for creating entries for a critical apparatus. For this revision, the breaking down of variants, as far as possible, to the level of single words is far more useful, and the occasional necessity of making larger units out of some of those 'atoms' is far less time-consuming than recording the sometimes lengthy sequences of words between two matches as a single long variant.

This solution, which we have chosen in the TUSTEP program VERGLEICHE (cf. the examples in Ott, 1979a: 46; 1979b: 34), has recently been pleaded for by Robinson: 'The fewer cases of variants involving more than one word found by COLLATE the more useful its results' (Robinson, 1989: 102); when he wrote that 'it was early clear that it is just in this that the method of earlier machine collations fail', he apparently did not know the TUSTEP program VERGLEICHE.

Collating many versions of a text   The need for collating more than two versions of a text can be solved in different ways: either the program itself allows a certain number of input files to be read in parallel, or provisions are made for the output of successive pair-wise collations of a text to the same 'basic' text to be cumulated according to the needs of a project. It is this solution which we have chosen in TUSTEP (cf. Ott, 1979a: 41), thus avoiding any limits which may be imposed by the availability of central computer memory or the number of files which an operating system allows to be open at the same time. What seems, at first glance, to be a limitation, namely that only two files are collated at a time, is in reality the condition which avoids any technical limits regarding the number of collations to be performed: by subsequent sort and merge runs, one can cumulate as many 'variant reading' files as required by a project. And in cases where, in a later stage of the work, it becomes necessary to include a further text in the collation, only this one collation must be made, and its results merged with those of the previous collations.

Recording the variant readings for further processing   When the variants are to be recorded, each entry must show at least the following elements:

1   Complete indication of the location where the variant reading occurs (e.g. page-, line- and word-number or, for multi-word variants, pair of such references).
2   A sign for the kind of variant (omission, addition, replacement).
3   For additions or replacements, the wording of the variant reading.

These three elements allow a complete description of the differences contained in two texts. For the purpose of collecting variant readings for a variorum edition, there must be added a fourth element which makes possible the identification of the source of a variant after merging the different variant files resulting from the single pair-wise collations:

4   Code identifying the text bearing the variant reading (manuscript code).

The four elements mentioned hitherto allow the sorting and merging of variant readings as required for a critical apparatus: location of variant reading, sign for kind of variant (omission, addition, replacement), wording of variant, and code for the witnesses bearing this variant. Also, all the technical information necessary for preparing a genetic apparatus, which shows in parallel lines the different stages of the development of the text, is contained in these four elements.

In a critical apparatus, normally also the wording of the edited text ('lemma') is repeated, followed by a square bracket. Though it can be retrieved easily by program through the location element contained in each entry in the variant file, it is useful to add it as a fifth element to each entry:

5 Wording of the text of the collation basis.

This fifth element is required if the recorded variants are the basis for further research on their character and on the character of the texts in which they are contained. Variant spellings which are typical for the single witnesses may easily be found after a sort-run in which the first sorting criterion is not the location of a variant reading, but this fifth element which contains the wording of the text used as collation basis; the second sorting criterion will be the wording of the variant reading (element 3); the manuscript code (element 4) which will serve as the reference in the resulting list must be used as the third criterion.

(For performing those sorts efficiently, TUSTEP adds further fields containing those elements in the form of sort keys; they need not be discussed here. For a more detailed description, see Ott (1979a). Some details have been changed in the meantime; they are described completely in TUSTEP (1989: 441–57) and, for additional sort keys, pp. 417–30.)

8.3 Integrating the Tasks

Under the title 'A Text Processing System for the Preparation of Critical Editions', in a paper given at the 4th ALLC Conference (April 1976) at the University of Oxford, I described some basic principles of the system we were developing at Tübingen. (The paper has been published in *Computers and the Humanities*, 1979. A more up-to-date description may be found in Butler and Stoneman, 1988: 81–103.)

The goal of this development was 'to get the preparatory work and the composing stage into one system' (p. 12) where 'the output of any one program, including the composing program' (which also adds information, namely the new page- and line-divisions of the text, which may be needed subsequently as references for indexes, concordances, cross-references, table of contents etc.), 'may serve as input for any other program of the same group' (p. 12); 'what counts here . . . is that there is one program covering the text processing requirements of an editor from the first input up to the final output on the composing machine', a system 'which has been designed to be used by non-programmers' (Ott, 1979b: 35).

These requirements have been rediscovered and formulated still more explicitly by Shillingsburg (1986: 135):

It seemed to us that a really good computer-assisted process must have certain basic characteristics: First, it must be an integrated system in which the output from any one stage of computer work would be usable as input for the next stage . . . . Second, a good process must start at the beginning of the examination of source texts and carry through to the typesetting and printing of the end product . . . . Third, nothing of a mechanical or repetitive nature should of necessity be done by hand and eye . . . . Fourth, every stage in the process must be interruptable, reviewable, revisable, and, if necessary, re-doable.

It is this integration which makes consistent computer application to the scholarly tasks of critical editing easy (and therefore feasible). I shall briefly demonstrate this by means of the application of the collation program.

Before the collation of the different versions of a text can be started in order to collect the variant readings they offer, the texts themselves must be entered and carefully corrected in order to avoid the recording of transcription errors among the variants. As indicated briefly above, automatic collation can be an economic replacement for conventional proofreading and interactively correcting a text. We had our first experiences with this method of double transcription and automatic collation for correcting a text when the text of the Vulgate was transcribed for the preparation of the *Novae Concordantiae Bibliorum Sacrorum iuxta Vulgatam Versionem Critice Editam* which B. Fischer has published in five volumes (Stuttgart: Frommann-Holzboog, 1977). I have described them in Ott (1970); on the economics of this procedure, see also Ott (1989a: 421). It is based on the fact that, as long as both transcriptions do not show exactly the same error at the same location, a difference will be found by the collation program. There are, of course, cases where one cannot rely on probability; e.g. when old spelling texts are transcribed, and the modern language has slightly different spelling of words, the probability that the modern spelling shows up in both transcriptions at the same place is relatively high. These problems must be attacked by other means.

When applied for the purpose of proofreading and correcting only, two transcriptions of the same text are collated by program, and the differences are both listed and recorded in a file. The records in this file are later interpreted as correcting instructions. This is possible, because the elements 1, 2 and 3 of these records described above (p. 220) which allow the complete description of the variants contained in the second one of the two compared texts, are also the elements required for an instruction to perform appropriate changes to a text: at the location given (element 1), delete, add or replace (element 2) one or more words contained in the text file by the word(s) contained in this record (element 3) of the 'corrections file'. Starting from the results of the collation, one needs only to check the printed list of differences. In every instance, where the second transcription is wrong, one then deletes the corresponding entry from the 'variant file' with the help of an editor; the remaining 'variants' are those where the first transcription was wrong and the second one has the right wording. Only in the rare instances where both transcriptions contain an error in the same word must the 'correcting instruction' generated by the collation program itself be corrected. Then the batch correcting program KAUSFUEHRE is run, taking as input both the file containing the first transcription and the file containing the remaining (corrected) variants of the second transcription; the program interprets the variants as correcting instructions and writes the corrected text to an output file.

As soon as the texts to be collated have been corrected, automatic collation can be used to collect the variants contained in these texts.

It has often been argued that for many purposes this procedure – computer collation from machine-readable versions of a text – is too expensive in time and money, because the texts must be transcribed (or scanned by optical character recognition) and corrected before they can be collated.

For these cases, the modular procedure described above supports the mixing of automatic and conventional collation, since it separates the recording of the variant readings from any evaluation of these variants. To integrate the results of conventional collation, one need only transcribe these results in the syntax described above and required also by the batch correcting program: it consists of the location (page-, line- and word-number) of the word where the variant is found (or where it begins and ends, in the case of variants containing more than one word), a symbol ('+', '−' or '=') for 'addition', 'omission', 'replacement' and (except for omission) the wording of the variant. The code of the manuscript can be added by program after the whole file has been transcribed. This format allows merging of variants collected manually and recorded in a second step with variants collected by automatic collation. As the format in which the variants are recorded is identical to the format of correcting instructions, it is also possible to reconstruct the whole text of the version containing those variants, which may then be collated to the other versions if required. This reconstruction will be as accurate as the manual collation itself and the transcription of its results; it will show up everything except (if not recorded) the page and line divisions of the version collated manually.

The evaluation of the collation results is done with the help of the other programs of the system, of which the role of the sorting program has just been mentioned. The variants are handled in a similar way as index entries collected by other programs; sort keys are added before sorting, and groupings are carried out after the sort by the same programs which are used for preparing (hierarchically structured) indexes, including frequency counts and other operations. The selection of variants to be used for different purposes (such as, on the one hand, the description of a certain manuscript, for which purely orthographic subtleties not to be included in the apparatus are also important, and the compilation of the critical apparatus) will be supported by the same programs which allow manual selection (based on markings added to the text) or automatic selection (based on pattern-matching and other algorithms) for other purposes.

When, in the course of the edition, the edition text changes, the collations can be repeated (which is feasible since collation is automatic) with this new text as the basis for collation. Even versions which have been collated only manually can be integrated in this procedure, as shown above, by first reconstructing the full text on the basis of the (first) collation basis and the results of this manual collation which have been transcribed as indicated above.

The work on the edition text, on the apparatuses, on the preface, the comments and the indexes will generate many different versions of all these parts during the process of editing. Some of the relevant work will be carried out interactively, using an editor to insert, exchange or delete single characters or whole paragraphs. Other procedures are carried out automatically by search and replace operations or more sophisticated replacement algorithms. In every case, the editor must rely on the exact execution of the manual operations and on the adequate formulation of the replacement rules. This makes it advisable to check the results of each of these operations.

The procedures to be carried out for automatic collation are so convenient that we recommend this to our users even for checking ordinary corrections, e.g. of typesetting errors. Before they correct texts interactively with the help of a text editor, or make students carry out those corrections, they are advised always to make a copy of the text before starting their corrections. So, after correction, they can run an automatic collation of the uncorrected and the corrected file and can check in the resulting printer listings if all and only those corrections have been carried out which had been intended. Of course, in addition to working automatically, without human intervention, the program must be fast enough, and not rely on identical line divisions of the two files to be collated: it must be possible to collate text versions which have been refor-matted between two collations.

The possibility of automatically checking the results of all operations may lead to otherwise unattainable reliability of scholarly work, which is especially important in the preparation of critical editions. A short but impressive report on the importance of automatic collation, the automatic transfer of collation results into a critical text and perfect control over every alteration made to the text, may be found in the afterword of Hans Walter Gabler's edition of James Joyce's *Ulysses* (New York: Garland, 1984).

Automatic collation is not only a tool for the first step necessary for critical editions, the collection of the variant readings. It is a tool which may give perfect control over every stage of manual or automatic work on a text. The consistent and steady application of this tool in everyday scholarly work will however depend to a large extent on the question whether it is integrated into the computer-based working environment.

This integration of the collation program is still more important than it is for other computerized steps of editorial work as e.g. for the programs for index or concordance preparation, or for the typesetting program which is used for the final publication. For this last step to be carried out in the preparation of a critical edition, the necessity of changing the system or of transforming files to other formats may be tolerable. In the case of automatic collation, this necessity would prevent its steady use as a daily tool.

Further Reading

As stated above, good overviews of computer applications to all stages of the preparation of critical editions are contained in chapter 7, 'Textual Criticism', of Hockey (1980) and in chapter 6, 'Textual Editing with a Computer', of Oakman (1980) (the revised edition of 1984 has identical text, but added an introduction and bibliographic references up to 1983). In both cases, discussion concentrates on the questions of automatic collation and on discovering genealogical relations, as did Oakman (1975).

In 1978, an international colloquium 'La pratique des ordinateurs dans la critique des textes' took place in Paris; its acts have been published in CNRS (1979). This publication starts with a paper by Jacques Froger (who, with his 1968 book, had initiated a great number of publications on computerized analysis of stemmatic relationship) and concentrates on the question of manuscript classification and stemmatic questions, whose solution was attempted by 'méthodes statistiques', 'méthodes algorithmiques', 'méthodes formelles' (these are the section headings under which the single papers are published); a final section entitled 'de la collation automatique à la photocomposition' collects five papers regarding the other steps occurring in the preparation of critical editions.

The bibliography Ott (1980) (published in 1983 only due to delay in printing the journal) gives the titles of relevant publications up to March 1983. Since then, the discussion of questions regarding computerized manuscript classification and stemmatology seems to have almost stopped; the enthusiasm of the 1960s and 1970s has given place to a methodological scepticism regarding the application of mathematical and statistical methods (cf. Pierce, 1988).

Among the publications which take into account all the steps necessary in the preparation of critical editions, it is still worth mentioning Praschek (1965) who distinguished seven steps in the third phase of an editorial project – a distinction which has been useful in further discussions of computer applications (see the beginning of this chapter). He then concentrates on collation, on stemmatological questions (including an excursion into questions of authorship), and on typesetting and correcting printer's proofs.

An attempt to give a short introduction (40 pages only, including title page and glossary) to computers and critical editing has been undertaken by Ott, Gabler and Sappler (1982). Without giving any details of specific hardware and software, the booklet concentrates on the technical background (computerized photocomposition; computer tools for the preparation of the manuscript of the edition; information storage and retrieval; the necessity for technical coordination) and on the organization of computerized editorial work.

Scholarly Editing in the Computer Age: Theory and Practice by P. Shillingsburg (1986) has, as the title says, two parts; the first one concentrates on editorial concepts; 'Practice' itself is subdivided into two parts, 'practice' and 'practicalities'; it is in this third part where, after a chapter on 'Economics and editorial goals', there follow two chapters on 'Computer assistance to scholarly editing' and on 'Computer typesetting'. Both chapters are based on personal experience and contain valuable hints: for computer typesetting, they include a passage on 'what the editor needs to know about running computers and using software appropriate to the typesetting process' and a plea for professionality. From the chapter on computer assistance to scholarly editing, some central passages are quoted above.

The latest conference on the subject of which published proceedings are known to me is the conference on 'historical edition and computer' (Graz, Austria, 23–30 October 1988). The title of the conference and its proceedings (Schwob, Kranich-Hofbauer and Suntinger, 1989) is misleading in as far as of the six sections, only the following three contain contributions to the field: 1: Profiles of requirements for a historical and critical edition from the humanist's view; 4: Typesetting, Layout, Wordprocessing; 5: Database contra edition: systems of storage, possibilities of storing etc. (section titles: my translation).

9 Computers and Language Learning: Past, Present – and Future?

Rex Last

9.1 Introduction

The idea of employing an electronic computer to play even a modest part in the teaching of a modern language may at first sight seem to be a striking contradiction in terms. The computer is perceived as a rigid device, dealing with the equivalent of black and white issues, and alien to the infinite subtleties and richness of natural language. Language and the computer appear on the surface at least to be worlds apart from each other. Surprisingly, though, linguists were among the very first non-scientists to recognize the fact that the full potential of the computer was not being achieved by those who regarded it almost exclusively in terms of a number-crunching tool, but that its storage and manipulative capabilities rendered it particularly appropriate to a wide range of quantitative applications within the fields of linguistic and literary studies.

In what follows, I shall use the commonest acronym for computer-assisted language learning, CALL, which in the United States has the alternative name of CALI, in which the I stands for Instruction.

9.2 The Prehistory of CALL

In order to explain how CALL originated and the form its development took, it is necessary first briefly to consider the history of the application of the computer to language and literature in general. And in the context of cryptographical investigations in the Second World War, language applications were involved in the very earliest developments of the electronic digital computer.

The first well-publicized computing applications undertaken in the field of mechanical translation date from the 1940s. This enterprise, fuelled by the explosion of scientific papers published particularly in Russian, unfortunately foundered, partly because of the lack of power in early post-war computers, but chiefly because of a failure to recognize that the act of translation is not a simple linear and fundamentally mechanical process akin to the decryption of a complex code which is ultimately breakable by deterministic algorithmic techniques. In other words, it was wrongly assumed that natural language in its written form contained all the information necessary for a complete and unambiguous process of analysis and subsequent synthesis, possibly via a metalanguage, to accommodate a wide variety of language pair interchanges, into the target language, an attitude heavily conditioned by the success of computing machines in breaking complex enemy codes in wartime.

After the failure of the American MT programme and the withdrawal of its government funding, computer applications in languages appeared to have been discredited and have gone into decline. By the end of the 1960s, however, the University of Cambridge boasted a Literary and Linguistic Computer Centre, and sufficient impetus had been gathered among humanities scholars working with computers for a newsletter to originate from the University of Manchester Regional Computing Centre edited by Joan Smith, which led directly to a conference on humanities applications and the founding of the Association for Literary and Linguistic Computing in 1972.

Apart from work in areas such as the law, music, history and archaeology, the dominant figures in the early days of humanities computing were linguists, many of them Germanists. They had recognized at an early stage that the computer possessed considerable potential in creating concordances of literary texts, and of processing natural language in various ways not hitherto possible. Output such as reverse indexes and frequency listings using the same raw input data became more or less commonplace. Even in those pioneering days, the computer was being applied to contentious areas such as the quantification of style and disputed authorship (determining by various statistical techniques who was the likely author of a particular text). In other words, the computer was not merely cast in a clerical role, taking the drudgery out of scholarship, but also in a more advanced set of applications, not just doing more quickly what scholars had done very slowly in the past, but moving into areas which it would be impossible to contemplate exploring by old pencil and paper methods. However, of computer-assisted language learning (CALL) there was as yet no sign.

The reason for this was quite simple. Until the advent of the microcomputer, the standard mode of interaction between user and computer was largely 'off-line', in other words, program and data would be keyed in on punched cards or paper tape, presented at computer reception, and the output in the form of a lineprinter listing would emerge some hours (or even days, in the not infrequent event of system crashes) later. Direct 'on-line' interaction, where it existed, was either by teletype machine or a similar line-by-line scrolling video screen. Response times were not reliable, and many systems offered only upper-case characters. Foreign language accents were an unheard-of luxury.

9.3 The First Experiments

Despite these severe shortcomings on the side of the technology, a few linguists were none the less keen to extend the role of the computer from off-line batch processed research work into on-line interactive teaching. One of the earliest experiments took place in the Department of German and subsequently also the Department of Dutch at the University of Hull and demonstrated that, within certain strict limitations, even the mainframe computer had a potential role to play. Using programs devised by Last, Last and King incorporated CALL for beginners in German and Dutch into undergraduate teaching courses. Davies in Ealing College, London, was another early pioneer working on related lines.

The Hull package, called EXERCISE, was typical of much early CALL in that it offered the learner a tutorial mode of interaction. In other words, the computer acted as the questioner, and the learner was required to reply accurately to the question.[1]

The package consisted of a series of tests in which the learner could either make two attempts at each answer, or could ask for the answer to be shown. At the end of each test, a score was given, and the learner invited to have another attempt at questions not correctly answered the first time round. Despite the simplicity of design (or maybe even because of its unfussy format), with the incorporation of alternative answers and a comment facility, it was recognized that there was a clear function for such a package. The computer, then, was within a precisely defined set of constraints able to perform a remedial role, assisting in the necessary process of reinforcing vocabulary and grammatical material, rather than introducing new subject matter and taking over the role of teacher. (And it still is: see Fox, 1989). It was able to be fully incorporated into teaching modules by a feature which – with the students' knowledge, of course – kept a full record of log-on times and, much more importantly, of all the incorrect responses keyed in by students. This enabled the teacher to pinpoint weaknesses in individual and group performance, and, more chasteningly, inadequacies in the design of the tests themselves. A full account of the project will be found in Last (1984).

Learning a foreign language is a discipline which demonstrates a number of particular and peculiar characteristics. First, it is necessary to proceed along a given learning curve in a step-by-step manner. It is not possible, so to speak, to miss out units along the way without prejudicing the whole programme of learning. In a subject such as geography, one might study the littoral habitation patterns of the eastern seaboard of a country or those of the west, or both, without prejudice. In language, however, it is not possible to decide to concentrate on just the present and future tenses of verbs, or the nominative and dative of nouns. Progress is conditional on mastering all the aspects of a language in some kind of appropriate sequential pattern, unless of course one is dealing strictly with a 'survival' level of conversational language learning. Secondly, it is essential that the learner should not just passively recognize the learned material but also be capable of applying the appropriate transformations and other rules, thus producing it in the correct grammatical form instantaneously in both oral and written situations. The fact that learners vary widely in the rate at which they cope with this second process causes special difficulties in the classroom, and the involvement of a patient electronic tutor which will happily retest the learner without getting bored or prejudicing the learning rate of the group as a whole marked a significant potential step forward in language learning. This is particularly true in the case of the Dutch and German courses in Hull, since both were intensive beginners' groups, and King particularly records his recognition of the increased motivation and faster progress by learners cushioned by this remedial role which the computer was particularly suited to play within this framework.

This simple tutorial mode of interaction formed the basis of the first generation of CALL software, although the ingenuity of the software writers caused it to extend far beyond the question-and-answer mode of Last's early programs. Two factors emerged at this early stage of experimentation with CALL which provided a keen focus for debate. The first concerns the nature of the answer to a tutorial question, the second relates to the matter of linearity.

It was recognized even by the first researchers that the crucial issue in tutorial CALL was the reaction of the computer to the learner's response to a stimulus from the screen. To put the issue in its simplest terms, if the computer is simply programmed to print 'Wrong' on the screen to an incorrect response, this is pedagogically a far from sound procedure, particularly when the learner is baffled as to why he or she is wrong. Even worse were the programs which allowed for one answer, and one answer only, when a number of answers might justifiably be regarded as either equally correct, or more or less correct on a scale of some kind. When asked: 'What is the German for *car*?' the learner might type *Auto*, but if the program has been written in such a way that it can only accept *das Auto* or even *PKW*, typed accurately in upper and lower case, or worse still, *der Wagen* and nothing else, the learner is simply on the receiving end of a lesson on how not to program a tutorial CALL package.

From this awareness of the complexity of the interaction at this level of the learner response, the issue rapidly broadened into a recognition of the importance of the user interface as a whole in promoting good CALL practice and encouraging the learner to treat the computer as a reliable and non-threatening tutor. This is particularly important when the computer is used for remedial teaching among students who might otherwise be intimidated by the personality of the human teacher and who are particularly sensitive to the weaknesses in their own performance. Now it is recognized that the human–computer interface in all its aspects plays a crucial role in the promotion of a profitable interaction between learner and CALL package. This aspect of CALL is discussed at length in Last (1989).

The second question is that of linearity. The first programs were strictly linear, in that a sequence of question and answers was presented in the same sequence to all learners, not – as some critics supposed – out of an increasingly outdated allegiance to behaviourism, but simply because it had not occurred to the first programmers to do otherwise. Some packages sought to circumvent this limitation by incorporating a measure of random selection, but that concept does not admit of any real progress along a learning curve. Very soon, the concept of branching programs gained ground, and this raised the other key issue after that of the human–computer interface (HCI) namely, the question as to who should be at the controls of the CALL process. Should the teacher determine the path which the learner must take, or was this an opportunity to introduce an electronic dimension to learner-directed education? As in the case of the HCI, this debate has focused the minds of researchers in the field to the point at which some very high-quality CALL is now beginning to emerge.

But the tutorial mode of interaction does not exhaust the list of possibilities. As we shall see, the natural flair of the language teacher to exploit whatever tools and materials are at hand in the complex business of language teaching threw up a wide range of interesting and powerful applications.

9.4   Technology and the Language Tutor

At this point, two further issues emerge, that of technology push, and that of the intelligent tutor. The temptation exists among CALL practitioners – although, to their credit, it has largely been successfully resisted – to work outwards from the technology, to exploit it because it is there, so to speak, rather than to ask what is the most appropriate technology, if any, to use in a particular teaching situation. Those on the outside of CALL looking in are understandably fearful of a new technology which their pupils and students seem all too familiar with, and nurture the suspicion that much CALL consists of using technology for the sake of it rather than to enhance and extend the potential range of teaching tools for the benefit of the learner. This applies particularly to those disillusioned by the failure of the language laboratory to measure up to the promise which came at its inception.

The second issue is a demand which has been voiced in some quarters (Self, 1985) that the computer should interact 'intelligently' with the learner.[2] This is a stance which I have always found rather baffling, since none of the other common teaching aids, from reference book to film library, has been burdened with the prerequisite requirement of intelligence. The computer is no more innately intelligent than any other learning media. It may be faster, more flexible and may even be trained to simulate aspects of intelligent response, but it is certainly not endowed with human intelligence. Perhaps this demand is driven by an uncomfortable Calvinistic feeling that in requiring the computer to sit patiently waiting for a bored third-former to remember the French for *parrot* we are in some environmentally unfriendly way 'under-using' the computer. If so, then it is certainly the case that the vast majority of computer use involves a huge percentage of idle time as the machine waits, for example, in between key strokes as I type in this paragraph at the word-processor.

There is nothing inherently right or wrong in using a computer for simple interaction in a tutorial mode, not least because increasing the complexity of interaction, in whatever direction, brings with it a number of penalties which militate against the cost-effectiveness of the medium, and in educational technology that is an important consideration. There is no point, for example, in devising a vastly complex branching program at the expense of several hundred hours of effort, if there is no guarantee that in a given cohort of students, all the branching options will be used by a reasonable percentage of the group.

There is another, less obvious, cost factor at work here too, and that is that it is essential to maintain the integrity of the interaction between learner and computer. The learner should trust his electronic tutor, and if that trust is in any way prejudiced by over-complex programming, then the whole exercise is imperilled.

The arguments for the intelligent tutor, however, go beyond that level. They demand that the machine should be somehow 'customized' to meet the needs of individual learners at given stages of their study of a language. Beyond the very simplest level of knowing that student A has completed the first unit of a computer-based study programme with a 40 per cent accuracy in response, which means that A will have to revise the material again before progressing to the next unit, the complexities of designing a system that will function properly completely outweigh the cost-effectiveness of such a system.

In addition, I am far from convinced that the process of learning should or ought to be formalized in this mechanistic way. Learners have been seen to resent packages which insist that they respond correctly to a given question or set of questions before they proceed to the next frame. And if this model of the learning process were applied rigidly across the curriculum, I could envisage many of us still in our school uniforms struggling through the early stages of maths or physics.

Such approaches to CALL have, I feel, done little to contribute to its slowly growing acceptance as a respectable and potentially powerful learning tool, and seem to have grown out of a lack of recognition that, for all its supposed glamour, the computer is really no more than just one more learning tool in the whole range available to the teacher.

9.5   Lack of Progress in CALL

One of the most curious aspects of CALL is its comparative lack of progress over the decade or so that it has been in existence. Leaving aside the fact that it is still very much a minority interest amongst language teachers, software packages appear not to have kept pace with technological and software engineering advances.

There are three main reasons why this is the case. The first is that, in the overwhelming majority of cases, it is the enthusiast language teacher who has become his or her own programmer. Mastering a programming language to a sufficient degree to be able to devise a modest CALL package was no mean feat for a language teacher in the early days, and once that point had been reached there was little incentive to explore further, not least because the only courses and textbooks available were heavily geared towards the science disciplines.

The second reason is, quite simply, that relatively straightforward programs can achieve a great deal within the context of CALL. It may not be exploiting all the 'potential' of the computer, whatever that may be, but once a sufficiently sophisticated model of question and answer interaction has been devised, there is quite a substantial amount of varied learning activity that can be applied.

This is particularly the case when it was recognized that the most effective packages were those which were not dedicated programs which performed one task only, but template programs to which potentially unlimited amounts of data can be applied. This was the case right from the earliest days of the EXERCISE package, and enabled an exercise based on material just intro- duced in class to be put together quite literally in a matter of minutes. Having found the area of greatest effectiveness for CALL, there was again little incentive to range beyond that territory, not least because it was soon realized that the laws of diminishing returns set in at an early stage.

The humanities programmer rapidly discovered that there appeared to be an inverse relationship between the complexity of a program and its efficacy and robustness. Very straightforward programs deliver reliable and effective results, whereas attempts to move into more challenging areas offer marginal and often dubious gains at the expense of a disproportionate amount of programming effort. This is particularly true when the programmer seeks to move from the lexical to the semantic level, as we shall see later.

The third significant reason for the painfully slow pace of progress in CALL was the lack of funding and of general recognition of CALL as a worthwhile and 'respectable' activity, which forced researchers to operate on a shoestring, not infrequently purchasing their own hardware and researching in their own spare time. Now, after a decade and more, the situation is shifting, since the British government has somewhat belatedly awoken to the recognition that information technology in learning is a Good Thing. There are centres for

CALL on both sides of the binary divide, and a new journal devoted to the subject has recently started publishing from the University of Exeter.

There is one further reason for the slowness in gaining impetus on the part of CALL, and that has ironically to do with the early initiative of the BBC linked with education to introduce microcomputing in schools. The BBC microcomputer, for all its innovations, was seriously overpriced, required separate purchasing of a console screen, disk drives and other peripherals, lacked a RAM sufficiently large to encourage the development of sophisticated programs, and ultimately turned out to be non-standard in both education and business fields, from both the point of view of hardware and operating system (see Burgess, 1990).

The relatively small user base, seen from an international perspective, coupled with the fact that the IBM PC and clones seem set to dominate the world market for the next decade at least, have militated against the programmers who learned BBC BASIC and, to a smaller extent 6502 assembler, and has set the potential market for software at a point below that at which most major publishers would consider developing and producing. That is, however, no more than the result of a combination of circumstances, and it is clear that CALL programs are now being targeted much more strongly on the MS-DOS market, with its far greater potential for international sales.

9.6   Examples of Good CALL Practice

I turn now to consider what is currently available in the CALL market-place and what the merits and potential of the various programming initiatives might be. First, I consider tutorial programs, with which CALL really started, then cloze testing or gapping programs, and then a range of other programs including an ingenious computerized book package. For a thorough if slightly out-of-date account of actual products available, see Davies and Higgins (1985). A more up-to-date account can be found in Kenning and Kenning (1990).

9.6.1   Tutorial Programs

By far the most common kind of package is the question and answer routine, which, as I indicated earlier, is most effective when created in the form of a template program which can then be applied to a very large range of databases. As in any area of software engineering, there is a trade-off between the sophistication of a dedicated program on the one hand, and the more generalized features of a template program on the other. What you gain in fine-grain attention to detail is more than lost in cost-effectiveness and wide applicability.

A typical tutorial program might contain a mix of the following features. It will be based around a question-and-answer sequence, which will take advantage of screen addressing (that is, appropriately locating material on the screen) and involve some control over the attractiveness of layout, colour mix, and so forth. For any one question, the option of alternative responses will be available, as will context-sensitive help.

As for the answer, a wide range of different options is available. If the learner does not know the answer, the alternatives range from pressing a button and seeing the answer, being given help relevant to the question, being shown the first letter of the answer, being given the answer to a similar question, in the case of verb endings, for example, being shown the paradigms, and so on. The possibilities are limited only by the ingenuity of the package designer.

Good practice dictates that the learner should have a good degree of control over the learning process, that he or she can quit a test at any time, that there are no time constraints over the answering process, and that the learner should not be compelled to repeat answers until they are correct.

In addition, there should be a feeling of flexibility in the package as a whole; in other words, many packages have an extremely limited form of interaction. A word is flashed on the screen and you have to offer up the Spanish or French or German for that word. Nothing else is on parade – no contextualization, no tests of the gender, no listing of synonyms, no help panels, and in such circumstances the poverty of the learning environment soon causes the learner to tire of what ought to be recognized as a highly intensive interactive mode.

There should, then, be some variety available to the learner, whether in the form of a preview facility of a given test, or a browsing mode, or some other means of varying the range and format of interaction.

9.6.2 Cloze Testing

One of the most straightforward applications of the computer in language learning is in the field of clozentropy, or gap testing. The concept is based on a learning technique which involves taking a text and blanking out every n^{th} word. Used with appropriate care, this concept and its variations can be applied with considerable success to improve the learner's inferencing ability, or guessing strategy, to give it its other title.

One much neglected aspect of language learning, mainly because the principal thrust in the past has been to 'get it right', is that of trying to complete a sense using current knowledge as a platform for advancing the skill of inferencing ability. The programs can have three main variations. In the first, either the program or the learner can ask for one in every so many words to be blanked out. The advantage of this approach is that it is grammatically and semantically non-specific, in that the words omitted will test a wide variety of areas of knowledge more or less at random. The negative aspect of uniform gapping is that the text has to be chosen with some care to avoid gaps occurring where, say, dates or proper names may be located which the learner has no reasonable chance of guessing within the context of the passage. The second approach involves removing words to test particular aspects of the passage, whether vocabulary knowledge, use of pronouns or verb forms, or some other linguistic feature or features.

A third approach is to present the learner with a completely blank screen or one filled with dashes to represent individual words, and invite him or her to type in a word, which will then be written on screen in the appropriate locations. Initial candidates are obviously non-context specifics such as *and, but, the,* and so forth, but it requires quite a degree of skill and understanding to achieve success in this kind of test.

One common reaction among learners is to remark on how difficult it can be to arrive at an answer even if a large part of the context is already clear. In addition, a frustrating aspect of this kind of test is that there are in many instances clear alternative answers, which may be perceived to be correct by the learner, although the computer will of course only admit the answer which it has in its memory.

A positive benefit of cloze tests – although by no means restricted to this aspect of CALL – is the way in which it has been noted that the most effective way of implementing the tests has been with a group of students gathered round a computer, rather than individuals working alone. This mode of interaction, born of economic necessity rather than pedagogical farsightedness, has had the considerable merit of turning an isolated, individual-based interaction into a group social activity in which as much peer-to-peer interaction is stimulated as is between learner and machine, ironically underpinning the pyschological basis of the original concept of clozentropy as a group decision-based methodology.

As in other aspects of CALL, such challenges can be met by letting the learner see the length of the missing word represented by the same number of dashes, by allowing him or her to see the first and then other letters of the word, and generally by providing the kind of support which will guide into the correct solution.

9.6.3   General Programs

In all educational technology, one of the most important factors to consider is the imbalance between the man-hours input into the design and development of a package on the one hand, and the actual usage to which that package can be put on the other. Too often a great deal of work generates an insufficient amount of output to justify the effort involved, and in many cases a viable alternative is to explore the potential of software already available but written for purposes other than language teaching.

The most obvious candidate for such application to CALL is the word-processor, apart from the spreadsheet the most popular and widely used application in microcomputing. Using a modern word-processor for writing essays in the foreign language brings a whole range of additional benefits for the learner (see Poulsen, 1990).

The first and most obvious is the assistance available from dictionaries and spelling checkers, and in the most advanced word-processing systems a thesaurus too. However, as in all computing applications, the user must be made aware of the fact that a spelling checker cannot – yet – differentiate between a correctly spelled word and its inapposite application: *their* for *there*, for example. Some style-checking programs are beginning to work in this direction, and top-of-the-range word-processing systems are already promising these and similar features (see also Williams, this volume).

On the broader front, the word-processor enables the learner and the teacher to interact in a much more fluid and powerful way than has previously been possible, in that it is simplicity itself to produce an interim version of an essay for the teacher to correct and comment on before a final version is presented.

Most important of all, the old linear technology of pen and paper is replaced by an electronic worksheet on which the learner can check that the structure of the essay is correct – for example, that the length of introduction matches that of conclusion, and that the signposts set in the introduction actually point to achieved objectives by the end of the essay.

It is also much easier to overcome the common structural weakness in the central section of the essay where the learner is tempted to place the key point of the argument first and then tail off into lesser matters.

As can be readily recognized, writing an essay in a foreign language is one application suited mostly to the more advanced learner, and the value of the computer here clearly extends to work beyond the scope of this chapter, namely, essay writing in English or the foreign language on cultural, historical or literary themes.

The word-processor can also be used to help in the work of written translations, by giving the learner the source language double-spaced. The target language translation is then typed into the spaces in between, and although this is a very primitive use indeed of the computer, learners have found it most beneficial.

In addition to the word-processor, the computer adventure game, one of the cult leisure applications of the computer, can be applied to language learning. Foreign language versions of adventure games can be of particular value, not least because they offer an admixture of informality and application of the language to a particular purpose.

9.6.4 The Viewbook

One application which has not yet been adapted for language learning use is the Viewbook, but it clearly has a potential in this area. The concept revolves round the notion of an electronic book which can be read page by page on screen, with the additional benefits of instant switching between glossary pages relating to the current text page, or of notes. In addition, there are sophisticated search and notepad facilities. There are a number of Viewbook titles in print, ranging from subjects like economics and politics to Shakespearean texts, and the opportunity exists for users to design their own Viewbooks using the Viewbook Author system, published by Information Education Ltd (Stoke-on-Trent).

The nearest application to CALL yet applied is the edition being prepared of *L'Avare* by Molière, but the opportunities for language teaching proper are evident. The objective of this computerized version of the seventeenth-century French dramatist, which I am editing, is to accelerate the process by which the learner can come to terms with an unfamiliar text in an alien variety of French. One means by which this is achieved is to enable the learner, quite literally at the touch of a button, to alternate on screen between the text of the drama and a comprehensive glossary for that particular screen page. In addition, there is equally instant access to an English language commentary on the text, and facilities like being able to search through the text for a particular word or phrase, or to extract any page of text for separate word-processing, actually extend the experience of French literature without in any way diminishing its original strength and impact.

9.6.5   Business Language

It is clear that the business user is attracting most of the commercial interest, since it is here rather than in the impoverished education service that there is sufficient financially supported demand for a growing software base. Examples of such software include Linguawrite, from MultiLingua (reviewed in *Computer Assisted Language Learning*, I (1990), 111) and the comprehensive Tick-Tack package from Primrose Publishing, Cambridge.

Interestingly, the dominant role is being played by the translatable business letter, which is based on the notion that much international business is driven by standard correspondence, and that if you select from the appropriate list of inputs, you have achieved the equivalent of multi-language machine translation (MT – also known as mechanical translation; see Lewis, this volume), which has eluded the best efforts of researchers for decades.

However, converting a letter into a series of numbers and getting the computer to look up their equivalent in the selected target language does not constitute a genuine act of translation, although I can see a role for this kind of exercise in the training of bilingual secretarial staff. The fundamental puzzle is how to deal with the issue the other way round – in other words, when a letter arrives in a foreign language in reply to your apparent fluent knowledge of that language.

9.6.6   Maximizing the Program Range

All too often, CALL packages, particularly of the tutorial type, offer a pretty limited range of interaction possibilities with the learner. If you are restricted simply to answering straightforward vocabulary questions, this has a serious negative impact on the attention span of the learner. It is important to allow the learner the opportunity to interact with the package in a variety of different ways, at different levels of difficulty, and in different modes, from intensely active to passive observation.

I offer by way of example the German Verbs Program which I recently completed. It is targeted on PC compatibles. This package consists of a database of all the German strong, mixed and modal verbs, together with a representative selection of weak verbs which demonstrate particular features of their class. There is also a parallel database of notes to verbs in the main list. The database can be accessed in two distinct ways. First, there is a dictionary look-up program which enables the learner to conduct a search of the database for a particular English or German verb. Fuzzy matching is incorporated into the search patterns. When a match or partial match is found, the learner has the opportunity to inspect the principal parts of the verb, read the notes, or have listed in full any one or more of nine different tense forms.

In testing mode, the package allows for twelve levels of difficulty and nine tenses to be tested in any combination. By a randomization process, the program selects a question, such as 'Give the *du* form of the pluperfect subjunctive of the verb *to speak*', and at this point the learner has a number of options, ranging from trying to key in the answer directly at one extreme to switching off the scoring feature at the other and simply pressing a button to see the right answer. In between, there are various levels of help, from the German infinitive through to a complete listing of the tense, and the learner is allowed any number of attempts at the program.

This multiplicity of interactive possibilities enables programs like this to have a wide applicability at different levels of attainment and ability, and to match the learner's state of mind from one of passive observation to intense application of productive skills.

The most successful applications of CALL to date, then, have been those which have selected a clearly defined area of language teaching which is susceptible to computational processes and have worked within those limitations.

9.7 New Approaches in Hardware

So far, I have considered CALL as if it were exclusively a matter of interaction between learner and conventional desktop microcomputer, with keyboard input and screen output. It has been argued that this is hardly the most apposite modality of interaction between modern languages student and high technology. The danger is not only that of emphasis on written skills and accuracy rather than the spoken word and fluency (a debate in language teaching circles which is as old as the hills), but also one of diverting the learner away from language acquisition into other skill areas like learning how to type. Many packages have attempted to overcome the typing bottleneck by using single-key input where practicable, but a real breakthrough in interactive possibilities first came with the computer-controlled cassette recorder, manufactured by Tandberg.

This device has an on-board digital clock and can be directly controlled by the computer in a number of different ways. For example, it can be told to go to 10 minutes 23 seconds along the tape and play for 12 seconds, or until there is a 2 second silence. The tape can be moved backwards and forwards speedily and accurately, and thus a new possibility of audio input to the learner emerges. It enables questions to be asked verbally, or additional notes and information to support the on-screen material, and has clear applications in areas such as pronunciation. As the recorder is a language laboratory machine, the learner can also speak responses on to tape and listen back to them.

One opportunity which the recorder offers is to automate the process of dictation exercises, even to the point of giving verbal explanations to specific incorrect answers. One drawback of this technology is that it increases exponentially the input time required by the teacher in order to create a CALL exercise. A second disadvantage is that, for all its speed, there is inevitably a perceptible pause when winding over any significant length of tape.

In many respects, this technology is under threat from the CD-I (compact disc interactive) and videodisc technologies, which offer not only almost instant access to sound but also moving images and programs stored on the high-capacity disks. Here, though, the problem is one of cost: financing the mastering of a videodisc can cost tens of thousands of pounds. A recent account of CD-ROM technology can be found in Darby (1990). However, such is the storage capacity of these technologies that it may well soon be possible to purchase off the shelf discs containing complete pronouncing dictionaries of a particular language, or a comprehensive slide collection of the everyday life of a particular country, so that the software designer can selectively plunder them for particular programming ends (see Hancock, 1987; and for a complete recent account of the field, Coleman, 1987).

9.8   New Approaches in Software

The next step forward would seem to be a move in the direction of AI-like programs, but as I have sought to explain (Last 1987, 1989) there are serious and possibly intractable problems to be overcome both on the side of the software technology and on the side of language itself.[3]

One great merit of conventional, first-generation CALL is its deterministic structure and well-defined boundaries. Any step away from such constraints may appear to the imperfectly formed aspirations of the researcher a breaking free into new and exciting territory, but the reality is much less appetizing. For a robust defence of 'old-fashioned CALL', see Farrington (1989).

If you depart from deterministic programs, which in the last analysis present a pattern of black and white with no shades of grey in between, you are inevitably moving into areas where we are talking about approximation rather than accuracy, reasonable expectations rather than absolute dependency, and where the implied lack of robustness militates against the integrity of the learner–computer interaction.

The software that AI has as yet produced is in many respects an exercise in self-deception. The most 'successful' software is that which has stripped away the complexities which would militate against its achievement in the real world, and there are many AI-type problems, such as weather forecasting, where it is impossible to determine a starting point for the problem and to feed all the parameters in, and where all that can be stated with any certainty is that there are some weather conditions in which medium range forecasting is possible, and others where it simply cannot be done. For evaluation of a recent AI approach to CALL, see G. Brown (1990).

The complexities of natural language present similar hard problems for the researcher to resolve, and even the massive resources placed at the disposal of the EC's translation program called Eurotra (see Lewis, this volume) have so far yielded relatively modest results. My estimation is that we shall be able to make progress towards the semantic level of interaction provided we restrict ourselves to limited and relatively well-defined objectives.

Maybe in a decade or so the brute force approach of massive parallel programming systems plus huge fast access databases will overcome many of the difficulties which currently face the CALL researcher seeking to move into this kind of area, but the present signs are not good.

In addition, two points should not be overlooked: first, the quality of the output from such a system depends on the integrity of the database; and secondly, it is not simply a matter of 'feeding in' data and then allowing the system to function merrily away. Language in the modern world is changing and developing almost on a daily basis and any computerized system will have to be sensitive to such dynamism. For a general evaluation of quality in CALL, together with a recent bibliography on the subject, see Hamburger (1990). A general account of modern hardware and software in the humanities can be found in Rahtz (1987).

9.9 The Next Decade

Trying to determine the future pattern of developments in computing is a particularly hazardous occupation. Futurologists of computing began with confident predictions that there would be a demand only for a handful of computers for a limited range of numerical applications, and they continued by confidently predicting a decade ago that 'genuine' artificial intelligence (AI) would be a reality in the early 1990s. Now the harbingers of neural networks and distributed parallel processing are announcing the latest millenium, but the lessons of the past are clearly that predicting the future in computing is especially dangerous.

In tentatively seeking to anticipate the directions into which CALL might profitably move over the coming years, it is necessary to tease out a whole range of tangled threads in order to be able to determine clear opportunities for advance. What is unambiguously clear, though, is the fact that there is a huge gulf between the present state of CALL and the aspirations of those seeking to implement intelligent tutoring systems and AI-like programs.

The key issues, in my estimation, are those of robustness and knowledge. One of the key aspects of any learning system is that the relationship between tutor and learner should not be imperilled by anything which might cause a lack of confidence by the latter in the former. The more one moves from the level of the individual word and phrase out to the semantic level, and the more one progresses from a closed, deterministic programming environment, the greater is the danger that the relationship of trust between learner and computer will be inadvertently broken. Either the program will find itself unable to resolve a situation or it may do so with an incorrect or incomplete answer. Secondly, for any program to make such advances, it needs to have a satisfactory degree of knowledge of the environment within which it is functioning.

One program under development which seeks to come to terms with these somewhat intractable problems is the project I describe in Last (1989), and which I have called the 'inexpert system'. An attempt is made to reverse the roles of computer and learner and, on the basis of a minimal set of rules relating to simple declarative utterances in German, to 'teach' the computer to be able to parse such sentences, and to use the information gathered with each sentence understood in trying to tackle the next incoming sentence. When the computer has sufficient knowledge to be able to cope with teaching a learner up to a particular level, the program and data are turned to that purpose.

To explain in greater detail: the program is told, for example, that there are three genders of noun in German, that nouns begin with capital letters, and that the verb in a simple main clause comes 'second idea' in that clause. Assuming that the program is some way along the learning process, it might encounter the following sentence:

Die Dame ist gestern in die Stadt gefahren.

A dialogue with the human operator might take this pattern: the first noun is clearly feminine. Of the feminine nouns I know about, those ending in 'e' have plurals in 'n'. There is a 99 per cent chance that this noun falls into that category. Am I correct? What is the English for this noun? Does it relate to a person, an object or an abstract concept?

Ferney (1989) describes a related approach to determining the gender of French nouns. He has devised a program bearing the splendid title of Gender Mender which seeks, partly through inbuilt rules, partly by a list of exceptions, to determine the gender of French nouns. He is clearly working towards not just testing the learning, but to devising a means whereby the computer can model and make sense of the information it is giving the learner.

Similar problems are tackled by Galletly and Butcher (1989) in the context of the challenge of generating an intelligent syntax checker for French. Here too, as in the case of Last and Ferney, one of the key issues apart from the intractable ambiguities – let alone perversity – of natural language is the question of knowledge which the program must possess, employ and develop in order to be able to function effectively in the context of a situation where there are more imponderables than the first generations of CALL ventured to tackle. We are on ground where heuristics and probabilities rather than deterministic certainties are the order of the day.

So far, limited achievements have been made and the reports of this kind of work which is edging out from known territory in a practical and inventive fashion are impressive. The future for CALL, though, still remains a matter of speculation – and sheer hard research work.

9.10   Conclusion

Since the mid-1970s, CALL has made considerable, if patchy, progress. How little real progress has been made can be seen in some of the contributions to Cameron, Dodd and Rahtz (1986). It has still not achieved the 'critical mass' of a mature and universally supported discipline, and there are still many in the profession either antipathetic to technology, despite the siren voices of interactive video, direct broadcasting by satellite (DBS), and the like, or who are frankly suspicious that the computer is being applied to teaching the wrong things in the wrong way.

Their attitudes are understandable and some of the strictures on CALL and the way it has been applied are not without foundation. My own perception is that CALL has established a firm, limited base as one tool among many in the language teacher's resource cupboard, but that the difficulties as viewed from the present time of moving forward into AI-type CALL or hypertext CALL (see Harland, 1990; Scarborough, 1990) are substantial.

There is as yet too little awareness of the fact that what made early 'advances' in AI and hypertext so apparently successful is the easily overlooked fact that what made, for example, the 'micro worlds' of such programs appear to function so smoothly was that all those complex elements which would make the problems real-world, open-ended problems had been carefully eliminated. Equally, in hypertext the danger exists of creating an artificially restricted or blandly denatured version of the free-ranging aspiration of navigating the instructional nodes like a new generation of electronic explorers. (For further discussion of hypertext, see Burnard, this volume, also McAleese, 1988.)

And, finally, and very unfashionably for a CALL pioneer and long-standing enthusiast, I must add that in all the excited pursuit of career-enhancing hi-tech applications of the computer and related peripherals in language learning we should never lose sight of the fact that this is not, despite the propaganda, in any way better or more educationally powerful than the 'real thing' – a dedicated, live, human teacher motivating a class of eager learners. The computer can indeed achieve much in a supportive role, but can never replace humanity. If it does, we are all doomed.

9.11   Further Reading

Among the available introductory surveys of CALL, Last (1984), now somewhat out of date, gives an account of all aspects of CALL in the classroom, and Davies and Higgins (1985) presents a complete survey with a useful bibliography and index of software. A more limited survey is given in Ahmad et al. (1985). Kenning and Kenning (1990), Fox et al. (1990) and also the selected papers from the 1987 CALL conference held in the University of Exeter (Cameron, 1989), offer a clear indication of the current state of the art in CALL as a whole. Coleman (1987) offers a good introduction to interactive video, and Zettersten (1986) discusses new technologies in language learning. Sloan (1984) and Last (1989) both caution against the deleterious effects of bowing to pressure for 'progress' in information technology, the latter being concerned specifically with the dangers of too hasty a drive towards artificial intelligence techniques. Tannenbaum (1988) offers a valuable survey of computing in the humanities and social sciences.

There is one book on programming for CALL (Davies, 1985). Two shorter discussions on PROLOG as a potential CALL language, particularly for AI-like approaches, can be found in Cameron (1989). The now rather dated teaching language PILOT is described in Conlon (1984).

The ReCALL guide, published by the CTI Centre for Modern Languages at the University of Hull, is an important source of information about what is currently available in CALL software (ReCALL, 1990). Recent attempts at a comprehensive bibliography for CALL can be found in Jung (1988) and Levy (1990). The survey in Lancashire and McCarty (1988) is also useful. Useful journals include *Computer-assisted Language Learning*, published by Intellect, *ReCALL* and the *CTISS* documents, from the CTI Centre at the University of Hull, *Literary and Linguistic Computing*, published by OUP, and *Interactive Multimedia*, published by Sigma Press. A British-based newsletter for CALL is *Callboard*, from NCCALL at the Ealing College of Higher Education, London. Information on American CALL can be found in the *Athelstan Newsletter*, published by Athelstan Publications, La Jolla, California.

Notes

1 For a recent defence of basic interaction of this kind, see L'Huillier (1990).
2 For an account at a recent project in the intelligent tutoring field, see Horton, Ellis and Black (1990).
3 For a practical discussion of the problems involved in a reading skills project, and a bibliography, see Fox (1990).

10 Computers and Writing

Noel Williams

10.1 Introduction

One of the most recent and most rapid growth areas in applying computers to text is that of writing. It is a wide area, so there is insufficient space here to review all the issues. Instead I will concentrate upon some of the key areas, focusing particularly upon applications which are typical (e.g. represented in readily available systems) and on research and development work which, though not yet available in the form of actual software, addresses significant issues. (For up-to-date research papers, see Williams and Holt, 1989; Williams, 1990; and Williams, forthcoming.) Slightly old now, but nevertheless still a useful review of the basics of computers and writing is Daiute (1985).

Most software for writing is built around the traditional pattern of writing teaching, that of plan–draft–revise. Although much research in the 1980s questioned this as a model of what writers really do (the most commonly used model is that of Hayes and Flower, 1980; other models are discussed in Sharples and Pemberton, 1989), this straightforward linear model nevertheless remains the prevalent one in training and education. This is true whether writing training is explicitly or implicitly linked to a sense of how writing is done (a discussion of this can be found in Williams, 1987).

Researchers in the area of computerized writing tools generally make a distinction between tools to train writers and tools for supporting normal writing processes (see, for example, Williams, 1989a). In both cases the three-stage model of writing seems implicit in those tools that are available. Often that model is made explicit. For example the WRITER'S HELPER package has eleven programs grouped under the general heading 'Find and Organize a Subject', a word-processor (for composing) and ten programs grouped as 'Evaluate a Writing Project'. HBJ WRITER has three similar groups of programs.

It is convenient in a review of this kind, therefore, to review software which serves these three areas, and to examine both writing support and writing training tools. I will therefore examine writing tools in the three areas of pre-writing, composing and post-writing, whilst noting that this division is not necessarily a natural one, before briefly outlining some of the other new trends is using computers for writing.

10.2   Pre-writing

Pre-writing consists of all the activities a writer engages in before putting pen to paper, such actions as information gathering, planning and organizing information. In fact, when you examine what writers actually do, you find that these actions typically are not only performed before the composing process but continually within it. Indeed some writers may start their task by writing something before they know what they are going to write about, and only when they have brainstormed some text onto the page or the computer screen will they then have a clearer idea of what information they need and what organizing and planning strategies might best serve them.

From the computational point of view, there are three types of program designed to aid these processes (though obviously programs like databases and information search facilities will also help the writer, as in any other information-intensive task). These three are:

- Dialogue and prompting programs
- Planning and outlining programs
- Notetaking tools

10.2.1   Dialogue Programs

Dialogue programs simply take a writer through a series of questions designed either to get the writer to analyse the writing task or to analyse that task for the writer. Most systems in use do the former. Generally they are little more than adaptations of (well-tried and successful) classroom techniques for getting students to articulate their knowledge (or lack of knowledge) of their purpose, audiences, material, task and context. One pre-writing technique for getting over writer's block, invisible writing, works very well on computer (see Marcus and Blau, 1983). As an example of dialogue systems, Hugh Burns' TOPOI uses a dialogue which is essentially that of Aristotle (Burns, 1984). It asks random questions designed to guide a student through the business of generating and clarifying a topic for writing, and will reward the student for input with random exhortations ('Well done! Excellent!'). It also is able to recognize some patterns in input which trigger particular trains of output. For example, if the student types 'Why . . . ' the system responds with 'Why not?' If the student types a string which includes 'do not under' then an explanation of the last question is given. Even such simple devices prove highly successful in encouraging students to develop their ideas.

The pre-writing tools in the WRITER'S HELPER package provide a good illustrative example of the typical offering in this field. It includes questioning programs aimed at finding a subject to write on, describing different facets of a topic, comparisons and contrasts, together with a prompting program which takes the student through the stages of debating an issue. Other programs help with the development of single paragraphs, organizing information hierarchically, finding original descriptions for topics and developing paragraph structures.

10.2.2 Outliners

Outliners aim to ease the task of planning and organization of a text by getting a writer to structure his or her ideas from the start. Commercial outliners generally force a hierarchical tree structure on the writer and do so through purely textual building of labels for the different parts of the tree. In the research and development laboratories graphical and hypertext tools are being worked on to allow different ways in to the same structure-building and planning exercise.

BRAINSTORM is a typical outliner. Essentially it enables a writer to create a hierarchy of topics and subtopics in a straightforward way. The writer creates a list of topics, then associates lists of subtopics with each item on the topic list, then sub-subtopics with the subtopics and so on. Individual labels, or groups of labels can be moved to different positions on the tree and the program has a degree of intelligence (removing some of the difficulties of housekeeping complex trees) which allows it to identify the use of the same label at different places in the tree (i.e. the need for cross-references). Text is produced in a form that can be immediately used by a word processor.

10.2.3 Notetaking Tools

These take many different forms. The simplest is simply a word-processor on a laptop computer, such as the Cambridge Computer Z88. So portable are such machines that minutes or lecture notes can be taken using them, and the notes then can be taken straight into a database for reference, or used as the basis of the write-up of the talk.

Mainstream programs such as SIDEKICK can 'pop-up' inside other programs, allowing a writer to make a note at any time while using the computer to do something else. The note is then stored and can be imported into other documents later on. One of the best implementations of this idea is on the Macintosh, whose built-in software allows the temporary storage of text and/or graphics for movement between any two applications.

Using such tools a writer can be generating ideas and notes for one text as she or he is working on the detailed draft of another. This sort of application is much closer to addressing the actual behaviour of working writers than a prompting program they must run before getting down to the business of producing text.

Probably the most sophisticated set of writing support tools currently in development, providing a combination of prewriting and composing tools, is the WRITER'S ASSISTANT being developed by Mike Sharples, Lyn Pemberton and James Goodlet at Sussex University (Sharples, Goodlet and Pemberton, 1989). This system differs from almost all others available or under development in two important ways:

1   It is built upon a wide-ranging description of user needs and user writing processes. A great deal of fundamental research has taken place to give the WRITER'S ASSISTANT as much theoretical and pragmatic value as possible. This contrasts markedly with typical post-writing tools, for example, which rely on textbook descriptions of what is good and bad in English, but typically carry out no research themselves on what users do with such textbooks, or would like to see changed. (Some of the theoretical thinking behind the WRITER'S ASSISTANT can be found in Sharples and Pemberton, 1989, 1990.)

2   It is a flexible support tool, designed to make the writer's natural writing processes more efficient. As Steven George recently remarked while delivering a paper at *Computers and Writing 3* in Edinburgh, 'Thirty-five different writers describe thirty-five different ways of writing.' So writing tools need the maximum of flexibility. The research team expect different writers to use the tools differently. This philosophy again is markedly different from typical post-writing tools, which impose a particular set of operations on the writer whether the writer wants them or not and whether they are good for that particular writer or not. (See below.)

10.3   Composing

By composing is meant the actual action of writing, putting ideas into form. Typically, composing goes on concurrently with the so-called pre-writing activities, and, as words appear on the page, post-writing activities begin as well, editing the text as it appears. Most writers engage in a complex series of iterative procedures, whereby they persistently generate plans and ideas which they realize wholly or partly as words, then test the words to check the idea and perhaps thereby generate more ideas, but in testing the words they also perform editorial checks which might lead them back to word generation. Writers are constantly moving back and forth around the words they create.

Obviously, word-processing and text editing tools serve the composing need. There is no need for an extensive review of different word-processing facilities in this brief space. The major characteristics of word-processing are well known: the ability to store, edit, remove, copy, format and present text more flexibly, more speedily and more efficiently than by any other means. However, there are characteristics of word-processors that affect the way writers work, and the documents they produce, and there are some significant differences between different word-processors.

The most obvious differences seen by a user are those in the 'user interface'. This is not the place to discuss human–computer interaction. Let me simply note that there are several different ways to approach the way users control, and get information from, computers. In word-processing, there are three ways that a user might control the software and two ways that the results of their actions might be presented to them (these are features of interfaces not restricted to word-processing, of course).

Control may be through commands, by menus controlled from the keyboard or by mouse. Display may be *WYSIWYG* (What You See Is What You Get) or not. In some word-processors, generally older ones, but often very powerful ones, the user has to remember a long list of esoteric keyboard commands that carry out operations on the text. In WORDSTAR, for example, which is about seven years old, ^OL will allow you to change the left margin. If you type **.p170** at the beginning of your text then it will be printed out with a page length of seventy lines.

These older word-processors are seldom completely WYSIWYG. The user may get a good idea of what the text will look like, but it will not be printed in exactly the same way as on the screen. (The exact relation between what appears on the screen and what appears on the printer is very complex, depending on the word-processing software, the screen being used, the printer used, and the options which have been selected within those offered by the software and the printer). So, for example, a text prepared for TROFF formatting will be full of single line commands that begin with a dot and contain a coded instruction, but you will not see the effects of those codes until you run the TROFF program and get output. TROFF is however much more than a word-processor, it is a complete typesetting language, giving a great deal more control than typical word-processors. This means that using TROFF demands a great deal of experience and esoteric knowledge.

From the user's point of view, selecting options from menus and seeing the results immediately on screen is much more satisfactory. The user need not remember complex commands to achieve particular effects, nor need he or she consult elaborate manuals, and the effect of actions is shown immediately on screen.

WORDSTAR is one of the most popular word-processors on microcomputers, which uses keyboard commands and only limited WYSIWYG. (The most recent version has added menus which make the system much more usable.) WORD 4.0 on the Apple Macintosh is one of the most popular modern word-processors and close to state of the art in its user interface and the quality of its WYSIWYG display.

Probably the most significant characteristic of word-processors for jobbing writers and students alike is the possibility of 'error-free' text. Of course, the errors removed by word-processing are only those of presentation, not structure or content. Even so, it is well known that the psychological effect of well-presented material better disposes the reader towards the content. Most of the commonly used features of word-processing are those which govern the attractiveness of the final document.

However, there are other features of word-processing which can significantly affect writing, especially for writers with some sophistication in the way they use the technology or address their tasks. Three notable ones are:

10.3.1 Search and Replace

Word-processing offers, with varying degrees of control, facilities for automatically searching through text and finding instances of particular character strings. Such a string, when found, can be automatically replaced with a different string. So, for example, if you know you often spell 'separate' as 'seperate', you can instruct the word-processor to search for all instances of 'seperate' and replace them with 'separate'. However, more sophisticated use enables writing (or rather typing) in a kind of shorthand. For each common phrase or word used in the text, a brief unique string can be invented and these can be typed in instead. For example, I use the word *computer* quite a lot in this chapter. So I've been typing in c@, and when I've finished my draft I will search for all instances of c@ and replace them with 'computer'.

10.3.2 Redrafting

Nothing in a word-processed text is permanent, so it need not be perfect. Only the final printout need be of the highest quality. This simple fact, that everything in a word-processed document can be changed, from the spelling to the organization to every item of content, allows writers a great deal more freedom in the way they write than they find with any other medium. Writers can happily throw down the first words that come into their heads, in any order they like, knowing that they can change the whole thing at any time they like.

One of the consequences of this (coupled with the improvements word-processing leads to in output) is that writers typically produce more and spend more time on their work. Student writers in particular, knowing that they can play around at will, typically run through more drafts and make more alterations during drafting than they would using conventional means.

10.3.3 Re-usable Text

Even more powerful, though it usually takes a writer some time to realize this, is the notion that the text is not fixed and unique, but re-usable. Once typed into a word-processor and stored, it can be used over and over again in many different contexts.

For example, the references used in this chapter were not compiled from scratch for this text, but copied from parts of four different files held in different places on computers I use, and amended accordingly. Only three of the references were typed in from scratch. Some of the others were typed eighteen months before I began this article. For anyone who writes more than a little about a restricted area, re-usable text is a major benefit in several ways.

First, it increases productivity. You can produce documents of a given length in less time by synthesizing material you already have. Second, the kind of writing you do may become more focused on the task in hand rather than on the content. If you have already produced the content (in a different context) and now have to adapt it, then you spend more time thinking about how you would adapt it and why, rather than about generating new content. For example, it is quite likely that I shall adapt some of the material in this chapter for future classes I give on computers and writing. In which case I shall be adapting an 8,000-word review in prose, written for a large audience I shall never meet, into a one-hour lecture with a smallish audience of people I know. What pieces can be dropped out? What else will I need to provide? How do I change the style? Should the order of the material be altered?

There are drawbacks to re-usable text, of course. Copyright law is one. While I may have the original on a floppy disk, my contract with the publishers will not allow me simply to print it out and give it to my students. Slightly more difficult to monitor is the agreement most authors have with publishers' contracts along the lines of the following: 'The author warrants that the said contribution is original, has not been published in any material form and is in no way whatever a violation of existing copyright.' Under such an agreement, if I simply take large chunks of material from books or articles I have already published, I am likely to upset both the publisher of the previous material and my current publisher.

Re-using text also means that the subsequent text is likely to lack originality and may represent a kind of tunnel vision, such that the author always deals with the same topic in the same way. If the original items were of poor quality then this also may well be preserved in future adaptation of it.

One slightly unusual word-processor is MINDREADER. It is quite an attractive, run-of-the-mill word-processor with one interesting feature, the sort of feature that is typically presented as 'intelligence'. It attempts to guess the word the writer is currently trying to type. It does this by comparing the letters typed so far with a dictionary of possible words. As someone uses it, however, it learns the words used most frequently and alters its guesses appropriately so, theoretically at least, it should gradually accommodate itself to the user's personal habits of writing.

Arguably this could be useful, especially for slow typists or those who have persistent spelling problems. However, for fast typists and experienced writers it simply seems to get in the way of normal typing. Yet this special feature can be taken advantage of. By training it to accept certain keypresses as signals of words and phrases you typically use a great deal or have some difficulty with, the program can fill in the difficult blanks.

This application illustrates one of the key attractions of software for writing. Whatever the functions are intended for, however they are intended to be used, there will be other, possibly better, uses which writers will discover.

10.4　Post-writing

Post-writing is analysis carried out upon a draft. The draft may be seen by the author as an interim document or as the 'final' text which simply has to be 'corrected'. (I put these words in inverted commas, as it seems to me odd to say that a text is finished when you expect to make further corrections to it!)

The most common post-writing tasks carried out by computer are spelling correction, grammar correction and stylistic analysis.

Spelling correction, by the use of spelling checkers, is now commonplace. Most word-processing systems either include built-in spelling checkers or are supported by additional spelling checkers from third party suppliers.

However, no spelling checker actually checks spelling. Although mechanisms vary a little, essentially a spelling checker simply compares every word in its target text with the words in its dictionary of English (or whatever language the spelling checker uses). If the target word is not in the dictionary it is regarded as misspelled. (Peterson, 1980, reviews some of the main techniques for spelling checking.) For this reason spelling checkers vary in their specification and performance. Dictionary sizes vary markedly, and are difficult to compare, as some are measured in word forms (i.e. where all different types, or inflectional forms, are classed as different words) while others sum the total lexemes.

These two ways of counting result from two approaches to spelling checking. The first involves holding a dictionary of literal strings, i.e. every word-form to be found in the target text is held within the dictionary. This approach has the advantage that the dictionary can be easily examined and updated (so that, for example, the user can add specialized vocabulary such as technical jargon). But it has several drawbacks. Computationally, holding literal strings is expensive. It uses up a great deal of memory and processing time. Linguistically, it means that legitimate neologisms (such as 'computerese', 'keyboarding', 'translation-less') will always be seen as spelling errors.

So a better computational and linguistic approach is to use a dictionary of base lexical forms augmented by rules for morphological derivation of legitimate word-forms. Processing becomes slightly more complicated, but probably more efficient than lookup of large dictionaries, neologisms are accepted and the solution is more attractive theoretically as it (presumably) is a closer model of the way humans store and use word-forms. However, it also has drawbacks. It is harder to update such a dictionary, as it may not be simply a matter of adding new forms, but also of connecting them to the appropriate morphological rules. Furthermore legitimate morphological rules can lead to illegitimate word analysis.

A simple example (though not a spelling error) is 'notable', which by the right rules is seen as 'note' + able' and by the wrong rules as 'not + able'. Another is the 'verb + ion = abstract noun' rule, as in 'abstraction', 'distraction' and 'action'. By this rule we can derive the verbs 'to dandel'(= 'dandelion') and 'to sc' (= 'scion'). Obviously the morphological rules necessary to support spelling checking are many and complex.

No spelling checker employs semantic or pragmatic knowledge, and no commercial systems use syntactic information. Thus each of the following spelling errors will be missed by a commercial spelling checker:

- She used to write memos on headed stationary (syntactic anomaly)
- The buoy ate fish and chips (semantic anomaly)
- At the birthday party every child had a peace (pragmatic anomaly)

However, as such errors are generally mistakes in the choice of homonyms, or near-homonyms, many style checkers and grammar checkers contain dictionaries of commonly confused homophones which alert the writer to the possibility of confusion. These style checkers still lack any information other than that of word-forms, but their dictionaries are designed on the criteria of common confusion, thus containing pairs such as *effect/affect* and *practice/practise*.

As most dictionaries used by spelling checkers are only dictionaries of word-forms, they cannot usually be used as we use paper dictionaries. They lack any information other than the form, so you cannot consult them for derivations, definitions, pronunciation or syntactic information. In the last two years a few systems have begun to combine the spelling checker with a dictionary and/or a thesaurus. A good example is the LITERACY TUTOR developed by System Applied Technology (Horton, Ellis and Black, 1990). This is a system designed for Basic English adult literacy students, who have their own distinct needs. The system integrates word-processor, spelling checker, dictionary of definitions, thesaurus and grammar checker, together with teaching materials which use the dictionary. Students can move at will between the different components and, apparently, find it an extremely helpful system.

Thesauruses and conventional dictionaries are available, usually as separate tools. As they use large amounts of memory, until recently they have not been very marketable except in large corporations. Now, with the advent of large and relatively cheap mass storage devices like CD-ROM (computer disks, similar to CD audio disks, which can store very large volumes of text) large-scale electronic storage of text is very cheap and new applications appear daily. One example is available from the publishers Houghton Mifflin. On a single disk are stored 240,000 words of the American Heritage Electronic Dictionary, including spelling, definitions, pronunciation, grammatical information, hyphenation points, synonyms, etymologies, usage notes, sample text and quotations, phrasal verbs and homographs.

Typically such disks only offer conventional lookup functions, equivalent to traditional use of paper thesauruses. Developers have only just begun to create new functions, uses and access to such information. However with recent developments, especially the rapid growth in the use of hypertext (see below), this may shortly change.

10.4.1 Stylecheckers and Grammar Checkers

Stylecheckers are, perhaps surprisingly, more common than grammar checkers. Linguists know that analysis of style is more complex than that of grammar, because grammatical variation is subsumed within stylistic variation. As with spelling checkers, most stylecheckers do not incorporate full syntactic analysis. Some, like WRITER'S WORKBENCH (Macdonald et al., 1982) and RUS-KIN (Williams, Holt and Cashdan, 1988; Williams, 1989a) have partial syntactic analysis, which is not perfect as it expects grammatical text and carries out its analysis based on the statistical probabilities of word form collocations, rather than a parse of syntactic structures. (The main advantage of this statistical approach is that it needs only a small dictionary of function words, whereas full syntactic parsers require complete dictionaries with syntactic feature marking.)

WRITER'S WORKBENCH WRITER'S WORKBENCH (WWB) is one of the oldest stylecheckers, being first in use in 1981 (MacDonald et al., 1982). Still in use, it contains most of the elements imitated by all other stylecheckers. It consists of a suite of programs that use specialist dictionaries and/or pattern-matching techniques to find possible flaws in text and to compile statistics of various linguistic characteristics of the text, such as number of nominalizations and passives, amount of abstraction, kinds of sentence opener, number of compound sentences, and so on (a simple account of some of these techniques can be found in Williams, 1988).

One feature possessed by WWB, but not by many of its followers, is the 'style table'. This is a set of normative statistics that can be compiled from any corpus of twenty or more texts chosen by the user. Such a table is time-consuming to compile, and its value is solely dependent on the relevance of the stylistic information it gathers, yet the style table is a very useful tool for comparing genres, authors or student essays against 'good' essays.

Evaluations of WWB in the classroom found it aided students at least as effectively as human tutors (see Kiefer and Smith, 1983, 1984, for USA data; Cashdan, Holt and Williams, 1986, for UK evaluation). In the United States the system has been used extensively, though in Britain less so. Its major effect, however, seems to have been the spawning of a brood of copies.

RUSKIN RUSKIN is a context-sensitive stylechecker developed with funding from the Training Agency in 1986–8 (then the Manpower Services Commission). It was built as an improvement on the WWB concept using what was then a novel notion, that of style rules. The style rule is a simple concept, yet potentially quite powerful as a way of conceptualizing the relation between context and text in computational terms.

A style rule is little more than a simple 'production rule', a rule with **IF...THEN...** structure which correlates a contextual variable, such as age of readership, with a textual variable, such as word length. Thus a possible rule might be:

IF average age of audience is low
THEN average word length should be low.

More generally the rules takes the form:

IF contextual variable **IS** value
THEN text variable **SHOULD BE** value

Linguists will be aware that the correspondence between text and context is seldom as simple as this concept suggests. Attempts to formalize stylistic variation have only ever proved partially successful, and, in some areas, almost completely unsuccessful. Computer scientists will observe that the rules use words like 'low', which need precise definition to be of use to a computer and must therefore have empirically determined values. Writers, and writing teachers, will also wonder about the efficacy of such rules. So it is unlikely that the style rule concept will improve our understanding of the relationships or correlations between text and context. All it does is allow us to specify those correlations which seem generally acceptable in a form which a computer can also readily accept. Not only can the computer process such a formalism, it can do so employing expert system terminology which can be used to reconcile conflict between different rules, calculate the reinforcement of resonant rules and aggregate the judgements of rules.

RUSKIN is not, however, an expert system, except in the very simple sense that it employs this formalism to judge texts. Its value over most other stylecheckers is that it recognizes contextual information in making its analyses.

It has other virtues as well, though these are vitiated to some extent by problems which limit RUSKIN's attraction. Consequently, it has never developed beyond being a rather fragile prototype. Nevertheless it has been disseminated and is in use, with many users finding it of value. Its main attractions, other than its use of contextual information, are that its interface presents information in different forms for different types of user, that 'click-on' explanations are provided for its jargon and it offers a range of different analyses, including phrasal, lexical and syntactic analysis. It also gives statistical analysis of text features, including readability formulae. However the most atttractive use of readability formulae is in the program simply called 'READABILITY'.

READABILITY   Readability formulae are popular measures of style, especially among those who believe that quantitative data is more valuable than qualitative, or where enforceable standards of text are supposed to be achieved (e.g. in technical writing where exact house styles are observed). However, readability formulae can only indicate the probable difficulty of text. As they are based on sentence-length (variously measured, but usually simply a word-count) and word-length (either measured in characters or syllables), any worth they have in judging syntactic or semantic complexity comes from the rough correlation between sentence length and sentence syntactic complexity and between word length and semantic density. To the extent that these do not correlate, readability formulae are of little value.

READABILITY, however, does attempt to place readability formulae in a more usable context, by providing a scattergram of sentence readability within a text and mapping that against the equivalent scattergrams for one of a selected set of model texts. On the scattergram outliers (sentences within the measured text that fall outside the range of the target text type) are identified and the user can see at once, visually, how her or his text falls within the paradigm and where it deviates. READABILITY thus provides a stylistic comparison without trying to evaluate the adequacy of the measured text. Evaluation is left to the user, yet because the visual data is simply presented, any novice can carry out the evaluation.

Even so it is still built on the simple measures of word and sentence length which are not true indicators of the density, abstractness, complexity or indeed readability of a text.

Possibly more useful are those programs that flag problem phrases, as these are more likely to be sources of real problems for readers. RUSKIN does this, as does WRITER'S WORKBENCH. However, GRAMMATIK IV is probably the best of the current systems.

GRAMMATIK IV   GRAMMATIK is one of the most venerable of style-checkers, with an ancestry that goes back to 1983, the days of the early CP/M text edtiors. At its heart, then and now, is a dictionary based on analysis of text features, largely lexical and phrasal, such as cliché, idiom, jargon and so on. GRAMMATIK IV, however, available for the IBM and the Macintosh, is impressively different from its forebears in the quality of its interface. While there is still much that the average user might desire changed, it provides one of the best presentations of style checking output currently available. Although its comments still take no account of the communicative context (unlike RUSKIN, for example), so advice is typically of a general or uncommitted kind, they are supported by explanatory help messages which take away much of the burden of the jargon from the user.

RIGHTWRITER   Compared to GRAMMATIK IV, RIGHTWRITER represents the norm in stylecheckers. It has some syntactic knowledge, it operates quite quickly, it has no contextual knowledge and no real intelligence, it provides numerical measures of text characteristics, operates in batch mode (i.e. you run it after you have finished your text rather than while you are writing it) and it inserts comments into that text for you to edit out or make some use of subsequently. In many ways it is like a slightly improved, slightly faster but cut down WRITER'S WORKBENCH, but because it runs on IBM PCs is more likely to be used by more writers. It is also comparatively cheap.

To use it a writer must have a definite desire to know more about specific features of his or her text. In other words, an extra stage is added to the writing process:

plan
draft
RIGHTWRITER review
author review
publish

As we have already noted, most writers do not operate in this straightforward fashion, but in a way which looks more haphazard and fragmentary (even though it may well have a perfectly reasonable internal logic). Systems like RIGHTWRITER (and, indeed, WRITER'S WORKBENCH, RUSKIN, PC STYLE and many others) which demand that the reader uses them at a definite stage in the writing process necessarily constrain the writer. Often, therefore, writers will not use such systems, judging them too inconvenient, though they may decide on occasional use for special documents or where their writing reaches a stage which does seem to correspond to an 'almost finished draft'.

This is why GRAMMATIK IV scores, for it can be used within the user's normal word-processor. Most users seem to require such use, stylechecking which is interactive, immediately available and provides information that can be fed straight into the current document. However, different writing tools offer different facilities and users will find a range of facilities offered by the different systems (a good review of some major writing tools is Hazen et al., 1986).

10.5   Other Tools for Writers

Pre-writing, composing and post-writing software have been in use in the classroom for many years, and are now infiltrating the office and other environments. As our understanding of writing improves and technology develops, these systems are now beginning to approach the kind of functions that truly support real writing use. However, there are new developments in writing software which may have even more profound effects on the way we write. Most notable among these are hypertext (see also chapter 1) and desk-top publishing.

10.5.1   Using Hypertext

Hypertext is currently an increasingly popular concept with a wide range of workers and researchers. It is not simply writing software – many hypertext systems are really hypermedia systems (they incorporate graphics, animation and sound), which means that if the writer is to use them then that writer needs to acquire other expertise, if only to decide when to refer the production of his/her material to other experts. Hypertext systems can also be viewed as database systems, so have raised substantial interest amongst people other than writers.

Nevertheless the fundamental characteristic of hypertext is a textual one – it employs non-linear rather than linear text. (It can, of course, be used for linear text, but this would defeat the object of most hypertext systems.) Linear text is text read from beginning to end without interruption or digression. A conventional novel is a good example. Non-linear text is any text that deviates from the linear paradigm. Many written texts are used in non-linear ways – i.e. not read from start to finish in paginated order. Obvious examples are children's adventure game or 'create your own story' decision-making books, where the choice of the reader alters the outcome of the narrative.

Less obvious, perhaps, is a wide range of documents in which people move backwards and forwards. Newspapers are one common one, which people flick through, selecting the articles, or parts of articles that they want. A reader might go first to the sports page, read a few items, be referred to the continuation of an article on another page, so go to that page, and then find something else of interest upon that new page. Then the reader might turn to the front page and read the headlines, then perhaps the leader and so on. Reference documents of all types, such as manuals and textbooks, are used in a similar way. Probably you have used this book non-linearly a little, as you skipped to the chapters you were most interested in, checked out the occasional reference, looked something up in the index and so on.

Print privileges linear text by the physical characteristics of the medium and by the dominant narrative paradigm. Hypertext privileges non-linear text, having as yet no dominant paradigm and providing a medium which can be used for just about any textual purpose where a computer is an appropriate delivery tool.

For the writer hypertext offers a great deal, yet also brings along some quite significant problems. For the reader also, it brings both attractions and drawbacks. As a hypertext is essentially a series of paragraphs or pages linked together in any way the author thinks reasonable, the problems are largely the obverse of the attractions. A writer can link anything to anything else, but then the reader has to guess where these links are leading and what they are for. The writer can construct a complex web of subtle interrelationships between chunks of text, but the reader can become lost in the web (see e.g. Edwards and Hardman, 1989). Each reader can take a route through the information which exactly suits his or her personal desires, but only if the writer has been able to anticipate those desires (McKnight, Richardson and Dillon, 1989).

Hypertext, in removing many of the constraints that apply in conventional writing, gives so much freedom that both writers and readers find it hard to cope with the potential richness and complexity (for a discussion of some of the complexity see McAleese, 1989b; Wright and Lickorish, 1989).

10.5.2 *Story Writing and Computers*

Computers are used, of course, in teaching children story writing. By and large teachers build classes around whatever conventional word-processors are available to them. However there are projects developing specialist systems tailored for just this purpose. One is Rosetta McLeod's STORYBASE (McLeod, 1990a, 1990b). Though the idea for this system is simple, the implementation and use is powerful. The astounding measure of its success is that children in test schools have come asking for more homework and for holiday homework, which is a rare phenomenon indeed.

STORYBASE is essentially a database of places, people, objects and events. The original version held only text, the latest version uses Interactive Video to store high quality pictures along with text description. The computer selects a subset of the database to form a child's writing assignment. Its unique value is that the asignment is personalized for that particular child. The child receives a unique writing task, unlike those received by anyone else in the class. This may then involve specialist research and activities to carry out in order to complete the assignment. The system appears to provide a very high level of motivation among children.

Of course, computers can be used not only as tools for learning how to write stories, but also as delivery vehicles for real narrative. Many attempts have been made to create programs that could write stories. Klein was able to produce plausible detective stories using a simple semantic database (Klein et al., 1979), but his approach proved extremely limited. Meehan constructed stories as accounts of the problem-solving activities of characters but these were very artificial constructs (Meehan, 1981). In practice, however, no program that can produce *interesting* stories has yet been written. Yazdani (1989) outlines some of the reasons for this. It seems unlikely that worthwhile story generators will arrive in the near future.

One of the most exciting areas for writers, but one which seems already to generate heated debate, is the area of Interactive Fiction (IF). IF is fiction in which the reader takes part, either making choices which affect the storyline, or perhaps even writing additional material him or herself. The phrase usually refers to hypertext fiction but there are literary precursors (see Howell and Douglas, 1990) and as we have seen, printed text, whilst apparently linear, may well be used in complex ways.

Machine-based fiction seems to many to be a logical continuation of the experimental tradition in fiction, though it also owes much of its stimulus to text based adventure games like Infocom's ZORK. However, existing game structures are more limited than the kind of writing normally thought of under the IF umbrella. It is more limited because it is essentially story-telling, is based on limiting the reader's choices to a relatively narrow set of simple actions and has clearly defined goals, pathways and win/lose situations. IF, which is not game-oriented, looks to create a rich imaginative experience, like that of a conventional novel, yet through unconventional means. Writers of IF see hypertext as a tool for a completely new kind of creativity.

For example, STORYSPACE (Bolter, 1989) is a system for writing hypertext fiction which links paragraphs or pages of text through keywords. The same keywords may link to different paragraphs on different visits to the same keyword, so a reader may quickly be led into a maze of complex links between chunks of text.

It is this fundamental feature, that the reader makes some of the story decisions and can thus wander through a very large number of possible storylinks, that causes both the excitement and the problems in IF. It creates excitement as it means that the reader effectively makes up the story, the writer simply provides the material (though the writer will always limit the number of routes through the system). It creates problems because readers can become lost, confused and frustrated within the narrative.

The primary source of frustration for readers is the lack of closure of such narratives. Naive readers are raised on a diet of narrative closure which, despite the prevalence of post-structural analysis in literary theory, holds most territory in the battle for making sense of narrative. While literary theorists argue that no story ends, that all stories are read differently by different people, that reading to recover the author's intentions is a mistake because they are irrecoverable and anyway unknowable and so on, most readers go blithely on believing that a good story has a beginning, middle and end, a clearly defined storyline which the author intended to achieve and works by relating events in logical sequence.

This is not the view that stories written in hypertext promote. While it is possible for someone reading an IF text on one occasion to achieve a single storyline that comes to a close, on a different occasion not only may he or she make a different choice so follow a different route and end with different closure, he or she may well discover new aspects of the previous reading of the story which 'open up' the original reading. Not only does the fiction change on each reading but previous readings are changed interpretatively on each re-reading.

For some creative writers, especially experimental writers and writing theorists, a computer tool which allows them to experiment with and construct new forms of narrative is the most exciting prospect any technology could ever offer. In the discussion of IF at the Second UK Conference on Computers and Writing delegates enthused over: reader creativity; endless fictions; communal fictions; fiction structured by reader associations; fictions that could mutate through different styles and genres; and fictions that could answer whatever questions the reader might want to ask. (Papers from the conference are published as Williams, 1990b. A brief account of the IF debate is Williams, 1989b.)

Worries are that passing control to the reader gives responsibility to the unskilled, so there will be many stories written by poor writers, and that such stories will inevitably be more about actions, simple narrative links, than richness of symbolism, metaphor, characterization or social and historical depth. The hypertext structure seems almost inevitably to lead to an episodic narrative.

10.5.3 Desk-top Publishing

One final area we should consider briefly, though it is properly not the province of writers but of printers, editors and typesetters, is desk-top publishing (DTP). A desk-top publishing system places sophisticated presentational tools in the hands of the ordinary micro user so that any writer, sufficiently resourced, can take a manuscript to the point where it can be printed and bound. To achieve the necessary quality a laser printer is needed, so the total cost of a DTP system including appropriate computer, software and printer might be about £8,000. Such facilities are therefore not within the reach of every writer. They are, however, much more accessible than any previous print technology.

Desk-top publishing takes over where the writer leaves off. It allows high precision control over such features of text as fonts, positioning and spacing of text, incorporation of graphics into text and so on, as well as automating such tasks as indexing, creating Tables of Contents, linking individual chapters into complete books with consistent pagination and so on. In other words it is a technology that can turn a text into a book.

The effect on writers is both enabling and disabling. It enables because it places control over every aspect of a text into the writer's hands. A writer can almost become a publisher through DTP. A book produced through DTP technology is almost indistinguishable to the non-expert eye from one produced by conventional print procedures. Writers also find it an extremely rewarding tool to use. They see their text transformed into professional quality print.

However, to use DTP well expertise is needed. Producing attractive text is not merely a matter of using a laser printer. Pages must be laid out with both text and graphics arranged to carry their logical purposes and yet achieve attractive design. This needs at least a good eye on the part of the user and preferably design expertise. DTP is also a technology riddled with complex terminology (derived from printing and typesetting) and unfamiliar concepts. Given that many writers have difficulty coping with proofreading marks on page proofs, many would be well advised to leave DTP systems to those who have print and graphical design skills (see also Ott's comments in chapter 8, this volume).

10.6   Conclusion

In summary, computers provide both training and support for writers which is exciting and rewarding, adding a great deal to the flexibility, control and productivity of most writers. At the same time the growth in this technology brings some dangers, and some of it does not provide what writers (and teachers) would hope it provided. Post-writing software in particular has to be used with particular care in a context which cushions the software's judgements with reason (for a discussion of the problems of post-writing software, see Williams, 1990a). Some of the most exciting writing software can also add to the burden of the writer, through requiring new skills (e.g. in hypertext and desk-top publishing) and through the problems that computer technology can bring to almost any situation, such as expense, hardware failure, ergonomic, health and safety considerations, poorly designed manuals and so on (see Williams 1990a).

Despite the problems, the field of computers and writing is rapidly expanding. The United Kingdom has an annual conference in the field, as does the United States, and there are at least four journals devoted to aspects of the field. It is expanding largely because of the benefits computers bring to writers, but also because computers offer new ways of writing. Computers do not just enable writers to do better the things they already do, they allow them to do new things, to write in different ways. Techniques such as invisible writing, outlining and re-usable writing, applications such as desk-top publishing and hypertext and functions such as search and replace, cross-reference checking and style checking give the writer new ways to manipulate text which seem to be producing both new kinds of writing and new theories of the writing process.

Further Reading

Colette Daiute's *Computers and Writing* (1985), though slightly old now, is still a very useful review of the basics of computers and writing in the United States, as is Robert Shostak's collection of papers, though these are beginning to assume the status of historical documents in the field (Shostak, 1984). Both texts cover most of the main ground, though not more recent developments such as desk-top publishing and hypertext. For UK material, the papers from the first two UK conferences on 'Computers and Writing', edited by myself and Patrik Holt, provide comprehensive overviews of what is currently going on (Williams and Holt, 1989; Williams, 1990b). My synthesis of the entire field of computers and writing, concentrating on UK activity but also reporting much US work (Williams, 1991) is the only UK book providing such an overview of the field.

Probably the most important paper in the literature on writing and cognition, is Flower and Hayes' paper 'The Dynamics of Composing', which examines the way writers create plans to solve writing problems (Flower and Hayes, 1980). It has influenced much of the cognitive and computer work on writing support.

If you have a specific interest in hypertext, probably currently the most rapidly expanding area in the field, Ray McAleese's collection of papers on hypertext provides a good start, covering issues from both the reader's and the writer's point of view (McAleese, 1989a).

Bibliography

Aarts, J. and Meijs, W. J. (eds) (1984) *Corpus Linguistics: Recent Developments in the Use of Computer Corpora in English Language Research*. Amsterdam: Rodopi.

Aarts, J. and Meijs, W. J. (eds) (1986) *Corpus Linguistics II: New Studies in the Analysis and Exploitation of Computer Corpora*. Amsterdam: Rodopi.

Aarts, J. and Meijs, W. J. (eds) (1990) *Theory and Practice in Corpus Linguistics*. Amsterdam: Rodopi.

Aarts, J. and van den Heuvel, T, (1985) Computational tools for the syntactic analysis of corpora. *Linguistics*, 23, 303–35.

Ahmad, K., Corbett, G., Rogers, M. and Sussex, R. (1985) *Computers, Language Learning and Language Teaching*. Cambridge, New York and Melbourne: Cambridge University Press.

Ahmad, K., Rogers, M. and Thomas, P. (1987) Term banks: a case study in knowledge representation and deployment. In H. Czap and C. Galinksi (eds) *Terminology and Knowledge Engineering*, Frankfurt-an-Main: INDEKS Verlag, 341–55.

Akkerman, E. (1989) An independent analysis of the LDOCE grammar coding system. In B. Boguraev and E. J. Briscoe (eds), *Computational Lexicography for Natural Language Processing*. London and New York: Longman: 65–83.

Akkerman, E., Masereeuw, P. C. and Meijs, W. J. (1985) *Designing a Computerized Lexicon for Word-level Tagging: ASCOT Report No. 2*. Amsterdam: Rodopi.

Al, B. F. (1988) Langue source, langue cible et métalangue. In R. Landheer (ed.), *Aspects de Linguistique Française*, Amsterdam: Rodopi, 15–29.

Aland, K. (ed.) (1987) *Text und Textwert der Griechischen Handschriften des Neuen Testaments. I. Die Katholischen Briefe*, 3 volumes. Berlin and New York: De Gruyter.

ALLC-ACH (1990): *ALLC-ACH 90: The New Medium. Book of Abstracts and Conference Guide*. 17th International Association for Literary and Linguistic Computing Conference; 10th International Conference on Computers and the Humanities. Siegen: University of Siegen.

Allen, J. (1987) *Natural Language Understanding*. Menlo Park, Calif: Benjamin/Cummings.

Allen, J., Hunnicutt, M. S. and Klatt, D., with Armstrong, R. C. and Pisoni, D. B. (1987) *From Text to Speech: the MITalk System*. Cambridge: Cambridge University Press.

Allen, J. F. and Perrault, C. R. (1986) Analyzing intention in utterances. In B. J. Grosz et al. (eds), *Readings in Natural Language Processing*, Los Altos: Morgan Kaufmann, 440–58. Also appears in *Artificial Intelligence* 15, 1980, 143–78.

Alshawi, H., Boguraev, B. K. and Briscoe, E. J. (1985) Towards a dictionary support environment for real-time parsing. In *Proceedings of the Second Conference of the European Chapter of the Association for Computational Linguistics*, Geneva, 171–8.

Altenberg, B. (1987) *Prosodic Patterns in Spoken English: Studies in the Correlation between Prosody and Grammar for Text-to-Speech Conversion. Lund Studies in English*, 76. Lund: Lund University Press.

Altenberg, B. (1991) A bibliography of publications relating to English computer corpora. In S. Johansson and A.-B. Stenström (eds) *English Computer Corpora: Selected Papers and Bibliography*, Boston: Mouton de Gruyter, 355–96. Original version (1986) in *ICAME News*, 10, 62–79.

Amsler, R. A. (1980) *The Structure of the Merriam-Webster Pocket Dictionary*, Doctoral Thesis, University of Texas at Austin.

Amsler, R. A. (1981) A taxonomy for English nouns and verbs, *Proceedings of the 19th Annual Meeting of the Association for Computational Linguistics*, Stanford, California, 133–8.

Amsler, R. A. and Tompa, F. W. (1989) *An SGML-based Standard for English Monolingual Dictionaries*. Waterloo, Ontario: Bellcore and the Centre for the New Oxford English Dictionary.

Ananiadou, S. (1987) A brief survey of some current operational systems. In M. King *Machine Translation Today*. Edinburgh: Edinburgh University Press, 171–91.

Appelt, D. E. (1985) *Planning English Sentences*. Cambridge: Cambridge University Press.

Arnold, D. (1986) General review of the design methodology. *Multilingua*, 5, 136–8.

Arthern, P. J. (1979) Machine translation and computerized terminology systems – a translator's viewpoint. In. B. M. Snell (ed.) *Translating and the Computer*. Amsterdam: North-Holland, 77–108.

Ashford, J. H. (1987) Text storage and retrieval in the ORACLE relational database management system: design study and intended application. *Program*, 21/2, 108–23.

Ashford, J. H. and Willett, P. (1988) *Text Retrieval and Document Databases*. London: Chartwell-Bratt.

Association for Computing Machinery (1989) *Hypertext '89 Proceedings*. 5–7 November 1989, Pittsburgh and New York: Association for Computing Machinery.

Atwell, E. and Elliott, S. (1987) Dealing with ill-formed English text. In R. Garside, G. Leech and G. Sampson (eds) *The Computational Analysis of English*. London and New York: Longman, 120–38.

Austin, J. L. (1962) *How to do Things with Words*. New York: Oxford University Press.

Bahl, L. R., Jelinek, F. and Mercer, R. L. (1983) A maximum likelihood approach to continuous speech recognition. *IEEE Transactions on Pattern Analysis and Machine Intelligence*, 5/2, 179–90.

Bailey, B. J. R. (1990) A model for function word counts. *Applied Statistics*, 39, 107–14.

Bailey, R. W. (1979) The future of computational stylistics. *ALLC Bulletin*, 7, 4–11. Reprinted in R. G. Potter (ed.) (1989a) *Literary Computing and Literary Criticism*, Philadelphia: University of Pennsylvania Press, 3–12.

Bain, M., Bland, R., Burnard, L., Duke, J., Edwards, C., Lindsey, D., Rossiter, N. and Willett, P. (1989) *Free Text Retrieval Systems: A Review and Evaluation*. London: Taylor Graham.

Barnard, D. T. (1988) SGML-based markup for literary texts: two problems and some solutions. *Computers and the Humanities*, 22, 265–76.

Bateman, J. A. (1985) *Utterances in Context: Towards a Systemic Theory of the Intersubjective Achievement of Discourse*. PhD dissertation, University of Edinburgh.

Bateman, J. A. (1990) Upper modeling: a level of semantics for natural language processing. Presented at the 5th International Workshop on Language Generation, Pittsburgh.

Bateman, J. A. and Paris, C. L. (1989) Phrasing a text in terms the user can understand. In *11th IJCAI Conference Proceedings*, Detroit. Also available as USC/Information Sciences Institute Research Report RR-89-240.

Battestin, M. C. (ed.) (1989) *New Essays by Henry Fielding: His Contributions to 'The Craftsman' (1734–1739) and other early journalism, with a stylometric analysis by Michael G. Farringdon*. Charlottesville, Va.: University of Virginia Press.

Beale, A. D. (1989) *The Development of a Distributional Lexicon: A contribution to computational lexicography*. Doctoral thesis. Lancaster: Department of Linguistics and Modern English Language, University of Lancaster.

Becker, J. D. (1975) *The Phrasal Lexicon*. Cambridge, MA: Bolt, Beranek and Newman, Technical Report 3081.

Becker, M. (1988) *Electronic Data Processing in Practice* (translated by D. Lewis). Chichester: Ellis Horwood.

Bender, T. K. and Briggum, S. M. (1982) Quantitative stylistic analysis of impressionistic style in Joseph Conrad and Ford Madox Ford. In R. W. Bailey (ed.) *Computing in the Humanities*. Amsterdam: North-Holland, 59–64.

Benduhn-Mertz, A. (1985) Methodological aspects in automatically discovering genealogical dependencies among Greek New Testament Manuscripts. *ALLC Journal*, 5, 31–5.

Biber, D. (1988) *Variation across Speech and Writing*. Cambridge: Cambridge University Press.

Billing, H. (1987) Machine translation summit, Hakone, 17–19 September 1987: eine bewertende Beschreibung der vorgestellten Systeme und Projekte im Bereich der maschinellen Übersetzung (MT). *Sprache und Datenverarbeitung*, 11, 5–5.

Blatt, A., Freigang, K.-H., Schmitz, K.-D. and Thome, G. (1985) *Computer und Übersetzen: eine Einführung*, Hildesheim, Zurich and New York: Georg Olms Verlag.

Bock, J. K. (1982) Toward a cognitive psychology of syntax: Information processing contributions to sentence formulation. *Psychological Review*, 89, 1–47.

Boden, M. A. (1987) *Artificial Intelligence and Natural Man*, 2nd edn. Brighton: Harvester Press.

Boguraev, B. and Briscoe, E. J. (eds) (1989) *Computational Lexicography for Natural Language Processing*. London and New York: Longman.

Boguraev, B., Briscoe, E., Calzolari, N., Cater, A., Meijs, W., Picchi, E. and Zampolli, A. (1989) *Acquisition of Lexical Knowledge for Natural Language Processing Systems*, Project Description and Technical Annexe for Esprit Basic Research Action, Pisa.

Bolter, J. D. (1989) *Storyspace 7.05d*. Riverrun Ltd, 1703 East Michigan Ave, Jackson, Michigan 49202.

Brainerd, B. (1977) *Weighing Evidence in Language and Literature: A Statistical Approach*. Toronto: University of Toronto Press.

Brainerd, B. (1979) Pronouns and genre in Shakespeare's drama. *Computers and the Humanities*, 13, 3–16.

Brainerd, B. (1980) The chronology of Shakespeare's plays: a statistical study. *Computers and the Humanities*, 14, 221–30.

Bratley, P. and Ross, D. Jr (1981) Syllabic spectra. *ALLC Journal*, 2, 41–50.

Bresnan, J. (1978) A realistic transformational grammar. In M. Halle, J. Bresnan and G. Miller (eds), *Linguistic Theory and Psychological Reality*, Cambridge, MA.: MIT Press, 39–49.

Bresnan, J. (1982) *The Mental Representation of Grammatical Relations*. Cambridge, MA: MIT Press.

Briscoe, E. (1985) *Report of the Dictonary Syndicate*. Alvey Speech Club Workshop, Warwick University.

Brower, R. A. (1951) *The Fields of Light: an experiment in critical reading*. London: Oxford University Press.

Brown, E. K. (1984) *Linguistics Today*. London: Fontana.

Brown, G. (1990) eL: a tool for language learning. *Computer Assisted Language Learning*, 2, 83–91.

Brown, P. F., Cocke, J., Della Pietra, S. A., Della Pietra, V. J., Jelinek, F., Lafferty, J. D., Mercer, R. L. and Roossin, P. S. (1990) A statistical approach to machine translation. *Computational Linguistics*, 16, 79–85.

Budd, T. (1987) *A little Smalltalk*. Reading, MA: Addison-Wesley.

Burgess, G. (1990) Time for evaluation, time for change: CALL past, present, and future. *Computer Assisted Language Learning*, 1, 11.

Burnard, L. (1987) Principles of database design. In S. Rahtz (ed.) *Information Technology in the Humanities*, Chichester: Ellis Horwood, 54–68.

Burnard, L. (1988) The Oxford Text Archive: principles and prospects. In J.-P. Genet (ed.) *Standardisation et Echange des Bases de Données Historiques*, Paris: Editions du CNRS, 191–203.

Burnard, L. (forthcoming) The Text Encoding Initiative: a progress report. *Proceedings of the Eleventh ICAME Conference*, Berlin, July 1990.

Burns, H. (1984) Recollections of first-generation computer-assisted prewriting. In W. Wresch (ed.), *The Computer in Composition Instruction*. Urbana, Ill.: National Council of Teachers of English, 15–33.

Burrows, J. F. (1983) 'Nothing out of the ordinary way': differentiation of character in the twelve most common words of *Northanger Abbey*, *Mansfield Park*, and *Emma*. *British Journal for Eighteenth-Century Studies*, 6, 17–41.

Burrows, J. F. (1986a) Modal verbs and moral principles: an aspect of Jane Austen's style. *Literary and Linguistic Computing*, 1, 9–23.

Burrows, J. F. (1986b) The reciprocities of style: literary criticism and literary statistics. *Essays and Studies*, new series 39, 78–93.

Burrows, J. F. (1987a) *Computation into Criticism: A study of Jane Austen's novels and an experiment in method*. Oxford: Clarendon Press.

Burrows, J. F. (1987b) Word-patterns and story-shapes: the statistical analysis of narrative style. *Literary and Linguistic Computing*, 2, 61–70.

Burrows, J. F. (1989a) 'A Vision' as a revision? *Eighteenth-Century Studies*, 22, 551–65.

Burrows, J. F. (1989b) 'An Ocean where each Kind . . . ': statistical analysis and some major determinants of literary style. *Computers and the Humanities*, 22, 309–21.

Burrows, J. F. and Hassall, A. J. (1988) Anna Boleyn and the authenticity of Fielding's feminine narratives. *Eighteenth-Century Studies*, 21, 427–53.

Burton, D. M. (1973) *Shakespeare's Grammatical Style: A computer-assisted analysis of 'Richard II' and 'Antony and Cleopatra'*. Austin: University of Texas Press.

Busemann, S. (1984) Surface transformations during the generation of written German sentences. Report ANS-27, Research Unit for Information Science and Artificial Intelligence, University of Hamburg, Hamburg. Also in D. D. McDonald and L. Bolc (eds) (1988) *Natural Language Generation Systems*, New York: Springer-Verlag, 98–165.

Butler, C. S. (1981) *Poetry and the Computer: some quantitative aspects of the style of Sylvia*

Plath. London: Oxford University Press. (From the *Proceedings of the British Academy*, 65, 1979, 291–312.)

Butler, C. S. (1985a) Computerized text processing in linguistic and literary research. *Linguistics Abstracts*, 1, 53–67.

Butler, C. S. (1985b) *Statistics in Linguistics*. Oxford: Basil Blackwell.

Butler, C. S. (1985c) *Computers in Linguistics*. Oxford: Basil Blackwell.

Butler, C. S. (1990) Language and computation. In N. E. Collinge (ed.) *An Encyclopaedia of Language*. London and New York: Routledge, 611–67.

Butler, S. and Stoneman, W. P. (eds) (1988) *Editing, Publishing and Computer Technology. Papers Given at the Twentieth Annual Conference on Editorial Problems*. University of Toronto, 2–3 November 1984. New York: AMS Press.

Byrd, R., Calzolari, N., Chodorow, M., Klavans, J., Neff, M. and Rizk, O. (1987) *Tools and Methods for Computational Lexicology*, RC-12642, IBM, Yorktown Heights.

Cameron, K. (ed.) (1989) *Computer-assisted Language Learning. Program structure and principles*. Oxford: Blackwell Scientific.

Cameron, K., Dodd, W. S. and Rahtz, S. (eds) (1986) *Computers and Modern Language Studies*. Chichester: Ellis Horwood.

Campbell, J. (1983) *Grammatical Man: Information, entropy, language, and life*. London: Allen Lane.

Cannon, R. L. and Oakman, R. L. (1989) Interactive collation on a microcomputer: the URICA! approach. *Computers and the Humanities*, 23, 469–72.

Carcagno, D. and Iordanskaya, L. (1989) Content determination and text structuring in GOSSIP. Presented at the 2nd European Workshop on Text Generation, Edinburgh.

Carroll, J. B. (1971) Statistical analysis of the corpus. In J. B. Carroll, P. Davies and B. Richman (eds) *The American Heritage Word Frequency Book*. New York: American Heritage.

Carter, D. (1989) LDOCE and speech recognition. In B. Boguraev and E. J. Briscoe (eds) *Computational Lexicography for Natural Language Processing*. London and New York: Longman.

Cashdan, A., Holt, P. and Williams, N. (1986) *Report to the Manpower Services Commission on a Pilot Investigation into the Assessment of Written Style by Computer*. Sheffield: Training Agency.

Catach, N. (ed.) (1988) *Les Editions critiques. Problèmes techniques et éditoriaux. Actes de la Table Ronde Internationale de 1984*. Paris: Les belles lettres.

Cater, J. P. (1983). *Electronically Speaking: Computer speech generation*. Indianapolis: Howard W. Sams.

Cawsey, A. (1990) Generating communicative discourse. In R. Dale, C. Mellish and M. Zock (eds), *Current Research in Natural Language Generation*. New York: Academic Press, 75–101.

Cercone, N. and Murchison, C. (1985) Integrating artificial intelligence into literary research: an invitation to discuss design specifications. *Computers and the Humanities*, 19, 235–43.

Cherry, C. (1957) *On Human Communication*. Cambridge, MA: MIT Press.

Chomsky, N. (1957) *Syntactic Structures*. The Hague: Mouton.

Chomsky, N. (1965) *Aspects of the Theory of Syntax*. Cambridge, MA: MIT Press.

Clark, H. H. and Murphy, G. L. (1982) Audience design in meaning and reference. In J. F. Le Ny and W. Kintsch (eds), *Language and Comprehension*, Amsterdam: North-Holland, 287–99.

Clifford, J. L. (ed.) (1964) *Peregrine Pickle*. London: Oxford University Press.

Clippinger, J. A. (1974) *A Discourse Speaking Program as a Preliminary Theory of Discourse Behavior and a Limited Theory of Psychoanalytic Discourse.* PhD dissertation, University of Pennsylvania.

Clocksin, W. F. and Mellish, C. S. (1987) *Programming in Prolog,* 3rd revised and extended edition. Berlin and Heidelberg: Springer Verlag.

CNRS (1979) *La Pratique des ordinateurs dans la critique des textes.* Colloques Internationaux du Centre National de la Recherche Scientifique, no. 579. Paris: Editions du CNRS.

Coleman, J. (ed.) (1987) *The Interactive Video Disc in Language Teaching.* New Alyth, Perthshire: Lochee Publications.

Conlon, T. (1984) *PILOT – the language and how to use it.* New Jersey: Prentice Hall.

Coombs, J., De Rose, S. and Renear, A. (1987) Markup systems and the future of scholarly text processing. *Communications of the ACM,* 30/11, 933–47.

Copestake, A. (1990) *An Approach to Building the Hierarchical Element of a Lexical Knowledge Base from a Machine-Readable Dictionary.* ACQUILEX Working Paper. Cambridge: Computer Laboratory, Cambridge University.

Crookes, D. (1988) *Introduction to Programming in Prolog.* New York: Prentice Hall.

Cullingford, R. (1986) SAM. In B. J. Grosz, K. Sparck-Jones and B. L. Webber (eds) *Readings in Natural Language Processing.* Los Altos: Morgan Kaufmann, 627–49.

Dahlgren, K. (1988) *Naïve Semantics for Natural Language Understanding.* Boston, MA: Kluwer Academic Publishers.

Dahlgren, K. and McDowell, J. (1989) Knowledge representation for commonsense reasoning with text. *Computational Linguistics,* 15/3, 149–70.

Daiute, C. (1985) *Computers and Writing.* Reading, MA: Addison-Wesley.

Dale, R. (1990) Generating recipes: an overview of EPICURE. In R. Dale, C. Mellish and M. Zock (eds) *Current Research in Natural Language Generation.* New York: Academic Press, 229–55.

Dale, R., Mellish, C. and Zock, M. (eds) (1990) *Current Research in Natural Language Generation.* New York: Academic Press.

Danlos, L. (1987) *Génération Automatique de Textes en Langues Naturelles.* PhD dissertation, University of Paris. Also in English translated by D. Debize and C. Henderson, *The Linguistic Basis of Text Generation.* Cambridge: Cambridge University Press.

Darby, J. (ed.) (1990) *Computers in Teaching Initiative Report.* Oxford: CTISS Publications.

Date, C. J. (1987) *Database: A Primer,* 4th edn. Reading, MA: Addison-Wesley.

Date, C. J. (1988) *A Guide to the SQL Standard,* 2nd edn, Reading, MA: Addison-Wesley.

Davey, A. (1979) *Discourse Production.* Edinburgh: Edinburgh University Press.

Davies, G. (1985) *Talking BASIC. An Introduction to BASIC Programming for Users of Language.* London: Cassell.

Davies, G. and Higgins, J. (1985) *Using Computers in Language Learning: A teacher's guide,* 2nd edn. London: CILT.

Davies, T. (1989) TERMDOK: the ultimate translator's tool? *LT Electric Word,* 16, 51–2.

De Rose, S. J., Durand, D. and Mylonas, E. (1990) What is text, really? *Journal of Computers in Higher Education,* 1/2, 3–26.

De Smedt, K. J. M. J. (1990) *Incremental Sentence Generation.* PhD dissertation, University of Nijmegen.

De Smedt, K. J. M. J. and Kempen, G. (1987) Incremental sentence production. In Kempen (ed.) *Natural Language Generation*. Boston, MA: Kluwer Academic, 356–70.

Dik, S. C. (1978) *Functional Grammar*. Amsterdam: North-Holland.

Dik, S. C. (1989a) *The Theory of Functional Grammar. Part I: The Structure of the Clause*. Dordrecht: Foris.

Dik, S. C. (1989b) Relational reasoning in functional logic. In J. H. Connolly and S. C. Dik (eds) *Functional Grammar and the Computer*. Dordrecht: Foris, 273–88.

Dik, S. C. (1989c) *The Lexicon in a Computational Functional Grammar*. Amsterdam: General Linguistics Institute, Amsterdam University.

Dilligan, R. J. and Lynn, K. (1972–3) Computers and the history of prosody. *College English*, 34, 1103–4, 1113–23.

Edwards, D. M. and Hardman, L. (1989) 'Lost in hyperspace': cognitive mapping and navigation in a hypertext environment. In R. McAleese (ed.) (1989a) *Hypertext: Theory into Practice*. Oxford: Intellect, 105–25.

Efron, B. and Thisted, R. (1976) Estimating the number of unseen species: how many words did Shakespeare know? *Biometrika*, 63, 435–47.

Efron, B. and Thisted, R. (1987) Did Shakespeare write a newly-discovered poem? *Biometrika*, 74, 445–55.

Ellegård, A. (1962) *A Statistical Method for Determining Authorship: the 'Junius' letters 1769–1772*. Gothenburg: University of Gothenburg.

Ellegård, A. (1978) *The Syntactic Structure of English Texts: A computer-based study of four kinds of text in the Brown University Corpus. Gothenberg Studies in English*, 43. Gothenburg: Acta Universitatis Gothoburgensis.

Emele, C. (1986) *FREGE: Entwicklung und Implementierung eines objektorientierten FRont-End-GEnerators für das Deutsche*. PhD dissertation, University of Stuttgart.

Fabian, B. and Kranz, D. (1971) Interne Kollation. Eine Einführung in die maschinelle Textvergleichung. In G. Martens and H. Zeller (eds), *Texte und Varianten. Probleme ihrer Edition und Interpretation*, Munich: C. H. Beck, 385–400.

Fallside, F. and Woods, W. (eds) (1985) *Computer Speech Processing*. New York: Prentice Hall.

Farrington, B. (1989) AI 'grandeur' or 'servitude'? In K. Cameron (ed.) *Computer-assisted Language Learning*. Oxofrd: Blackwell Scientific, 67–80.

Fass, D. (1989) An account of coherence, semantic relations, metonymy, and lexical ambiguity resolution. In S. L. Small, G. W. Cottrell and M. K. Tanenhaus (eds) *Lexical Ambiguity Resolution*, San Mateo, California: Morgan Kaufmann.

Fawcett, R. P. (1990) The COMMUNAL project: Two years old and going well. *Network*, 13/14, 35–9.

Feeney, M. and Merry, K. (eds) (1990) *Information Technology and the Research Process*. London: Bowker-Saur.

Ferney, D. (1989) Small programs that 'know' what they teach. In K. Cameron (ed.) *Computer-assisted Language Learning*. Oxford: Blackwell Scientific, 14–27.

Fish, S. (1980) What is stylistics and why are they saying such terrible things about it? In S. Fish, *Is there a Text in this Class?* Cambridge, MA: Harvard University Press, 68–96.

Flower, L. S. and Hayes, J. R. (1980) The dynamics of composing: making plans and juggling constraints. In Gregg L. W. and Steinberg E. (eds) *Cognitive Processing in Writing*. Hillsdale, NJ: Lawrence Erlbaum, 31–50.

Fortier, P. A. (1985) Using the computer for literary criticism: theoretical underpinnings and cost factors. In B. Derval and M. Lenoble (eds), *La Critique littéraire et l'ordinateur.* Montreal: Derval and Lenoble.

Fortier, P. A. (1989a) Some statistics of themes in the French novel. *Computers and the Humanities*, 23, 293–9.

Fortier, P. A. (1989b) Analysis of twentieth-century French prose fiction: theoretical context, results, perspective. In R. G. Potter (ed.) (1989a) *Literary Computing and Literary Criticism.* Philadelphia: University of Pennsylvania Press, 77–95.

Foucault, M. (1967) *Madness and Civilization,* translated by Richard Howard. London: Tavistock Publications. (Originally *Histoire de la folie,* 1961.)

Fox, J. (1990) A microcomputer-based approach to training in second language reading skills. *Computer Assisted Language Learning*, 1, 29–40.

Fox, J., Matthews, A., Matthews, C. and Rope, A. (1990) *Educational Technology in Modern Language Learning.* Sheffield: Training Agency.

Francis, W. N. (1980) A tagged corpus – problems and prospects. In S. Greenbaum, G. Leech and J. Svartvik (eds) *Studies in English Linguistics – for Randolph Quirk.* London: Longman 192–209.

Francis, W. N. (1982) Problems of assembling and computerizing large corpora. In S. Johansson (ed.) *Computer Corpora in English Language Research.* Bergen: Norwegian Computing Centre for the Humanities, 7–24.

Francis, W. N. and Kučera, H. (1979) *Manual of Information to Accompany 'A Standard Sample of Present-day Edited American English, for Use with Digital Computers'* (augmented and revised edition). Providence, RI: Department of Linguistics, Brown University. (Original edition 1964, revised 1971.)

Francis, W. N. and Kučera, H. (1982) *Frequency Analysis of English Usage: Lexicon and grammar.* Boston, MA: Houghton Mifflin.

Friedman, D. P. and Felleisen, F. (1987) *The Little Lisper.* Boston, MA: MIT Press.

Froger, J. (1964–5) La collation des manuscrits à la machine électronique. *Institut de Recherche et d'Histoire des Textes. Bulletin*, 135–71.

Froger, J. (1968) *La Critique des textes et son automatisation.* (Initiation aux nouveautés de la science, 7). Paris: Dunod.

Gabler, H. W. and Kreitmair, W. (1986) Der Computer als Arbeitshilfe für das wissenschaftliche Edieren. In B. Gregor and M. Krifka (eds) *Computerfibel für die Geisteswissenschaften,* Munich: C. H. Beck, 203–11.

Gabler, H. W., with W. Steppe and C. Melchior (eds) (1984) *Ulysses,* 3 vols. New York and London: Garland.

Galletly, J. E. and Butcher, C. W. (1989) Towards an intelligent syntax checker. In K. Cameron (ed.) *Computer-assisted Language Learning.* Oxford: Blackwell Scientific, 81–100.

Garrett, M. (1990) Sentence processing. In D. N. Osherson and H. Lasnik (eds) *Language.* Cambridge, MA: MIT Press, 132–75.

Garside, R., Leech, G. and Sampson, G. (eds) (1987) *The Computational Analysis of English: A corpus-based approach.* London and New York: Longman.

Garvin, P. L. (1963a) *Natural Language and the Computer.* New York: McGraw-Hill.

Garvin, P. L. (1963b) Syntax in machine translation. In P. L. Garvin (1963a) *Natural Language and the Computer.* New York: McGraw-Hill, 223–32.

Gazdar, G. and Mellish, C. (1987) Computational linguistics. In J. Lyons, R. Coates, M. Deuchar and G. Gazdar (eds) *New Horizons in Linguistics 2.* London: Penguin, 225–48.

Gazdar, G. and Mellish, C. (1989a) *Natural Language Processing in LISP.* Reading, MA: Addison-Wesley.

Gazdar, G. and Mellish, C. (1989b) *Natural Language Processing in PROLOG: An introduction to computational linguistics*. Reading, MA: Addison-Wesley.

Gelernter, D. and Jagannathan, S. (1990) *Programming Linguistics*. Cambridge, MA: MIT Press.

George, S., Ghaoui, C., Rada, R. and Beer, M. (1990) Text to hypertext and back again. Paper delivered to Computers and Writing III. P. Holt and N. Williams (eds) (forthcoming) *Computers and Writing*. Oxford: Intellect.

Goetschalckx, J. (1979) EURODICAUTOM. In B. M. Snell (ed.) *Translating and the Computer*. Amsterdam: North-Holland, 71–5.

Goldfarb, C. (1990) *The SGML Handbook*. Oxford: Oxford University Press.

Goldfield, J. D. (1989) Computational thematics, a selective database, and literary criticism: Gobineau, tic words, and Riffaterre revisited. In R. G. Potter (ed.) (1989a) *Literary Computing and Literary Criticism*. Philadelphia: University of Pennsylvania Press, 97–122.

Goldman, N. M. (1975) Conceptual generation. In R. C. Schank, *Conceptual Information Processing*. Amsterdam: North-Holland, 289–371.

Gonnet, G. H. and Tompa, F. W. (1987) *Mind Your Grammar: A new approach to modelling text*. Technical Report OED-87-01, Waterloo, Canada: UW Centre for the New OED.

Greenbaum, S. (1990) The International Corpus of English. *ICAME Journal*, 14, 106–8.

Greenblatt, D. L. (1973) Generative metrics and the authorship of 'The Expostulation'. *Centrum*, 1, 87–104.

Greenblatt, D. L. (1977) Using statistics for the historical study of style. *Style*, 11, 251–61.

Grice, H. P. (1971) Meaning. In D. D. Steinberg and L. A. Jacobovits (eds) *Semantics: An interdisciplinary reader in philosophy, linguistics, and psychology*. Cambridge: Cambridge University Press.

Grimes, J. E. (1975) *The Thread of Discourse*. The Hague: Mouton.

Grishman, R. (1986) *Computational Linguistics*. New York: Cambridge University Press.

Grishman, R. and Kittredge, R. (eds) (1986) *Analyzing Language in Restricted Domains: Sublanguage description and processing*. Hillsdale, NJ: Lawrence Erlbaum.

Griswold, R. E. and Griswold, M. T. (1990) *The Icon Programming Language*, 2nd edn. Englewood Cliffs, NJ: Prentice Hall.

Grosz, B. J. (1980) Focusing and description in natural language dialogs. In A. Joshi et al. (eds) *Elements of Discourse Understanding* (Proceedings of a workshop on computational aspects of linguistic structure and discourse setting). Cambridge: Cambridge University Press, 115–31.

Grosz, B. J. and Sidner, C. L. (1986) Attention, intentions, and the structure of discourse. *Computational Linguistics*, 12, 175–204.

Grosz, B. J., Sparck-Jones, K. and Webber, B. L. (eds) (1986) *Readings in Natural Language Processing*. Los Altos: Morgan Kaufmann.

Guinn, D. M. (1980) The making of a masterpiece: Stephen Crane's 'The Red Badge of Courage'. *Computers and the Humanities*, 14, 231–9.

Halliday, M. A. K. (1978) *Language as Social Semiotic*. London: Edward Arnold.

Halliday, M. A. K. (1985) *An Introduction to Functional Grammar*. London: Edward Arnold.

Hamburger, H. (1990) Evaluation of L2 systems: Learners and theory. *Computer Assisted Language Learning*, 1, 19–27.

Hancock, R. (1987) Non-verbal communication on interactive videodisc as an adjunct to language learning. In G. Chesters and N. Gardner (eds) *The Use of Computers in the Teaching of Language and Languages*. Bath: University of Bath, 99.

Harland, M. (1990) Hypercard: assessing its potential in CALL programming. *Computer Assisted Language Learning*, 1, 41–50.

Hasan, R. (1978) Text in the systemic-functional model. In W. Dressler (ed.) *Current Trends in Text Linguistics*, Berlin: De Gruyter, 111–42.

Hayes, J. R. and Flower, L. (1980) Identifying the organization of writing processes. In L. W. Gregg and E. Steinberg (eds) *Cognitive Processes in Writing*. Hillsdale, NJ: Lawrence Erlbaum, 3–30.

Hays, D. G. (1963) Research procedures in machine translation. In P. L. Garvin (1963a) *Natural Language and the Computer*. New York: McGraw-Hill, 183–214.

Hazen, M., Eichelberger, J., Killion, S. and O'Shields, M. E. (1986) *Report on the Writer's Workbench and Other Writing Tools*. Instructional Computing, Microcomputer Support Center, 402 Hanes 019A, University of North Carolina.

Hinman, C. (1947) Mechanized collation. A preliminary report. *Papers of the Bibliographical Society of America*, 41, 99–106.

Hirsch, E. D. Jr (1987) *Cultural Literacy*. Boston, MA: Houghton Mifflin.

Hobbs, J. R. (1979) Coherence and coreference. *Cognitive Science*, 3, 67–90.

Hobbs, J. R. (1986) Overview of the TACITUS project. *Computational Linguistics*, 12, 220–2.

Hockey, S. (1980) *A Guide to Computer Applications in the Humanities*. London: Duckworth and Baltimore: The Johns Hopkins University Press.

Hockey, S. M. (1985) *SNOBOL Programming for the Humanities*. Oxford: Clarendon Press.

Hockey, S. M. (1986) OCR: The Kurzweil Data Entry Machine. *Literary and Linguistic Computing*, 1/2, 63–7.

Hockey, S. and Martin, J. (1988) *The Oxford Concordance Program: Users' Manual Version 2*. Oxford: Oxford University Computing Service.

Hofland, K. and Johansson, S. (1982) *Word Frequencies in British and American English*. Bergen: Norwegian Computing Centre for the Humanities/London: Longman.

Holmes, J. N. (1988) *Speech Synthesis and Recognition*. Wokingham: van Nostrand Reinhold.

Holt, P. and Williams, N. (eds) (forthcoming) *Computers and Writing: State of the art*. Oxford: Intellect, Blackwells, Ablex.

Horacek, H. (1990) The architecture of a generation component in a complete natural language dialogue system. In R. Dale, C. Mellish and M. Zock (eds) *Current Research in Natural Language Generation*. New York: Academic Press, 193–227.

Hornby, A. S. (ed.) (1974) *Oxford Advanced Learner's Dictionary of Current English*, (3rd edn). London: Oxford University Press.

Horton, J., Ellis, D. and Black, P. (1990) The design and development of an intelligent tutoring system for adult literacy students. In Williams (1990b) CALL. Oxford: Intellect.

Hovy, E. H. (1988a) *Generating Natural Language under Pragmatic Constraints*. Hillsdale, NJ: Lawrence Erlbaum.

Hovy, E. H. (1988b) Planning coherent multisentential text. In *26th ACL Conference Proceedings*, Buffalo, 163–9.

Hovy, E. H. (1988c) On the study of text planning and realization. In E. H. Hovy, D. D. McDonald and S. R. Young (eds) *Proceedings of the AAAI Workshop on Text Planning and Realization*. AAAI, St. Paul, 17–29.

Hovy, E. H. (1990) Unresolved issues in paragraph planning. In R. Dale, C. Mellish and M. Zock (eds) *Current Research in Natural Language Generation*. New York: Academic Press, 17–45.

Howard-Hill, T. H. (1973) A practical scheme for editing critical texts with the aid of a computer. *Proof*, 3, 335–56.

Howell, G. and Douglas, J. Y. (1990) The evolution of interactive fiction. In N. Williams (1990b) *CALL*. Oxford: Intellect, 93–109.

Hughes, J. J. (1987) *Bits, Bytes and Biblical Studies*. Grand Rapids, Mi: Zondervan.

Hutchins, W. J. (1986) *Machine Translation: Past present and future*. Chichester: Ellis Horwood.

Ide, N. M. (1987a) *Pascal Programming for the Humanities*. Philadelphia: University of Pennsylvania Press.

Ide, N. M. (1987b) Image patterns and the structure of William Blake's the Four Zoas. *Blake: An Illustrated Quarterly*, 20, 125–33.

Ide, N. M. (1989a) A statistical measure of theme and structure. *Computers and the Humanities*, 23, 277–83.

Ide, N. M. (1989b) Meaning and method: computer-assisted analysis of Blake. In R. G. Potter (ed.) (1989a) *Literary Computing and Literary Criticism*. Philadelphia: University of Pennsylvania Press, 123–41.

Ide, N. and Sperberg-McQueen, C. M. (1990) Outline of a standard for encoding literary and linguistic data. In Y. Choueka (ed.) *Computers in Literary and Linguistic Research: Proceedings of the 15th ALLC Conference, 1988*. Geneva: Slatkine, 215–32.

ISO 8879 (1986) *Information Processing – Text and Office Systems – Standard Generalized Markup Language (SGML)*. International Organization for Standardization.

Jacobs, P. S. (1985) *A Knowledge-Based Approach to Language Production*. PhD dissertation, University of California (Berkeley).

Jameson, A. (1987) How to appear to be conforming to the 'maxims' even if you prefer to violate them. In G. Kempen (ed.) *Natural Language Generation*. Boston, MA: Kluwer Academic, 19–42.

Janssen, S. (1990) Automatic sense disambiguation with LDOCE: enriching syntactically analyzed corpora with semantic data. In J. Aarts and W. J. Meijs (eds) *Theory and Practice in Corpus Linguistics*. Amsterdam: Rodopi, 105–35.

Jelinek, F. (1985a) The development of an experimental discrete dictation recognizer. *Proceedings of the IEEE*, 73, 1616–24.

Jelinek, F. (1985b) *Self-organized Language Modeling for Speech Recognition*. IBM Research Report, T. J. Watson Research Center, Yorktown Heights, NY.

Jespersen, O. (1909–49) *A Modern English Grammar on Historical Principles, I–VII*. Copenhagen: Munksgaard.

Johansson, S. (1980) The LOB corpus of British English texts: presentation and comments. *ALLC Journal*, 1, 25–36.

Johansson, S. (ed.) (1982) *Computer Corpora in English Language Research*. Bergen: Norwegian Computing Centre for the Humanities.

Johansson, S. (1985) Word frequency and text type: some observations based on the LOB corpus of British English texts. *Computers and the Humanities*, 19, 23–36.

Johansson, S., Atwell, E., Garside, R. and Leech, G. (1986) *The Tagged LOB Corpus, Users' Manual*. Bergen: Norwegian Computing Centre for the Humanities.

Johansson, S. and Hofland, K. (1989) *Frequency Analysis of English Vocabulary and Grammar* (2 vols). Oxford: Clarendon Press.

Johansson, S., Leech, G. and Goodluck, H. (1978) *Manual of Information to Accompany* the *'Lancaster-Oslo/Bergen Corpus of British English, for Use with Digital Computers'.* Oslo: Department of English, Oslo University.

Johansson, S. and Stenström, A. -B. (eds) (1991) *English Computer Corpora: Selected papers and bibliography.* Berlin: Mouton de Gruyter.

Johnson, R., King, M. and des Tombe, L. (1985) EUROTRA: a multilingual system under development. *Computational Linguistics,* 11, 155–69.

Johnson, R. and Varile, N. (1986) Software; an overview. *Multilingua,* 5, 163–5.

Jones, R. L. (1987) Accessing the Brown Corpus using an IBM PC. *ICAME Journal,* 11, 44–7.

Joshi, A. K. (1987) Tree adjoining grammars and their relevance to generation. In G. Kempen (ed.) *Natural Language Generation.* Boston, MA: Kluwer Academic, 233–52.

Jung, U. O. H. (1988) *An International Bibliography of Computer-Assisted Language Learning with Annotations in German.* Frankfurt-am-Main: Peter Lang.

Kamp, H. (1981) A theory of truth and semantic representation. In J. A. G. Groenendijk, Th. M. V. Janssen and M. B. J. Stokhof (eds) *Formal Methods in the Study of Language,* Amsterdam: Mathematisch Centrum Tracts 135, 25–37.

Kaplan, R. M. and Bresnan, J. (1982) Lexical functional grammar: a formal system for grammatical representation. In J. Bresnan, *The Mental Representation of Grammatical Relations.* Cambridge, MA: MIT Press, 173–281.

Kay, M. (1979) Functional grammar. In *5th Berkeley Linguistics Society Meeting Proceedings,* Berkeley, 133–7.

Kaye, G. (1989) *KAYE the KWIC Analyser: User's Manual.* Winchester: IBM Scientific Centre.

Kempen, G. (1986) Language generation systems. In I. Batori, W. Lenders and W. Putschke (eds) *Computational Linguistics: An international handbook on computer-oriented language research and applications.* Berlin: Walter de Gruyter, 79–86.

Kempen, G. (ed.) (1987) *Natural Language Generation: Recent advances in artificial intelligence, psychology, and linguistics.* Boston, MA: Kluwer Academic.

Kenning, M.-M and Kenning, M. J. (1990) *Computers and Language Learning. Current theory and practice.* Chichester: Ellis Horwood.

Kenny, A. (1978) *The Aristotelian Ethics.* Oxford: Clarendon Press.

Kenny, A. (1982) *The Computation of Style: An introduction to statistics for students of literature and humanities.* Oxford: Pergamon.

Kenny, A. (1986) *A Stylometric Study of the New Testament.* Oxford: Clarendon Press.

Keulen, F. (1986) The Dutch Computer Pilot Project. In J. Aarts and W. J. Meijs (eds) *Corpus Linguistics II.* Amsterdam: Rodopi, 127–61.

Kiefer, K. E. and Smith, C. R. (1983) Textual analysis with computers: tests of Bell Laboratories' computer software, *Research in the Teaching of English,* 17/3, 201–14.

Kiefer, K. E. and Smith, C. R. (1984) Improving students' revising and editing: the Writer's Workbench system. In W. Wresch (ed.) *The Computer in Composition Instruction.* Urbana, Ill: National Council of Teachers of English, 65–82.

King, M. (ed.) (1983) *Parsing Natural Language.* London: Academic Press.

King, M. (1987) *Machine Translation Today: The state of the art.* Edinburgh: Edinburgh University Press.

Kingscott, G. (1989) *Applications of Machine Translation. A Study for the Commission of the European Communities.* Nottingham: Praetorius Ltd.

Kittredge, R., Polguere, A. and Goldberg, E. (1986) Synthesizing weather forecasts from formatted data. In *11th Computational Linguistics Conference Proceedings.* Bonn, 563–5.

Klein, S., Aeschlimann, J. F., Balsiger, D. F., Converse, S. L., Court, C., Foster, M., Lao, R., Oakley, J. D. and Smith, J. (1979) Automatic novel writing: a status report. In W. Burghardt and K. Holler (eds) *Text Processing*. New York: Walter de Gruyter, 338–413.

Knowles, F. (1979) Error analysis of SYSTRAN output. In B. M. Snell (ed.) *Translating and the Computer*. Amsterdam: North-Holland, 109–33.

Knowles, G. and Lawrence, L. (1987) Automatic intonation assignment. In R. Garside, G. Leech and G. Sampson (eds) *The Computational Analysis of English*. London and New York: Longman, 139–48.

Koller, W. (1979) *Einführung in die Übersetzungswissenschaft*. Heidelberg: Quelle and Meyer.

Kolotka, G. (1986) Shakespeare's new poem: an ode to statistics. *Science*, 231, 335–6.

Kučera, H. and Francis, W. N. (1967) *Computational Analysis of Present-day American English*. Providence, RI: Brown University Press.

Kukich, K. (1983) *Knowledge-Based Report Generation: A knowledge-engineering approach*. PhD dissertation, University of Pittsburgh.

Kukich, K. (1987) Where do phrases come from: some preliminary experiments in connectionist phrase generation. In G. Kempen (ed.) *Natural Language Generation*. Boston, MA: Kluwer Academic, 405–22.

Kytö, M. (1989) Progress report on the diachronic part of the Helsinki Corpus. *ICAME Journal*, 13, 12–15.

Kytö, M. and Rissanen, M. (1988) The Helsinki Corpus of English Texts: classifying and coding the diachronic part. In M. Kytö, O. Ihalainen and M. Rissanen (eds) *Corpus Linguistics*. Amsterdam: Rodopi, 169–80.

Kytö, M., Ihalainen, O. and Rissanen, M. (eds) (1988) *Corpus Linguistics Hard and Soft*. Amsterdam: Rodopi.

Lancashire, I. (1991) *The Humanities Computing Yearbook 1989–90*. Oxford: Oxford University Press.

Lancashire, I. and McCarty, W. (1988) *The Humanities Computing Yearbook 1988*. Oxford: Clarendon Press.

Landow, G. P. (1989) Hypertext in literary education, criticism and scholarship. *Computers and the Humanities*, 23/3, 173–98.

Last, R. W. (1984) *Language Teaching and the Microcomputer*. Oxford: Basil Blackwell.

Last, R. W. (1987) Artificial intelligence – the way forward for CALL? In G. Chesters and N. Gardner (eds) *The Use of Computers in the Teaching of Language and Languages*. Bath: University of Bath, 61–6.

Last, R. W. (1989) *Artificial Intelligence Techniques in Language Learning*. Chichester: Ellis Horwood.

Last, R. W. (ed.) (in press) *Molière, L'Avare, Viewbook*. Stoke-on-Trent: Information Education, Ltd.

Lawson, V. (1982) *Practical Experience of Machine Translation: Proceedings of a conference. London, 5–6 November*. Amsterdam: North-Holland.

Lawson, V. (1985) *Tools for the Trade. Translating and the Computer 5*. London: Aslib.

Ledger, G. R. (1985) A new approach to stylometry. *ALLC Bulletin*, 13, 67–72.

Leech, G. and Garside, R. (1991) Running a grammar factory: the production of syntactically analysed corpora or 'treebanks'. in S. Johansson and A.–B. Stenström (eds) *English Computer Corpora*. Berlin: Mouton de Gruyter, 15–32.

Lehrberger, J. and Bourbeau, L. (1988) *Machine Translation: Linguistic characteristics of MT systems and general methodology of evaluation*. Amsterdam: John Benjamins.

Lemmens, M. and Wekker, H. (1986) *Grammar in English Learners' Dictionaries.* Tübingen: Niemeyer Verlag.

Levelt, W. J. M. and Schriefers, H. (1987) Stages of lexical access. In G. Kempen (ed.) *Natural Language Generation.* Boston: Kluwer Academic, 395–404.

Levy, M. (1990) *Call Bibliography.* Gold Coast, Queensland: Language Centre, Bond University.

Lewis, D. (1985) The development and progress of machine translation systems. *ALLC Journal*, 5, 40–52.

L'Huillier, M. (1990) Evaluation of CALL programs for grammar. *Computer Assisted Language Learning*, 1, 79–86.

Liberman, M. (1989) Text on tap: the ACL/DCI. In *Proceedings of the DARPA Speech and Natural Language Workshop, October 1989.* San Mateo, CA: Morgan Kaufmann.

Lockwood, D. G. (1972) *Introduction to Stratificational Linguistics.* New York: Harcourt Brace Jovanovich.

Logan, H. M. (1982) The computer and metrical scansion. *ALLC Journal*, 3, 9–14.

Logan, H. M. (1985) 'Most by Numbers judge a Poet's Song'. *Computers and the Humanities*, 19, 213–20.

Love, H. H. R. (1971) The computer and literary editing: achievements and prospects. In R. A. Wisbey (ed.) *The Computer in Literary and Linguistic Research.* Cambridge: Cambridge University Press, 47–56.

MacDonald, N. H., Frase, L. T., Gingrich, P. S. and Keenan, S. A. (1982) The Writer's Workbench – computer aids for text analysis. *IEEE Transactions on Communications*, vol. COM-30, 1, 105–10.

MacWhinney, B. and Snow, C. (1990) The Child Language Data Exchange System. *ICAME Journal*, 14, 3–25.

Maegaard, B. (1988) Eurotra: the machine translation project of the European Communities. *Literary and Linguistic Computing*, 3, 61–5.

Mann, W. C., Bates, M., Grosz, B. J., McDonald, D. D., McKeown, K. R., and Swartout, W. R. (1981) Text generation: the state of the art and the literature. USC/Information Sciences Institute Research Report RR-81-101.

Mann, W. C., and Matthiessen, C. M. I. M. (1983) Nigel: a systemic grammar for text generation. USC/Information Sciences Institute Technical Report RR-83-105.

Mann, W. C. and Thompson, S. A. (1988) Rhetorical structure theory: toward a functional theory of text organization. *Text*, 8, 243–81. Also available as USC/Information Sciences Institute Research Report RR-87-190.

Marcus, S. and Blau, S. (1983) Not seeing is relieving: invisible writing with computers, *Educational Technology*, April, 12–15.

Martindale, C. (1973) An experimental simulation of literary change. *Journal of Personality and Social Psychology*, 25, 319–26.

Martindale, C. (1981) Evolutionary trends in English poetry. *Perspectives in Computing*, 1, 17–22.

Martindale, C. (1984) Evolutionary trends in poetic style: the case of English metaphysical poetry. *Computers and the Humanities*, 18, 3–21.

Matthiessen, C. M. I. M. (1984) Systemic grammar in computation: the Nigel case. In *1st European ACL Conference Proceedings*, Pisa, 155–64. Also available as USC/Information Sciences Institute Research Report RR-84-121.

Matthiessen, C. M. I. M. (1991) Lexicogrammatical choice in text generation. In C. L. Paris, W. R. Swartout and W. C. Mann (eds.) *Natural Language in Artificial Intelligence and Computational Linguistics*. Dordrecht and Boston, MA: Kluwer Academic, 249–92.

Maybury, M. T. (1989) Enhancing explanation coherence with rhetorical strategies. In *4th European ACL Conference Proceedings*. Manchester, 65–8.

McAleese, R. (ed.) (1989a) *Hypertext: Theory into practice*. Oxford: Intellect.

McAleese, R. (1989b) Navigating and browsing in Hypertext. In McAleese (ed.) (1989a) 6–44.

McCoy, K. F. (1985) *Correcting Object-Related Misconceptions*. PhD dissertation, University of Pennsylvania.

McDonald, D. D. (1980) *Natural Language Production as a Process of Decision Making Under Constraint*. PhD dissertation, Massachusetts Institute of Technology.

McDonald, D. D. and Bolc, L. (eds) (1988) *Natural Language Generation Systems*. New York: Springer-Verlag.

McDonald, D. D., Vaughan, M. W. and Pustejovsky, J. D. (1987) Factors contributing to efficiency in natural language generation. In G. Kempen (ed.) *Natural Language Generation*. Boston, MA: Kluwer Academic, 159–182.

McKeown, K. R. (1985) *Text Generation: Using discourse strategies and focus constraints to generate natural language text*. Cambridge: Cambridge University Press.

McKeown, K. R. and Swartout, W. R. (1987) Language generation and explanation. *Annual Reviews of Computer Science*, 2, 401–49.

McKnight, C., Richardson, J. and Dillon, A. (1989) The authoring of hypertext documents. In R. McAleese (ed.) (1989a) *Hypertext*. Oxford: Intellect, 138–47.

McLeod, R. (1990a) Magic lectern, *Times Educational Supplement*, 30 March.

McLeod, R. (1990b) IV Storybase. Paper delivered to Computers and Writing III. In P. Holt and N. Williams (eds) (forthcoming) *Computers and Writing*. Oxford: Intellect.

Meehan, J. (1976) *The Metanovel: Writing stories by computer*. PhD dissertation Yale University.

Meehan, J. R. (1981) TALE-SPIN. In R. C. Schank and C. K. Riesbeck (eds) *Inside Computer Understanding*. Hillsdale, NJ: Lawrence Erlbaum, 197–258.

Meijs, W. J. (1982) Exploring BROWN with QUERY. In S. Johansson (ed.) *Computer Corpora in English Language Research*. Bergen: Norwegian Computing Centre for the Humanities, 34–48.

Meijs, W. J. (1984) Data and theory in computer corpus research. In J. L. Mackenzie and H. Wekker (eds) *English Language Research: The Dutch contribution, I*. Amsterdam: Free University Press, 85–99.

Meijs, W. J. (1986) Links in the lexicon: the dictionary as a corpus, *ICAME News*, 10, 26–8.

Meijs, W. (ed.) (1987) *Corpus Linguistics and Beyond: Proceedings of the Seventh International Conference on Language Research on Computerized Corpora*. Amsterdam: Rodopi.

Meijs, W. J. (1988) Knowledge-activation in a large lexical data-base: problems and prospects in the LINKS-project. In *Amsterdam Papers in English (APE) No. 1*. Amsterdam: Amsterdam University English Department, 101–23.

Meijs, W. J. (1989) Spreading the word: knowledge-activation in a functional perspective. In J. H. Connolly and S. C. Dik (eds) *Functional Grammar and the Computer*. Dordrecht: Foris, 201–15.

Melby, A. (1987a) Creating an environment for the translator. In M. King (1987) *Machine Translation Today*. Edinburgh: Edinburgh University Press, 124–32.

Melby, A. (1987b) On human-machine interaction in translation. In S. Nirenburg (ed.) *Machine Translation*. Cambridge: Cambridge University Press, 145–54.

Mellish, C. (1988) Natural language generation from plans. In M. Zock and G. Sabah (eds) *Advances in Natural Language Generation, Vol. 1*. London: Pinter Publishers, 131–45.

Merideth, E. (1989) Gender patterns in Henry James: a stylistic approach to dialogue in *Daisy Miller, The Portrait of a Lady*, and *The Bostonians*. In R. G. Potter (ed.) (1989a) *Literary Computing and Literary Criticism*. Philadelphia: University of Pennsylvania Press, 189–206.

Merriam, T. (1982) The authorship of Sir Thomas More. *ALLC Bulletin*, 10, 1–7.

Merriam, T. (1986) Smith on Morton: the authorship controversy of Sir Thomas More. *Literary and Linguistic Computing*, 1, 104–6; with a rejoinder by M. W. A. Smith: pp. 106–8.

Meteer, M. W. (1990) *The 'Generation Gap': The problem of expressibility in text planning*. PhD dissertation, University of Massachusetts (Amherst). Available as BBN Technical Report 7347.

Meteer, M. W., McDonald, D. D., Anderson, S., Forster, D., Gay, L., Huettner, A. and Sibun, P. (1987) Mumble-86: Design and Implementation. COINS Technical Report 87-87, University of Massachusetts (Amherst).

Meyer, C. F. (1987) *A Linguistic Study of American Punctuation*. Frankfurt-am-Main: Peter Lang.

Miles, J. (1964) *Eras and Modes in English Poetry*. Berkeley: University of California Press.

Milic, L. T. (1967) *A Quantitative Approach to the Style of Jonathan Swift*. The Hague and Paris: Mouton.

Milic, L. (1981) Stylistics + computers = pattern stylistics. *Perspectives in Computing*, 1, 4–11.

Milic, L. (1985) Contra Fish: the arrogance of misreading. *Style*, 19, 385–94.

Milic, L. (1990) A new historical corpus. *ICAME Journal*, 14, 26–39.

Moore, J. D. (1989) *A Reactive Approach to Explanation in Expert and Advice-Giving Systems*. PhD dissertation, University of California (Los Angeles).

Moore, J. D. and Swartout, W. R. (1991) Dialogue-based explanation. In C. L. Paris, W. R. Swartout and W. C. Mann (eds) *Natural Language in Artificial Intelligence and Computational Linguistics*. Dordrecht and Boston, MA: Kluwer Academic, 3–48.

Moore, R. K. (1990) Speech technology corpora. Background paper for the SALT workshop on corpus resources. In *SALT Proceedings of a Workshop on Corpus Resources, 3–4 January 1990, Wadham College, Oxford*. London: Department of Trade and Industry/Speech and Language Technology Club, 11–12.

Morton, A. Q. (1978) *Literary Detection*. Epping: Bowker.

Morton, A. Q. (1986) Once: a test of authorship based on words which are not repeated in the sample. *Literary and Linguistic Computing*, 1, 1–8.

Morton, A. Q. (1989) Authorship: the nature of the habit. *Times Literary Supplement*, 17–23 February 1989, 164, 174.

Mosteller, F. and Wallace, D. L. (1964) *Inference and Disputed Authorship: 'The Federalist'*. Reading, MA: Addison-Wesley.

Nelson, T. H. (1987) *Literary Machines*. Swathmore, PA: privately published.

Neuman, M. (forthcoming) States of the art: the development and cataloguing of electronic text. *Proceedings of the 17th International ALLC Conference*, Siegen, June 1990.

Nirenburg, S. (ed.) *Machine Translation: Theoretical and methodological issues*. Cambridge: Cambridge University Press.

Nirenburg, S., McCardell, R., Nyberg, E., Huffman, S., Kenschaft, E. and Nirenburg, I. (1988) Lexical realization in natural language generation. In *2nd Machine Translation Conference Proceedings*, Pittsburgh, 53–9.

Novak, H.-J. (1987) Strategies for generating coherent descriptions of object motions in time-varying imagery. In G. Kempen (ed.) *Natural Language Generation*. Boston, MA: Kluwer Academic, 117–32.

Oakman, R. L. (1972) The present state of computerized collation: a review article. *Proof*, 2, 333–48.

Oakman, R. L. (1975) Textual editing and the computer. Review essay. *Costerus: Essays in English and American Language and Literature. New Series Vol. IV*, Amsterdam, 79–106.

Oakman, R. L. (1980) *Computer Methods for Literary Research*. Columbia: University of South Carolina Press. Revised edition 1984: Athens (Georgia): The University of Georgia Press.

Oostdijk, N. (1988) A corpus linguistic approach to linguistic variation. *Literary and Linguistic Computing*, 3/1, 12–25.

Oppenheim, R. (1988) The mathematical analysis of style: a correlation-based approach. *Computers and the Humanities*, 22, 241–52.

Ott, W. (1970) Transcription and correction of texts on paper tape. Experiences in preparing the Latin Bible text for the computer. *Revue (LASLA)*, 51–66.

Ott, W. (1973) Computer applications in textual criticism. In A. J. Aitken et al. (eds) *The Computer and Literary Studies*, Edinburgh: University Press, 199–223.

Ott, W. (1974) Bibliograpie: Computer in der Editionstechnik. *ALLC Bulletin*, 2, 74–7.

Ott, W. (1975) Automatisierung von Seitenumbruch und Register-Erstellung beim Satz wissenschaftlicher Werke. In H. Heilmann (ed.) *4. Jahrbuch der EDV*, Stuttgart/Wiesbaden: Forkel, 123–43.

Ott, W. (1976) Integrierte Satzherstellung für wissenschaftliche Werke. *Der Druckspiegel*, 31, 35–44.

Ott, W. (1979a) A text processing system for the preparation of critical editions. *Computers and the Humanities*, 13, 29–35.

Ott, W. (1979b) The output of collation programs. In D. E. Ager et al. (eds) *Advances in Computer-aided Literary and Linguistic Research*. Birmingham: The University of Aston, Dept of Modern Languages, 41–51.

Ott, W. (1980) Bibliographie: EDV im Editionswesen. *Sprache und Datenverarbeitung*, 4, 179–84.

Ott, W. (1989a) Transcription errors, variant readings, scholarly emendations: software tools to master them. In Association Internationale Bible et Informatique, *Actes du Second Colloque International Bible et Informatique: méthodes, outils, résultats', Jerusalem, 9–13 June 1988*. Paris and Geneva: Champion-Slatkine, 419–34.

Ott, W. (1989b) Vom Manuskript zur Edition. Das Programm SATZ als Baustein in TUSTEP. In A. Schwob et al. (eds) *Historische Edition und Computer. Möglichkeiten und Grenzen interdisziplinärer Textverarbeitung und Textbearbeitung*. Graz: Leykam-Verlag, 153–76.

Ott, W. (1990) Edition und Datenverarbeitung. In H. Kraft, *Editionsphilologie*. Darmstadt: Wissenschaftliche Buchgesellschaft, 59–70.

Ott, W., Gabler, H. W. and Sappler, P. (1982) *EDV-Fibel für Editoren*. Stuttgart: Holzboog; Tübingen: Niemeyer.

Oxford University Computing Service (1983) *Text Archive*. Document available from OUCS, 13 Banbury Road, Oxford OX2 6NN.

Palmer, F. (1972) *Grammar*. London: Penguin Books.

Paris, C. L. (1987) *The Use of Explicit User Models in Text Generation: Tailoring to a user's level of expertise*. PhD dissertation, Columbia University.

Paris, C. L. (1988) Planning a text: can we and how should we modularize this process? In E. H. Hovy, D. D. McDonald and S. R. Young (eds) *Proceedings of the AAAI Workshop*. AAAI: St Paul, 55–62.

Paris, C. L. (1991) Generation and explanation: building an explanation facility for the Explainable Expert Systems framework. In C. L. Paris, W. R. Swartout and W. C Mann (eds) *Natural Language in Artificial Intelligence*. Dordrecht and Boston, MA: Kluwer Academic, 49–82.

Paris, C. L., Swartout, W. R. and Mann, W. C. (eds) (1991) *Natural Language in Artificial Intelligence and Computational Linguistics*. Dordrecht and Boston: Kluwer Academic.

Patten, T. (1986) *Interpreting Systemic Grammar as a Computational Representation: A problem-solving approach to text generation*. PhD dissertation, University of Edinburgh.

Penman (1989) *The Penman Documentation*. Unpublished documentation for the Penman language generation system, USC/Information Sciences Institute.

Pereira, F. C. N. and Warren, D. H. D. (1986) Definite clause grammars for language analysis – a survey of the formalism and a comparison with augmented transition networks. In B. J. Grosz, K. Sparck-Jones and B. L. Webber (eds) *Readings in Natural Language Processing*. Los Altos: Morgan Kauffman, 101–24. Also in *Artificial Intelligence* 13, 1980, 231–78.

Perrault, R. and Grosz, B. (1988) Natural-language interfaces. In H. E. Shrobe, and the American Association for Artificial Intelligence (eds) *Exploring Artificial Intelligence*, San Mateo: Morgan Kaufmann, 133–72. Also in *Annual Review of Computer Science* 1, 1986, 47–82.

Peterson, J. L. (1980) Computer programs for detecting and correcting spelling errors, *Communications of the ACM*, 23 December, no. 12.

Pierce, R. H. (1980) Multivariate numerical techniques applied to the study of manuscript tradition. In B. Fidjestøl et al. (eds) *Tekstkritisk Teori og Praksis. Nordisk symposium i tekstkritikk. Godøysund 19–22 May 1987*. Oslo: Novus Forlag, 24–45.

Pollard, C. and Sag, I. (1987) *Information-Based Syntax and Semantics, Vol. 1*. CSLI Lecture Notes.

Poritz, A. B. (1988) Hidden Markov models: a guided tour. In ICASSP 88: *1988 International Conference on Acoustics, Speech and Signal Processing*, vol. 1, 7–13. New York: IEEE.

Potter, R. G. (1980) Towards a syntactic differentiation of period style in modern drama. *Computers and the Humanities*, 14, 187–96.

Potter, R. G. (1982) Reader responses and character syntax. In R. W. Bailey (ed.) *Computing in the Humanities*. Amsterdam: New-Holland, 65–78.

Potter, R. G. (ed.) (1989a) *Literary Computing and Literary Criticism*. Philadelphia, Pa: University of Pennsylvania Press.

Potter, R. G. (1989b) From literary output to literary criticism. *Computers and the Humanities*, 23, 333–40.

Potter, R. G. (1989c) Changes in Shaw's dramatic rhetoric. In R. G. Potter (ed.) *Literary Computing and Literary Criticism*. Philadelphia, Pa: University of Pennsylvania Press, 225–58.

Poulsen, E. (1990) Evaluation of CALL from a classroom perspective. *Computer Assisted Language Learning*, 1, 73–8.

Praschek, H. (1965) Die Technifizierung der Edition – Möglichkeiten und Grenzen. In H. Kreuzer and G. Gunzenhäuser (eds) *Mathematik und Dichtung. Versuche zur Frage einer exakten Literaturwissenschaft*. Munich: Nymphenburger Verlagsbuchhandlung, 123–42.

Procter, P. (ed.) (1978) *Longman Dictionary of Contemporary English*. Harlow: Longman.

Proud, J. K. (1989) *The Oxford Text Archive*. British Library R&D Report no. 5985.

Rahtz, S. (ed.) (1987) *Information Technology in the Humanities: Tools, techniques and applications*. Chichester: Ellis Horwood.

Rasborg, B. (1989) *Machine Translation and its History to EUROTRA – with Special Reference to Factors of Evaluation*. MA thesis, University of Exeter.

ReCALL (1990) *ReCALL Software Guide*, Issue 2. Hull: CTI Centre for Modern Languages, University of Hull.

Reichman, R. (1978) Conversational coherency. *Cognitive Science*, 2, 283–327.

Reiter, E. B. (1990) *Generating Appropriate Natural Language Object Descriptions*. PhD dissertation, Harvard University.

Reithinger, N. (1987) Generating referring expressions and pointing gestures. In G. Kempen (ed.) *Natural Language Generation*. Boston, MA: Kluwer Academic, 1–82.

Renouf, A. (1987a) Lexical resolution. In W. Meijs (ed.) (1987) *Corpus Linguistics and Beyond*. Amsterdam: Rodopi, 121–31.

Renouf, A. (1987b) Corpus development. In J. M. Sinclair (ed.) *Looking Up*. London and Glasgow: Collins, 1–40.

Ritchie, G. (1983) Semantics in parsing. In M. King (ed.) *Parsing Natural Language*. London: Academic Press, 199–218.

Ritchie, G. D., Pulman, S. G., Black, A. W. and Russell, G. J. (1987) A computational framework for lexical description. *Computational Linguistics*, 13, 290–307.

Ritter, M. A. (1980) Stemmatisierungsversuche zum Corpus Dionysiacum Areopagiticum im Lichte des EDV-Verfahrens. *Nachrichten der Akademie der Wissenschaften in Göttingen, I. Philologisch-Historische Klasse* Nr. 6, 95–134.

Robinson, J. J. (1986) DIAGRAM: a grammar formalism for dialogues. In B. J. Grosz, K. Sparck-Jones and B. L. Webber (eds) *Readings in Natural Language Processing*. Los Altos: Morgan Kauffman, 139–59.

Robinson, P. M. W. (1989) The collation and textual criticism of Icelandic manuscripts. (1): collation; (2): textual criticism. *Literary and Linguistic Computing*, 4, 99–105, 174–81.

Rösner, D. (1986) *Ein System zur Generierung von Deutschen Texten aus Semantischen Repräsentationen*. PhD dissertation, University of Stuttgart.

Rosner, M. and Petitpierre, D. (1986) Description of the virtual machine implementation. *Multilingua*, 5, 166–8.

Ross, D. Jr (1977) Differences, genres, and influences. *Style*, 11, 262–73. Reprinted in R. G. Potter (ed.) (1989a) *Literary Computing and Literary Criticism*. Philadelphia: University of Pennsylvania Press, 45–57.

Sabol, C. R. (1982) Focus and attribution in Ford and Conrad. In R. W. Bailey (ed.) *Computing in the Humanities*. Amsterdam: North-Holland, 47–58.

Sabol, C. R. (1989) Reliable narration in *The Good Soldier*. In R. G. Potter (ed.) (1989a) *Computing and Literary Criticism*. Philadelphia: University of Pennsylvania Press, 207–23.

Sacks, H., Schegloff, E. A. and Jefferson, G. (1974) A simplest systematics for the organization of turn-taking for conversation. *Language*, 50, 696–735.

SALT (1990) *Proceedings of a Workshop on Corpus Resources, 3–4 January 1990, Wadham College, Oxford*. London: Department of Trade and Industry/Speech and Language Technology Club.

Salton, G. (1989) *Automatic Text Processing: The transformation analysis and retrieval of information by computer*. Reading, MA: Addison-Wesley.

Sampson, G. (1987) Probabilistic models of analysis. In R. Garside, G. Leech and G. Sampson (eds) *The Computational Analysis of English*. London and New York: Longman, 16–29.

Sampson, G. (1989) How fully does a machine-usable dictionary cover English text? *Literary and Linguistic Computing*, 4, 29–35.

Sanford, A. J. (1987) *The Mind of Man. Models of Human Understanding*. Brighton: Harvester Press.

Scarbrough, D. (1990) Shareware hypertext for CALL on the PC. *Computer Assisted Language Learning*, 1, 65–72.

Schank, R. C. (1975) *Conceptual Information Processing*. Amsterdam: North-Holland.

Schank, R. (1986) Language and memory. In B. J. Grosz, K. Sparck-Jones and B. L. Webber (eds) *Readings in Natural Language Processing*. Los Altos: Morgan Kauffman, 171–91.

Schepers, H. (1981) EDV-Erfahrungen einer Edition. *Philosophisches Jahrbuch*, 88, 159–164.

Schmitt, P. A. (1987) Fachtexte für die Übersetzerausbildung: Probleme und Methoden der Textauswahl. In R. Ehnert and W. Schleyer. *Übersetzen im Fremdsprachenunterricht* Beiträge zur Übersetzungs-wissenschaft-Annäberungen an eine Übersetzungsdidaktik. DAAD Armin Wolff: Regensburg.

Schwob, A., Kranich-Hofbauer, K. and Suntinger, D. (eds) (1989) *Historische Edition und Computer. Möglichkeiten und Probleme interdisziplinärer Textverarbeitung und Textbearbeitung*. Graz: Leykam-Verlag.

Sclater, N. (1983) *Introduction to Electronic Speech Synthesis*. Indianapolis: Howard W. Sams.

Scott, D. R. and De Souza, C. (1990) Getting the message across in RST-based text generation. In R. Dale, C. Mellish and M. Zock (eds) *Current Research in Natural Language Generation*. New York: Academic Press, 47–73.

Self, J. (1985) *Microcomputers in Education*. Brighton: Harvester Press.

Shann, P. (1987) Machine translation: a problem of linguistic engineering or of cognitive modelling? In M. King, *Machine Translation Today*. Edinburgh: Edinburgh University Press, 71–90.

Shannon, C. E. and Weaver, W. W. (1949) *The Mathematical Theory of Communication*. Urbana: University of Illinois Press.

Sharples, M., Goodlet, J. and Pemberton, L. (1989) Developing a Writer's Assistant. In N. Williams and P. Holt (eds) *Computers and Writing*. Oxford: Intellect, 22–37.

Sharples, M. and Pemberton, L. (1989) *Representing Writing: An account of the writing process with regard to the writer's external representations*, unpublished MS, School of Cognitive Sciences, University of Sussex.

Sharples, M. and Pemberton, L. (1990) Starting from the writer: guidelines for the design of user-centred document processors. In N. Williams (1990b) *CALL*. Oxford: Intellect, 37–57.

Shieber, S. M. (1986) *An Introduction to Unification-Based Approaches to Grammar*. CSLI Lecture Notes, Chicago University Press.

Shieber, S. M., Van Noord, G., Moore, R. C. and Pereira, F. C. N. (1989) A semantic-head-driven generation algorithm for unification-based formalisms. In *27th ACL Conference Proceedings*, Vancouver, 7–17.

Shillingsburg, P. L. (1986) *Scholarly Editing in the Computer Age. Theory and Practice.* Athens (Georgia) and London: University of Georgia Press.

Shneiderman, B. and Kearsley, G. (1989) *Hypertext Hands On!.* Reading, MA: Addison-Wesley.

Shostak, R. (ed.) (1984) *Computers in Composition Instruction.* University of Oregon: International Council for Computers in Education.

Sidner, C. L. (1979) *Toward a Computational Theory of Definite Anaphora Comprehension in English.* PhD dissertation, Massachusetts Institute of Technology.

Simmons, R. F. (1984) *Computations from the English. A Procedural Logic Approach for Representing and Understanding English Texts.* Englewood Cliffs, NJ: Prentice Hall.

Simmons, R. F. and Slocum, J. (1972) Generating English discourse from semantic networks. *Communications of the ACM*, 15, 891–905.

Sinclair, J. M. (ed.) (1987) *Looking Up: An account of the Cobuild project in lexical computing.* London and Glasgow: Collins.

Sinclair, J., Hanks, P., Fox, G., Moon, R. and Stock, P. (eds) (1987) *Collins COBUILD English Language Dictionary.* London and Glasgow: Collins.

Skolnik, J. (1980) *L-trees*, Technical Report. Amsterdam: Arts Faculty Computer Department, University of Amsterdam.

Slater, E. (1975a) Shakespeare: word links between poems and plays. *Notes and Queries*, 220, 157–63.

Slater, E. (1975b) Word links with *The Merry Wives of Windsor. Notes and Queries*, 220, 169–71.

Slater, E. (1977) Word links with *All's Well that Ends Well. Notes and Queries*, 222, 109–12.

Slater, E. (1978) Word links between *Timon of Athens* and *King Lear. Notes and Queries*, 223, 147–9.

Slater, E. (1982) Edmund Ironside. *Times Literary Supplement*, 13 August, 879.

Slater, E. (1983) Edmund Ironside. *Times Literary Supplement*, 18 March, 268.

Sloan, D. (ed.) (1984) *The Computer in Education: A critical perspective.* New York: Columbia University Press.

Slocum, J. (ed.) (1987) *Machine Translation Systems.* Cambridge: Cambridge University Press.

Slype, G. van, Guinet, G. F. and Seitz, F. (1981) *Mieux Traduire pour Mieux Communiquer. Etude Prospective du Marché de la Traduction Préparée pour la Commission des Communautés Européennes.* Brussels and Luxembourg: Direction générale Marché de l'information et innovation.

Smith, J. B. (1978) Computer criticism. *Style*, 12, 326–56. Reprinted in R. G. Potter (ed.) (1989a) *Literary Computing and Literary Criticism.* Philadelphia: University of Pennsylvania Press, 13–44.

Smith, J. B. (1980) *Imagery and the Mind of Stephen Dedalus: A computer-assisted study of Joyce's 'A Portrait of the Artist as a Young Man'.* Lewisburg, Pa: Bucknell University Press.

Smith, J. B. (1985) ARRAS and literary criticism. In B. Derval and M. Lenoble (eds) *La Critique littéraire et l'ordinateur.* Montreal: Derval and Lenoble, 79–93.

Smith, M. W. A. (1985) An investigation of Morton's method to distinguish Elizabethan playwrights. *Computers and the Humanities*, 19, 3–13.

Smith, M. W. A. (1986) A critical review of word-links as a method for investigating Shakespearean chronology and authorship. *Literary and Linguistic Computing*, 1, 202–6.

Smith, M. W. A. (1987a) Hapax legomena in prescribed positions: an investigation of recent proposals to resolve problems of authorship. *Literary and Linguistic Computing*, 2, 145–52.

Smith, M. W. A. (1987b) The authorship of Pericles: new evidence for Wilkins. *Literary and Linguistic Computing*, 2, 221–9.

Smith, M. W. A. (1988) The authorship of Acts I and II of *Pericles*: a new approach using first words of speeches. *Computers and the Humanities*, 22, 23–41.

Smith, M. W. A. (1989) A procedure to determine authorship using pairs of consecutive words: more evidence for Wilkins's participation in *Pericles*. *Computers and the Humanities*, 23, 113–29.

Snell, B. M. (ed.) (1983) *Term Banks for Tomorrow's World. Translating and the Computer 4*. Aslib: London.

Sowa, J. F. (1984) *Conceptual Structures*. Reading, MA: Addison-Wesley.

Sperberg-McQueen, C. M. and Burnard, L. (eds) (1990) *Guidelines for the Encoding and Interchange of Machine-readable Texts*. (TEI Document no. P1, version 1.1) Chicago and Oxford: ACH–ACL–ALLC Text Encoding Initiative.

Stevenson, B. (1989) Adapting hypothesis testing to a literary problem. In R. G. Potter (ed.) (1989a) *Literary Computing and Literary Criticism*. Philadelphia: University of Pennyslvania Press, 61–74.

Svartvik, J. (1986) For W. Nelson Francis. *ICAME News*, 10, 8–9.

Svartvik, J. (ed.) (1990) *The London-Lund Corpus of Spoken English: Description and research. Lund Studies in English 82*. Lund: Lund University Press.

Tannenbaum, R. S. (1988) *Computing in the Humanities and Social Sciences. Vol. 1. Fundamentals*. Rockville, MD: Computer Science Press.

Taylor, L. (1988) *Concordancing a Corpus: A guide to concordancing machine-readable corpora on the Sequent Symmetry Computer*. Lancaster: Department of Linguistics and Modern English Language, Lancaster University.

Taylor, L., Leech, G. and Fligelstone, S. (1991) A survey of English machine-readable corpora. In S. Johansson and A.-B. Stenström. *English Computer Corpora*. Berlin: Mouton de Gruyter, 319–54.

Thomson, N. (1989) How to read articles which depend on statistics. *Literary and Linguistic Computing*, 4, 6–11.

Tompa, F. (1986) *Database Design for a Dictionary of the Future*, Preliminary Report. Waterloo, Ontario: Centre for the New Oxford English Dictionary, University of Waterloo.

Tribble, C. and Jones, G. (1990) *Concordances in the Classroom: A resource book for teachers*. London: Longman.

Trilling, L. (1961) Manners, morals, and the novel. In L. Trilling, *The Liberal Imagination*. London: Mercury Books, 205–22. (Original edition: London: Secker & Warburg, 1951.)

TUSTEP (1989) *TUSTEP. Tübinger System von Textverarbeitungsprogrammen*. Tübingen: Zentrum für Datenverarbeitung der Universität.

Ule, L. (1977) Vocabulary richness in Shakespeare. *ALLC Bulletin*, 5, 174–7.

Ule, L. (1982) Recent progress in computer methods of authorship determination. *ALLC Bulletin*, 10, 73–89.

van Dijk, T. (1985) *Studies in the Pragmatics of Discourse*. The Hague: Mouton.

van Halteren, H. (1984) User interface for a Linguistic Data Base. *ICAME News*, 8, 31–40.

van Herwijnen, E. (1990) *Practical SGML*. Dordrecht: Kluwer Academic.

van Peer, W. (1989) Quantitative studies of literature: a critique and an outlook. *Computers and the Humanities*, 23, 301–7.

van Sterkenburg, P. G. J. and Pijnenburg, W. J. J. (eds) (1984) *Van Dale Groot Woordenboek Hedendaags Nederlands*. Utrecht and Antwerp: Van Dale Lexicografie.

Varile, G. B. (1983) Charts: a data structure for parsing. In M. King (ed.) *Parsing Natural Language*. London: Academic Press, 73–87.

Voogt-van Zutphen, H. J. (1987) *Constructing an F. G. Lexicon on the Basis of LDOCE* (Working Papers in Functional Grammar No. 24). Amsterdam: Dept of Linguistics, University of Amsterdam.

Voogt-van Zutphen, H. J. (1989) Towards a lexicon of Functional Grammar. In J. H. Connolly and S. C. Dik (eds) *Functional Grammar and the Computer*. Dordrecht: Foris, 151–76.

Vossen, P. (1989) The structure of lexical knowledge as envisaged in the LINKS-project. In J. H. Connolly and S. C. Dik (eds) *Functional Grammar and the Computer*. Dordrecht: Foris, 177–99.

Vossen, P. (1990a) Polysemy and vagueness of meaning descriptions in the Longman Dictionary of Contemporary English. ACQUILEX Working paper no. 001. Amsterdam: English Department, University of Amsterdam. To appear in J. Svartvik and H. Wekker (eds) *Topics in English Linguistics*. The Hague: Mouton/De Gruyter.

Vossen, P. (1990b) The end of the chain: where does decomposition of lexical knowledge lead us eventually? ACQUILEX Working paper no. 010. Amsterdam: English Department, University of Amsterdam. In *Proceedings of the 4th Conference on Functional Grammar, June 1990, Copenhagen* (provisional title) (forthcoming).

Vossen, P., den Broeder, M. and Meijs, W. J. (1988) The LINKS project: building a semantic database for linguistic applications. In M. Kytö, O. Ihalainen and M. Rissanen (eds) *Corpus Linguistics Hard and Soft*. Amsterdam: Rodopi, 279–93.

Vossen, P., Meijs, W. J. and den Broeder, M. (1989) Meaning and structure in dictionary definitions. In B. Boguraev and E. J. Briscoe (eds) *Computational Lexicography for Natural Language Processing*. London and New York: Longman, 171–92.

Vossen, P. and Serail, I. (1990) *Devil: A taxonomy-browser for decomposition via the lexicon*, ACQUILEX Working Paper, Amsterdam University.

Waggoner, J. (1989) *Samson Agonistes*: Milton's use of syntax to define character. In R. G. Potter (ed.) (1989a) *Literary Computing and Literary Criticism*. Philadelphia: University of Pennsylvania Press, 145–65.

Ward, N. (1990) A connectionist treatment of grammar for generation. Presented at the 5th International Workshop on Language Generation, Pittsburgh.

Wehrli, E. (1987) Recent developments in theoretical linguistics and implications for machine translation. In M. King, *Machine Translation Today*. Edinburgh: Edinburgh University Press, 58–70.

Weiner, J. L. (1980) BLAH: A system which explains its reasoning. *Artificial Intelligence*, 15, 19–48.

Wheeler, P. J. (1987) SYSTRAN. In M. King, *Machine Translation Today*. Edinburgh: Edinburgh University Press, 192–208.

Whitelock, P. J. and Kilby, K. J. (1983) *Linguistic and Computational Techniques in Machine Translation System Design*. Manchester: UMIST.

Whitelock, P., Wood, M., Somers, H., Johnson, R. and Bennett, P. (eds) (1987)

Linguistic Theory and Computer Applications. New York: Academic Press.

Wilensky, R. (1981a) Meta-planning: representing and using knowledge about planning in problem solving and natural language understanding. *Cognitive Science*, 5, 197–235.

Wilensky, R. (1981b) A knowledge-based approach to natural language processing: a progress report. In *7th IJCAI Conference Proceedings*, Vancouver, 493–6.

Wilks, Y. (1983) Deep and superficial parsing. In M. King (ed.) *Parsing Natural Language*. London: Academic Press, 219–46.

Wilks, Y., Fass, D., Guo, C., McDonald, J., Plate, T. and Slator, B. (1989) A tractable machine dictionary as a resource for computational semantics. In B. Boguraev and E. J. Briscoe (eds) *Computational Lexicography for Natural Language Processing*. London and New York: Longman, 193–228.

Williams, C. B. (1940) Sentence-length as a criterion of literary style. *Biometrika*, 31, 356–61.

Williams, N. (1987) Computer assisted writing instruction. In G. Chesters and N. Gardner (eds) *The Use of Computers in the Teaching of Language and Languages*. Bath: University of Bath, 84–94.

Williams, N. (1988) Style Wars – Writing a PC stylechecker, *Personal Computer World*, January, 140–3 and 202–7.

Williams, N. (1989a) What IF? A symposium on Interactive Fiction, *Computers and Writing Newsletter*, 3, October, 13–15.

Williams, N. (1990a) Writers' problems and computer solutions. In N. Williams (1990b) *CALL*. Oxford: Intellect, 5–25.

Williams, N. (1990b) *CALL: Special Issue on Computers and Composition, June*. Oxford: Intellect, Basil Blackwell, Ablex.

Williams, N. (1991) *The Computer, the Writer and the Learner*. London: Springer-Verlag.

Williams, N. and Holt, P. (eds) (1989) *Computers and Writing: Models and tools*. Oxford: Intellect, Basil Blackwell, Ablex.

Williams, N., Holt, P. and Cashdan, A. (1988) *Expert System for Report Writing. A report to the Manpower Services Commission*. Sheffield: Training Agency.

Winograd, T. (1972) *Understanding Natural Language*. Edinburgh: Edinburgh University Press.

Winograd, T. (1983) *Language as a Cognitive Process: Volume 1: Syntax*. Menlo Park: Addison-Wesley.

Witten, I. H. (1982) *Principles of Computer Speech*. London: Academic Press.

Wright, P. and Lickorish, A. (1989) The influence of discourse structure on display and navigation in hypertexts. In N. Williams and P. Holt (eds) *Computers and Writing*. Oxford: Intellect, 90–124.

Yang, H. (1985) The JDEST Computer Corpus of Texts in English for Science and Technology. *ICAME News*, 9, 24–5.

Yazdani, M. (1989) Computational story writing. In N. Williams and P. Holt (eds) *Computers and Writing*. Oxford: Intellect, 125–47.

Yule, G. U. (1939) On sentence-length as a statistical characteristic of style in prose. *Biometrika*, 30, 363.

Yule, G. U. (1944) *The Statistical Study of Literary Vocabulary*. Cambridge: Cambridge University Press.

Zampolli, A. (1990) A survey of European corpus resources. In *SALT. Proceedings of a Workshop on Corpus Resources*. London: DTI/Speech and Language Technology Club, 64–84.

Zettersten, A. (1986) *New Technologies in Language Learning*. Oxford: Pergamon.

Zgusta, L. (1970) *Manual of Lexicography*. The Hague: Mouton.

Zhu, Q. (1989) A quantitative look at the Guangzhou Petroleum English Corpus. *ICAME Journal*, 13, 28–38.

Zukerman, I. and Pearl, J. (1986) Comprehension-driven generation of meta-technical utterances in math tutoring. In *5th AAAI Conference Proceedings*, Philadelphia, 606–11.

Index of Names

Index of Subjects

Index of Software, Computer Languages, Projects, etc.

Index of Languages other than Modern English